CAREER GUIDE

Road Maps to Meaning in the World of Work

Career Guide

Road Maps to Meaning in the World of Work

Gary Lynn Harr
Florida Community College at Jacksonville

Brooks/Cole Publishing Company
I(T)P ™ An International Thompson Publishing Company

Pacific Grove • Albany • Bonn • Boston • Cincinnati • Detroit • London • Madrid • Melbourne
Mexico City • New York • Paris • San Francisco • Singapore • Tokyo • Toronto • Washington

A CLAIREMONT BOOK

Sponsoring Editor: *Claire Verduin*
Marketing: *Roxane Buck-Ezcurra*
Editorial Associate: *Gay C. Bond*
Production Editor: *Marjorie Z. Sanders*
Manuscript Editor: *Judith Johnstone*
Permissions Editor: *May Clark*

Cover Design: *Cloyce J. Wall*
Interior Design: *Jim Love/Publishers Design Studio, Inc.*
Illustration: *Margot Koch/Publishers Design Studio, Inc.*
Typesetting: *Publishers Design Studio, Inc.*
Printing and Binding: *Malloy Lithographing, Inc.*

COPYRIGHT © 1995 by Brooks/Cole Publishing Company
A division of International Thomson Publishing Inc.
I(T)P   The ITP logo is a trademark under license.

For more information, contact:

BROOKS/COLE PUBLISHING COMPANY
511 Forest Lodge Road
Pacific Grove, CA 93950
USA

International Thomson Publishing Europe
Berkshire House 168-173
High Holborn
London WC1V7AA
England

Thomas Nelson Australia
102 Dodds Street
South Melbourne, 3205
Victoria, Australia

Nelson Canada
1120 Birchmount Road
Scarborough, Ontario
Canada M1K 5G4

International Thomson Editores
Campos Eliseos 385, Piso 7
Col. Polanco
11560 México D. F. México

International Thomson Publishing GmbH
Königswinterer Strasse 418
53227 Bonn
Germany

International Thomson Publishing Asia
221 Henderson Road
#05-10 Henderson Building
Singapore 0315

International Thomson Publishing Japan
Hirakawacho Kyowa Building, 3F
2-2-1 Hirakawacho
Chiyoda-ku, 102 Tokyo
Japan

Printed in the United States of America

10 9 8 7 6 5 4 3 2 1

Library of Congress Cataloging-in-Publication Data
Harr, Gary, [date]
    Career guide: road maps to meaning in the world of work/ Gary Lynn Harr.
        p.   cm.
    Includes bibliographical references and index.
    ISBN 0-534-21942-X
    1. Career development I. Title.
HF5381.H147 1994
650.14—dc20   94-21083
                                                 CIP

Those who dare to *fly* fear no abyss.

Contents

PART ONE   Career Exploration

PART THREE Education

PART FOUR Further Exploration

Appendices

Preface

"This book . . . is about a search . . . for daily meaning as well as daily bread . . ." These words were written by Studs Terkel in the introduction of his book *Working*; they represent his conclusion after dozens of interviews with people from many different walks of life. This emphasis upon "daily meaning as well as daily bread" represents an underlying principle of *Career Guide*. Two assumptions underlie this approach:

- **An essential driving force of career development is the search for meaning**—the quest for a sense of individual purpose and significance. There are other motivations at work in this process, but *meaning* is the most important in terms of human growth and development.
- **The most generative concept of career planning is that of discovering your Way**—a path through work and life that allows you to express and create what is most meaningful to you.

You don't have to agree completely with either of these assumptions in order for this book to be of value to you; *Career Guide* was designed to be approachable from a variety of levels and perspectives. However, if you do incorporate these assumptions into your perspective, the outcome of your career planning is likely to be more rewarding.

Career Guide is written for students and other adults who desire some simple and straightforward guidance toward a meaningful direction and purpose in their lives. This book is suitable as a text in a career planning course as well as for self-directed use by individuals faced with a career choice or transition. *Career Guide* provides a practical, yet comprehensive, introduction to career planning, placed within a larger developmental framework.

A Practical Model of Career Planning

Career Guide is based on a set of straightforward career planning principles:

- **The selection of an occupation is both an expression of one's meaning in life and a way to achieve this meaning.** Career planning is a process that can be used to help manifest meaning in peoples' lives. This is a concept that is addressed from the very beginning in this text.

■ **A holistic concept of clear and creative thinking is a fundamental element in the career planning process.** Such thinking takes emotions and intuition into consideration as integral elements of thought, rather than competing or separate functions. For healthy people, thinking is a holistic process that guides their lives, underwrites their emotional balance, nourishes their creative potential, and expresses the uniqueness of their being. Such thinking also includes the deliberate and practical consideration of philosophical premises.

■ **A person's philosophy is a fundamental influence in his or her life.** One's philosophy is a set of beliefs and principles that serve as a foundation for the conduct of day-to-day living. It is a discipline devoted to understanding reality, life, and the nature of human beings. Chapter Nine includes a brief introduction to key philosophical terms and issues, providing a framework for understanding how our premises directly affect the career planning process.

■ **Different people prefer different learning styles.** The concept and application of learning preferences are addressed in the Introduction, providing an opportunity to explore their impact on the career planning process. In addition, the text itself is designed to appeal to a variety of styles.

■ **People can benefit by using self-assessment to find out more about themselves.** The structure and focus provided by assessment make it an important element in career decision making. Self-assessment also personalizes the process, thereby increasing motivation and involvement.

■ **People can benefit by exploring different kinds of occupational options.** Most people have mistaken conceptions about occupations, founded on stereotypes or lack of knowledge. The media, television in particular, is a source of many such preconceptions.

■ **Career planning should address human development and the process of transition.** These factors are significant influences in people's lives and play an important part in career development.

■ **Decision making is a vital skill.** Factors that can influence decision effectiveness (such as critical and creative thinking skills) are important elements of career planning. An understanding of the method of decision making is equally important. Logical *and* intuitive models are presented as complementary processes that can strengthen each other.

These simple principles form the basis of an approach to career planning that is both practical and comprehensive. A number of key elements have been incorporated in this book to support these principles and to enhance the educational process.

Key Elements of This Book

Career Guide provides a useful mixture of elements that enhances its effectiveness:

- **Computer software is provided** to supplement the assessment in Chapter Two. This IBM-DOS-compatible software provides an automated way to generate a Career Profile (more than ten pages of narrative printout) based on the assessment used in this book. The Software Supplement also provides the user with the option of entering objective skills data and selected results from Holland's *Self-Directed Search (SDS)* to verify the students' self-estimates. Additional information on this software is provided in Appendix C.

- **Key resources are included within the text.** Reference material from the *Occupational Outlook Handbook* (and other career information sources) is reproduced within the text, providing the reader with direct access to important information—an advantage when career resource materials are in limited supply or are not easily accessible. The specific occupations listed in this book are the same ones listed in the *Occupational Outlook Handbook*—perhaps the most accessible and useful print resource available for exploring occupations.

- **An integrated system of occupational classification is used throughout.** This system is structured in a way that is easy to understand and simple to use. The assessment results (interests, skills, and values) are integrated by seven occupational clusters of Worker Trait Groups developed by the U.S. Department of Labor. The seven occupational clusters are cross-indexed to John Holland's widely used classification codes.

- **Self-assessment options are presented.** Provision is made for those who wish to supplement the interest and skill assessment with results from Holland's *Self-Directed Search.* The software associated with this text also permits objective skills analysis.

- *Career Guide* **focuses primarily upon the career exploration and decision-making process.** It does not include employability information, which is readily available in many other books and which is not usually the immediate focus of people trying to select an occupation. For those who want information on employability skills, a number of excellent references are suggested in the Bibliography.

- **Learning and motivation devices are incorporated.** These devices are designed to structure and expand the learning process.

  - A **Preview** describes each major section of the chapter. The Preview serves to establish a cognitive map of the content, enhancing comprehension and motivation.

  - **Travelog** exercises are questions and self-assessment exercises designed to stimulate thinking about the personal implications—and applications—of what is being read.

- The **Quiz** at the end of each chapter is a device to help readers test their knowledge of the material covered.

- The **To Consider** . . . section presents a few issues and ideas related to the chapter content and is intended to facilitate reflection, debate, and discussion.

- **Suggested Activities** suggests follow-up activities that can expand the reader's experience and knowledge of selected chapter topics.

- **Parables** are presented between chapters to appeal to an additional learning modality, thereby enriching the learning experience. Readers familiar with *Thus Spoke Zarathustra* will recognize the inspiration for the style of these stories.

Career Guide **is designed to facilitate a constant interaction between what is written and the experiences and thoughts of the reader.** Completing the Travelogs, doing the self-assessments, answering the quizzes, conducting the worker interviews, and working through the other suggested assignments will greatly enhance the benefits that may be derived from this work. The writing involved in these exercises strengthens learning; many people find that writing something down enhances their memory and clarifies their thinking.

It is recommended that you use these exercises to create the basis for a separate "Career Planning Journal," thereby documenting your progress. The pages of this text are perforated to facilitate removal.

Acknowledgments

This book would not be in your hands without the encouragement and assistance of many people. My parents, M. Charles and Leota Harr, have always encouraged my creative endeavors with the kindness and appreciation that only parents can generate. My brother, Christopher Harr, and my sister, Sandra Lyons, have always been enthusiastically supportive. My friends and colleagues at Florida Community College at Jacksonville, especially Charles Dassance, Charles Smires, Gerald Patterson, Susan Hayes, Martha Phillips, and Tessie Bond, have contributed to my life and work in many significant ways. "Steve" Stevenson has helped in many ways with his wise understanding. Elizabeth Scott has kindly provided support, practical insight, and thoughtful review to this book and to my life.

The staff at Brooks/Cole has been a pleasure to work with. Claire Verduin is especially appreciated for recognizing the possibilities inherent in a rather crude initial manuscript and for patiently nurturing its development. Marjorie Sanders has expertly guided the book through the production process.

The reviews were valuable sources of suggested revisions. I extend my appreciation to George Barnett, Richland Community College; Al Butler, Monroe Community College; Donald Cochran, Illinois State University; Lynne P. Hall, Bakersfield College; and Charles J. Pulvino, University of Wisconsin, Madison.

My debt to the philosopher Henry David Thoreau will be obvious by the use of a number of quotes from his book *Walden*—a document reflecting *his* search for purposeful occupation and meaning in the world. I am also indebted to the thinking and writing of many others. I have tried to identify these people and their work throughout the book and in the Bibliography.

It was Thoreau who asserted: "The universe constantly and obediently answers to our conceptions . . ." I am thankful for the answer that has resulted in this work.

Gary Lynn Harr

CAREER GUIDE

The Search for Meaning in the World of Work

Introduction

All [people] want, not something to do with, but something to do, or rather something to be.

HENRY DAVID THOREAU

Thoreau went to Walden pond to confront his destiny. Although you may not have a cabin in the woods, your purpose must ultimately be the same as his. Your career path is an important part of this purpose, and every step you take toward your future is a step toward what you *will be.*

The Career Guide is designed to guide you through a systematic process of thinking, planning, and exploring. It will provide you with a series of conceptual road maps that can be used to plot a course toward a meaningful and satisfying career. A few operational definitions provide a useful beginning.

In Friedrich Nietzsche's *Thus Spake Zarathustra*, the prophet is asked about "The Way." Zarathustra responds: "This - is now my way: where is yours?" Your Way will be unique. There is no one given path that everyone can follow to achieve meaning and fulfillment in life.

Your **Way** is the path that gives meaning to your life. Some people think of this as a calling in life; others think of it as a significant purpose, or an overriding value that provides them with a sense of their place in the universe. Your Way is not something you are born with; it is something that you must discover, or create, for yourself. "To educate others and to help them develop their capacity to think clearly and effectively" is one example of such a sense of purpose.

Your **career** is the overall path you will take through your work life. Ideally, your career will be a reflection or expression of your Way. Following up on the example given, a career decision leading to teaching would represent an opportunity "to educate others and to help them develop their capacity to think clearly and effectively." During your career, you may engage in one or more occupations.

Your **occupation** is the specific form that your career may take at any given point in time (for example, college educator). Your occupation is the *how* of your work life — how your Way takes shape within the boundaries of your career.

Your **job** is defined by the specific job duties you fulfill within your occupation (for example, English professor at Galt University). Your job is composed of the day-to-day responsibilities you fulfill as a member of your occupation.

It is a premise of this book that "Jobs are too small for people"—that jobs can rarely sustain a search for meaning and purpose unless they are somehow related to a larger sense of meaning. *The Career Guide* will encourage you to think in terms of this larger perspective, to think about your Way. Of course, it will also provide specific tools to direct you toward a job of your choice.

Career exploration is as much an art as it is a science; there are no strict rules about the "right" path to follow. There is, however, a general sequence of considerations that proves helpful to most people. *The Career Guide* is designed around these considerations.

An Overview

A brief description of each chapter is now provided to guide you through this book.

Part One: Career Exploration

Chapter One: Planning Your Route covers the significance of the search for meaning, some common reasons why people work, common myths about the career planning process, and the importance of goals. This chapter concludes with a discussion of the importance of assuming responsibility for your own career planning.

Chapter Two: Getting Underway provides self-assessment exercises that will help you evaluate your interests, skills, and work values. It also helps you select compatible occupational clusters for further exploration.

Chapter Three: Resources and Rest Stops provides an overview of several key career exploration resources, including two publications by the U.S. Department of Labor. This chapter also includes an Occupational Listing that directly links the results of your self-assessment with occupations listed in the *Occupational Outlook Handbook*.

Chapter Four: Exploring Career Territory takes you through a step-by-step process of finding out more about the careers you want to consider. Special emphasis is put on nonprint information resources.

Part Two: Decisions

Chapter Five: Down the Road describes how the economy and the workforce are changing and provides projections of what this means for tomorrow's jobs. This chapter highlights the 25 fastest-growing, and the 25 slowest-growing, occupations and provides an overview of issues related to workplace diversity.

Chapter Six: Navigation Aids will explore some of the most important factors involved in career decision making, including a systematic decision-making model, strategies to improve your critical thinking skills and to enhance your creative thinking potential, and an introduction to intuitive decision making.

Part Three: Education

Chapter Seven: Getting There from Here explains some things you will need to know if you select a career that involves further education, including a section on methods to better prepare yourself for any kind of testing.

Chapter Eight: On-the-Road Assistance describes some of the key elements of the academic planning and advising process, provides a list of Secrets to College Success, and evaluates a number of vital study skills.

Part Four: Further Exploration

Chapter Nine: Life's Crossroads is designed to set your career planning within the larger framework of your life. This chapter briefly touches upon five key life issues that you must address to be more effective in your career and your life, and discusses the importance and influence of your world view. Some instructors using this text may want to assign Chapter Nine after the Introduction in order to provide an overall theoretical context for the career planning process; others may prefer to work toward these more abstract elements and will choose the chapters' original order.

Chapter Ten: Transitions explores the nature of change and transition. This chapter describes methods of approaching change, stages of transition, and strategies to avoid transition difficulties.

The **Conclusion** provides closure to the process set forth in this book.

The **Bibliography** provides recommended reading for further career planning and exploration.

Appendix A includes the complete text of "The Job Outlook in Brief," reprinted from the *Occupational Outlook Quarterly*, a publication of the U.S. Department of Labor.

Appendix B provides a valuable table of occupational matching information, reproduced from the *Occupational Outlook Quarterly*.

Appendix C supplies a description of the computer software available to supplement this book.

I hope this overview has given you a sense of where you are going and what you'll be exploring as you work through this book. Before you get started, look at one factor that might determine how you approach this book: your learning preferences.

Approaches to Learning

*L*earning is not something that everyone does in exactly the same manner. All of us have preferences that influence how we approach a learning situation. It may help to think in terms of differing *learning styles*. No one learning style is better than another; they are just different ways of approaching the learning task.

David Kolb is a learning theorist who has developed one of the most commonly used learning style models. His model of *experiential learning* provides a structure that may help you understand the learning process and how people differ in their approach to it. Kolb describes two learning dimensions (perception and processing) that we will adapt to our purposes, and to which we will add a third (organization). Each dimension will be described in terms of two preferences. Read the descriptions and then think about the preferences that are closest to your natural learning style.

Perception has to do with a preference for a certain manner of approaching the learning process.

- **Concrete experience** is a preference for tangible details, facts, and figures. *Concrete learners* want specific examples and hands-on involvement related to what they are learning. They may be impatient with theoretical or conceptual discussions. They often learn best by having something either demonstrated to them or explained in terms of everyday experience. They like field trips, internships, class activities, and other opportunities to get directly involved with the specific elements of what they are learning. Concrete learners prefer that a teacher starts with specific details and works up to more general ideas about a subject.

- **Abstract conceptualization** is a different approach to perception—a preference for theory, concepts, generalizations, and the "big picture." *Abstract learners* may be impatient with specific details, facts, and figures that must be memorized. They usually learn best if they can grasp the general concept of what they are learning before digging into the details. They prefer theoretical models, discussions of concepts, exploration of implications of ideas, and analysis of general elements of what they are learning. Abstract learners prefer that a teacher start with the main concepts of a subject and then fill in the details.

Processing **has to do with the methods people prefer for getting involved with what they are learning.**

■ **Reflective observation** is a preference for a detached involvement. *Reflective learners* like to observe what is going on and then think about it. They enjoy using their imagination to mull over possibilities, implications, and applications related to what they are learning. They usually learn best if they have time to process new ideas, they like quiet concentration, and they often prefer to work on independent projects. Reflective learners prefer that a teacher challenges their thinking, them allows them to mull it over before they have to respond to questions about it.

■ **Active experimentation** is a different kind of involvement with learning. *Active learners* like to experiment with what they are learning. They are interested in the direct application of new ideas. They usually learn best if given the opportunity to participate in class projects, experiments, and group activities that demonstrate what they are learning. Active learners prefer that their teacher maintain a lively approach to learning that lets them explore its application.

Organization **is a third dimension, not directly approached by Kolb, dealing with preferences related to the structure of the learning process.**

■ **Structured learners** want a step-by-step approach to learning. They are systematic in their approach, complete assignments in the sequence assigned, and like to have an overview of the process and a plan in mind before they commit themselves to assignments. They learn best if the learning experience is carefully outlined and sequenced and if the instructor follows this structure. Structured learners prefer that their teacher establishes clear parameters and expectations.

■ **Flexible learners** feel somewhat constrained by a lock-step approach to learning. They usually prefer a flexible approach that allows alternatives, options, and individual preferences. They may prefer to read through the text in a different order than presented and to revise assignments in a way that is more appealing to them. They learn best if given some latitude to direct their own learning and to modify assignments to meet their individual needs. Flexible learners prefer an instructor who varies the approach to learning and introduces the novel and unexpected into the learning process.

Everyone has the ability to learn using all six preferences. Kolb's theory states that learning progresses through all four of his preferences, usually starting with concrete experience, that leads to reflective observation, which results in the formulation of abstract concepts, upon which the student bases active exploration. This results in more concrete experience, and the cycle starts all over again.

Your preferred strategies will usually be easier for you, and more enjoyable. To the extent your preferences match an instructor's classroom format, you are likely to learn more easily in that instructor's class.

Your learning preferences also have a direct influence on how you are likely to approach the learning involved in the career planning process.

- **Concrete learners** will prefer the sections of the text that provide specific details related to down-to-earth aspects of career exploration. The Suggested Activities sections will appeal to them, since these are usually specific tasks to accomplish. In the classroom, they will prefer examples from daily life, detailed explanations provided in handouts, and demonstrations of the application of principles. These learners can enhance their flexibility by being open to the more abstract elements such as the Parables and the theoretical fundamentals covered in Chapters Nine and Ten.

- **Abstract learners** will prefer the sections that involve theory (such as Chapters One, Nine, and Ten), metaphor (such as the Parables) and the To Consider . . . sections. In the classroom, they will prefer theoretical lectures and debates, as well as the discussion of abstract principles related to what they are learning. These learners can enhance their flexibility by being patient with detailed explanations and by being open to the specific details of sections like those found in Chapters Two, Three, and Four.

- **Reflective learners** will especially enjoy the sections on human development and philosophy, the To Consider . . . exercises found at the end of each chapter, and the Travelogs that let them reflect upon how their learning applies to their own experience. In the classroom, they will prefer a relaxed atmosphere that allows for thought before answering and will appreciate time for individual pursuits and research. These learners can enhance their flexibility by actively participating in class and by volunteering for group projects.

- **Active learners** will enjoy activities like the Worker Interviews, which involve some activity related to what they are learning. They will also prefer a classroom that is a high-energy place, where many activities are provided to demonstrate what is being taught. These learners can enhance their flexibility by spending some time alone, thinking about what they are learning, and by spending extra time on the Travelogs.

- **Structured learners** will like the logical organization of the book and the structure that is repeated from chapter to chapter. In the classroom, they will prefer a consistent, planned, sequenced, and carefully organized presentation of what is to be learned. These learners can enhance their flexibility by being open to occasional changes in routine and by allowing themselves to "go with the flow" at times.

■ **Flexible learners** will probably prefer to skip around a bit, and to add their own personal twist to the assignments. In the classroom, they will feel constrained by too much structure, preferring variety and change in format and presentation. These learners can enhance their flexibility by disciplining themselves to follow the structure provided by this book and—if used in the context of a class—their instructor.

It is also important to develop your less-preferred strategies of learning. By becoming a more flexible, balanced, and capable learner, you can be more adaptable in your approach to learning. This is important, since instructors will have differing teaching styles, to which you will have to adapt. To this end, you might actually seek out instructors that ask you to exercise a preference you would ordinarily seek to avoid. It's also useful to get some advice from others who prefer an approach that you do not, asking them to explain and to model how they tackle their learning assignments.

The following Travelog is the first in a series of exercises you will find throughout this book. The purpose of the Travelogs is to help you explore the personal relevance of what you are reading and to document this exploration in a format that you can choose to share with others (your friends, parents, counselor, or instructor). Please complete this exercise before you continue your reading.

Travelog #1

*B*ased upon your responses to what you have read, mark a point that best represents your own preferences along the continuum for each of the three (3) learning dimensions.

PERCEPTION

Concrete		Abstract

PROCESSING

Reflective		Active

ORGANIZATION

Structured		Flexible

- What three (3) things could you do to better match course requirements to your learning preferences?

  1.

  2.

  3.

- What is your *least* natural learning preference? Why?

- What related assignments or learning activities would you prefer to *avoid* if possible?

■ List two (2) possible benefits that you might derive from completing the learning activities you might prefer to avoid.

1.

2.

■ If you had the opportunity to make suggestions to a career planning instructor concerning how his or her course might better appeal to your natural learning preferences, what would you suggest?

As you might guess, no single approach can successfully address all the possible combinations of these various learning styles. The *Career Guide* attempts to provide a wide variety of learning alternatives, some of which will appeal to each of these preferences. Although you may find some of these alternatives more interesting than others, you should find all of them of some benefit.

A knowledge of your learning style can provide you with a valuable tool if you assume the responsibility to understand and apply it. The depth and scope of David Kolb's work is only suggested by what has been presented. For further information on learning styles, refer to Kolb's work, listed in the Bibliography.

Now that you have a feel for the structure of this book and how you may approach it, you are ready to start the career planning process.

The Parable of Zara's Return

*A*t the age of 50, Zara left the world. For ten years he lived in solitude, surrounded by the womb of the whistling wind and succored by the silence of the stony mountains. In the canyons of these mountains he found the meaning that had eluded him among men. In the canyons, he found a healing for the wounds of his youth. In the silent depth of his spirit, he found his Way and his connection to the Creative Force that maintains all existence. It was time for his return.

As he reached the foot of the mountain, he came upon a young woman heading in the opposite direction. Her head was lowered and her steps were slow and unsure. "Greetings, young traveler!" said Zara. The woman raised her eyes—sad eyes, heavy with the sights of an unkind world.

Zara spoke to her with compassion. "I recognize you, young one. I know the path you are taking, where you come from, and where you are going. I can see you carry with you the heaviness of this world. Gravity—the enemy of all who would fly—holds you tight in its grasp, squeezing the breath from your life and your dreams." The young woman began to stare intently at this old hermit who seemed to know the nature of her being so precisely.

Zara continued: "I too have felt this awful weight. I too fled to the mountains in hope of escaping the enemy of the spirit's flight. I know the weight upon your wings. I know the suffering of your journey. I know what it feels like to be lost among the living, to struggle for a purpose, a direction, a meaning to guide the yearnings of your soul. I am here to tell you that your journey is not away from the world but toward yourself. Turn from the mountain and follow me for awhile. I know the signs of that which you are tracking. The signs do not lead toward the mountains; they lead toward a place you have yet to know. Follow me and my eagle that circles above; we no longer fear the abyss that surrounds your destination. The abyss is feared only by those without wings!"

She looked into Zara's eyes and felt the depth, compassion, and power of his gaze. Without hesitation she turned and followed him.

PART ONE

Career Exploration

The first four chapters cover the basic elements of the career exploration process. Chapter One begins by introducing a number of important concepts that form a foundation for career planning. Chapter Two provides a structured series of self-evaluations that focuses on more tangible elements of career planning: interests, skills, and values. Using the resources in Chapter Three and the step-by-step exploration procedure in Chapter Four, you should be able to generate a tentative list of occupations that are compatible with your own interests, skills, and values.

CHAPTER ONE

Planning Your Route

Preview

I went to the woods because I wished to live deliberately, to front only the essential facts of life, and to see if I could not learn what it had to teach, and not, when I came to die, discover that I had not lived. I did not wish to live what was not life, living is so dear; nor did I wish to practice resignation, unless it was quite necessary. I wanted to live deep and suck out all the marrow of life, to live so sturdily and Spartan-like as to put to rout all that was not life . . . .

HENRY DAVID THOREAU

*B*efore you set out on a journey of any kind, it's important to be properly prepared. This preparation often involves defining a purpose and a destination, clearing up any confusion about your route, and accepting some responsibility for your own direction and destiny. This chapter will focus on the preparation necessary for the career exploration you are about to undertake. The main sections of this chapter are as follows.

- **The Search for Meaning** explores the significance of career planning in terms of finding and expressing meaning in life.
- **Reasons to Work** explains that there are many reasons to work other than to earn a living.
- **Career Myths** will explore some of the more common misunderstandings about the career exploration process.
- **Your Destination** asks you to look at short-term and long-term goals and the reality testing that helps assure their realism and practicality.
- **Taking the Wheel** describes the importance of assuming responsibility for your own future and why some people do so more naturally than others.

By the time you finish this chapter, you will be ready to get started with some self-assessment that will form the basis for your career exploration.

Your Way is pregnant with possibility. Rollo May, a philosopher and psychologist, wrote: "We stand on the edge of life, each moment comprising that edge. Before us is only possibility." One of the most important factors affecting this possibility is what you *will* for yourself. Webster's New World Dictionary defines *will* as "the power of making a reasoned choice or decision . . ." It is this power that differentiates you as a rational and conscious being capable of influencing your future.

The use of this power of reasoned choice is volitional—it is not automatic. You must *choose* to use your power to influence your own possibilities. One of the most fundamental reasons that people choose to exercise their will is to establish meaning in their lives—which is the starting point for the journey you are about to begin.

The Search for Meaning

*T*he quest for meaning in life can take many forms. Some people find meaning in terms of their religious beliefs; others find meaning in devotion to country, family, creative expression, or personal achievement. Because this is a career planning book, we will focus on the possibility of establishing meaning through the work you choose to do. This emphasis is not meant to minimize other sources of meaning in peoples' lives; it merely focuses attention on the more immediate issues facing those involved in the career planning process.

The choice of a career direction is often the anvil upon which meaning is forged. Whatever the presenting motivation may be—a well-paying job, personal status, satisfaction that comes from helping others—the foundation of the career search is usually a deeper desire for meaning in life. Everyone wants to feel that what they do for a living has significance, that their work fulfills some purpose beyond the humdrum tasks it may involve. On some level, everyone wants what Thoreau wanted: "to live deliberately . . . and not, when I came to die, discover that I had not lived."

This book takes an optimistic view of human potential and emphasizes your ability to shape your future into a meaningful and fulfilling life. However, to fully understand the nature and challenge of this task, we must take a few moments to survey the "dark side" of the social situation that serves as the context for this task.

Meaning is a quality in short supply in modern-day America. Traditional institutional sources of meaning and belonging—family, church, employer, nation—have been weakened by a fragmented social environment caught in a whirlwind of accelerated change. Eric Hoffer, writer and social analyst, observed: "The accelerating rate of change . . . is upsetting and weakening traditions, customs, habits, routines . . . the commonplaces of everyday life can no longer be taken for granted." Almost 25 years ago, Alvin Toffler wrote *Future Shock*, a signal flare that documented the acceleration of technological change and its social affects. Toffler maintained that this acceleration has already resulted in "the death of permanence," which includes many aspects of life that people have traditionally depended upon to give meaning to their lives.

Futurist John Naisbitt pointed out that "When people are buffeted by change, the need for spiritual belief intensifies." Organized, orthodox religion is the most common manner of meeting this need. However, today membership in traditional churches has actually declined, while participation in unorthodox religions and cults has increased as people attempt to replace a sense of belonging and meaning that is missing in their lives. Many Baby Boomers, now reaching middle age, are feeling the need for spiritual guidance, but most are not returning to the churches in which they were raised. Newspaper columnist Jack Anderson claims that there are up to 5000 cults in America today (even the most conservative estimates place the number at 700), with 5 to 10 million people belonging to such a group at one time or another. In *Megatrends 2000*, Naisbitt states that " . . . millions today are attracted to the unorthodox ends of the religious spectrum: from New Age channelers to 'speaking in tongues' charismatics to scandal prone TV preachers." He estimates the number of "New Agers" to be 10 or 12 million and found that "Ninety-five percent of the readers of *New Age Journal* are college-educated, with average household incomes of $47,500"—a powerful economic and social force.

In *The Third Wave*, Toffler offers three reasons for this phenomenal growth of unorthodox religious groups: (1) the feeling of community that comes from membership, (2) the need for life structure that comes from tightly prescribed behavior, and (3) the meaning that seems to come with adoption of the cults' version of reality understood to be Truth (their doctrine). Toffler concludes that these apparent benefits come " . . . at an extremely high price: the mindless surrender of self"— a price that an increasing number of people seem willing to pay.

Membership in youth gangs serves the same kind of functions as cults do, and has contributed to an explosion of violent crime. The U.S. Department of Justice reports that over 80% percent of the population can expect to be victims of a violent assault sometime during their lifetime. Over 57% of urban and suburban adults surveyed by an August 23, 1993, *Time*/CNN poll indicated that they worried about being the victim of a crime. Much of the increase in crime is associated with drug trafficking and use; nearly 12 times as many drug offenders were sent to state prisons in 1990 as in 1980 (*Harper's Index*, July, 1993). Cultic extremism, increasing violent crime, and widespread drug abuse are obvious symptoms of a society in trouble.

The American Dream—the use of technology to raise the quality of life, an optimistic view of the future, an environment of opportunity and freedom, and rewards based on self-reliance and individual achievement—is alive, but it is not well. An out-of-control national debt casts a dark shadow over a shaky and seemingly unpredictable economy. Adjusted for inflation, worker wages have remained stagnant for over 20 years. Government regulation alternates between strangling Americans with red tape (try reading the U.S. tax code) and leaving them unprotected against corruption and avarice (witness the savings and loan scandal/bailout).

Business bankruptcies are at an all-time high. The manufacturing industries that have traditionally formed the backbone of the economy—auto, steel, textiles—are, to use Toffler's words, "in terminal agony." Although the auto industry is showing some signs of a resurgence, the hundreds of thousands of high-paying jobs lost in the industrial sector are gone forever; and the people who held these jobs are having difficulty finding another job at the same pay. In his book *The Adaptive Corporation*, Toffler describes the modern corporate environment as " . . . increasingly unstable, accelerative, and revolutionary." Further evidence of this trend is found in a *Time* magazine cover story (November 22, 1993), "America's Frightening New World of Work," which included a survey showing that 66% of those polled thought job security worse than it was two years ago. Of those polled with this opinion, 53% saw this decline as a long-term trend.

In this environment, there has been a lowering of expectations. Many young people no longer think they will improve upon their parents' standard of living—a goal commonly achieved by previous generations. Fewer college students consider it important to develop a philosophy of life (an understanding of life). For many workers, careers are not expected to be a source of meaning and personal satisfaction.

Fortunately, life provides many sources of meaning other than work. However, there is a cost to be paid when work is separated from a larger sense of meaning. To the extent that work is alienated from meaning, it violates a basic need within most peoples' lives. Studs Terkel recognized the cost of such alienation after interviewing many people, concluding that work without meaning "is by its very nature, about violence—to the spirit as well as to the body." Meaning cannot be separated from work with impunity.

Fortunately, this seemingly gloomy picture may be viewed from another perspective. America remains a land of opportunity. Eric Hoffer wrote that " . . . as long as a country has courage and a passion for excellence, it can face the future confidently no matter how fearsome its difficulties." The America of today, as in the past, has no shortage of either courage or excellence. America leads the world in new patents and Nobel laureates. Many new industries are developing to fill the vacuum left by the decline of manufacturing: computers, electronics, robotics, genetic engineering, environmental technology, information services, and alternative energy sources, to name a few. The job outlook for many occupations remains very favorable. (More data on this will be provided in a later chapter). A federal-level focus upon the national debt, the educational system, and crime promises the possibility of significant improvements on all three fronts. In the beginning of 1994, the economy began to show signs of regaining strength and vitality. World trade agreements promise to open up new foreign markets to U.S. products and services. A world turning away from totalitarianism and toward democracy suggests the possibility of lessened conflict and higher regard for human rights. Summarizing these trends, John Naisbitt, author of *Megatrends* and *Megatrends 2000*, wrote that "The economic forces of the world are surging across national borders, resulting in more democracy, more freedom, more trade, more opportunity, and greater prosperity."

Alvin Toffler, one of the most astute observers of social trends, contends that " . . . beneath the clatter and jangle of seemingly senseless events there lies a startling and potentially hopeful pattern." He believes that many of the personal and social dislocations we are now experiencing are symptoms of a transition between the dying of one age and the birth of another—the birth of what he calls "The Third Wave"—a postindustrial, information-based economy. No less an authority than the comic character Pogo summarized the situation: "It seems like we are now confronted with a number of insurmountable opportunities."

Whatever its social and economic problems, America remains a land of opportunity and talent, a land of wealth, and a monument to individual freedom. Founded on the principles of peoples' inherent right to direct their own destiny and to pursue their own happiness, America provides the freedom, rewards, values, principles, ideas, and opportunities requisite for the achievement of meaning.

Meaning is not something you are born with. It is not something that you can buy or hoard. It is not something that can be redistributed or legislated. It is not an entitlement. Meaning is something you, as an individual, must *create*. If you believe in a Higher Power that sustains meaning in the world, it is *your choice* to accept this belief. By making such a choice, you create meaning in your life.

It is also up to you to create the clear understanding that leads to a sense of meaning and to the formulation of a *Weltanschauung*— (world view). This creation depends upon what philosopher Ayn Rand describes as " . . . a fundamental conviction . . . that *ideas matter* . . . . That ideas matter means that knowledge matters, that truth matters, that one's mind matters." Without this conviction, you have surrendered your most powerful tools in your search for meaning and fulfillment.

The significance of your world view for your life and your career planning is covered in a section on "Practical Philosophy" in Chapter Nine. Readers who prefer to begin their career planning with a Big Picture—a philosophical or theoretical context—should read Chapter Nine before continuing.

Given the importance of the search for meaning in life, there are many other reasons that people work. The level at which you approach career planning is often determined by the kind of needs that motivate the process.

Reasons to Work

Most people have to work for a living. Earning the money required to maintain a comfortable and secure life-style would be on most peoples' list of reasons for working. Unless you have a generous family inheritance or have won the lottery, you will trade the value of your thought and/or your muscle for the symbolic value of pieces of green paper bearing pictures of dead presidents. This money will then be traded for other things of value that sustain and enrich your life.

There are many other reasons to work. One approach to understanding the motivation to work is to examine it in terms of psychological theory. Abraham Maslow was a psychologist who did some pioneering work that sheds light on this subject.

Maslow's work is significant because he chose to study *healthy* people. He made this choice at a time when most psychological research was focused on neurosis and psychosis—a legacy from Sigmund Freud and a *medical* model of mental health. As a result of his research, Maslow developed a theory of motivation based on a hierarchy of five primary human needs, each level of which must be satisfied before the next level is operational:

- *Physiological needs* are the most basic. The need for adequate food, clothing, and shelter are survival requirements that, until they are satisfied, take precedence over other needs.

- *Safety needs* become important once survival needs are met. If personal safety is seriously at risk, this becomes a dominant focus of one's energy and effort.

- *Belonging and love needs* are motivational factors once physiological and safety needs are satisfied. This level represents the more social elements of human life.

- *Self-esteem needs* become dominant once a sense of belonging is established. A feeling of self-worth, and confidence in one's abilities and capacities, are important at this level of motivation.

- *Self-actualization needs* are at the pinnacle of Maslow's hierarchy. The realization and fulfillment of one's potential, of one's Way, can only be accomplished at this level of functioning.

Your motivation to work and your approach to career planning may be analyzed in reference to this hierarchy of needs.

Establishing economic security is important to most people, a desire directly related to physiological and safety needs. The desire for adequate compensation and job opportunity are reflections of this level of need.

Contributing to the welfare of others is an important element of belonging for many people, particularly those who choose to go into fields like social service or health care. Also, providing for the welfare of their family is a motivating factor related to the need for belonging for most people. *Belonging to a work group* is another common source of personal satisfaction. The work setting often provides an opportunity to satisfy social as well as personal needs. Ideally, the workplace is an environment that brings together people who share common interests and values.

Achievement and productivity are important sources of self-esteem for many people. Work can provide many direct opportunities for the expression of these motivations. *Challenging one's limitations* can be another important source of self-esteem. Work provides the opportunity to stimulate the development of skills, to encourage a broader range of interests, and to facilitate new methods of interacting with others.

Status, prestige, and power are other paths that people choose to satisfy self-esteem needs in the world of work. Some people choose occupations that reward them in terms of these kinds of values.

Expressing and developing creative talents is another aspect of self-actualization. Whether the talent is artistic, technical, interpersonal, or intellectual, there are many occupations that allow for the expression and development of such skills. *The power to express and create meaning* also falls within the province of self-actualization. If you are working in an occupation that has personal meaning for you, and that allows you to express this meaning, you will be among an elite group of the very fortunate. Everyone has this potential, but it is something that must be *achieved*, and that must be preceded by the satisfaction of other, more basic needs.

Your decision to pursue a given career direction is likely to be a combination of many of these factors. As you can see, working is more than just "bringing home the bacon." According to Maslow's theory, the kind of work you decide to do is a reflection of the level of satisfaction of your needs. This decision will have a major influence on many parts of your life. It will affect the kind of life-style you can maintain, the people you socialize with, and, very often, the kind of activities you pursue outside of work.

Research done in 1983 by The Public Agenda Foundation resulted in a list of the top ten characteristics people seek in their work. These characteristics are listed below (with an addition, corresponding Maslow need categories, in parentheses). Check those items that represent characteristics important to you (regardless of order).

☐	(1)	Respect from their co-workers	(Belonging)
☐	(2)	Work that is of some personal interest	(Self-Actualization)
☐	(3)	Recognition for work well done	(Self-Esteem)
☐	(4)	Opportunity to develop new skills	(Self-Actualization)
☐	(5)	Power to improve work methods and procedures	(Self-Actualization)
☐	(6)	Latitude to apply one's own thinking	(Self-Actualization)
☐	(7)	Ability to see tangible end results	(Belonging)
☐	(8)	Efficient management	(Safety)
☐	(9)	Work that is challenging	(Self-Actualization)
☐	(10)	Information about what is going on at work	(Belonging)

Interestingly enough, high pay and job security didn't make the top ten, though they weren't far behind.

Because the level of need satisfaction is a dynamic and developmental process, your motivation to work is likely to change as you gain life experience. What is most important at one stage of motivation recedes in importance once satisfaction of the primary need at that level is achieved. When this occurs, a different source of motivation becomes dominant. In practical terms, this means that the lower your dominant motivation for occupational choice falls within Maslow's hierarchy of needs, the more likely your motivation will change as you grow and develop as a person. The following Travelog will help you explore some of these motivational issues.

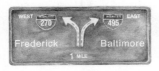

Travelog #2

As we have seen, your career choices are influenced by many motivational factors. The following questions will help you consider these influences.

■ How important is the satisfaction of *physiological* needs in your occupational selection? Describe how working will help you satisfy these needs.

■ How important is the satisfaction of *safety* needs in your selection of an occupation? Describe how working will help you satisfy these needs.

■ How important is the satisfaction of *belonging* needs in your selection of an occupation? Describe how working will help you satisfy these needs.

■ How important is the satisfaction of *self-esteem* needs in your selection of an occupation? Describe how working will help you satisfy these needs.

■ How important is the satisfaction of *self-actualization* needs in your selection of an occupation? Describe how working will help you satisfy these needs.

■ What is your *dominant* level of need at the present stage of your career development? Why is this significant for your career planning?

Travelog #3

*T*est yourself on the following items by circling "T" for True or "F" for False.

1. T F   Career testing will tell me exactly what occupation is right for me.

2. T F   There is one perfect occupation waiting somewhere out there for me.

3. T F   I'll only have to do career planning once in my life.

4. T F   I already know everything I need to know about my occupation of choice.

5. T F   I don't have enough time to spend on career planning right now.

6. T F   The best place for me to start looking for an occupation is where employers are doing lots of hiring now.

7. T F   I can trust in fate to bring me to the right occupation.

All of the items in this exercise are false. (How many did you get right?) Such myths are thought to be true by many people. This makes myths hard to distinguish from facts and often creates problems in the career planning process. A few common myths are described in the following pages.

Because of the importance of your career decision, it is vital that you have a clear understanding of career planning as you begin this journey. A clear understanding must be based upon fact rather than fiction. The next section will help you separate myth from reality concerning the career planning process.

Career Myths

*I*n any kind of search for truth and meaning, one of the things you must do is to separate myth from reality. People's ideas about career planning are often enmeshed in myth. Travelog #3 provides a quiz that addresses many common misconceptions about the career planning process.

MYTH 1   "Career testing will tell me exactly what occupation is right for me."

FACT 1   **Test results can provide you with additional information** that may be helpful as a part of the career planning process. **No test, however, can provide infallible predictions.** Tests take a sample of certain kinds of knowledge or attitudes and draw conclusions based upon this sample. Test results can be confounded by many things: a lack of reliability, cultural differences, unrepresentative samples, and unintentionally biased items, to name a few. The self-assessment exercises in this text are meant to point you in a direction for further exploration, not to be infallible guides. Use tests with caution, and critically examine test results in terms of your own experience and knowledge. Chapter Two will provide you with an opportunity for some self-assessment.

MYTH 2   "There is one perfect occupation waiting somewhere out there for me."

FACT 2   **Many occupations have the potential to satisfy your career goals.** Once you have more clearly defined what you are looking for in a career, you will find that there are any number of occupations that match these criteria. For example, you may narrow down your search to health care professions. You are still faced with a choice among dozens of occupations in this career field (physician, nurse, physical therapist, respiratory therapist, medical lab technologist, veterinarian, pharmacist). As you explore such options and find out more about each, you can compare what they offer in terms of advantages and disadvantages.

MYTH 3   "I'll only have to do career planning once in my life."

FACT 3   **Career planning is an ongoing process.** You will probably readdress your career plans several times during your life. It is estimated that the typical person entering the work force at this time in history will have as many as five or six different occupations by the time he or she retires. Important as it is to find an occupation that will be rewarding, it is not likely to be a final decision. Many occupations that will be available within your lifetime do not even exist yet! Twenty years ago, who would have imagined the need for microcomputer specialists or computer-aided drafting and design technicians? The skills and understanding that you will develop as you work through this book will serve you well each time you deal with career planning choices.

MYTH 4   "I already know everything I need to know about my occupation of choice."

FACT 4   **Most people's knowledge of occupations is incomplete.** The media often provide a glamorized and unrealistic picture of occupations. Most of what passes as knowledge is really based upon stereotypes. The television show may depict police work as an exciting occupation dedicated to putting the bad guys behind bars. It is less likely to show the hours spent doing paperwork, directing traffic, or responding to domestic disputes where there is no clearly defined "bad guy." Likewise, the occupation of a pilot is often depicted as a swashbuckling adventure of tearing through the skies at mach speed. It is less likely to show the hours spent poring over weather maps, sitting in airports between flights, reading instruments in the cockpit, waiting on the ground for takeoff, or reading flight regulation updates. As you narrow down your occupational options, be sure you are getting a balanced and accurate picture of the occupations you are considering. A number of methods designed to help you in this task will be suggested later in this text.

MYTH 5   "I don't have enough time to spend on career planning right now."

FACT 5   **Timely and effective career planning can save you a lot of wasted time, money, and effort.** Unrealistic or misguided career plans may cause you to take unnecessary courses, do poorly in courses not matched to your skills, or extend the time needed to complete your goals. Also, once you have a clear goal in mind, it will be easier to do what it takes to get there. If you are heading down the road with no destination in mind, there is a tendency to get sidetracked by things that look interesting but make no lasting contribution to your life. If you have a destination in mind, the choices you make are more likely to contribute meaningfully to your goals. This process of career planning may take considerable time and effort, but it is time and effort well spent.

MYTH 6   "The best place for me to start looking for an occupation is where employers are doing lots of hiring now."

FACT 6   **The job market is in constant flux.** Employment opportunities can change dramatically as a function of economic conditions, advances in technology, and the labor supply. Although projections are available from information resources, this data should be used with caution. It could change by the time you are ready to enter the job market. There is an inevitable lag time between the demand for certain kinds of occupations and the response to this demand. For example, today there may be a dramatic need for nurses. This demand outstrips the supply with a resulting increase in salary, fringe benefits, and opportunity as employers compete for the limited supply of trained workers. College students who decide they want to become nurses primarily because of this increased opportunity may be disappointed after years of training because they are competing with thousands of people with the same idea who are flooding the job market and thus creating a supply that exceeds the demand. This kind of changing demand and supply situation can happen with any occupation. Nonetheless, job outlook trends can be useful information if used cautiously and not as the primary factor in a career choice.

MYTH 7   "I can trust in fate to bring me to the right occupation."

FACT 7   **Most people can benefit from a systematic investigation and consideration of different occupations.** You won't just "run into" the occupation that will match your skills, be compatible with your interests, reward you in terms of your values, and reflect a meaningful Way. The more information you gather about yourself and the occupations you are considering, the more likely it is you will make a wise career decision. Fate will play a role in your career path—some things beyond your control will have an influence on your life—but you have an active role to play in determining your own fate.

Myths can be a significant obstacle to someone beginning the career planning process. The clearer your thinking is about this process, the more likely it will be beneficial. As you start to think about choosing an occupation, it will be helpful to think in terms of the goals you want to accomplish.

Your Destination

Goals will establish a direction and a context for your career planning efforts. Before you get too far down the road, you need to consider your goals in the context of career decision making. For this purpose, we will divide goals into two categories:

- **Short term goals are destinations that can be reached within the immediate future.** Completing this book and doing some career exploration are examples of short-term goals.
- **Long-term goals extend further out into your future.** Establishing yourself in a rewarding occupation and starting a family are examples of this kind of goal.

Ideally, short-term goals are related to, and contribute to, long-term goals. For example, the short-term goal of completing this book contributes to a long-term goal of establishing yourself in a rewarding occupation. If short-term goals are not related to long-term goals, they may actually undermine your long-term goals. For example, a short-term goal of buying a new car may result in the choice to work a second job instead of going to school, possibly limiting future career opportunities because of a lack of educational credentials. On the other hand, a short-term goal of finishing your college degree will greatly enhance your earning power and your choice of possible occupations.

By thinking through your goals, you can help ensure that the decisions you make will move you toward your chosen career destination. The following two Travelogs ask you to think about your goals. Referring to the previous section on reasons to work may be helpful.

Travelog #4

*P*lease answer the following questions:

■ What are your three (3) most important short-term goals related to your career development?

   1.

   2.

   3.

■ What are your three (3) most important long-term goals related to your career development?

   1.

   2.

   3.

■ Describe how your short-term goals contribute to your long-term goals.

■ Are you satisfied with your present goals?

■ Are your goals clear enough to provide direction for the career planning process?

Travelog #5

*A*nother important consideration has to do with "reality testing" of goals. Once you have an idea of short- and long-term goals, you should determine the feasibility of such goals. This usually involves collecting additional information related to your goals—something you will be doing in later chapters of this book.

There are some basic questions that you should keep in mind to help determine whether your goals are realistic. Select one of the short-term goals you listed in Travelog #4 and answer the following questions.

SHORT-TERM CAREER GOAL:

■ What kinds of skills are required to accomplish this goal?

■ What personality characteristics are required to reach this goal?

■ What things beyond my control must fall into place?

■ What kinds of resources (money, time) are required?

■ What other qualifications must I satisfy?

■ Can I realistically meet these requirements?

■ How can I test whether I have what it takes to achieve this goal?

Goals will be of little benefit unless you assume the responsibility to do what it takes to achieve them. The next section presents several views concerning personal responsibility.

Taking the Wheel

You have already shown that you are capable of one of the most fundamental keys to the career planning process—taking responsibility for the direction of your own life. If this were not the case, you wouldn't have picked up this book.

In his autobiography, *Warrior's Way*, Robert de Ropp describes something he learned that applies to the topic at hand: "It is our privilege as human beings to live either as Warriors or slaves. A Warrior is master of his [or her] fate." Warriors will take what fate provides them and use it to achieve what is within the power of their mind and their will. Slaves allow themselves to be crushed by fate, surrendering their life to circumstance without a significant or effective struggle. Which are you: Warrior or slave?

If you do not assume responsibility for your own career planning, a number of unpleasant consequences are likely to result:

- *Wasting time in indecision.* Decision making is an *active* process. Unless you take the initiative in this process, important decisions may stay in limbo for a long time. Actually, it may be argued that, by not taking such initiative, you are actually making a decision to remain in a state of indecision. While in this state, your life remains in a holding pattern.

- *Wasting money on the wrong kind of training.* Since life must go on in the face of indecision, many people make commitments without a clear sense of their own goals. For example, if you go too far in college without having made an occupational choice, you may take courses that will not apply to the major you eventually select. Though such work might be of some benefit (e.g., broadening your perspectives on life), if it occurs near the end of your program of study, it may delay your graduation.

- *Remaining in a job that doesn't meet your needs.* While you are waiting for fate to intervene, you remain where you are, doing what you've always been doing. If this involves continuing in a job that is unsatisfying, frustrating, or limiting, then you are subjecting yourself to physical and psychological stress. This kind of stress can often lead to physical illness or psychological problems such as depression or irritability.

■ *Missing opportunities*. Opportunities are constantly walking by your door. If you are waiting behind the door, you will miss many opportunities. Open the door by actively seeking your goals and invite opportunity to walk in!

The next two Travelogs will help you explore issues related to the amount of control you choose to exercise over your own decision making. Decision making is a behavior that varies for individuals, and it can have a marked influence on your career planning.

Travelog #6

*T*hink about a time in your past when you were faced with making a difficult decision related to school or work.

■ What was the decision?

■ What elements of the decision were under your direct control?

■ What elements of the decision were outside your direct control?

■ To what extent did you assume responsibility for making the decision?

■ What would you do differently if you faced that situation again?

■ Think of a situation when you clearly took an active part in making a decision. How did you feel about it?

■ Think of a situation when you let circumstances, or other people, make your decision. How did you feel about the outcome of the situation?

Travelog #7

*P*sychological researchers have found that people differ in how much influence they feel they can exercise over what happens to them. These researchers have labeled what they are investigating as "locus of control" and have discovered that people's attitudes fall on a continuum ranging from an "external" to an "internal" locus of control. This exercise will help you determine your own attitudes toward this concept; an explanation of these terms will follow. Answer the following questions by circling the answer of your choice.

PART A

- Is your future mostly determined by forces beyond your control?   Yes   No

- Does fate or luck play a major role in your life?   Yes   No

- Is it usually the fault of someone else when things turn out poorly?   Yes   No

- Do you feel you can make little difference in how things happen?   Yes   No

- Is it best just to accommodate yourself to things as they occur?   Yes   No

PART B

- Do you have a responsibility actively to direct your own future?   Yes   No

- Do you think fate or luck has little or no influence on outcomes?   Yes   No

- Are you primarily responsible if your decisions turn out poorly?   Yes   No

- Do your decisions have a direct effect on how things occur?   Yes   No

- Do you plan toward the outcomes you desire?   Yes   No

If you answered yes to more than three items in Part A *or* no to more than three items in Part B, you probably have an *external locus of control*—a belief that your life is strongly influenced by factors beyond your control. Julian Rotter, the researcher who pioneered these concepts, described this belief as the understanding that outcomes were the " . . . result of luck, chance, fate, as under control of powerful others, or as unpredictable because of the great complexity of the forces [at work] . . ."

If you answered no to more than three items in Part A *or* yes to more than three items in Part B, you probably have an *internal locus of control*—the belief that outcomes in your life may be attributed to personal abilities, characteristics, attitudes, and other factors under your control.

A mixture of answers would indicate a mixed locus of control, with no clear belief in one direction or another.

Researchers have also shown that how you think about locus of control can influence you personal well-being. Generally, "Internals" have an advantage in terms of overall satisfaction with their life. In terms of career planning, it is obvious that an internal locus of control is an advantage. Why bother with such planning if you have little control over the outcome (as the "External" might think)?

This not to say that your career path will be totally determined by your decisions. There will always be events and circumstances that you cannot predict or influence, some of which will send you in a direction different than you might have planned. Such unpredictable elements of life play a role in everyone's career. Yet Rollo May reminds us that "Freedom is how we relate to our destiny, and destiny is significant only because we have freedom." Warriors (in De Ropp's sense of the term) will *use* the consequences of fate to direct their own destiny, as fuel for the fire that lights their Way.

The key to assuming control of your life is to understand that you are a being of *volitional* consciousness; you must *freely choose* to exercise your mind's capacity for thought in order to fulfill your potential. Your mind will *not automatically* tell you what occupation is best suited to your interests or what values will further your life. Your mind will *not automatically* generate independence, self-esteem, or personal meaning.

To live up to your potential you must consciously engage in a process of clear and creative thinking, guided by values that reflect the requirements of reality and your essential human nature. The first step of this process is to assume responsibility for achieving such a goal and to assume that you have the power to influence your destiny. People with an internal locus of control will be predisposed to this approach to life; those with an external locus of control must start from a different place.

You *can* choose an occupation that is well matched to your skills, interests, values, and goals—a path that will lead you to self-actualization and a sense of meaning. The next chapter begins to guide you through an important part of this process.

Quiz 1

*P*lease answer the following questions. Continue answers on the reverse side if additional space is needed.

1. Why is the analysis of motivation important in career planning?

2. Why should you be concerned about career planning myths?

3. Name two (2) advantages of clearly identifying your goals:
   a.

   b.

4. How can learning style influence the manner in which you approach career planning?

5. Why is it an advantage to have an internal locus of control when it comes to career planning?

6. What is the most important thing that you learned about yourself by working through this chapter?

7. What topic covered in this chapter would you like to explore further?

To Consider . . .

1. Some futurists think that we are moving toward a world in which all work will be done by machines.

   How would society be different if people did not have to work in order to make a living?

   What would you do if you didn't have to work in order to make a living?

2. The myth that the Earth is flat was widely held until relatively recent times.

   How do myths like this get started?

   Do myths serve a purpose?

   Why do some myths persist for so long?

Suggested Activities

1. Talk to some of your parents and friends about why they work. What kinds of rewards do they get from their work?

2. Watch how various occupations are portrayed on television. How realistic are the portrayals? In what manner are the portrayals inaccurate, glamorized, or stereotyped?

3. Interview someone who has a locus of control different from your own. How do his or her perceptions of reality differ from yours?

The Parable of the Magician

As they entered the town at the foot of the mountains, Zara and his young companion came upon a crowd. The gasping crowd was watching a magician seem to pull rabbits out of his hat and to conjure birds from hardboiled eggs.

The magician spoke to the crowd: "All is illusion in this life. Rabbits appear from nowhere. Life flies from death. Nothing is as it appears. The real is hidden, while the imaginary parades about in plain sight. Who are you to know the difference between the real and the unreal? You seek the truth in vain; it is forever disguised. Truth is the province of magicians!"

Zara pushed to the front of the crowd. "Liar! Emissary of Darkness, be silent!" cried Zara. The crowd fell silent, as did the startled magician. A hundred widened eyes fell upon the old mountain hermit.

Zara spoke to them. "Reality is not the province of magicians and soothsayers and prophets of other-worlds! Doubt the ground you stand upon and you will fall dizzily to your knees. And on your knees is where the preachers of illusion want you! The purpose of their magic tricks is to undermine your grasp of Reality, to make you doubt your senses and your reason. The weeds of doubt create fertile soil for tyranny and slavery. Listen to this magic man, and tyranny and slavery will be your reward."

Zara continued: "Reality is as clear as the sky on a cloudless day. Nothing is hidden from you. The world is open to your mind if your mind is open. Run from the dust devils that spin in circles, raising clouds to obscure your vision and choke your reason."

Zara then turned to the magician, who was hurriedly gathering his belongings. "According to you, magic man, this staff is an illusion. Let's see if this illusion will bounce off your hard little head!" Before Zara had fully raised his staff, the magician was in full flight, pulling his trunk behind him, rabbits jumping out and birds taking flight from every pocket of his overcoat.

"Reality is as clear as your mind," spoke Zara to the remaining crowd. "Talk of illusion and blind belief is spread by magicians, other-worlders, and other dust devils seeking applause, coins from your pockets, and blood from your veins."

Zara raised his staff once again and spoke: "Test their heads for hollowness before you believe what comes from their mouths!"

Getting Underway

Preview

*Many [people] go fishing all of their lives without knowing that it is not
fish that they are after.*

HENRY DAVID THOREAU

The truth is not always obvious. You must usually look below the surface to
catch what you are really after, be it fish or truth. Career planning usually
begins with a self-evaluation that encourages you to look below your surface, focusing on interests, skills, and values. This chapter provides you the opportunity to
take a look at these factors in a manner that relates them to different kinds of
occupations. The results you obtain will prepare you to use the career exploration
resources described in Chapter Three. The main sections of this chapter are described next.

- **Occupational Interests** describes kinds of activities that can be a part of various occupations.
- **Occupational Skills** defines differing abilities that may be required in various
  kinds of occupations.
- **Work Values** explains various kinds of rewards that may be realized from
  work.
- **Self-Assessment** presents an evaluation instrument that measures interests,
  skills, and values, and relates the results to six general occupational clusters.
- **Steps to Interpret Your Results** provides a step-by-step procedure to explore
  the meaning of your assessment results.

By the end of this chapter you will have what you need to get started with
your career exploration.

Assessment of your interests is a good place to begin this evaluation process. The most common type of occupational assessment tries to relate your interests and preferred activities to the activities of various kinds of work. This is the focus of the next section.

Occupational Interests

*I*nterests are an important factor in career satisfaction. The reason is really quite simple: If the occupation you select involves activities you enjoy, you will probably like your work. Many people, however, make career decisions before they really know what kinds of day-to-day activities are involved in a given occupation. Such uninformed decision making can lead to unpleasant surprises and significant disappointments.

For purposes of career exploration, you will be looking at occupations in terms of seven general occupational clusters—groupings of occupations that are related in terms of interests, skills, and values. John Holland, a pioneering career development theorist, was one of the first to use a small number of general occupational clusters as the basis for career exploration. Holland proposed six occupational groupings or occupational themes: Realistic, Investigative, Artistic, Social, Enterprising, and Conventional. Subsequently, many systems of career planning have adopted variations of his concept. A brief description follows of activities related to the seven clusters used in this guide.

I-1 Mechanical	Working with the hands; with things, tools, instruments, and/or machines.
I-2 Analytical	Working with the mind; focusing on ideas, data, and technical concerns.
I-3 Technical	Working with information and things; involving inspecting, trouble-shooting, adjusting, or calibrating activities.
I-4 Expressive	Working with things and ideas; involving artistic and creative activities.
I-5 Empathic	Working with people; providing assistance, support, and/or education.
I-6 Persuasive	Working with people; involving leadership, politics, sales, promotion, and/or supervision.

I-7 Clerical   Working with data and details; maintaining
                                  records, schedules, and other paperwork.

Your self-assessment results will provide an indication of which clusters are likely to contain occupations that match your interests.

Travelog #8

*U*sing the descriptions of interests provided on the previous pages, describe an activity or project you have experienced that is related to each area of interest.

■ Mechanical

■ Analytical

■ Technical

■ Expressive

■ Empathic

■ Persuasive

■ Clerical

Occupational interests are a valuable guide to the career direction you will want to explore. You will also need to consider the skills you have (or need to develop) and how these relate to a career decision.

Occupational Skills

Skills are useful as a indicator of training and employment success. If the occupation you choose calls upon your strengths, you are more likely to succeed than if it requires you to exercise skills that you have not yet developed. Skills can often *be* developed, but a basic aptitude for a given type of task is a significant head start toward success. Aptitudes govern the speed and extent to which skills may be acquired. This section will deal with your current level of skills (also frequently called *abilities*). You can contact your counselor or teacher about further testing options.

Different occupations require varying combinations of skills. Very few people will have a high level of aptitude for every skill required by an occupation; this is rarely necessary for success. Your assessment results will be based on your estimation of your current skill level related to seven different abilities. These skills are widely recognized as relevant to occupational success, and variations of them are commonly used in objective testing batteries such as the General Aptitude Test Battery (GATB), the Differential Aptitude Test (DAT), and the Career Ability Placement Survey (CAPS). Such testing instruments are commonly available in college career centers, counseling offices, and school guidance departments. Here is a list of skills used in this guide:

S-1 Mechanical   The ability to understand and apply mechanical principles, work with tools, fix machines, and so on.

S-2 Spatial   The ability to visualize objects in space, estimate distances, see how objects fit together, and so on.

S-3 Reasoning   The ability to understand and use logical and rational thinking to solve problems.

S-4 Numerical   The ability to solve numerical problems through computation, applying mathematical rules, and so on.

S-5 Language

The ability to recognize and use standard English, spoken and written, including a wide variety of words.

S-6 Perceptual

The ability, rapidly and accurately, to observe detail, proof text for errors, and so on.

S-7 Dexterity

The ability to make rapid and accurate hand movements, utilize tools, make manual adjustments, and so on.

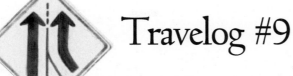

Travelog #9

*F*or each skill, identify two (2) occupations for which you think the skill would be a major factor in work performance and success.

Mechanical
  1. _____ 2. _____

Spatial
  1. _____ 2. _____

Reasoning
  1. _____ 2. _____

Numerical
  1. _____ 2. _____

Language
  1. _____ 2. _____

Perceptual
  1. _____ 2. _____

Dexterity
  1. _____ 2. _____

When you get to a later section of this chapter (the Occupational Cluster Sheets), these skills will be related to seven occupational clusters. At that point you can turn back and check your answers.

At least one more factor has to be considered in your initial career exploration—your values. As with interests and skills, values can provide a useful road sign pointing toward your occupational destination.

Work Values

Values reflect what you consider to be most important in life. This section will examine a narrower concept—*work* values—having to do with the kinds of rewards you desire from your work. Ideally, the rewards from your work would be compatible with what is most important to you. The closer this match, the more likely you will be satisfied with the work.

Different occupations provide varying opportunities for the expression of work values. This does *not*, however, mean that any given individual within an occupation holds any given set of values. Values are grouped with occupational clusters in terms of *opportunity for expression* and should not be taken as an "acid test" for occupational selection.

As you grow up, your work values are shaped by other people (parents, relatives, friends), by various social institutions (school, church, mass media), and by your own reflection upon what you have learned and experienced. Until you have taken the time to examine critically what you have "inherited," you can't be sure that these values are truly your own. Such an examination is an important part of career planning.

Your self-assessment will generate feedback related to a number of work values:

V-1 Achievement	To accomplish a goal resulting in increased efficiency, productivity, or competency.
V-2 Caring	To assist, care for, comfort, instruct, or encourage others.
V-3 Creativity	To exercise talents for innovation, originality, or the generation of new methods of doing things.
V-4 Independence	To work under your own direction, with a minimal degree of supervision.

V-5 Influence	To affect the opinions, attitudes, or actions of others.
V-6 Knowledge	To inquire, research, analyze, and otherwise extend the scope of what you know.
V-7 Leadership	To provide supervision, direction, and guidelines to others.
V-8 Order	To maintain a systematic, accurate, and carefully organized manner of doing things.
V-9 Persistence	To hold to a consistent and determined course of action until you accomplish your goal.
V-10 Growth	To expand self-knowledge and to pursue personal growth experiences.
V-11 Stability	To be assured of a settled, stable, and dependable manner of doing things.
V-12 Status	To enjoy respect, honor, and deference from others.
V-13 Variety	To pursue a wide range of different activities in a flexible environment.

Travelog #10

*L*ist one (1) value that is likely to be strongly associated with each of the following occupations. If you wish, you will be able to check your answers against the occupational cluster information provided later in this book.

Occupation	Associated Value
Police officer	_____
Nurse	_____
Accountant	_____
Scientist	_____
Artist	_____
Writer	_____
Lawyer	_____

The process of career decision making involves the consideration of all three factors (interests, skills, and work values) and many more. The following exercises will help you collect some data related to all three factors.

Self-Assessment

General Instructions

This survey is designed to collect information about what interests you, the current level of your skills, and what you feel is important. This information will be used to generate results that you will use for your own benefit. In order for these results to have any value to you, it is very important that you rate yourself as honestly as possible.

Please try to *rate yourself as you actually are today*, rather than how you would like to be or wish to appear to others; otherwise, your results will have little meaning to you. Also, try to *spread your ratings along the rating scale*, rather than giving many items exactly the same rating. Be sure to complete all parts. There is no time limit.

Special Note for SDS Users

If you have access to John Holland's *Self-Directed Search (SDS)*, you may choose to use the results of this instrument instead of (or in addition to) completing the following interest and skills self-assessments. In any case, do complete the *values assessment* that follows, since the SDS does not measure this variable. You will be instructed how to apply your SDS results in a later section.

Interest Assessment

*L*isted below are several kinds of work activities. Please read each item and decide how much the indicated activity interests (is appealing to) you. For the purpose of this exercise, do not consider your ability to do the activity, only your interest in it. Rate your INTEREST LEVEL (1–9) according to this scale:

1	2	3	4	5	6	7	8	9
NOT INTERESTED				SOMEWHAT INTERESTED			VERY INTERESTED	

For each cluster of six items, add your ratings for a TOTAL SCORE.

Ask Yourself: How Interested Am I In . . .

Working with hand tools   _____

Constructing or repairing things   _____

Working with machinery   _____

Enforcing safety regulations   _____

Reading *Popular Mechanics* magazine   _____

Working outdoors   _____

_____   I-1 TOTAL SCORE

Reading *Popular Science* magazine   _____

Visiting a scientific laboratory   _____

Analyzing theoretical problems   _____

Problem solving and experimenting   _____

Conducting medical research   _____

Analyzing statistical results for trends   _____

_____   I-2 TOTAL SCORE

Working with electronic instruments   _____

Collecting scientific data   _____

Reading *Popular Electronics* magazine   _____

Monitoring quality standards   _____

Checking compliance with regulations   _____

Conducting lab tests   _____

_____   I-3 TOTAL SCORE

Expressing myself in writing or art   _____

Taking an art course   _____

Expressing my ideas in an original manner   _____

Viewing works created by talented artists   _____

Reading photography or art magazines   _____

Visiting an art museum or a gallery   _____

_____   I-4 TOTAL SCORE

Providing care for children or the elderly   _____

Working in a social service agency   _____

Taking a human relations course   _____

Teaching, training, or advising others   _____

Assisting others who need help   _____

Working closely with others   _____

   _____   I-5 TOTAL SCORE

Selling products or ideas   _____

Promoting or marketing activities   _____

Motivating or leading others   _____

Providing legal advice   _____

Reading *Business Week* magazine   _____

Taking a business course   _____

   _____   I-6 TOTAL SCORE

Following office procedures   _____

Visiting a clerical operations center   _____

Maintaining financial records   _____

Typing, filing, and record keeping   _____

Scheduling activities or events   _____

Keeping track of schedules and details   _____

   _____   I-7 TOTAL SCORE

Skills Assessment

*L*isted below are several kinds of abilities. Read each item and then estimate (as objectively as you can) your current level of skill related to each ability, compared to others your age. Do not consider your interest in using that ability, only your skill in performing it. Rate your level of SKILL (1–9) according to the scale presented below:

1	2	3	4	5	6	7	8	9
LOW		BELOW AVERAGE		AVERAGE		ABOVE AVERAGE		HIGH

For each cluster of four items, add your ratings for a TOTAL SCORE.

Ask Yourself: How Skilled Am I At . . .

Fixing broken mechanical objects   _____

Figuring out how to put things together   _____

Understanding how mechanical things work   _____

Taking things apart to fix them   _____

_____   S-1 TOTAL SCORE

Estimating distances and dimensions   _____

Visualizing furniture placement in a room   _____

Finding locations on a road map   _____

Following floor plans or blueprints   _____

_____   S-2 TOTAL SCORE

Understanding theoretical relationships   _____

Following a complex logical argument   _____

Analyzing the main idea of a story   _____

Using abstract concepts to explain ideas   _____

_____   S-3 TOTAL SCORE

Doing arithmetic calculations   _____

Solving mathematical word problems   _____

Balancing my checkbook   _____

Calculating percentages and ratios   _____

_____   S-4 TOTAL SCORE

Using correct grammar in writing   _____

Writing a well-constructed paper or report   _____

Using proper capitalization and punctuation   _____

Understanding the words in college textbooks   _____

_____   S-5 TOTAL SCORE

Proofreading rapidly and accurately   _____

Spotting details that are out of place   _____

Checking over paperwork for errors   _____

Inspecting parts for possible defects   _____

    _____   S-6 TOTAL SCORE

Making quick and coordinated hand movements _____

Using my hands to move small objects   _____

Shuffling and dealing a deck of cards   _____

Sorting objects by hand   _____

    _____   S-7 TOTAL SCORE

Values Assessment

*L*isted below are a number of work objectives. Please read each item and rate it from 1–9, depending upon how IMPORTANT the described objective is to you. The rating scale is as follows:

1	2	3	4	5	6	7	8	9
NOT IMPORTANT				SOMEWHAT IMPORTANT			VERY IMPORTANT	

For each cluster of four items, add your ratings for a TOTAL SCORE.

Ask Yourself: How Important Is It for Me To . . .

Achieve my work objectives   _____

Feel that I am being productive   _____

Accomplish my work with increasing skill   _____

Accomplish above and beyond my objectives   _____

    _____   V-1 TOTAL SCORE

Assist those less fortunate than myself   _____

Be helpful to others   _____

Educate or guide others   _____

Serve others who are in poor health   _____

    _____   V-2 TOTAL SCORE

Express my creative talents   _____

Participate in innovative projects   _____

Try different methods of doing things   _____

Explore new and interesting discoveries   _____

_____   V-3 TOTAL SCORE

Work independently on projects   _____

Follow my own manner of doing things   _____

Work without close supervision from others   _____

Pretty much establish my own work priorities   _____

_____   V-4 TOTAL SCORE

Know what it takes to influence decisions   _____

Influence the actions of others   _____

Figure out how to present an idea to someone   _____

Persuade others to think in a given manner   _____

_____   V-5 TOTAL SCORE

Have an in-depth knowledge of my work   _____

Learn new skills and methods of work   _____

Continually study and to expand my knowledge   _____

Maintain my curiosity about my field of interest   _____

_____   V-6 TOTAL SCORE

Have planning and decision-making authority   _____

Direct and supervise the work of others   _____

Utilize my leadership skills   _____

Exercise significant decision-making authority   _____

_____   V-7 TOTAL SCORE

Have orderly work procedures _____

Have a systematic method to get things done _____

Maintain an organized work space _____

Have a clear standard to guide my work _____

_____ V-8 TOTAL SCORE

See projects through from start to finish _____

Overcome problems or difficulties _____

Finish work that is assigned to me _____

Follow through on tough assignments _____

_____ V-9 TOTAL SCORE

Pursue personal growth opportunities _____

Increase my level of self-awareness _____

Increase my self-knowledge _____

Work toward a sense of personal fulfillment _____

_____ V-10 TOTAL SCORE

Have a consistent pattern of work assignments _____

Be a part of a stable work environment _____

Work in an environment with clear expectations _____

Have a strong sense of job security _____

_____ V-11 TOTAL SCORE

Have status among my fellow workers _____

Be publicly recognized by my supervisor _____

Enjoy a sense of respect among my peers _____

Hold a position of high visibility _____

_____ V-12 TOTAL SCORE

Work in an environment without too many rules _____

Pursue a wide range of different activities _____

Vary my work tasks on a regular basis _____

Avoid doing the same thing over and over again _____

_____ V-13 TOTAL SCORE

Assessment Summary Sheet

*I*f you take the time to summarize your scores on this sheet, it will simplify the next section of this chapter. In the next section you will be applying your scores to seven occupational clusters. Please refer back to the totals on each of the assessments and copy them onto this sheet in the appropriate spaces. Make sure the score codes (I-1, S-3) match.

Interest Scores

I-1	_____	Mechanical	I-5	_____	Empathic
I-2	_____	Analytical	I-6	_____	Persuasive
I-3	_____	Technical	I-7	_____	Clerical
I-4	_____	Expressive			

Skills Scores

S-1	_____	Mechanical	S-5	_____	Language
S-2	_____	Spatial	S-6	_____	Perceptual
S-3	_____	Reasoning	S-7	_____	Dexterity
S-4	_____	Numerical			

Values Scores

V-1	_____	Achievement	V-8	_____	Order
V-2	_____	Caring	V-9	_____	Persistence
V-3	_____	Creativity	V-10	_____	Growth
V-4	_____	Independence	V-11	_____	Stability
V-5	_____	Influence	V-12	_____	Status
V-6	_____	Knowledge	V-13	_____	Variety
V-7	_____	Leadership			

Travelog #11

I hope the self-assessment you have completed has given you some useful information to consider as part of your career planning. Please think about, and provide written responses for, the following questions.

■ What were your highest two (2) *interest* factors?
   1.

   2.

■ Would you have predicted this result? Why or why not?

■ What were your highest two (2) *skill* factors?
   1.

   2.

■ Would you have predicted this result? Why or why not?

- What are your two (2) highest work *value* factors?

  1.

  2.

- Would you have predicted this result? Why or why not?

- Why is it important to consider all three factors (interests, skills, and values)?

- How will your results make you think differently about yourself and your career possibilities?

Occupational Cluster Sheets

The next pages present seven occupational clusters, each of which contains many different occupations. You will be transferring your assessment results onto these sheets in order to get an idea of the degree to which each cluster is compatible with your interests, skills, and values. Each cluster sheet contains the interests, skills, and values most commonly associated with that cluster.

Refer to the Assessment Summary Sheet and copy your scores onto the cluster sheets in the appropriate spaces. Be sure that score codes (I-1, V-6) match. Then, for each score, read across the sheet and find the score range that contains your score. Starting at the left end of the scale, draw a straight, dark line across to the end of the range that contains your score. The label above the end of this line will give you an idea of how to interpret your score (Low, Moderately Low, Moderate, Moderately High, or High).

Example: For the first section of the Mechanical Cluster, if your Mechanical Interest score (designated as score code I-1 on your Assessment Summary Sheet) was 38, the top of your cluster sheet would look like this:

Mechanical Cluster

INTERESTS	Low	Moderately Low	Moderate	Moderately High	High
Mechanical					
I-1 Score 38	6-18	19-23	24-36	37-42	43-54

This would indicate a *moderately high* score.

Special Note: Optional SDS Results

If you have access to the *Self-Directed Search (SDS)* by John Holland (a common, standardized self-assessment instrument), you can transfer some of your scores from the SDS to the following cluster sheets, providing you with additional interest and skills information. The results of the SDS section on **Activities** (pp. 4–5 of that booklet) can be used to supplement your *interest* results; the SDS section on **Competencies** (pp. 6–7) can be used to supplement your *skills* results. The results of your Career Travel Guide self-assessment and the SDS results should be very close (within one category of each other); if this is not the case, you may want to discuss possible sources of variation with your instructor or a career counselor.

If you do *not* choose to use supplemental SDS results, simply leave these sections of the cluster sheets blank.

Go ahead and complete each of the seven Occupational Cluster Sheets at this time. At the bottom of each sheet you will see that there is a place for you to mark your impression of the Overall Compatibility between your interests, skills, and values and that particular occupational cluster. You will complete this as part of the next section, so leave it blank for now.

Mechanical Cluster

INTERESTS	Low	Moderately Low	Moderate	Moderately High	High
Mechanical I-1 Score _____	6–18	19–23	24–36	37–42	43–54
Optional: SDS Activities (p. 4) Realistic (R) No. of L's _____	1–2	3–4	5–6	7–9	10–11

SKILLS	Low	Moderately Low	Moderate	Moderately High	High
Mechanical S-1 Score _____	4–12	13–15	16–24	25–27	28–36
Spatial S-2 Score _____	4–12	13–15	16–24	25–27	28–36
Perceptual S-6 Score _____	4–12	13–15	16–24	25–27	28–36
Dexterity S-7 Score _____	4–12	13–15	16–24	25–27	28–36
Optional: SDS Competencies (p. 6) Realistic (R) No. of Y's _____	1–2	3–4	5–6	7–9	10–11

VALUES	Low	Moderately Low	Moderate	Moderately High	High
Independence V-4 Score _____	4–12	13–15	16–24	25–27	28–36
Order V-8 Score _____	4–12	13–15	16–24	25–27	28–36
Persistence V-9 Score _____	4–12	13–15	16–24	25–27	28–36
Stability V-11 Score _____	4–12	13–15	16–24	25–27	28–36

OVERALL COMPATIBILITY	Low	Moderately Low	Moderate	Moderately High	High

Analytical Cluster

INTERESTS	Low	Moderately Low	Moderate	Moderately High	High
Analytical I-2 Score _____	6–18	19–23	24–36	37–42	43–54
Optional: SDS Activities (p. 4) Investigative (I) No. of L's _____	1–2	3–4	5–6	7–9	10–11

SKILLS	Low	Moderately Low	Moderate	Moderately High	High
Reasoning S-3 Score _____	4–12	13–15	16–24	25–27	28–36
Numerical S-4 Score _____	4–12	13–15	16–24	25–27	28–36
Language S-5 Score _____	4–12	13–15	16–24	25–27	28–36
Perceptual S-6 Score _____	4–12	13–15	16–24	25–27	28–36
Optional: SDS Competencies (p. 6) Investigative (I) No. of Y's _____	1–2	3–4	5–6	7–9	10–11

VALUES	Low	Moderately Low	Moderate	Moderately High	High
Achievement V-1 Score _____	4–12	13–15	16–24	25–27	28–36
Creativity V-3 Score _____	4–12	13–15	16–24	25–27	28–36
Independence V-4 Score _____	4–12	13–15	16–24	25–27	28–36
Knowledge V-6 Score _____	4–12	13–15	16–24	25–27	28–36

OVERALL COMPATIBILITY

	Low	Moderately Low	Moderate	Moderately High	High

Technical Cluster

INTERESTS

	Low	Moderately Low	Moderate	Moderately High	High
Technical I-3 Score _____	6–18	19–23	24–36	37–42	43–54
Optional: SDS Activities (p. 4) Investigative (I) No. of L's _____	1–2	3–4	5–6	7–9	10–11

SKILLS

	Low	Moderately Low	Moderate	Moderately High	High
Mechanical S-1 Score _____	4–12	13–15	16–24	25–27	28–36
Spatial S-2 Score _____	4–12	13–15	16–24	25–27	28–36
Reasoning S-3 Score _____	4–12	13–15	16–24	25–27	28–36
Numerical S-4 Score _____	4–12	13–15	16–24	25–27	28–36
Perceptual S-6 Score _____	4–12	13–15	16–24	25–27	28–36
Dexterity S-7 Score _____	4–12	13–15	16–24	25–27	28–36
Optional: SDS Competencies (p. 6) Investigative (I) No. of Y's _____	1–2	3–4	5–6	7–9	10–11

VALUES

	Low	Moderately Low	Moderate	Moderately High	High
Order V-8 Score _____	4–12	13–15	16–24	25–27	28–36
Persistence V-9 Score _____	4–12	13–15	16–24	25–27	28–36

VALUES	Low	Moderately Low	Moderate	Moderately High	High
Stability V-11 Score _____	4–12	13–15	16–24	25–27	28–36

OVERALL COMPATIBILITY	Low	Moderately Low	Moderate	Moderately High	High

Expressive Cluster

INTERESTS	Low	Moderately Low	Moderate	Moderately High	High
Expressive I-4 Score _____	6–18	19–23	24–36	37–42	43–54
Optional: SDS Activities (p. 4) Artistic (A) No. of L's _____	1–2	3–4	5–6	7–9	10–11

SKILLS	Low	Moderately Low	Moderate	Moderately High	High
Spatial S-2 Score _____	4–12	13–15	16–24	25–27	28–36
Language S-5 Score _____	4–12	13–15	16–24	25–27	28–36
Perceptual S-6 Score _____	4–12	13–15	16–24	25–27	28–36
Dexterity S-7 Score _____	4–12	13–15	16–24	25–27	28–36
Optional: SDS Competencies (p. 6) Artistic (A) No. of Y's _____	1–2	3–4	5–6	7–9	10–11

VALUES	Low	Moderately Low	Moderate	Moderately High	High
Creativity V-3 Score _____	4–12	13–15	16–24	25–27	28–36
Independence V-4 Score _____	4–12	13–15	16–24	25–27	28–36

VALUES	Low	Moderately Low	Moderate	Moderately High	High
Growth V-10 Score _____	4–12	13–15	16–24	25–27	28–36
Variety V-13 Score _____	4–12	13–15	16–24	25–27	28–36

OVERALL COMPATIBILITY	Low	Moderately Low	Moderate	Moderately High	High

Empathic Cluster

INTERESTS	Low	Moderately Low	Moderate	Moderately High	High
Empathic I-5 Score _____	6–18	19–23	24–36	37–42	43–54
Optional: SDS Activities (p. 5) Social (S) No. of L's _____	1–2	3–4	5–6	7–9	10–11

SKILLS	Low	Moderately Low	Moderate	Moderately High	High
Reasoning S-3 Score _____	4–12	13–15	16–24	25–27	28–36
Numerical S-4 Score _____	4–12	13–15	16–24	25–27	28–36
Language S-5 Score _____	4–12	13–15	16–24	25–27	28–36
Optional: SDS Competencies (p. 7) Social (S) No. of Y's _____	1–2	3–4	5–6	7–9	10–11

VALUES	Low	Moderately Low	Moderate	Moderately High	High
Caring V-2 Score _____	4–12	13–15	16–24	25–27	28–36
Influence V-5 Score _____	4–12	13–15	16–24	25–27	28–36

VALUES	Low	Moderately Low	Moderate	Moderately High	High
Growth V-10 Score _____	4–12	13–15	16–24	25–27	28–36
Stability V-11 Score _____	4–12	13–15	16–24	25–27	28–36

OVERALL COMPATIBILITY	Low	Moderately Low	Moderate	Moderately High	High

Persuasive Cluster

INTERESTS	Low	Moderately Low	Moderate	Moderately High	High
Persuasive I-6 Score _____	6–18	19–23	24–36	37–42	43–54
Optional: SDS Activities (p. 5) Enterprising (E) No. of L's _____	1–2	3–4	5–6	7–9	10–11

SKILLS	Low	Moderately Low	Moderate	Moderately High	High
Reasoning S-3 Score _____	4–12	13–15	16–24	25–27	28–36
Numerical S-4 Score _____	4–12	13–15	16–24	25–27	28–36
Language S-5 Score _____	4–12	13–15	16–24	25–27	28–36
Optional: SDS Competencies (p. 7) Enterprising (E) No. of Y's _____	1–2	3–4	5–6	7–9	10–11

VALUES	Low	Moderately Low	Moderate	Moderately High	High
Achievement V-1 Score _____	4–12	13–15	16–24	25–27	28–36
Influence V-5 Score _____	4–12	13–15	16–24	25–27	28–36

VALUES	Low	Moderately Low	Moderate	Moderately High	High
Leadership V-7 Score _____	4–12	13–15	16–24	25–27	28–36
Status V-12 Score _____	4–12	13–15	16–24	25–27	28–36

OVERALL COMPATIBILITY	Low	Moderately Low	Moderate	Moderately High	High

Clerical Cluster

INTERESTS	Low	Moderately Low	Moderate	Moderately High	High
Clerical I-7 Score _____	6–18	19–23	24–36	37–42	43–54
Optional: SDS Activities (p. 5) Conventional (C) No. of L's _____	1–2	3–4	5–6	7–9	10–11

SKILLS	Low	Moderately Low	Moderate	Moderately High	High
Perceptual S-6 Score _____	4–12	13–15	16–24	25–27	28–36
Dexterity S-7 Score _____	4–12	13–15	16–24	25–27	28–36
Optional: SDS Competencies (p. 7) Conventional (C) No. of Y's _____	1–2	3–4	5–6	7–9	10–11

VALUES	Low	Moderately Low	Moderate	Moderately High	High
Order V-8 Score _____	4–12	13–15	16–24	25–27	28–36
Persistence V-9 Score _____	4–12	13–15	16–24	25–27	28–36
Stability V-11 Score _____	4–12	13–15	16–24	25–27	28–36

OVERALL COMPATIBILITY	Low	Moderately Low	Moderate	Moderately High	High

Steps to Interpret Your Results

Now you have a summary of interests, skills, and values for each of the seven occupational clusters. What you are ideally looking for is a cluster where you have moderate or higher ratings for the related interests, skills, and values. This would indicate an area that is worth further exploration.

The following step-by-step guide may be useful in this process. Complete the steps for each occupational cluster.

Action Step #1   **Locate your interests.** Refer back to the seven Occupational Cluster Sheets (starting with the Mechanical cluster). Review the Interest rating at the top of the sheet (and the SDS Activities rating, if you used this as well). This score should normally be the moderate range or higher for this cluster to qualify for further exploration.

Action Step #2   **Review your skills ratings** for this cluster. If the related skills (and the SDS Competencies rating, if you used this as well) are rated moderate or higher, these scores confirm that the occupations in this cluster may be suitable. If one or more of the skills are rated lower than moderate, you will need to consider if these are skills that you can develop through further training, and whether further ability testing may be useful in helping you analyze your skills more objectively.

Action Step #3   **Review your values.** Now move to your values ratings for the cluster you are examining. As with the skills, if the related values are rated moderate or higher, this indicates a degree of opportunity for expressing these values within the occupations in this cluster. If one or more of these values are rated lower than moderate, less opportunity for expression is indicated, and this may be an area you need to explore further with the assistance of a counselor.

Action Step #4   **Rate overall compatibility**. Review the interest, skill, and value ratings for the cluster and determine an overall rating. For example, if all the ratings were high, the overall compatibility would be high; if some were moderately high and others moderately low, the overall compatibility might be moderate. You don't have to be exact about this; just get a sense of whether this cluster is promising enough to justify further exploration. At the bottom of the Cluster Sheet, draw a horizontal line across the page (as you did with your other scores) to indicate your overall compatibility rating for this cluster.

Action Step #5   Repeat steps 1–4 for each of the other clusters.

Action Step #6   **Possibly reconsider your interests**. If you have any clusters where both skills and values are rated high, but a less-than-moderate interest is indicated, you may want to review these clusters in more detail to be sure they do not merit further consideration.

Action Step #7   Rank the seven occupational clusters according to overall compatibility. The cluster with the highest overall compatibility would be listed first; the one with the lowest overall compatibility would be last.

1.

2.

3.

4.

5.

6.

7.

If you have any difficulty completing this exercise, please make an appointment with a counselor or career planning instructor for further explanation and assistance.

Travelog #12

*T*he occupational clusters you have been examining may be subdivided into more specific Worker Trait Groups (for example, 3.01 Managerial Work: Nature). These groups may then be used to guide your exploration and to generate specific occupations for your consideration. Based on your priority listing, you should have an idea of which clusters are most compatible with your interests, skills, and values.

Start with the cluster that you have listed as your first priority. Find the title of this cluster in the following table and review the Worker Trait Groups listed under it. **Circle the Worker Trait Group numbers of the groups that you want to explore in more detail.**

Example: If your first priority was Analytical, you might look through the list and decide that Medical Sciences and Social Research looked interesting. You would then circle 2.03 and 11.03. After you have finished with your first priority cluster, repeat this process for at least your second and third priority clusters. Continue until you have circled at least five Worker Trait Group numbers.

MECHANICAL

3.01	Managerial Work: Nature
4.01	Safety and Law Enforcement
4.02	Security Services
5.04	Air and Water Vehicle Operation
5.05	Craft Technology

ANALYTICAL

2.01	Physical Sciences
2.02	Life Sciences
2.03	Medical Sciences
11.01	Math and Statistics
11.03	Social Research
11.06	Finance

TECHNICAL

2.04	Laboratory Technology
5.01	Engineering
5.03	Engineering Technology
5.07	Quality Control
11.10	Regulations Enforcement
11.12	Contracts & Claims

EXPRESSIVE

1.01   Literary Arts
1.02   Visual Arts
1.03   Drama
1.04   Music
1.05   Dance
11.08 Communications

EMPATHIC

10.01 Social Services
10.02 Nursing, Therapy, Teaching
10.03 Child and Adult Care
11.02 Educational and Library
       Services

PERSUASIVE

8.01   Sales Technology
8.02   General Sales
9.02   Barber and Beauty Services
11.04 Law
11.05 Business Administration
11.07 Services Administration
11.09 Promotion
11.11 Business Management

CLERICAL

7.01   Administrative Detail
7.02   Mathematical Detail
7.03   Financial Detail
7.04   Oral Communications
7.05   Records Processing
7.06   Machine Operation

Travelog #13

*L*ist in priority from high to low, five (5) Worker Trait Groups that seem to be the most promising for further exploration. To the right of the group, place a check mark under those factors that *most strongly support* your selection.

EXAMPLE	Interests	Skills	Values
1. 2.03 Medical Sciences	☑	☑	☐

	Interests	Skills	Values
1. _____	☐	☐	☐
2. _____	☐	☐	☐
3. _____	☐	☐	☐
4. _____	☐	☐	☐
5. _____	☐	☐	☐

■ Do you see anything that these groups have in common? If so, what?

■ Which of these groups would you have expected to pick before the assessment?

■ Which of these groups would you probably *not* have chosen before the assessment?

■ How difficult do you think it will be to select an occupation from among these groups?

Quiz 2

*P*lease answer the following questions. Continue answers on reverse side if additional space is needed.

1. Why is it important to evaluate your interests when trying to select an occupation?

2. What does an evaluation of skills contribute to the career planning process?

3. What does it mean if your most important values do not match up with the highest reward values of the occupations you are considering?

4. What should you do if one or more factors (interests, skills, or values) do not match up with the pattern for an occupation you are considering?

5. What is the most important thing that you learned about yourself by working through this chapter?

6. What topic covered in this chapter would you like to explore further?

To Consider . . .

1. A student decides that he wants to become a rocket scientist. His interest and value results confirm this choice, but his skills scores are below average for this occupation.

   If you were his career counselor, how would you advise him?

   When should someone be told that their career plans are unrealistic?

2. A student has taken all the tests available, but still has no idea what she wants to do.

   What might be the reasons for this?

   What are some possible reasons for someone to resist the clarification of a career direction?

Suggested Activities

1. Ask several friends to review your assessment results. Pay attention to how they interpret them. How does their interpretation differ from your own? Why is there a difference?

2. Ask someone who knows you well to take the assessment as if he or she were you. How do the perceptions of this person (about your interests, skills, and values) differ from your own? How do you account for such differences?

3. Arrange to take an objective skills test. This can usually be done through a career counselor or instructor. Compare the results with your own self-estimates. How do the results differ? How do you account for such differences?

The Parable of the Sea

Zara stopped on a cliff overlooking the sea. The wind was blowing violently, swirling the dark clouds like smoke rings blown from the mouth of heaven, driving great waves to crash against the rocky shore.

Zara spoke to his disciple: "Like a ship at sea, we are most aware of the waves that toss us about. But there are deeper currents that flow beneath the surface. Where your rudder cannot reach. Where, from the surface, your eye cannot see. In these bottomless depths, destiny is formed and flows silently beneath the waves.

"Surface beings will forever be tossed about by the waves and blown to and fro by the wind. They will suffer the seasickness of despair that engulfs those who float along without power and direction. They will suffer the scurvy of those who never know the true source of their sustenance. The surface beings will cry out against the wind and the waves: 'We are lost! We at at the mercy of powers beyond our control! Life is suffering and without direction, purpose, or meaning! Who will deliver us?'

"If you would dare to know the depths, you must enter its darkness. You must dive through the turbulent waves of your life and enter into deeper currents of thought. Only those willing to leap into the depths will come to know the slow and sure movements of their destiny. Only the deep beings will come to know their Way."

Zara continued: "But the pressure increases with the depth. Not every being can endure the pressures and dangers of the deep. You must be strong of will, clear of thought, and powerful of spirit; otherwise, you will be crushed by the depth and dashed into the rocks by the currents. Deep ones must be prepared for the abyssal zones they enter. Their minds must grow gills that can extract air from the liquid of life and meaning from fathomless Being."

Zara turned to his disciple and asked her: "Would you be a deep one? Are you prepared to dive into the depths of your destiny? Would you know your Way? Then . . . show me your gills!"

CHAPTER THREE

Resources and Rest Stops

Preview

*How many a man has dated a new era in his life from the reading of
a book!*

HENRY DAVID THOREAU

As we have previously discussed, myths, preconceptions, and stereotypes about occupations are often the rule rather than the exception. Reference books and other information resources are important tools for uncovering the nature of occupations. Now that you have narrowed down your career search, you will need to become familiar with these resources and what they have to offer. The main sections of this chapter are as follows.

- *Guide for Occupational Exploration* describes a valuable resource published by the U.S. Department of Labor that is organized by the same Worker Trait Groups you have been working with.

- **Occupational Listing** provides a resource to translate Worker Trait Groups into specific occupations for further exploration.

- *Occupational Outlook Handbook* introduces the resource you will use to collect specific information about the occupations you decide to explore.

- **Other Career Resources** lists a number of other information resources commonly available for your use in career centers and libraries.

By the time you finish this chapter, you will be ready for the exploration of specific occupations.

Resources described in this chapter provide information that will help you make a career decision, but this information is in no way a complete picture of the occupation itself. These books contain much useful information, but it is important to verify this information before you base a life-changing decision on it. By all means, read everything you can get your hands on about the occupations you are considering, but don't make up your mind based solely on this information. Other techniques, such as the worker interview (described later in this book), need to be used to supplement what you have read.

Using this chapter, you will learn about a number of important information resources. Such resources are commonly found in local libraries, high school or college counseling centers, or the offices of professional career counselors.

The specific information provided by the Occupational Listing will be useful if you are not able to locate other resources, but you'll still want to narrow your career search to some specific occupations.

Guide for Occupational Exploration (GOE)

The *GOE* is a good reference to use in order to explore and expand your list of occupational groups; it is ordered by the same Worker Trait Groups with which you have been working. For the occupations that fall within each group, it provides answers to the following questions:

- What kind of work would you do?
- What skills and abilities do you need for this kind of work?
- How do you know if you would like, or could learn, to do this kind of work?
- How can you prepare for and enter this kind of work?
- What else should you consider about these jobs?

The *GOE*, originally published by the U.S. Department of Labor, also provides a complete list of occupations that fall within each group. Some of the following information is excerpted from that source. Other publishers have developed their own versions of the *GOE*; these versions will vary in format and content to some degree, but should be based on the same Worker Trait Group categories. These sections of the *GOE* are reproduced for your information:

The **Introduction** will explain the purpose and organization of the *GOE*.

Use of the *Guide* in Career Exploration explains how to approach the material in this reference as an aid to career planning.

A **Sample Worker Trait Group Description** (11.04 Law) is reproduced to give you an example of the information provided within the *GOE*.

I. Introduction

Purpose of the Guide

One of the first objectives of the U.S. Federal-State Employment Service System is to help people see themselves realistically in regard to their ability to meet job requirements. The *Guide for Occupational Exploration* is designed for that purpose. By providing information about the interests, aptitudes, adaptabilities, and other requisites of occupational groups, the *Guide* makes possible a comparison of these requirements with what the individual knows about himself or herself. It is also a tool for counselors assisting individuals in self-assessment and occupational choice.

The language of the text is simple and nontechnical, intended for any reader's use, with or without counseling help: the youth who is planning a career; the person who must, or wishes to, change jobs; the partially qualified or unqualified jobseeker; and the counselor or vocational adviser who assists others with career exploration and planning and occupational choices or changes.

Organization

The data in this publication are organized into 12 interest areas, 66 work groups, and 348 subgroups.

INTEREST AREAS

The interest areas correspond to the interest factors which were identified from the research and development activities in interest measurement conducted by the Division of Testing in the U.S. Employment Service. The interest factors represent the broad interest requirements of occupations as well as the vocational interests of individuals. Both the factors and the areas are identified by a two-digit code, for example:

01   An interest in creative expression of feelings or ideas.

WORK GROUPS

Within each interest area are work groups - jobs suitable for exploration by those who have the particular interest. Each work group contains descriptive information and a listing of jobs. Within each group, the jobs are of the same general type of work and require the same adaptabilities and capabilities of the worker. Each group has its unique four-digit code and title, for example:

01.01   Literary Arts

The number of groups in each area varies from 2 in Area 12 to 12 in Area 5.

SUBGROUPS

Within each work group, jobs are subgrouped to make it easier for the reader to distinguish among jobs. Each subgroup has its six-digit unique code and title, for example:

01.01.02 Creative Writing

Because of the number of jobs within some of the subgroups, a further clustering of these jobs by industry is made, for example, aircraft manufacturing, iron and steel, motion picture. Within the same industry designation occupations are listed in alphabetical order and also within each subgroup. If an occupation has more than one industry designation, it is listed under that which occurs first alphabetically; for example, a job having the industry designations of motion picture, radio, and tv broadcasting would be listed under "motion picture."

The following illustrates the components of the structure:

01   Artistic (Interest area)

01.01   Literary Arts (Work group)

01.01.02 Creative Writing (Subgroup)

     Screen Writer (motion pic, radio & tv broad.) 131.087-018

     Crossword-Puzzle Maker (print. & pub.) 139.087-010

     Editorial Writer (print. & pub.) 131.067-022

     Biographer (profess. & kin.) 052.067-010

     Copy Writer (profess. & kin.) 131.067-014

     Humorist (profess. & kin.) 131.067-026

     Lyricist (profess. & kin.) 131.067-034

Poet (profess. & kin.) 131.067-042
Writer, Prose, Fiction and Nonfiction
(profess. & kin.) 131.067-946
Continuity Writer (radio & tv broad.)
131.087-010

Descriptive information for each group gives the kinds of job activities performed, the requirements made on the worker, clues for relating individuals to the type of work, preparation for entry into jobs, and other pertinent items.

To meet the needs of all the users of this publication, four appendixes are added.

Appendix A: Background and Technical development of the Interest Factors and the *Guide*. Describes the concepts and procedures for the development of the interest factors, and the methodology for their use in determining interest areas in this publication. Includes the techniques and procedures used in developing the work groups and subgroups.

Appendix B. Uses Interest and Aptitude Tests (measurement tests oriented to utilization of the *Guide*). Provides (1) a brief description of the USES Interest Inventory and General Aptitude Test Battery (GATB)

(measures of an individual's occupational interests and aptitudes oriented to the *Guide* and its use); and (2) a listing of occupations for which specific Aptitude Test Batteries (SATB's) have been developed to aid counselors who have access to the GATB.

Appendix C: Use of the *Guide* in organizing career and occupational information resources. Contains techniques and procedures for cataloging and filing occupational information materials according to the structure in the *Guide*.

Appendix D: Alphabetic Arrangement of Occupations. Lists all the occupations in the *Guide*. Bridges the occupations in the *Dictionary of Occupational Titles* (DOT) and the sub-groups in the *Guide*. Includes all occupations in the DOT, fourth edition, excepting those specifically related to the military. Occupational titles are the same as those in the *Dictionary*, followed by the industry designation(s), the *Dictionary* code, and the six-digit code from this publication. Base titles are in capital letters; undefined related titles, in initial capital letters; and alternate titles, in lower case letters.

II. Use of the Guide in Career Exploration

An essential ingredient of vocational counseling is occupational and labor market information. Although the counseling process involves far more than providing such information, any instrument that organizes the world of work and provides information about occupational duties and requirements is valuable both to the counselor and to the counselee. Because vocational counseling services are not available to large numbers of potential counselees, the *Guide* is intended to help such persons make more informed vocational decisions than they might otherwise.

In this section of the *Guide*, both the individual who must make occupational choices without benefit of vocational counseling and the vocational counselor who assists counselees are instructed in how to use the *Guide*.

Use by Individuals Without Counselor Assistance

If you need help in deciding what kind of work you should choose, you can use the *Guide* to help you plan your career or get ready to find a job: not just any job, but one you can do or learn to do and which will be satisfying to you.

Different people like, and are good at, different things. To find the job that is right for you, you need two kinds of information:

1. You need information about yourself. You need to know the kind of work you would like to do and whether you are able to do such work. If you can't do it now, can you learn to do it and is a training program available?

GUIDE FOR OCCUPATIONAL EXPLORATION

2. You need information about occupations that sound interesting to you. What does the worker do on such jobs? What knowledge and skills must the worker have? What training is required?

This *Guide* tells you about occupations that relate to your interests and abilities. When you have used it properly, you will be better prepared to plan your career or seek employment, whether you do so through your public employment service office, an employment agency, a school placement program, answers to want ads, or applications directly to employers. Taking the following steps, you will learn about many jobs, including some you never knew existed. You should then be able to decide what type of work you can do and will find satisfaction in doing.

STEP 1. THINK ABOUT YOUR INTERESTS

What kind of work would you most like to do? Did you know that all jobs in the world of work have been organized into groups according to the interests of the workers?

Some workers like to help others. Some would rather do mechanical work with their hands or tools. Others prefer artistic work, or writing, or selling, or clerical work. These are just a few examples. The *Guide for Occupational Exploration* has taken all jobs in the United States and organized them into 12 areas on the basis of worker interest. They are called Interest Areas. Each of these 12 interest areas has been given a name, a code number, and a brief description. You will find these on page 9 of the *Guide*.

In order to learn more about the relation of your interests to occupations, turn to page 8 of the *Guide* and read the titles and descriptions of each interest area. Select one or more areas you think you would like to explore.

STEP 2. SELECT ONE OR MORE WORK GROUPS TO EXPLORE

In order to know what work groups to explore, you need to decide whether you would find satisfaction in work activities such as those required by occupations in the group. To do this, turn to the Summary Listing of Interest Areas, Work Groups, and Subgroups on pages 9–12 in the *Guide*. Look up the page numbers for each interest area you selected in Step 1. Turn to that page and read the description of the area. Then read the titles of each work group within the area. Think about what you like to do and what you think you can do. The following information will help you select the work groups that interest you.

Many of the jobs listed in the interest areas you have selected may require knowledge and skills that you do not have or would have difficulty acquiring. There should be occupations in some of these areas, however, that fit your interests and that you can do or learn to do. The jobs in each Interest Area have been divided into groups of jobs having similar worker requirements. These are called work groups.

Some work groups are made up of jobs requiring little specialized training or experience. Jobs in these groups are open to nearly anyone who is willing to work. Other groups include jobs requiring special courses in school or special training or education after high school. For example, some jobs require knowledge of subjects such as physics or chemistry. Others require accuracy and speed in working difficult math problems. You must think about what courses you have taken in school, how well you did in those subjects, and whether or not you might like a job that uses such knowledge and skill. You also have to think about whether you might be able to get the necessary additional training.

The groups that require the most education, training, and experience are usually listed first among the work groups in most interest areas. For example, in Area 05, Mechanical, the first work group is 05.01, Engineering. Most jobs in this group require 4 or more years of college.

The last work group in this area is 05.12, Elemental Work, Mechanical. In this group, many jobs are open to workers who have little formal education. As you make your selection of work groups to explore, you need to think about the difficulty of the work involved in each group, and about the training and experience that are required.

When you have made your selection of work groups from the first interest area, follow this same process for any other areas you selected in Step 1.

STEP 3. EXPLORE THE WORK GROUPS YOU SELECTED

To explore a work group, look up its description in the *Guide for Occupational Exploration* and read it very carefully. As you read about a group, you may discover that it is not what you thought it would be and that you are not interested in it. Or you may find that the training requirements are more difficult than you want. If you find for any reason that you no longer want to consider the group, stop exploring it, and go on to the next group you wish to consider.

STEP 4. EXPLORE SUBGROUPS AND SPECIFIC OCCUPATIONS

Each work group in the *Guide* contains occupations that have been organized into subgroups.

Each subgroup is identified by a six-digit code and a title, and contains a list of all the occupations assigned to it.

After you have studied a work group description and decided that you are interested in considering it further, you should examine its subgroups to see if one or more of them appears to suit your interests and qualifications better than the others. If you need further information to help you decide, you should select one or more of the occupations in the subgroups and look them up in the *Dictionary of Occupational Titles*. You can do this by using the nine-digit DOT code, which is shown in the subgroups immediately following the title of each occupation.

Job definitions in the *Dictionary of Occupational Titles* (DOT) are listed in numerical order by DOT code. For example, to look up Editor, Film, you would look in the DOT under code 962.264-010, which is on page 930.

When you have completed your exploration of all groups that interest you and have identified subgroups, and possibly occupations of particular interest, you are in a position to organize the information you have collected. You can then make some decisions and plan your next steps.

STEP 5. GET IT ALL TOGETHER

Compare your present qualifications with those needed for the groups you are considering. You may have the training and experience necessary for immediate employment. On the other hand, you may have to make plans that include additional training or work experience at a lower level to help qualify you for the work of your choice.

At any rate, list those occupations or subgroups of occupations you are now interested in and think you

can learn to do. Then plan to get training or a job.

If you still don't know what you should do, you can probably be helped by a vocational counselor or by a course or program designed for people who want assistance in vocational planning. If you are a student, you should arrange to meet with your school counselor, who can help you personally or tell you about any special programs available. If you are already in contact with a specialized agency such as the Bureau of Vocational Rehabilitation, a halfway house, or a CETA program, the counselor or caseworker in that program should be able to help you or refer you to someone who can.

If you are completely on your own, you should try to locate a private or public organization that offers vocational guidance services. Your library can probably help you identify such organizations. One such agency, which should be able to give you both employment counseling and job placement service, is the local office of the State employment service.

Use by Vocational Counselors

The counselor who assists individuals to choose a suitable occupational or vocational goal may function in any of a variety of settings - the school, the college, the public employment service, the private employment service, the vocational rehabilitation agency, or the community or private vocational guidance center.

In virtually every setting in which such counselors operate, they wish to help the individual evaluate his or her occupational interests, skills, and potentials, relate them to occupational requirements and opportunities, and arrive at a suitable occupational goal and a plan for achieving it.

To assist the counselee in this analysis, the counselor uses various tools and sources of information. The counselor helps the applicant or client to analyze his or her work experience (regular, casual, part-time, summer, military), education and training, voluntary and leisure-time activities, and other relevant experiences that may provide evidence of occupational preferences, skills, and potentialities. The counselor may administer or arrange for the administration of interest inventories or check lists, aptitude tests such as the USES General Aptitude Test Battery, and other tests and inventories.

Employment or vocational counseling, however, cannot be effective if it is limited to information about the counselee. Information is necessary about the world of work, to which the knowledge acquired about the individual can be related in arriving at a suitable occupational choice.

For some time now, the counselor has had available sources of occupational information, published by the Department of Labor, such as the *Occupational Outlook Handbook*, the *Occupational Outlook Quarterly*, the *Job Guide for Young Workers*, *Occupations in Demand at Job Service Offices*, and the *Dictionary of Occupational Titles*, as well as State occupational guides and labor market area reports prepared by State employment security agencies. These and similar publications provided useful information about labor market trends and opportunities and descriptions of occupations. However, a practical grouping of jobs in terms of occupational interest and work requirements was lacking.

The *Guide for Occupational Exploration* fills this longfelt need of vocational counselors. The thousands of occupations in the world of work are grouped by interests and by traits required for successful performance. The *Guide* provides a convenient crossover from information about the counselee to potentially suitable fields of work.

ROLE OF *GUIDE* IN COUNSELING AND GUIDANCE

The *Guide for Occupational Exploration* provides a clustering of occupations into fields of work within each major interest area—broad fields (through four-digit groups) and narrower fields (through six-digit subgroups)—which the counselor and counselee can explore and to which they can relate occupationally significant information about the counselee. Rather than attempting to explore the entire world of work, the counselor and counselee can identify those areas of work in which the counselee has the strongest interest and, within the interest areas, those work groups that are most closely related to the interests, skills, aptitudes, education and training, and physical abilities of the counselee.

The *Guide* may be used particularly (1) to give the counselee an overview of the world of work and thus widen his or her understanding of occupations and (2) to help the counselee determine his or her occupational goal by offering a choice of fields of work and occupations that best reflect the interests, abilities, and potentials of the counselee.

TIE-IN WITH THE GENERAL APTITUDE TEST BATTERY (GATB)

The *Guide* joins the General Aptitude Test Battery (GATB) and the forthcoming Interest Inventory and revised Interest Check List to form a coordinated assessment-occupational exploration system developed by the USES for use in the counseling process. To facilitate use of GATB results with the *Guide*, a new set of Occupational Aptitude Patterns (OAP's) has been developed based on work groups in the *Guide*. (The new OAP's are scheduled for publication soon.)

USE OF THE *GUIDE* IN THE COUNSELING PROCESS

The *Guide* may be used at any point in the counseling process: (1) to enable the counselee to obtain a better understanding of the variety of interest areas and fields of work that constitute the world of work and (2) to assist the counselee to explore areas of interest, fields of work, and specific occupations in order to identify occupational groups and specific jobs that are most in line with the counselee's interests, abilities, and potentials.

Widening Understanding of World of Work

If the counselee's experience and understanding of the world of work is limited, it will be desirable for him or her, during the early stages of the counseling process, to obtain an overview of the various interest areas and work groups covered in the *Guide*. The *Guide* lists 12 Interest Areas, 66 Work Groups, and 348 subgroups.

The counselor may review these sections with the counselee or suggest that the counselee review them independently, to become generally familiar with the various interest areas and with the work groups covered in each area, especially in those areas in which he or she has a particular interest. If the counselee wishes to know more about an interest area or work group, there are brief descriptions at the beginning of the interest area and of the work group starting on page 13 in the *Guide*.

This overview should be helpful not only in giving the counselee an overall "feel" of the world of work but also in providing a background against which to

GUIDE FOR OCCUPATIONAL EXPLORATION

relate elements in his or her work experience, education and training, leisure time activities, and other experiences that point to possible suitable fields of work and occupations in the analysis that takes place during the course of the counseling process.

Determining Occupational Goal

During the counseling process, the counselor assists the counselee to choose an occupational field that best represents the counselee's interests, skills, and potential abilities, and that offers opportunity for employment. Analysis of occupationally related experiences, application of aptitude and interest tests, and relation of the resulting information to occupational groupings in the *Guide for Occupational Exploration* are major steps in this process.

Analysis of Occupationally Related Experiences. The counselor assists the counselee to analyze occupationally related experiences that may indicate his or her true occupational interests, aptitudes, acquired skills, personal traits, and any environmental and financial factors that may have vocational significance. Thus, the counselor explores with the counselee past work history, school courses, leisure-time activities, hobbies, voluntary activities, and other experiences for indications of kinds of work the counselee particularly liked and seemed to do well in and those he or she disliked or did poorly in. Out of this analysis will emerge indications of types of work to consider seriously or to avoid.

The overview of the world of work, seen through the *Guide* as suggested above, when received early in the counseling process, will provide an occupational information base that will be useful in analyzing past experiences for occupationally significant elements.

Aptitude and Interest Testing

In addition to obtaining information about the counselee's background during the counseling interview, the counselor will often administer, or arrange for administration of, the USES Interest Inventory or Interest Check List and/or the General Aptitude Test Battery (GATB) or other tests for further indications of interests and potential ability.

The USES Interest Inventory (to be published in 1979) will provide formal measures of occupational interests that can be related directly to the Interest

Areas in the *Guide*. Meanwhile, a newly revised Interest Check List will give helpful information on occupational interests of the counselee and a tie-in with the *Guide* because the results will relate directly to the work groups in the *Guide*.

The occupational preferences that derive from the interview(s) and the use of the interest tools will serve as entries to the 12 Interest Areas in the *Guide for Occupational Exploration.* The GATB results can also serve as entries to the *Guide* because the new OAP structure will relate directly to occupational groups in the *Guide*.

Use of *Guide* in Determining Occupational Goal

After occupationally significant information is obtained about the counselee through the counseling interview(s) and the use of the various tools, the counselor and the counselee can use the *Guide* to explore fields of work and to help the counselee select a suitable occupational goal.

Steps suggested in this process are the following:

STEP 1. HELP THE COUNSELEE IDENTIFY AREAS TO BE CONSIDERED

The information obtained about the counselee will reveal broad areas of particular interest to him or her. A list of these Interest Areas may be made to insure exploration of all pertinent areas. The counselee should be encouraged to read the description of the selected areas to verify further the relevance of his or her interests. A review may also be made of the descriptions of other interest areas for the possible identification of further areas to be explored.

STEP 2. HELP THE COUNSELEE SELECT AND EXPLORE WORK GROUPS

When interest areas to explore further are chosen, the client may review the description of all work groups (indicated by four-digit code) within these interest areas to help decide which work groups to explore. Sometimes a glance at the work group title may be enough to identify a type of activity the client does not wish to investigate further. The counselee may then return to each group selected for further exploration. Alternatively, as the counselee reads a group title and description and expresses interest in the work group, he or she may explore it immediately, before moving on to the next work group.

In exploring the work group, the counselor should help the counselee determine the suitability of the group from the standpoint of his or her true interests, aptitudes, skills and traits required, further preparation needed, and other relevant considerations.

To explore each selected work group, it is suggested that the counselee review each of the five items under the work group description. During the course of discussion of each item, the counselor should help the counselee try to relate occupationally significant information known about the counselee to the information in the item.

The first item, *"What kind of work would you do?"* provides examples of *types of work activities* included in the group, for example, "Write dialogue for television program" and "Set up and operate a lathe." These examples, along with the description of the work group, will help the counselee to get a "feel" of the kind of work involved and to determine then if it is a type of activity in line with his or her interests, skills, and potentials. These activities do not apply to a single occupation but are illustrative of the kind of work performed in various jobs in this group.

The second item, *"What skills and abilities do you need for this kind of work?"* names *characteristics required of the worker* to perform successfully in occupations in this group. For example, it points up such actual or potential abilities needed as "influencing people's opinions, attitudes, and judgments" and "willingness and ability to work within precise limits or standards of accuracy." This information should help the counselee determine whether these are the kinds of work situations and requirements that would appeal to him or her.

The third item, *"How do you know if you would like or could learn to do this type of work?"* mentions *work experience, extracurricular activities, hobbies,* and other activities and experiences, as well as *skills, potentials, and interests* relevant to occupations in this work group. This item provides clues concerning the counselee's possible ability to do, or learn to do, and want to do this kind of work.

Questions such as "Have you written an original story?", "Can you create original characters or situations that interest and entertain others?", and "Have you taken an industrial arts or machine shop course?", "Do you like to set up machines according to written standards?" help the counselee think through whether he or she has the interest and ability to do, or learn to do, types of work included in this group. The counselor should help the counselee relate these kinds of personal experiences and interests to the work group being explored.

The fourth item, *"How can you prepare for and enter this type of work?"* describes the kind of *training, work, and other experience* usually required by or acceptable to employers and the means of entry into the field. The counselee, if interested in this work group, will consider at this point whether he or she has the kind of preparation usually needed or is willing to take further training that may be required.

The fifth item, *"What else should you consider about these jobs?"* provides a number of *other considerations* that the counselee will want to weigh in making up his or her mind about the satisfactions and suitability of this kind of work. For example, the counselee is advised "Most new workers in writing occupations start with routine assignments such as writing headlines." "Only in establishments where few writers are employed is the newcomer given creative writing assignments," and "Some workers are paid hourly wages. Other workers are paid according to the number of pieces they produce."

A simple record should be kept of all work groups reviewed and those identified for further exploration.

The counselor or counselee might prefer either to complete Step 3 for each work group being explored before moving on to the next work group, or to complete Step 2 for all work groups being considered, before exploring any of them further.

STEP 3. HELP THE COUNSELEE TO EXPLORE SUBGROUPS AND SPECIFIC OCCUPATIONS

After exploring the work group, the counselee will usually find either that he or she is not seriously interested in the type of work covered by the group or will want to explore it still further. Where the counselee is still interested in the work group, the counselor should help him or her to examine and interpret subgroup titles and to choose one or more for further investigation.

The specific occupations within each subgroup are arranged in clusters by the industry in which the jobs occur. Therefore, in examining subgroups and occupations, a factor to consider is whether the industry is located in the area in which the counselee lives or to which he or she is willing to go.

The counselee should be encouraged to identify subgroup titles that seem interesting and potentially suitable, based on all the information that the counselee now has about himself or herself. Then specific occupations that may tentatively appeal to the counselee could be identified.

The counselee should be helped to look up in the *Dictionary of Occupational Titles* the definitions of occupations that seem of particular interest. The subgroups and the specific occupations within them should be considered from the standpoint of opportunities available for placement or training, of the counselee's interests and qualifications, and of the occupational requirements.

STEP 4. HELP THE COUNSELEE TO SELECT HIS OR HER VOCATIONAL GOAL

A listing should be made of subgroups and specific occupations that appear to be particularly interesting and suitable for the counselee. The pros and cons of each should be weighed and the most desirable and suitable work groups, subgroups, or occupations selected by the counselee as his or her vocational goal. The goal may be expressed in terms of any of these three categories but most likely of the work groups, or subgroups, depending upon the individual's qualifications.

STEP 5. HELP THE COUNSELEE TO DEVELOP A PLAN FOR ATTAINING THE GOAL

As usual, the counselor will assist the counselee to develop a realistic vocational plan for reaching the goal; the plan should reflect actions to be taken by the local office and the counselee, either to enter a training program or to obtain suitable employment.

STEP 6. ASSIGN APPROPRIATE OCCUPATIONAL CLASSIFICATIONS

The counselor, particularly in the employment service setting, should assign one or more occupational classifications to reflect the occupational goal(s) arrived at by the counselee and to facilitate his or her selection for referral to suitable employment.

Two or more counseling interviews are usually required to help the counselee make a suitable occupational choice and to plan to implement that choice. The counselor may wish to suggest that, during one of the interviews or between interviews, the counselee review a copy of the *Guide for Occupational Exploration*. The section, "Use by Individuals Without Counselor Assistance," will provide helpful suggestions for reviewing the *Guide* even though the counselee is actually receiving assistance from the counselor.

The *Guide* thus serves as a useful reference tool in career exploration for the individual as well as an important tool for the counselor in helping develop a sound and realistic vocational goal for the counselee.

11.04 Law

Workers in this group advise and represent others in legal matters. Those in small towns and cities conduct criminal or civil cases in court, draw up wills and other legal papers, abstract real estate, and perform related activities. Those in large cities usually specialize in one kind of law, such as criminal, civil, tax, labor, or patent. They work in law firms, unions, government agencies, and commercial and industrial establishments. Some are self-employed and have their own office. Lawyers are frequently elected to public office, particularly as legislators. Many State Governors and U.S. Presidents have been lawyers.

What kind of work would you do?
Your work activities would depend upon your specific job. For example, you might
   —study court decisions and conduct investigations on claims filed against insurance companies.
   —prepare wills, deeds, and other legal documents for people.

—preside in a court of law or at a formal hearing.

—conduct research in technical literature to recommend approval or rejection of patent applications.

—represent union or management in labor negotiations.

—defend people during prosecution under the law.

—represent clients who are suing or being sued for money or legal action.

—give advice concerning federal, state, local, and foreign taxes.

What skills and abilities do you need for this kind of work?

To do this kind of work, you must be able to:

—understand, interpret, and apply legal procedures, principles, and laws.

—define problems, collect information, establish facts, and draw valid conclusions.

—deal with all kinds of clients, juries, judges, and other lawyers in a manner that will influence their opinions, attitudes, and judgments.

—read carefully and listen carefully to identify important details which could help a client win his case.

—use your judgment about how to conduct a case or deal with a problem.

How do you know if you would like or could learn to do this kind of work?

The following questions may give you clues about yourself as you consider this group of jobs.

—Have you taken debate or speech courses? Do you feel at ease presenting a point of view in front of a group?

—Have you taken courses in journalism or composition? Can you communicate complex ideas effectively?

—Have you watched detective or lawyer television programs? Do you understand the legal terminology used?

—Have you attended a trial or court proceeding? Would you like to work in this type of atmosphere?

How can you prepare for and enter this kind of work?

Occupations in this group usually require education and/or training extending from four years to over ten years, depending upon the specific kind of work. Lawyers are required to pass a bar examination and obtain a license for the particular state in which they want to practice. Educational requirements for taking the bar examination vary. Some states require proof of graduation from an approved law school. A four year college degree and completion of a program for law clerks may be accepted. Other states allow persons who study law with a licensed lawyer to take the bar examination. Correspondence courses in law are accepted as preparation for bar examinations in some states. Special requirements and licenses are necessary for those who wish to practice law in certain higher courts.

Entry requirements for law schools vary according to the institution. Some accept students directly from high school. Others require college graduation.

Some jobs in this group require legal education, but not a license. In these jobs, workers need legal knowledge, but do not practice law.

Licensed lawyers enter the field as junior partners in law firms, junior executives in business or industry, or workers in government agencies. A few establish their own law practices. However, self-employment is usually delayed because of the need for money, experience, and reputation. Some jobs in this group are elected or appointed positions.

Lawyers sometimes work long or irregular hours. They may be required to respond to emergency calls from clients. While the ability to see will make the study and practice of law easier, it is not required. There are many successful blind workers in this field.

If you think you would like to do this kind of work, look at the job titles listed on the following pages. Select those that interest you, and read their definitions in the Dictionary of Occupational Titles.

What else should you consider about these jobs?

The field of law is highly competitive, but salaried positions can be found in government agencies, private businesses, and in some law offices. Lawyers in private practice depend on collection of fees for their income. When they have several long-term retainers (fees paid in advance so that service is available when needed), they have a stable income.

Law

11.04.01 Justice Administration

Appeals Referee (gov. ser.) 119.267-014

Appeals Reviewer, Veteran (gov. ser.) 119.117-010

Hearing Officer (gov. ser.) 119.107-010
Judge (gov. ser.) 111.107-010
Magistrate (gov. ser.) 111.107-014

11.04.02 Legal Practice
District Attorney (gov. ser.) 110.117-010
Insurance Attorney (insurance) 110.117-014
Bar Examiner (profess. & kin.) 110.167-010
Lawyer (profess. & kin.) 110.107-010
Lawyer, Admiralty (profess. & kin.) 110.117-018
Lawyer, Corporation (profess. & kin.) 110.117-022
Lawyer, Criminal (profess.& kin.) 110.107-014
Lawyer, Patent (profess.& kin.) 110.117-026
Lawyer, Probate (profess. & kin.) 110.117-030
Lawyer, Real Estate (profess. & kin.) 110.117-034
Legal Investigator (profess. & kin.) 119.267-022

Paralegal Assistant (profess & kin.) 119.267-026
Tax Attorney (profess. & kin.) 110.117-038
Title Attorney (profess.& kin.) 110.117-042

11.04.03 Conciliation
Adjudicator (gov. ser.) 119.167-010
Commissioner of Conciliation (gov. ser.) 188.217-010
Arbitrator (profess. & kin.) 169.107-010
Conciliator (profess. & kin.) 169.207-010

11.04.04 Abstracting, Document Preparation
Tariff Publishing Agent (bus. ser.) 184.167-250
Customs-House Broker (finan. inst.) 186.117-018
Abstractor (profess. & kin.) 119.267-010
Patent Agent (profess. & kin.) 119.167-014

Occupational Listing

This occupational listing will be the resource used to translate Worker Trait Groups of interest into occupations for further exploration. Note that not all of the Worker Trait Groups are listed; those including mostly unskilled jobs were not included.

All of the occupations that are listed in the following Occupational Listing can be found in the *Occupational Outlook Handbook (OOH)*, described in the next section. Many of the listings are actually occupational groups that include several specific occupations, listed within the cited section of the *OOH*.

You might want to scan this list to familiarize yourself with its organization. You will not actually do anything with it until you get to the next chapter.

1.01 Literary Arts

GOE Worker Trait Group Description
Workers in this group write, edit, or direct the publication of prose or poetry. They find employment on newspapers or magazines, in radio and television studios, and in the theater and motion picture industries. Some writers are self-employed and sell stories, plays, and other forms of literary composition to publishers.

Related OOH Listings
Reporters and correspondents
Writers and editors

1.02 *Visual Arts*

GOE Worker Trait Group Description

Workers in this group create original works of art or do commercial art work, using such techniques as drawing, painting, photographing, and sculpting to express or interpret ideas or to illustrate various written materials. Some visual artists design products, settings, or graphics (such as advertisements or book covers), and oversee the work of other artists or craftsmen who produce or install them. Others teach art, or appraise or restore paintings and other fine art objects. Advertising agencies, printing and publishing firms, television and motion picture studios, museums and restoration laboratories employ visual artists. They also work for manufacturers and in retail and wholesale trade. Many are self-employed, operating their own commercial art studios or doing freelance work.

Related *OOH* Listings

Designers
Photographers and camera operators
Visual artists

1.03 *Drama*

GOE Worker Trait Group Description

Workers in this group produce, direct, and perform in dramatic productions and similar forms of entertainment. They also teach acting, choose performers for particular roles, and perform other "behind-the-scenes" work to make productions run smoothly. They are employed by motion picture, television, and radio studios, and by stock companies, theaters, and other places where plays or floor shows are presented. Schools and colleges hire performing artists both to teach drama and to produce and direct student productions. Fulltime employment in this field is found at educational institutions and at studios that have staff announcers, disc jockeys, and regularly scheduled talk shows or do dramatic presentations. However, most performing artists are not permanently employed, and must audition for roles in both short-term and long-run productions.

Related *OOH* Listings

Actors, directors, and producers
Radio and television announcers and newscasters

1.04 *Music*

GOE Worker Trait Group Description

Workers in this group sing or play instruments, teach, or direct vocal or instrumental music. They compose, arrange, or orchestrate musical compositions, and plan the presentation of concerts. They work for motion picture studios, television and radio networks or local stations, recording studios, night clubs, and other places where musical entertainment is regularly provided. They may be employed by orchestras, bands, or choral groups that give scheduled performances or are hired for special events. Composers, arrangers, and orchestrators work for music publishing companies and firms in the recording and entertainment fields. Schools and colleges hire musicians to teach and direct vocal and instrumental music. Many musicians are self-employed and, like all performing artists, must audition for parts in musical productions or for employment with an orchestra or other performing group.

Related *OOH* Listing
    Musicians

1.05 Dance

GOE Worker Trait Group Description

Workers in this group compose, perform, or teach dance routines or techniques. Performing dancers and composers (choreographers) work for motion picture and television studios, nightclubs and theaters, and other places where this kind of entertainment is regularly presented. Dance teachers are employed by schools and studios. Although some dancers work full time as performers or teachers, most must audition for both chorus and solo work in theatrical productions of all kinds. Many dancers are self-employed as teachers who give private lessons to children and adults, specializing in ballroom or ballet instruction.

Related *OOH* Listings
    Dancers and choreographers

2.01 Physical Sciences

GOE Worker Trait Group Description

Workers in this group are concerned mostly with nonliving things such as chemicals, rocks, metals, mathematics, movements of the earth and stars, and so forth. They conduct scientific studies and perform other activities requiring a knowledge of math, physics, or chemistry. Some workers investigate, discover, and test new theories. Some look for methods to develop new or improved materials or processes for use in production and construction. Others do research in such fields as geology, astronomy, oceanography, and computer science. Workers base their conclusions on information that can be measured or proved. Industries, government agencies, or large universities employ most of these workers in their research facilities.

Related *OOH* Listings
    Chemists
    Geologists and geophysicists
    Mathematicians
    Meteorologists
    Physicists and astronomers

2.02 Life Sciences

GOE Worker Trait Group Description

Workers in this group are concerned mostly with living things such as plants and animals. They conduct research and do experiments to expand humanity's knowledge of living things. Some may work on problems related to how the environment affects plant and animal life. Others may study causes of disease and methods to control disease. These workers are usually employed in the research facilities of hospitals, government agencies, industries, and universities.

Related *OOH* Listings

> Agricultural scientists
> Biological scientists
> Foresters and conservation scientists

2.03 Medical Sciences

GOE Worker Trait Group Description

Workers in this group are involved in the prevention, diagnosis, and treatment of human and animal diseases, disorders, or injuries. It is common to specialize in specific kinds of illnesses, or special areas or organs of the body. Workers who prefer to be more general may become general practitioners, family practitioners, or learn to deal with groups of related medical problems. A wide variety of work environments is available to medical workers, ranging from large city hospitals and clinics, to home offices in rural areas, to field clinics in the military or in underdeveloped countries.

Related *OOH* Listings

> Chiropractors
> Dentists
> Optometrists
> Physicians
> Podiatrists
> Speech pathologists and audiologists
> Veterinarians

2.04 Laboratory Technology

GOE Worker Trait Group Description

Workers in this group use special laboratory techniques and equipment to perform tests in the fields of chemistry, biology, or physics. They record information that results from their experiments and tests. They help scientists, medical doctors, researchers, and engineers in their work. Hospitals, government agencies, universities, and private industries employ these workers in their laboratories and research facilities.

Related *OOH* Listings
    Clinical laboratory technologists and technicians
    Dental laboratory technicians
    Ophthalmic laboratory technicians
    Pharmacists
    Science technicians

3.01 Managerial Work: Nature

GOE Worker Trait Group Description

Workers in this group operate or manage farming, fishing, forestry, and horticultural service businesses of many kinds. Some of them breed specialty plants and animals. Others provide services to increase production or beautify land areas. Many of them work in rural or woodland areas, on farms, ranches, and forest preserves. Others find employment with commercial nurseries, landscaping firms, business services, or government agencies located in large and small communities all over the country. Many are self-employed, operating their own large or small businesses.

Related *OOH* Listings
    Farm operators and managers
    Foresters
    Gardeners and groundskeepers

4.01 Safety and Law Enforcement

GOE Worker Trait Group Description

Workers in this group are in charge of enforcing laws and regulations. Some investigate crimes, while others supervise workers who stop or arrest lawbreakers. Others make inspections to be sure that laws are not broken. Many jobs are found in the federal, state, or local governments, such as the police and fire departments. Some are found in private businesses, such as factories, stores, and similar places.

Related *OOH* Listings
    Firefighting occupations
    Police, detectives, and special agents

4.02 Security Services

GOE Worker Trait Group Description

Workers in this group protect people and animals from injury or danger. They enforce laws, investigate suspicious persons or acts, prevent crime, and fight fires. Some of the jobs are found in federal, state, or local governments. Some workers are hired by railroads, hotels, lumber yards, industrial plants, and amusement establishments.

Related *OOH* Listings
> Corrections officers
> Firefighting occupations
> Guards

5.01 Engineering

GOE Worker Trait Group Description

Workers in this group plan, design, and direct the construction or development of buildings, bridges, roads, airports, dams, sewage systems, air-conditioning systems, mining machinery, and other structures and equipment. They also develop processes and techniques for generating and transmitting electrical power, manufacturing chemicals, extracting metals from ore, and controlling the quality of products being made. Workers specialize in one or more kinds of engineering, such as civil, electrical, mechanical, mining, and safety. Some are hired by industrial plants, petroleum and mining companies, research laboratories, and construction companies. Others find employment with federal, state, and local governments. Some have their own engineering firms and accept work from various individuals and companies.

Related *OOH* Listings
> Aerospace engineers
> Architects
> Chemical engineers
> Civil engineers
> Electrical and electronics engineers
> Industrial engineers
> Landscape architects
> Mechanical engineers
> Metallurgical, ceramic, and materials engineers
> Mining engineers
> Nuclear engineers
> Petroleum engineers

5.03 Engineering Technology

GOE Worker Trait Group Description

Workers in this group collect, record, and coordinate technical information in such activities as surveying, drafting, petroleum production, communications control, and materials scheduling. Workers find jobs in construction, factories, engineering and architectural firms, airports, and research laboratories.

Related *OOH* Listings
> Air traffic controllers
> Broadcast technicians
> Drafters

Engineering technicians

Surveyors

5.04 Air and Water Vehicle Operation

GOE Worker Trait Group Description

Workers in this group pilot airplanes or ships, or supervise others who do. Some instruct others in flying. Most of these workers are hired by commercial airlines and shipping companies. Some find jobs piloting planes or ships for private companies and individuals.

Related OOH Listings

Aircraft pilots

Water transportation occupations

5.05 Craft Technology

GOE Worker Trait Group Description

Workers in this group perform highly skilled hand and/or machine work requiring special techniques, training, and experience. Work occurs in a variety of nonfactory settings. Some workers own their own shops.

Related OOH Listings

Aircraft mechanics and engine specialists

Automotive body repairers

Automotive mechanics

Bindery workers

Bricklayers and stonemasons

Carpenters

Commercial and industrial electronic equipment repairers

Communications equipment mechanics

Computer and office machine repairers

Diesel mechanics

Electricians

Electronic equipment repairers

Electronic home entertainment equipment repairers

Farm equipment mechanics

General maintenance mechanics

Heating, air-conditioning, and refrigeration technicians

Home appliance and power tool repairers

Industrial machinery repairers

Machinists

Millwrights

Mobile heavy equipment mechanics

Motorcycle, boat, and small-engine mechanics

Numerical-control machine tool operators
Plumbers and pipefitters
Printing press operators
Sheet-metal workers
Telephone installers and repairers
Welders, cutters, and welding machine operators

5.07 *Quality Control*

GOE Worker Trait Group Description

Workers in this group inspect and/or test materials and products to be sure they meet standards. The work is carried out in nonfactory settings, and includes activities such as grading logs at a lumber yard, inspecting bridges to be sure they are safe, inspecting gas lines for leaks, and grading gravel for use in building roads. Jobs may be found with construction companies, sawmills, petroleum refineries, and utility companies.

Related OOH Listings

Inspectors, testers, and graders

7.01 *Administrative Detail*

GOE Worker Trait Group Description

Workers in this group perform clerical work that requires special skills and knowledge. They perform management activities according to established regulations and procedures. Jobs in this group are found in offices of businesses, industries, courts of law, and government agencies, as well as in offices of doctors, lawyers, and other professionals.

Related OOH Listings

Clerical supervisors and managers
Secretaries

7.02 *Mathematical Detail*

GOE Worker Trait Group Description

Workers in this group use clerical and math skills to gather, organize, compute, and record, with or without machines, the numerical information used in business or in financial transactions. Jobs in this group are found wherever numerical record-keeping is important. Banks, finance companies, accounting firms, or the payroll and inventory control departments in business and government are typical of places where this work is done.

Related OOH Listings

Credit clerks and authorizers
Billing clerks

Bookkeeping, accounting, and auditing clerks
Brokerage clerks and statement clerks
Payroll and timekeeping clerks
Traffic, shipping, and receiving clerks

7.03 Financial Detail

GOE Worker Trait Group Description

Workers in this group use basic math skills as they deal with the public. Keeping records, answering customers' questions, and supervising others is often part of the job. Jobs in this group are found where money is paid to or received from the public. Banks, grocery check-out counters, and ticket booths are typical places of employment.

Related OOH Listings

Bank tellers
Cashiers
Counter and rental clerks
Reservation and transportation ticket agents

7.04 Oral Communications

GOE Worker Trait Group Description

Workers in this group give and receive information verbally. Workers may deal with people in person, by telephone, telegraph, or radio. Recording of information in an organized manner is frequently required. Private businesses, institutions such as schools and hospitals, and government agencies hire these workers in their offices, reception areas, registration desks, and other areas of information exchange.

Related OOH Listings

Adjusters, investigators, and collectors
Dispatchers
Hotel and motel clerks
Information clerks
Interviewing and new account clerks
Order clerks
Receptionists
Telephone, telegraph, and teletype operators
Reservation and transportation ticket agents and travel clerks

7.05 Records Processing

GOE Worker Trait Group Description

Workers in this group prepare, review, maintain, route, distribute, and coordinate recorded information. They check records and schedules for accuracy. They may schedule the activities of people or the use of equipment. Jobs in this group are found in most businesses, institutions, and government agencies.

Related *OOH* Listings
> Credit clerks and authorizers
> File clerks
> General office clerks
> Mail clerks and messengers
> Material recording, scheduling, dispatching, and distributing occupations
> Medical records technicians
> Order clerks
> Personnel clerks
> Postal clerks and mail carriers
> Record clerks
> Stenographers and court reporters
> Stock clerks

7.06 *Clerical Machine Operation*

GOE Worker Trait Group Description

Workers in this group use business machines to record or process data. They operate machines that type, print, sort, compute, send, or receive information. Their jobs are found in businesses, industries, government agencies, or wherever large amounts of data are processed, sent, or received.

Related *OOH* Listings
> Computer and peripheral equipment operators
> Typists, word processors, and data entry keyers

8.01 *Sales Technology*

GOE Worker Trait Group Description

Workers in this group sell products such as industrial machinery, data processing equipment, and pharmaceuticals; services such as industrial shipping, insurance, and advertising. They advise customers of the capabilities, uses, and other important features of these products and services, and help them choose those best suited to their needs. They work for manufacturers, wholesalers, and insurance, financial, and business service institutions. Also included in this group are workers who buy products, materials, securities and properties for resale. Some work for themselves.

Related *OOH* Listings
> Insurance agents and brokers
> Manufacturers' and wholesale sales representatives
> Real estate agents, brokers, and appraisers
> Securities and financial services sales representatives
> Services sales representatives

8.02 *General Sales*

GOE Worker Trait Group Description

Workers in this group sell, demonstrate, and solicit orders for products and services of many kinds. They are employed by retail and wholesale firms, manufacturers and distributors, business services, and nonprofit organizations. Some spend all their time in a single location, such as a department store or automobile agency. Others call on businesses or individuals to sell products or services, or to follow up on earlier sales.

Related *OOH* Listings
Retail sales workers
Travel agents

9.02 *Barber and Beauty Services*

GOE Worker Trait Group Description

Workers in this group provide people with a variety of barbering and beauty services. These services involve care of the hair, skin, and nails. These workers find employment in barber and beauty shops, department stores, hotels, and retirement homes. A few workers find jobs on passenger ships. Some are self-employed and work in their own homes or go to the customer.

Related *OOH* Listings
Barbers and cosmetologists

10.01 *Social Services*

GOE Worker Trait Group Description

Workers in this group help people deal with their problems. They may work with one person at a time or with groups of people. Workers may specialize in problems that are personal, social, vocational, physical, educational, or spiritual in nature. Schools, rehabilitation centers, mental health clinics, guidance centers, and churches employ these workers. Jobs are also found in public and private welfare and employment services, juvenile courts, and vocational rehabilitation programs.

Related *OOH* Listings
Counselors
Human services workers
Protestant ministers
Psychologists
Rabbis
Roman Catholic priests
Recreation workers
Social workers

10.02 *Nursing, Therapy, Teaching*

GOE Worker Trait Group Description

Workers in this group care for, treat, or train people to improve their physical and emotional well-being. Most workers in this group deal with sick, injured, or disabled people. Some workers are involved in health education and sickness prevention. Hospitals, nursing homes, and rehabilitation centers hire workers in this group, as do schools, industrial plants, doctors' offices, and private homes. Some sports also have a need for workers in this group.

Related *OOH* Listings

Dental hygienists
Emergency medical technicians
Licensed practical nurses
Nuclear medicine technologists
Radiologic technologists
Occupational therapists
Physical therapists
Physician assistants
Recreational therapists
Registered nurses
Respiratory therapists

10.03 *Child and Adult Care*

GOE Worker Trait Group Description

Workers in this group are concerned with the physical needs and the welfare of others. They assist professionals in treating the sick or injured. They care for the elderly, the very young, or the handicapped. Frequently these workers help people do the things they cannot do for themselves. Jobs are found in hospitals, clinics, day care centers, nurseries, schools, private homes, and centers for helping the handicapped.

Related *OOH* Listings

Dental assistants
EEG technologists
EKG technicians
Homemaker–home health aides
Medical assistants
Nursing aides and psychiatric aides
Preschool workers
Private household workers
Surgical technicians
Teacher aides

11.01 *Mathematics and Statistics*

GOE Worker Trait Group Description

Workers in this group use advanced math and statistics to solve problems and conduct research. They analyze and interpret numerical data for planning and decision making. Some of these workers may first study and then determine how computers may best be used to solve problems or process information. Colleges, large businesses and industries, research organizations, and government agencies use these workers.

Related *OOH* Listings

Actuaries
Computer programmers
Computer systems analysts
Mathematicians
Operations research analysts
Statisticians

11.02 *Educational and Library Services*

GOE Worker Trait Group Description

Workers in this group do general and specialized teaching, vocational training, and library work of various kinds. Jobs are found in schools, colleges, libraries, and other educational facilities.

Related *OOH* Listings

Adult education teachers
College and university faculty
Dietitians and nutritionists
Kindergarten and elementary school teachers
Librarians
Library technicians
Secondary school teachers

11.03 *Social Research*

GOE Worker Trait Group Description

Workers in this group gather, study, and analyze information about individuals, specific groups, or entire societies. They conduct research, both historical and current, into all aspects of human behavior, including abnormal behavior, language, work, politics, lifestyle, and cultural expression. They are employed by museums, schools and colleges, government agencies, and private research foundations.

Related *OOH* Listings

Economists

Psychologists
Social scientists and urban planners
Sociologists
Urban and regional planners

11.04 Law

GOE Worker Trait Group Description

Workers in this group advise and represent others in legal matters. Those in small towns and cities conduct criminal or civil cases in court, draw up wills and other legal papers, abstract real estate, and perform related activities. Those in large cities usually specialize in one kind of law, such as criminal, civil, tax, labor, or patent. They work in law firms, unions, government agencies, and commercial and industrial establishments. Some are self-employed and have their own office. Lawyers are frequently elected to public office, particularly as legislators. Many state governors and U.S. presidents have been lawyers.

Related *OOH* Listings

Lawyers and judges
Paralegals

11.05 Business Administration

GOE Worker Trait Group Description

Workers in this group are top-level administrators and managers who work through lower-level supervisors to direct all or a part of the activities in private establishments or government agencies. They set policies, make important decisions, and establish priorities. These jobs are found in large businesses, industry, and government. Labor unions and associations will also hire these workers.

Related *OOH* Listings

Administrative services managers
Construction contractors and managers
Engineering, science, and data processing managers
Employment interviewers
Financial managers
General managers and top executives
Government chief executives and legislators
Industrial production managers
Management analysts and consultants
Personnel, training, and labor relations specialists and managers
Property and real estate managers
Purchasing agents and managers
Wholesale and retail buyers and merchandise managers

11.06 Finance

GOE Worker Trait Group Description

Workers in this group use mathematical and analytical skills to design financial systems and examine and interpret financial records. They are concerned with accounting and auditing activities, analysis of records systems, risk and profit analyses, brokering, and budget and financial control. They find employment in banks, loan companies, investment firms, colleges, government agencies, and business firms. Some workers, like accountants and appraisers, are self-employed.

Related *OOH* Listings

Accountants and auditors
Budget analysts
Cost estimators
Underwriters

11.07 Services Administration

GOE Worker Trait Group Description

Workers in this group manage programs and projects in agencies that provide people with services in areas such as health, education, welfare, and recreation. They are in charge of program planning, policy making, and other managerial activities. The jobs are found in welfare and rehabilitation agencies and organizations, hospitals, schools, churches, libraries, and museums.

Related *OOH* Listings

Archivists and curators
Education administrators
Health services managers

11.08 Communications

GOE Worker Trait Group Description

Workers in this group write, edit, report, and translate factual information. They find employment with radio and television broadcasting stations, newspapers, and publishing firms. Government agencies and professional groups provide some opportunities, as do large firms that publish company newsletters and brochures.

Related *OOH* Listings

Reporters and correspondents
Writers and editors

11.09 Promotion

GOE Worker Trait Group Description

Workers in this group raise money, advertise products and services, and influence people in their actions or thoughts. They find employment in business and industry, with advertising agencies, professional groups, unions, colleges, and government agencies.

Related *OOH* Listings
Marketing, advertising, and public relations managers

Public relations specialists

11.10 *Regulations Enforcement*

GOE Worker Trait Group Description
Workers in this group enforce government regulations and company policies that affect peoples' rights, health and safety, and finances. They examine records, inspect products, and investigate services, but do not engage in police work. Most workers find employment with government agencies, licensing departments, and health departments. Some are employed by retail establishments, mines, transportation companies, and nonprofit organizations.

Related *OOH* Listings
Construction and building inspectors

Inspectors and compliance officers

11.11 *Business Management*

GOE Worker Trait Group Description
Workers in this group manage a business, such as a store or cemetery, a branch of a large company, such as a local office for a credit corporation, or a department within a company, such as a warehouse. They usually carry out operating policies and procedures determined by administrative workers such as presidents, vice presidents, and directors. Some managers own their own businesses and are considered self-employed. Managers find employment in all kinds of businesses as well as government agencies.

Related *OOH* Listings
Hotel managers and assistants

Restaurant and food service managers

11.12 *Contracts and Claims*

GOE Worker Trait Group Description
Workers in this group negotiate contracts and settle claims for companies and individuals. Some make arrangements for agreements between buyers and sellers. Others investigate claims involving damage, injury, and losses. Jobs are found in insurance and transportation companies, businesses, construction companies, and government agencies. Some are found in booking agencies. These agents are frequently self-employed.

Related *OOH* Listings
> Adjusters, investigators, and collectors
> Purchasing agents and managers
> Real estate agents, brokers, and appraisers

Occupational Outlook Handbook (OOH)

The *Occupational Outlook Handbook* (*OOH*) is an excellent source for occupational information. The *OOH* is published by the U.S. Department of Labor and provides detailed information for the same occupations in the Occupational Listing. For each occupation, it explains:

Nature of the work

Working conditions

Employment

Training, other qualifications, and advancement

Job outlook

Earnings

Related occupations

Sources of additional information

Once you have read through this information, you will likely be able to tell whether this occupation deserves further consideration. Also, you will probably eliminate some occupations that you thought might be possibilities. For example, the training requirements might involve more time than you are willing to invest. The work environment might not be to your liking. Any number of such considerations may play a role in such a decision. The following sections of the 1994–1995 *OOH* are reproduced for your information:

Keys to Understanding What's in the Handbook provides an overview of the *OOH* and its organization.

A Sample Occupational Listing (for lawyers and judges) gives you an example of the information provided for various occupations listed within the *OOH*.

Sources of Information on Preparation and Training is reproduced to provide you with some information about other references and resources that may be helpful to you.

Copies of the *OOH* may be ordered from: Superintendent of Documents, P.O. Box 371954, Pittsburgh, PA 15250-7954. Call (202) 783-3238 (8A.M.–4P.M. EST, Monday–Friday) for specific pricing and ordering procedures. The *OOH* is now also available on CD-ROM for those with computers so equipped.

OCCUPATIONAL OUTLOOK HANDBOOK

Keys To Understanding What's in the Handbook

The *Occupational Outlook Handbook* describes about 250 occupations in detail—covering about 104 million jobs, or 85 percent of all jobs in the Nation. Occupations that require lengthy education or training are given more attention. In addition, summary information on 77 occupations—accounting for another 6 percent of all jobs—is presented in the chapter beginning on page 458. The remaining 9 percent of all jobs are mainly residual categories—such as all other management support workers—for which little meaningful information could be developed.

The *Handbook* is best used as a reference; it is not meant to be read from cover to cover. Instead, start by exploring the table of contents, where related occupations are grouped in clusters, or look in the alphabetical index at the end of the *Handbook* for specific occupations that interest you. This introductory chapter explains how the occupational descriptions, or statements, are organized. The next two chapters, Sources of Information on Career Preparation and Training, and Tomorrow's Jobs, tell you where to obtain additional information and discuss the forces that are likely to determine employment opportunities in industries and occupations through the year 2005.

For any occupation that sounds interesting to you, use the *Handbook* to find out what the work entails; what education and training you need; what the advancement possibilities, earnings, and job outlook are; and what related occupations you might consider. Each occupational statement in the *Handbook* follows a standard format, making it easier for you to compare occupations. The following describes each section of a *Handbook* statement, and gives some hints on how to interpret the information provided.

About Those Numbers at the Beginning of Each Statement

The numbers in parentheses that appear just below the title of most occupational statements are from the *Dictionary of Occupational Titles (D.O.T.)*, Fourth Edition, Revised 1991, a U.S. Department of Labor publication. Each number classifies the occupation by the type of work, required training, physical demands, and working conditions. D.O.T. numbers are used primarily by State employment service offices to classify applicants and job openings. They are included in the *Handbook* because some career information centers and libraries use them for filing occupational information.

An index at the back of this book beginning on page 468 cross-references the Revised Fourth Edition D.O.T. numbers to occupations covered in the *Handbook*.

Nature of the Work

This section explains what workers typically do on the job, what equipment they use, how closely they are supervised, the end product of their efforts, and how much variety there is in their daily routine. Technological innovations that are changing what workers do or how they do it, as well as emerging specialties, also are described here.

Responsibilities of workers in the same occupation usually vary by employer, industry, and size of firm. In small organizations, for example, workers generally perform a wider range of duties because the resources for specialization simply do not exist. In addition, most occupations have several levels of skill and responsibility. Trainees or those with little experience may start by performing routine tasks under close supervision. Experienced workers perform more difficult duties, with greater independence, while the most skilled and senior workers perform the most difficult and responsible jobs.

Working Conditions

This section describes work hours, the physical environment, workers' susceptibility to injury and illness, and protective clothing and safety equipment that commonly are worn. In many occupations, people usually work regular business hours—40 hours a week, mornings and afternoons, Monday through Friday. Others may work nights or weekends, or more than 40 hours—periodically or on a regular basis. Some workers have a degree of freedom in determining their hours—in occupations that lend themselves to temporary work or self-employment, for example. Some jobs are performed in pleasant surroundings, while others are in dirty, noisy, dangerous, or stressful ones. Workers may move around a lot or work in a confined space, with varying degrees of physical exertion. Some jobs require outdoor work or extensive travel. A growing number of employers require drug testing.

Employment

This section reports how many jobs this occupation provided in 1992, and in what industries they were found. Where significant, it also discusses the geographic distribution of jobs, the proportion of workers in the occupation who worked part time (fewer than 35 hours a week), and the proportion who were self-employed.

Training, Other Qualifications, and Advancement

You can be trained for jobs in high schools, colleges, postsecondary vocational schools, home study courses, government training programs, the Armed Forces, apprenticeships and other formal training programs offered by employers, or informally on the job. In most occupations, there are various ways to get training. This section identifies the different ways, and

indicates the most common or the type generally preferred by employers. It lists high school and college courses considered useful preparation for a job, discusses the nature and length of the training or education program, and reveals if continuing education is required to maintain the position. Remember, the amount of training you have often determines the level at which you enter an occupation and how quickly you may advance.

For entry level jobs in many occupations covered in the *Handbook*, employers do not require specific formal training but instead look for other qualifications. They hire people with good general skills and the proven ability to learn, then give them the specific training needed to do the job. Employers want people who get along with others; have good work habits; read, write, and speak well; and have basic mathematical and, increasingly, basic computer skills. They may require a high school diploma or college degree as evidence of good general skills. *Handbook* statements also list other desirable aptitudes and personal characteristics—such as mechanical aptitude, manual dexterity, patience, accuracy, and ability to work as part of a team or without close supervision.

This section also indicates whether a certificate, examination, or license is required for entry into the field or for independent practice, and if it is helpful for advancement. It also describes typical paths of advancement within the occupation, whether continuing education is required, and patterns of movement or advancement to other occupations.

Job Outlook

This section identifies the factors that will influence employment in the occupation through the year 2005. How will government spending, technological advances, changing business practices, or shifting population patterns affect the demand for workers?

The projections of job outlook presented in the *Handbook* are based on a set of assumptions about how the economy is likely to change between 1992 and 2005. After studying economic trends, how industries currently operate, and the directions in which they are moving, the number, distribution, and composition of jobs in 2005 were projected. Of course, no one can predict with certainty all the economic,

OCCUPATIONAL OUTLOOK HANDBOOK

political, social, and technological forces that will ultimately influence employment growth and job prospects in the future. A summary of the assumptions and methods used by the Bureau of Labor Statistics in making employment projections is presented on page 464. A detailed description is presented in *The American Work Force: 1992-2005*, BLS Bulletin 2452.

If an occupation grows rapidly, it obviously will provide more openings than if it grows slowly, Moreover, the strong demand for talent in a rapidly growing occupation generally improves chances for advancement and mobility. Keep in mind that slow-growing occupations, if large, also provide many job openings. The need to replace workers who transfer occupations or leave the labor force creates the majority of job openings in most occupations, regardless of the rate of growth. Large occupations generally have more replacement openings than small ones. Those with low pay and status, few training requirements, and a high proportion of young, old, or part-time workers generally have more turnover than those with high pay and status, lengthy training requirements, and many prime-working-age, full-time workers.

Besides describing projected employment change, this section also may discuss the degree of competition for jobs that applicants are likely to encounter. How easy or hard will it be to get a job in this field? Does the occupation attract many more jobseekers than there are openings to be filled? Do opportunities vary by industry, size of firm, or geographic location?

The accompanying box explains how to interpret the key phrases used to describe projected changes in employment. It also explains the terms used to describe the relationship between the number of job openings and the number of jobseekers. The descriptions of the relationship between the supply of and demand for workers in a particular occupation reflects the knowledge and judgment of economists in the Bureau's Office of Employment Projections.

Individuals might want to enter an occupation or specialty or locate in a geographic area that has fewer qualified workers than jobs. This is understandable because, under these shortage conditions, jobseekers generally can choose from more job offers, expect higher salaries, and advance faster. Keep in mind, however, that even in occupations with a rough balance of jobseekers and openings, almost all qualified applicants can usually find jobs, although perhaps not their first choice. When there are surpluses of workers, on the other hand, applicants may have to search for a longer time, accept a less desirable offer, find a job in another occupation, or face extended unemployment. But since job openings do exist even in overcrowded fields, good students or well-qualified individuals should not be deterred from undertaking training or seeking entry.

Some statements discuss job security—workers in some occupations are more likely than workers in other occupations to keep or lose their jobs during recessions or government budget cuts, or when new technologies are introduced.

Finally, it is possible that opportunities in your community or State are better or worse than those described in the *Handbook*, which discusses opportunities in the Nation as a whole. Therefore, it is important to check with local sources. (See the chapter on Sources of Information on Career Preparation and Training, beginning on page 5, and the list of State and local agencies, beginning on page 465.)

Key Phrases in the *Handbook*

Changing employment between 1992 and 2005

If the statement reads...	Employment is projected to...
Grow much faster than the average	Increase 41 percent or more
Grow faster than the average	Increase 27 to 40 percent
Grow about as fast as the average	Increase 14 to 26 percent
Little change or grow more slowly than the average	Increase 0 to 13 percent
Decline	Decrease 1 percent or more

Opportunities and competition for jobs

If the statement reads...	Job openings compared to jobseekers may be...
Excellent opportunities	Much more numerous
Very good opportunities	More numerous
Good or favorable opportunities	About the same
May face competition	Fewer
May face keen competition	Much fewer

Earnings

This section indicates how much workers in the occupation generally earn. Earnings are based on several types of pay plans. Workers may be paid a straight annual salary, an hourly wage, commissions based on a percentage of what they sell, or a piece rate for each item they produce. Others receive tips for services to customers. Workers also may be paid a combination of a salary plus commission, or a salary or hourly wage plus bonus, piecework, or tips.

Nearly all workers receive employer-paid benefits in addition to wages and salaries. Standard employee benefits such as health, pension, and vacation and sick leave generally are not mentioned in the detailed occupational statements. Instead, the statements focus on unique benefits, if any. Teachers, for example, get summers off; college faculty get sabbatical leave and tuition for dependents; pilots, flight attendants, and aircraft mechanics working for airlines get free or discounted air travel for themselves and their families; and retail sales workers get discounted merchandise.

In 1991, benefits comprised about 28 percent of total compensation costs, reflecting increases in social security and medical care benefits, as well as growth in benefits designed to meet the needs of a changing labor force—parental leave, child care, and employee assistance programs, for example (chart 1). In addition to medical care, most employees also receive pensions, paid vacations and holidays, and life insurance. Some also receive stock options, profit sharing plans, savings plans, tuition assistance, discounts on merchandise, and expense accounts.

Benefits vary depending on where an employee works and whether they work full time or part time. State and local government employees, for example, generally have a higher incidence of medical and dental care, life insurance, retirement plans, and different types of leave than workers in the private sector. Private sector employees, on the other hand, tend to have a higher incidence of holidays, vacations, and sickness and accident insurance.

Workers employed in medium and large firms with 100 or more employees enjoy better benefits than workers in small firms with fewer than 100 workers. Medium and large firms generally provided more medical and dental, life insurance, and retirement benefits, as well as more unpaid maternity leave and long term disability insurance. Paid vacations and holidays, and medical care and life insurance were the only benefits available to the majority of workers in small firms.

Similarly, full-time workers almost always receive more benefits than part-time employees. For example,

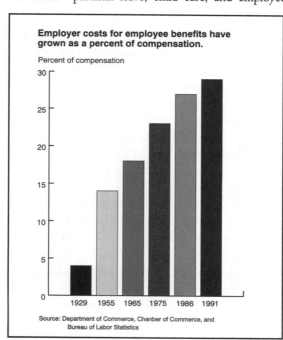

Employer costs for employee benefits have grown as a percent of compensation.

Percent of compensation

Source: Department of Commerce, Chanber of Commerce, and Bureau of Labor Statistics

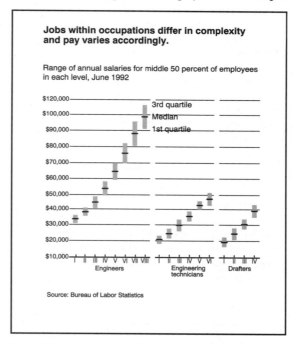

Jobs within occupations differ in complexity and pay varies accordingly.

Range of annual salaries for middle 50 percent of employees in each level, June 1992

Source: Bureau of Labor Statistics

OCCUPATIONAL OUTLOOK HANDBOOK

one third of part-time employees received paid vacations and holidays in 1991, compared to over four-fifths of full-time workers. Employee benefits also are discussed in the section on evaluating a job offer in the following chapter, Sources of Information on Career Preparation and Training, beginning on page 5.

About 8 percent of all workers were self-employed in 1992. Their earnings vary more than those of workers on wages or salaries and, unlike most wage and salary workers, they pay for their own benefits.

Within every occupation, earnings of workers vary depending on experience, level of responsibility, performance, industry, amount of unionization, and geographic area. Earnings generally are higher in cities than in rural areas, and vary by geographic region. Keep in mind that the geographic areas where earnings are higher often have higher costs of living as well.

The level of responsibility that goes with a job affects earnings, too. Annual salaries for eight levels of engineers, five levels of engineering technicians, and five levels of drafters are illustrated in chart 2. These reflect different work levels, starting with entry level jobs and continuing up the career ladder to more complex and responsible supervisory positions. Therefore, it is rarely accurate to say that all people in one occupation earn more than those in another. We can say

that the average is higher or that the middle range of earnings is higher, but there usually is some overlap.

Many *Handbook* statements cite Current Population Survey (CPS) data. They show the median earnings of full-time salaried (but not self-employed) workers in 1992. (The median is the midpoint—half earned more than this and half earned less.) They generally also give the range of earnings of the middle 50 percent of workers, and earnings of the lowest and highest 10 percent. The earnings distribution of physical therapists in 1992, based on CPS data, is illustrated in chart 3. The shaded area under the curve indicates that the median was $35,500, with one-half earning between $26,600 and $43,600. The lowest 10 percent earned under $17,800, while the highest 10 percent earned more than $52,500. You can compare CPS earnings data between occupations or to the average for all occupations. The median for all full-time wage and salary workers in 1992 was $23,100; the middle 50 percent earned between $15,500 and $34,400; the highest 10 percent earned $48,500 or more, and the lowest 10 percent, $11,300 or less.

Some statements include earnings data from sources other than the CPS. The characteristics of these data vary, making it difficult to compare earnings precisely among occupations.

Related Occupations

When you find an occupation that appeals to you, also explore the jobs listed in this section. These occupations usually involve similar aptitudes, interests, education, and training.

Sources of Additional Information

This section lists names and addresses of associations, government agencies, unions, and other organizations that can provide useful information. For some occupations, this section also refers you to free or relatively inexpensive publications that offer more information. These publications also may be available in libraries, school career centers, or guidance offices.

(For additional sources of information, read the next chapter, Sources of Information on Career Preparation and Training.)

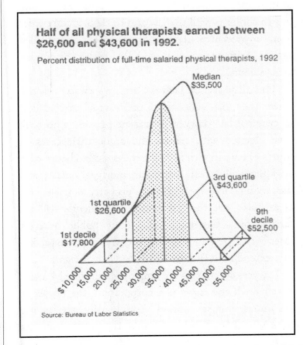

Half of all physical therapists earned between $26,600 and $43,600 in 1992.

Percent distribution of full-time salaried physical therapists, 1992

Median $35,500

3rd quartile $43,600

1st quartile $26,600

9th decile $52,500

1st decile $17,800

$10,000 15,000 20,000 25,000 30,000 35,000 40,000 45,000 50,000 55,000

Source: Bureau of Labor Statistics

Lawyers and Judges

(D.O.T.110; 111; 119.107, 117, 167-010, 267-014; 169.267-010)

Nature of the Work

Lawyers. Lawyers, also called attorneys, act as both advocates and advisors in our society. As advocates, they represent one of the opposing parties in criminal and civil trials by presenting evidence that support their client in court. As advisors, lawyers counsel their clients as to their legal rights and obligations and suggest particular courses of action in business and personal matters. Whether acting as advocates or advisors, all attorneys interpret the law and apply it to specific situations. This requires research and communication abilities.

Lawyers perform in-depth research into the purposes behind the applicable laws and into judicial decisions that have been applied to those laws under circumstances similar to those currently faced by the client. While all lawyers continue to make use of law libraries to prepare cases, some supplement their search of the conventional printed sources with computer software packages that automatically search the legal literature and identify legal texts that may be relevant to a specific subject. In litigation that involves many supporting documents, lawyers may also use computers to organize and index the material. Tax lawyers are also increasingly using computers to make tax computations and explore alternative tax strategies for clients.

Lawyers then communicate to others the information obtained by research. They advise what actions clients may take and draw up legal documents, such as wills and contracts, for clients, Lawyers must deal with people in a courteous, efficient manner and not disclose matters discussed in confidence with clients. They hold positions of great responsibility, and are obligated to adhere to strict rules of ethics.

The more detailed aspects of a lawyer's job depend upon his or her field of specialization and position. Even though all lawyers are allowed to represent parties in court, some appear in court more frequently than others. Some lawyers specialize in trial work. These lawyers need an exceptional ability to think quickly and speak with ease and authority, and must be thoroughly familiar with courtroom rules and strategy. Trial lawyers still spend most of their time outside the courtroom conducting research, interviewing clients and witnesses, and handling other details in preparation for trial.

Besides trials, lawyers may specialize in other areas, such as bankruptcy, probate, or international law. Environmental lawyers, for example, may represent public interest groups, waste disposal companies, or construction firms in their dealings with the Environmental Protection Agency (EPA) and other State and Federal agencies. They help clients prepare and file for licenses and applications for approval before certain activities can occur. They also represent clients' interests in administrative adjudications and during drafting of new regulations.

Some lawyers concentrate in the emerging field of intellectual property. These lawyers help protect clients' claims to copyrights, art work under contract, product designs, and computer programs. Still other lawyers advise insurance companies about the legality of insurance transactions. They write insurance policies to conform with the law and to protect companies from unwarranted claims. They review claims filed against insurance companies and represent the companies in court.

The majority of lawyers are in private practice where they may concentrate on criminal or civil law. In criminal law, lawyers represent persons who have been charged with crimes and argue their cases in courts of law. In civil law, attorneys assist clients with litigation, wills, trusts, contracts, mortgages, titles, and leases. Some manage a person's property as trustee or, as executor, see that provisions of a client's will are carried out. Others handle only public interest cases—civil or criminal—which have a potential impact extending well beyond the individual client.

Lawyers sometimes are employed full time by a single client. If the client is a corporation, the lawyer is known as "house counsel" and usually advises the company about legal questions that arise from its business activities. These questions might involve patents, government regulations, contracts with other companies, property interests, or collective bargaining agreements with unions.

Attorneys employed at the various levels of government make up still another category. Lawyers that work for State attorneys general, prosecutors, public defenders, and courts play a key role in the criminal justice system. At the Federal level, attorneys investigate cases for the Department of Justice or other agencies. Also, lawyers at every government level help develop programs, draft laws, interpret legislation, establish enforcement procedures, and argue civil and criminal cases on behalf of the government.

Other lawyers work for legal aid societies—private, nonprofit organizations established to serve disadvantaged people. These lawyers generally handle civil rather than criminal cases.

A relatively small number of trained attorneys work in law schools. Most are faculty members who specialize in one or more subjects, and others serve as administrators. Some work full time in nonacademic settings and teach part time. (For additional information, see the statement on college and university faculty elsewhere in the *Handbook*.) Some lawyers become judges, although not all judges have practiced law.

Judges. Judges apply the law. They oversee the legal process that in courts of law resolves civil disputes and determines guilt in criminal cases according to Federal and State laws and those of local jurisdictions. They preside over cases touching on virtually every aspect of society, from traffic offenses to disputes over management of professional sports, from the rights of huge corporations to questions of disconnecting life support equipment for terminally ill persons. They must insure that trials and hearings are conducted fairly and that the court administers justice in a manner that safeguards the legal rights of all parties involved.

Judges preside over trials or hearings and listen as attorneys representing the parties present and argue their cases. They rule on the admissibility of evidence and methods of conducting testimony, and settle disputes between the opposing attorneys. They insure that rules and procedures are followed, and if unusual circumstances arise for which standard procedures

have not been established, judges direct how the trial will proceed based on their knowledge of the law.

Judges often hold pretrial hearings for cases. They listen to allegations and, based on the evidence presented, determine whether they have enough merit for a trial to be held. In criminal cases, judges may decide that persons charged with crimes should be held in jail pending their trial, or may set conditions for release through the trial. In civil cases, judges may impose restrictions upon the parties until a trial is held.

When trials are held, juries are often selected to decide cases. However, judges decide cases when the law does not require a jury trial, or when the parties waive their right to a jury. Judges instruct juries on applicable laws, direct them to deduce the facts from the evidence presented, and hear their verdict. Judges sentence those convicted in criminal cases in many States. They also award relief to litigants including, where appropriate, compensation for damages in civil cases.

Judges also work outside the courtroom "in chambers." In their private offices, judges read documents on pleadings and motions, research legal issues, hold hearings with lawyers, write opinions, and oversee the court's operations. Running a court is like running a small business, and judges manage their courts' administrative and clerical staff, too.

Judges' duties vary according to the extent of their jurisdictions and powers. *General trial court judges* of the Federal and State court systems have jurisdiction over any case in their system. They generally try civil cases that transcend the jurisdiction of lower courts, and all cases involving felony offenses. Federal and State *appellate court judges*, although few in number, have the power to overrule decisions made by trial court or administrative law judges if they determine that legal errors were made in a case, or if legal precedent does not support the judgement of the lower court. They rule on fewer cases and rarely have direct contacts with the people involved.

The majority of State court judges preside in courts in which jurisdiction is limited by law to certain types of cases. A variety of titles are assigned to these judges, but among the most common are *municipal court judge, county court judge, magistrate,* or *justice of the peace.* Traffic violations, misdemeanors, small claims cases, and pretrial hearings constitute the bulk of the work of these judges, but some States allow them to handle cases involving domestic relations, probate, contracts, and selected other areas of the law.

Administrative law judges, formerly called *hearing officers*, are employed by government agencies to rule on appeals of agency administrative decisions. They make decisions on a person's eligibility for various Social Security benefits or worker's compensation, protection of the environment, enforcement of health and safety regulations, employment discrimination, and compliance with economic regulatory requirements.

Working Conditions

Lawyers and judges do most of their work in offices, law libraries, and courtrooms. Lawyers sometimes meet in clients' homes or places of business and, when necessary, in hospitals or prisons. They frequently travel to attend meetings; to gather evidence; and to appear before courts, legislative bodies, and other authorities.

Salaried lawyers in government and private corporations generally have structured work schedules. Lawyers in private practice may work irregular hours while conducting research, conferring with clients, or preparing briefs during nonoffice hours. Lawyers often work long hours, and about half regularly work 50 hours or more per week. They are under particularly heavy pressure, for example, when a case is being tried. Preparation for court includes keeping abreast of the latest laws and judicial decisions.

Although work generally is not seasonal, the work of tax lawyers and other specialists may be an exception. Because lawyers in private practice can often determine their own workload and when they will retire, many stay in practice well beyond the usual retirement age.

Many judges work a standard 40-hour week, but a third of all judges work over 50 hours per week. Some judges with limited jurisdiction are employed part time and divide their time between their judicial responsibilities and other careers.

Employment

Lawyers and judges held about 716,000 jobs in 1992. About four-fifths of the 626,000 lawyers practiced pri-

vately, either in law firms or in solo practices. Most of the remaining lawyers held positions in government, the greatest number at the local level. In the Federal Government, lawyers are concentrated in the Departments of Justice, Treasury, and Defense, but they work for other Federal agencies as well. Other lawyers are employed as house counsel by public utilities, banks, insurance companies, real estate agencies, manufacturing firms, welfare and religious organizations, and other business firms and nonprofit organizations. Some salaried lawyers also have part-time independent practices; others work as lawyers part time while working full time in another occupation.

Judges held 90,000 jobs in 1992. All worked for Federal, State, or local governments, with about half holding positions in the Federal Government. The majority of the remainder were employed at the State level.

Many people trained as lawyers are not employed as lawyers or judges; they work as law clerks, law school professors, managers and administrators, and in a variety of other occupations.

Training, Other Qualifications, and Advancement

Lawyers. To practice law in the courts of any State or other jurisdiction, a person must be licensed, or admitted to its bar, under rules established by the jurisdiction's highest court. Nearly all require that applicants for admission to the bar pass a written bar examination. Most jurisdictions also require applicants to pass a separate written ethics examination. Lawyers who have been admitted to the bar in one jurisdiction occasionally may be admitted to the bar in another without taking an examination if they meet that jurisdiction's standards of good moral character and have a specified period of legal experience. Federal courts and agencies set their own qualifications for those practicing before them.

To qualify for the bar examination in most States, an applicant must complete at least 3 years of college and graduate from a law school approved by the American Bar Association (ABA) or the proper State authorities. (ABA approval signifies that the law school—particularly its library and faculty—meets certain standards developed by the Association to promote quality legal education.) In 1992, the American Bar Association approved 177 law schools. Others were approved by State authorities only. With certain exceptions, graduates of schools not approved by the ABA are restricted to taking the bar examination and practicing in the State or other jurisdiction in which the school is located; most of these schools are in California. Seven States accept the study of law in a law office or in combination with study in a law school; only California accepts the study of law by correspondence as qualifying for taking the bar examination. Several States require registration and approval of students by the State Board of Law Examiners, either before they enter law school or during the early years of legal study.

Although there is no nationwide bar examination, 46 States, the District of Columbia, Guam, the Northern Mariana Islands, and the Virgin Islands require the 6-hour Multistate Bar Examination (MBE) as part of the bar examination; the MBE is not required in Indiana, Iowa, Louisiana, Washington, and Puerto Rico. The MBE, covering issues of broad interest, is given in addition to a locally prepared 6-hour State bar examination. The 3-hour Multistate Essay Examination (MEE) is used as part of the State bar examination in a few States. States vary in their use of MBE and MEE scores.

The required college and law school education usually takes 7 years of full-time study after high school— 4 years of undergraduate study followed by 3 years in law school. Although some law schools accept a very small number of students after 3 years of college, most require applicants to have a bachelor's degree. To meet the needs of students who can attend only part time, a number of law schools have night or part-time divisions which usually require 4 years of study. In 1991, about one 1 of 6 students in ABA-approved schools were part time.

Preparation for a career as a lawyer really begins in college. Although there is no recommended "prelaw" major, the choice of an undergraduate program is important. Certain courses and activities are desirable because they give the student the skills needed to succeed both in law school and in the profession. Essential skills—proficiency in writing, reading and analyzing, thinking logically, and communicating verbally—are learned during high school and college. An undergraduate program that cultivates these skills while broadening the student's view of the world is desirable. Courses in English, a foreign language, public speaking, government, philosophy, history, economics, mathematics, and computer science, among others, are useful. Whatever the major, students should not specialize too narrowly.

Students interested in a particular aspect of law may find related courses helpful; for example, many law schools with patent law tracks require bachelor's degrees, or at least several courses, in engineering and science. Future tax lawyers should have a strong undergraduate background in accounting.

Acceptance by most law schools depends on the applicant's ability to demonstrate an aptitude for the study of law, usually through good undergraduate grades, the Law School Admission Test (LSAT), the quality of the applicant's undergraduate school, any prior work experience, and sometimes a personal interview. However, law schools vary in the weight that they place on each of these factors.

All law schools approved by the American Bar Association require that applicants take the LSAT. Nearly all law schools require that applicants have certified transcripts sent to the Law School Data Assembly Service. This service then sends applicants' LSAT scores and their standardized records of college grades to the law schools of their choice. Both this service and the LSAT are administered by the Law School Admission Services.

Competition for admission to many law schools is intense. Enrollments rose very rapidly during the 1970's, with applicants far out-numbering available seats. Since then, law school enrollments have remained relatively unchanged, and the number of applicants has fluctuated. However, the number of applicants to most law schools still greatly exceeds the number that can be admitted. Enrollments are expected to remain at about their present level through the year 2005, and competition for admission to the more prestigious law schools will remain keen.

During the first year or year and a half of law school, students generally study fundamental courses such as constitutional law, contracts, property law, torts, civil procedure, and legal writing. In the remaining time, they may elect specialized courses in fields such as tax, labor, or corporation law. Law students often acquire practical experience by participation in school sponsored legal aid or legal clinic activities, in the school's moot court competitions in which students conduct appellate arguments, in practice trials under the supervision of experienced lawyers and judges, and through research and writing on legal issues for the school's law journal.

In 1992, law students in 36 States and 2 other jurisdictions were required to pass the Multistate Professional Responsibility Examination (MPRE), which tests their knowledge of the ABA codes on professional responsibility and judicial conduct. In some States, the MPRE may be taken during law school, usually after completing a course on legal ethics.

A number of law schools have clinical programs where students gain legal experience through practice trials and law school projects under the supervision of practicing lawyers and law school faculty. Law school clinical programs might include work in legal aid clinics, for example, or on the staff of legislative committees. Part-time or summer clerkships in law firms, government agencies, and corporate legal departments also provide experience that can be extremely valuable later on. Such training can provide references or lead directly to a job after graduation, and can help students decide what kind of practice best suits them. Clerkships also may be an important source of financial aid.

Graduates receive the degree of *juris doctor* (J.D.) or *bachelor of law* (LL.B.) as the first professional degree. Advanced law degrees may be desirable for those planning to specialize, do research, or teach. Some law students pursue joint degree programs, which generally require an additional year. Joint degree programs are offered in a number of areas, including law and business administration and law and public administration.

After graduation, lawyers must keep informed about legal and nonlegal developments that affect their practice. Thirty-seven States and jurisdictions mandate Continuing Legal Education (CLE). Furthermore, many law schools and State and local bar associations provide continuing education courses that help lawyers stay abreast of recent developments.

The practice of law involves a great deal of responsibility. Persons planning careers in law should like to work with people and be able to win the respect and confidence of their clients, associates, and the public. Integrity and honesty are vital personal qualities. Perseverance and reasoning ability are essential to analyze complex cases and reach sound conclusions. Lawyers also need creativity when handling new and unique legal problems.

Most beginning lawyers start in salaried positions. Newly hired salaried attorneys usually act as research assistants to experienced lawyers or judges. After several years of progressively more responsible salaried employment, some lawyers are admitted to partnership in their firm, or go into practice for themselves. Some lawyers, after years of practice, become full-time law school faculty or administrators; a growing number have advanced degrees in other fields as well.

Some persons use their legal training in administrative or managerial positions in various departments of large corporations. A transfer from a corporation's legal department to another department often is viewed as a way to gain administrative experience and rise in the ranks of management.

Judges. Most judges, although not all, have been lawyers first. All Federal judges and State trial and appellate court judges are required to be lawyers or "learned in law." About 40 States presently allow nonlawyers to hold limited jurisdiction judgeships, but opportunities are better with law experience. Federal administrative law judges must be lawyers and pass a competitive examination administered by the U.S. Office of Personnel Management. Many State administrative law judges and other hearing officials are not required to be lawyers, but law degrees are preferred for most positions.

Federal judges are appointed for life by the President, with the consent of the Senate. Federal administrative law judges are appointed by the various Federal agencies with virtually lifetime tenure. About half of all State judges are appointed, while the remainder are elected in partisan or nonpartisan State elections. Most State and local judges serve fixed terms, which range from 4 or 6 years for most limited jurisdiction judgeships to as long as 14 years for some appellate court judges. Judicial nominating commissions, composed of members of the bar and the public, are used to screen candidates for judgeships in many States, as

OCCUPATIONAL OUTLOOK HANDBOOK

well as for Federal judgeships.

All States have some type of orientation for newly elected or appointed judges. Thirteen States also require judges to take continuing education courses while serving on the bench.

Job Outlook

Persons seeking positions as lawyers or judges should encounter keen competition through the year 2005. Law schools still attract large numbers of applicants and are not expected to decrease their enrollments, so the supply of persons trained as lawyers should continue to exceed job openings. As for judges, the prestige associated with serving on the bench should insure continued intense competition for openings.

Lawyers. Employment of lawyers has grown very rapidly since the early 1970's, and is expected to continue to grow faster than the average for all occupations through the year 2005. New jobs created by growth should exceed job openings that arise from the need to replace lawyers who stop working or leave the profession. The strong growth in demand for lawyers will result from growth in the population and the general level of business activities. Demand also will be spurred by growth of legal action in such areas as employee benefits, consumer protection, criminal prosecution, the environment, and finance, and an anticipated increase in the use of legal services by middle-income groups through legal clinics and prepaid legal programs.

Even though jobs for lawyers are expected to increase rapidly, competition for job openings should continue to be keen because of the large numbers graduating from law school each year. During the 1970's, the annual number of law school graduates more than doubled, outpacing the rapid growth of jobs. Growth in the yearly number of law school graduates tapered off during the 1980's, but again increased in the early 1990's. The high number of graduates will strain the economy's capacity to absorb them. Although graduates with superior academic records from well-regarded law schools will continue to enjoy good opportunities, most graduates will encounter competition for jobs. As in the past, some graduates may have to accept positions in areas outside their field of interest or for which they feel they are over-

qualified. They may have to enter jobs for which legal training is an asset but not normally a requirement. For example, banks, insurance firms, real estate companies, government agencies, and other organizations seek law graduates to fill many administrative, managerial, and business positions.

Due to the competition for jobs, a law graduate's geographic mobility and work experience assume greater importance. The willingness to relocate may be an advantage in getting a job, but to be licensed in a new State, a lawyer may have to take an additional State bar examination. In addition, employers increasingly seek graduates who have advanced law degrees and experience in a particular field such as tax, patent, or admiralty law.

Employment growth of lawyers will continue to be concentrated in salaried jobs, as businesses and all levels of government employ a growing number of staff attorneys, and as employment in the legal services industry is increasingly concentrated in larger law firms. The number of self-employed lawyers is expected to continue to increase slowly, reflecting the difficulty of establishing a profitable new practice in the face of competition from larger, established law firms. Also, the growing complexity of law—which encourages specialization—and the cost of maintaining up-to-date legal research materials both favor larger firms.

For lawyers who nevertheless wish to work independently, establishing a new practice probably will continue to be easiest in small towns and expanding suburban areas, as long as an active market for legal services already exists. In such communities, competition from larger established law firms is likely to be less than in big cities, and new lawyers may find it easier to become known to potential clients; also, rent and other business costs are somewhat lower. Nevertheless, starting a new practice will remain an expensive and risky undertaking that should be weighed carefully. Most salaried positions will remain in urban areas where government agencies, law firms, and big corporations are concentrated.

Some lawyers are adversely affected by cyclical swings in the economy. During recessions, the demand for some discretionary legal services, such as planning estates, drafting wills, and handling real estate transactions, declines. Also, corporations are less likely to litigate cases when declining sales and profits result in budgetary restrictions. Although few lawyers actually lose their jobs during these times, earnings may decline for many. Some corporations and law firms will not hire new attorneys until business improves. Several factors, however, mitigate the overall impact of recessions on lawyers. During recessions, individuals and corporations face other legal problems, such as bankruptcies, foreclosures, and divorces, that require legal action. Furthermore, new laws and legal interpretations will create new opportunities for lawyers.

Judges. Employment of judges is expected to grow more slowly than average for all occupations. Contradictory social forces affect the demand for judges. Pushing up demand are public concerns about crime, safety, and efficient administration of justice; on the other hand, tight public funding should slow job growth.

Competition for judgeships should remain keen. Most job openings will arise as judges retire. Traditionally, many judges have held their positions until late in life. Now, early retirement is becoming more common, creating more job openings; however, becoming a judge will still be difficult. Besides competing with other qualified people, judicial candidates must gain political support in order to be elected or appointed.

Earnings

Annual salaries of beginning lawyers in private industry averaged about $36,600 in 1992, but top graduates from the Nation's best law schools started in some cases at over $80,000 a year. In the Federal Government, annual starting salaries for attorneys in 1993 were about $27,800 or $33,600, depending upon academic and personal qualifications. Factors affecting the salaries offered to new graduates include: Academic record; type, size, and location of employer; and the specialized educational background desired. The field of law makes a difference, too. Patent lawyers, for example, generally are among the highest paid attorneys.

Salaries of experienced attorneys also vary widely according to the type, size, and location of their employer. The average salary of the most experienced lawyers in private industry in 1992 was over $134,000 but some senior lawyers who were partners the Nation's top law firms earned over $1 million.

General attorneys in the Federal Government averaged around $62,200 a year in 1993; the relatively small number of patent attorneys in the Federal Governmnet averaged around $71,600.

Lawyers on salary receive increases as they assume greater responsibility. Lawyers starting their own practice may need to work part time in other occupations during the first years to supplement their income. Their incomes usually grow as their practices develop. Lawyers who are partners in law firms generally earn more than those who practice alone.

Federal district court judges had salaries of $133,600 in 1993, as did judges in the Court of Federal Claims. Circuit court judges earned $141,700 a year. Federal judges with limited jurisdiction, such as magistrates and bankruptcy court judges, had salaries of $122,900 in 1993. Full-time Federal administrative law judges had average salaries of $94,800 in 1993. The Chief Justice of the United States Supreme Court earned $171,500 in 1993, and the Associate Justices earned $164,100.

Annual salaries of associate justices of States' highest courts averaged nearly $89,570 in 1992, according to a survey by the National Center for State Courts, and ranged from about $62,500 to $121,207. Salaries of State intermediate appellate court judges averaged $88,435, but ranged from $79,975 to $113,632. Salaries of State judges with limited jurisdiction varied widely; many salaries are set locally.

Most salaried lawyers and judges were provided health and life insurance, and contributions were made on their behalf to retirement plans. Lawyers who practiced independently were only covered if they arranged and paid for such benefits themselves.

Related Occupations

Legal training is useful in many other occupations. Some of these are paralegal, arbitrator, journalist, patent agent, title examiner, legislative assistant, lobbyist, FBI special agent, political office holder, and corporate executive.

Sources of Additional Information

The American Bar Association annually publishes *A Review of Legal Education in the United States*, which

OCCUPATIONAL OUTLOOK HANDBOOK

provides detailed information on each of the 177 law schools approved by the ABA, State requirements for admission to legal practice, a directory of State bar examination administrators, and other information on legal education. Single copies are free from the ABA, but there is a fee for multiple copies. Free information on the bar examination, financial aid for law students, and law as a career may also be obtained from:

Member Services, American Bar Association, 541 North Fairbanks Court, Chicago, IL 60611-3314.

Information on the LSAT, the Law School Data Assembly Service, applying to law school, and financial aid for law students may be obtained from:

Law School Admission Services, P.O. Box 40, Newtown, PA 18940. Phone: (215) 968-1001.

The specific requirements for admission to the bar in a particular State or other jurisdiction may also be obtained at the State capital from the clerk of the Supreme Court or the administrator of the State Board of Bar Examiners.

Sources of Information on Career Preparation and Training

This chapter identifies selected sources of information about occupations, counseling, training and education, financial aid, and finding and evaluating potential jobs. Also, read the occupational statements in the Handbook, including the section on sources of additional information, which lists organizations you can contact for more information about particular occupations.

Career Information

A good place to start collecting information you need is from the people closest to you, your family and friends. These **personal contacts** are often overlooked, but can be extremely helpful. They may be able to answer your questions directly or, more importantly, put you in touch with someone else who can. This "networking" can lead to an "informational interview," where you can meet with someone who is willing to answer your questions about a career or a company, and who can provide inside information on related fields and other helpful hints. This is a highly effective way to learn the recommended type of training for certain positions, how someone in that position entered and advanced, and what he or she likes and dislikes about the work. While developing your network of contacts, you may want to begin exploring other avenues.

Public libraries, career centers, and guidance offices have a great deal of career material. To begin your library search, look in the card catalog or at the computer listings under "vocations" or "careers" and then under specific fields. Also, leaf through the file of pamphlets that describe employment in different organizations. Check the periodicals section, where you will find trade and professional magazines and journals about specific occupations and industries. Familiarize yourself with the concerns and activities of potential employers by skimming their annual reports and other information they distribute to the public.

You can also find occupational information on video cassettes, in kits, and through computerized information systems. Check career centers for programs such as individual counseling, group discussions, guest speakers, field trips, and career days.

Always assess career guidance materials carefully. Information should be current. Beware of materials produced by schools for recruitment purposes that seem to glamorize the occupation, overstate the earnings, or exaggerate the demand for workers.

You may wish to seek help from a counselor. **Counselors** are trained to help you discover your strengths and weaknesses, guide you through an evaluation of your goals and values, and help you determine what you want in a career. The counselor will not tell you what to do, but will administer interest inventories and aptitude tests, interpret the results, and help you explore your options. Counselors also

OCCUPATIONAL OUTLOOK HANDBOOK

may be able to discuss local job markets, and the entry requirements and costs of the schools, colleges, or training programs offering preparation for the kind of work that interests you. You can find counselors in:

- high school guidance offices,
- college career planning and placement offices,
- placement offices in private vocational/technical schools and institutions,
- vocational rehabilitation agencies,
- counseling services offered by community organizations,
- private counseling agencies and private practices,
- State employment service offices affiliated with the U.S. Employment Service.

Before employing the services of a private counselor or agency, seek recommendations and check their credentials. The International Association of Counseling Services (IACS) accredits counseling services throughout the country. To receive the listing of accredited services for your region, send a self-addressed, stamped, business-size envelope to IACS, 101 South Whiting St., Suite 211, Alexandria, VA 22304. The *Directory of Counseling Services*, an IACS publication providing employment counseling and other assistance, may be available in your library or school career counseling center. For a list of certified career counselors by State, contact the National Board of Certified Counselors, 3-D Terrace Way, Greensboro, NC 27403. Phone: (919) 547-0607.

Professional societies, trade associations, labor unions, business firms, and educational institutions provide a variety of free or inexpensive career material. Many of these are identified in the Sources of Additional Information section of each *Handbook* statement. For information on occupations not covered in the *Handbook*, consult directories in your library's reference section for the names of potential sources. You may need to start with *The Guide to American Directories* or *The Directory of Directories*. Another useful resource is *The Encyclopedia of Associations*, an annual multivolume publication listing trade associations, professional societies, labor unions. and fraternal and patriotic organizations.

The National Audiovisual Center, a central source for all audiovisual material produced by the U.S. Gov-

ernment, rents and sells material on jobs and careers. For a catalog, contact the National Audiovisual Center, 8700 Edgeworth Dr., Capitol Heights, MD 20743. Phone: 1-800-788-6282.

For first-hand experience in an occupation, you may wish to intern, or take a summer or part-time job. Some internships offer academic credit or pay a stipend. Check with guidance offices, college career resource centers, or directly with employers.

State and Local Information

The *Handbook* provides information for the Nation as a whole. For help in locating State or local area information, contact your **State occupational information coordinating committee (SOICC)**. These committees may provide the information directly, or refer you to other sources. Refer to the chapter beginning on page 465 for addresses and telephone numbers of the SOICC's.

Most States have career information delivery systems (CIDS). Look for these systems in secondary schools, postsecondary institutions, libraries, job training sites, vocational rehabilitation centers, and employment service offices. Jobseekers can use the systems' computers, printed material, microfiche, and toll-free hotlines to obtain information on occupations, educational opportunities, student financial aid, apprenticeships, and military careers. Ask counselors and SOICC's for specific locations.

State employment security agencies develop detailed information about local labor markets, such as current and projected employment by occupation and industry, characteristics of the work force, and changes in State and local area economic activity. Addresses and telephone numbers of the directors of research and analysis in these agencies are listed in the chapter beginning on page 465.

Education and Training Information

Colleges, schools, and training institutes normally readily reply to requests for information. When contacting these institutions, you may want to keep in mind the following items:

OCCUPATIONAL OUTLOOK HANDBOOK

- admission requirements
- courses offered
- certificates or degrees awarded
- cost
- available financial aid
- location and size of school

Check with professional and trade associations for lists of schools that offer career preparation in a field you're interested in. Guidance offices and libraries usually have copies of the kinds of directories listed below, as well as college catalogs that can provide more information on specific institutions. Be sure to use the latest edition because these directories and catalogs are often revised annually.

Information about home study programs appears in the *Directory of Accredited Home Study Schools,* published by the National Home Study Council. Send requests for the *Directory* and a list of other publications to the National Home Study Council, 1601 18th St. NW., Washington, DC 20009. Phone: (202) 234-5100.

Local labor unions, school guidance counselors, and State employment offices provide information about apprenticeships. Copies of *The National Apprenticeship Program and Apprenticeship Information* are available from the Bureau of Apprenticeship and Training, U.S. Department of Labor, 200 Constitution Ave. NW., Washington, DC 20210. Phone: (202) 219-5921.

Financial Aid Information

Information about financial aid is available from a variety of sources. Contact your high school guidance counselor and college financial aid officer for information concerning scholarships, fellowships, grants, loans, and work-study programs. In addition, every State administers financial aid programs; contact State Departments of Education for information. Banks and credit unions can provide information about student loans. You also may want to consult the directories and guides to sources of student financial aid available in guidance offices and public libraries.

The Federal Government provides grants, loans, work-study programs, and other benefits to students. Information about programs administered by the U.S.

Department of Education is presented in *The Student Guide to Federal Financial Aid Programs,* updated annually. To get a copy, write to the Federal Student Aid Information Center, c/o Federal Student Aid Programs, P.O. Box 84, Washingington, DC 20044, or phone, toll-free, 1-800-433-3243.

The National and Community Service Trust Act of 1993 allows individuals aged 17 and over, to serve in approved local programs before, during, or after post-secondary education, to earn money for education. A participant must complete at least 1 year of full-time or 2 years of part-time service to qualify. Awards may be used for past, present, or future expenses, including 2- and 4-year colleges, training programs, and graduate or professional programs. Information about service appointments may be found in high schools, colleges, and other placement offices, or can be obtained by contacting the commission on national service in your State, or by calling 1-800-94-ACORPS.

Meeting College Costs, an annual publication of the College Board, explains how student financial aid works and how to apply for it. The current edition is available to high school students through guidance counselors.

Need a Lift?, an annual publication of the American Legion, contains career and scholarship information. Copies cost $2 each, prepaid (including postage), and can be obtained from the American Legion, Attn: Emblem Sales, P.O. Box 1050, Indianapolis, IN 46206. Phone: (317) 635-8411.

Some student aid programs are designed to assist specific groups—Hispanics, blacks, native Americans, or women, for example. *Higher Education Opportunities for Minorities and Women,* published in 1991 by the U.S. Department of Education, is a guide to organizations offering assistance. This publication can be found in libraries and guidance offices, or copies may be obtained from the U.S. Department of Education, 400 Maryland Ave. SW., Washington, DC 20202. Phone: (202) 401-3550.

The Armed Forces have several educational assistance programs. These include the Reserve Officers' Training Corps (ROTC), the New G.I. bill, and tuition assistance. Information can be obtained from military recruiting centers, located in most cities.

OCCUPATIONAL OUTLOOK HANDBOOK

Information on Finding a Job

It takes some people a great deal of time and effort to find a job they enjoy. Others may walk right into an ideal employment situation. Don't be discouraged if you have to pursue many leads. Friends, neighbors, teachers, and counselors may know of available jobs in your field of interest. Read the want ads. Consult State employment service offices and private or nonprofit employment agencies or contact employers directly.

Where To Learn About Job Openings
- Parents, friends, and neighbors
- School or college placement services
- Classified ads
  - —Local and out-of-town newspapers
  - —Professional journals
  - —Trade magazines
- Employment agencies and career consultants
- State employment service offices
- Civil service announcements (Federal, State, local)
- Labor unions
- Professional associations (State and local chapters)
- Libraries and community centers
- Women's counseling and employment programs
- Youth programs
- Employers

Informal job search methods. It is possible to apply directly to employers without a referral. You may locate a potential employer in the *Yellow Pages*, in directories of local chambers of commerce, and in other directories that provide information about employers. When you find an employer you are interested in, you can file an application even if you don't know for certain that an opening exists.

Want ads. The "Help Wanted" ads in newspapers list hundreds of jobs. Realize, however, that many job openings are not listed there. Also, be aware that the classified ads sometimes do not give some important information. Many offer little or no description of the job, working conditions, or pay. Some ads do not identify the employer. They may simply give a post office box for sending your resume. This makes follow-up inquiries very difficult. Furthermore, some ads offer out-of-town jobs; others advertise employment agencies rather than employment.

Keep the following in mind if you are using want ads:
- Do not rely solely on the classifieds to find a job; follow other leads as well.
- Answer ads promptly, since openings may be filled quickly, even before the ad stops appearing in the paper.
- Follow the ads diligently. Check them every day, as early as possible, to give yourself an advantage.
- Beware of "no experience necessary" ads. These ads often signal low wages, poor working conditions, or straight commission work.
- Keep a record of all ads to which you have responded, including the specific skills, educational background, and personal qualifications required for the position.

What Goes Into a Resume
A resume summarizes your qualifications and employment history. It usually is required when applying for managerial, administrative, professional, or technical positions. Although there is no set format, it should contain the following information:
- Name, address, and telephone number.
- Employment objective. State the type of work or specific job you are seeking.
- Education, including school name and address, dates of attendance, curriculum, and highest grade completed or degree awarded.
- Experience, paid or volunteer. Include the following for each job: Job title, name and address of employer, and dates of employment. Describe your job duties.
- Special skills, knowledge of machinery, proficiency in foreign languages, honors received, awards, or membership in organizations.
- Note on your resume that "references are available upon request." On a separate sheet, list the name, address, telephone number, and job title of three references.

OCCUPATIONAL OUTLOOK HANDBOOK

Public employment service. The State employment service, sometimes called the Job Service, operates in coordination with the Labor Department's U.S. Employment Service. About 1,700 local offices, also known as employment service centers, help jobseekers locate employment and help employers find qualified workers at no cost to themselves. To find the office nearest you, look in the State government telephone listings under "Job Service" or "Employment."

A computerized job network system—*America's Job Bank*—run by the U.S. Department of Labor, lists 50,000 or so job openings each week, with plans to list 75,000 or more in the future. Jobseekers can access these listings through the use of a personal computer in any local public employment service office, as well as in several hundred military installations. In addition, some State employment agencies have set up *America's Job Bank* in other settings, including libraries, schools, shopping malls, and correctional facilities. A wide range of jobs are listed.

Tips for Finding the Right Job, a U.S. Department of Labor pamphlet, offers advice an determining your job skills, organizing your job search, writing a resume, and making the most of an interview. *Job Search Guide: Strategies For Professionals*, another U.S. Department of Labor publication, also discusses specific steps that jobseekers can follow to identify employment opportunities. This publication includes sections on handling your job loss, managing your personal resources, assessing your skills and interests, researching the job market, conducting the job search and networking, writing resumes and cover letters, employment interviewing and testing, and sources of additional information. Check with your State employment service office, or order a copy of these publications from the U.S. Government Printing Office. Phone: (202) 783-3238 for price and ordering information.

Job matching and referral. At a State employment service office, an interviewer will determine if you are "job ready" or if counseling and testing services would be helpful before you begin your job search. After you are "job ready," you may examine *America's Job Bank*, a computerized listing of public- and private-sector job openings that is updated daily. Select openings that interest you, then get more details from a staff member who can describe the job openings in detail and arrange for interviews with prospective employers.

Counseling and testing. Centers can test for occupational aptitudes and interests and then help you choose and prepare for a career.

Services for special groups. By law, veterans are entitled to priority at State employment service centers. Veterans' employment representatives can inform you of available assistance and help you deal with any problems.

Summer Youth Programs provide summer jobs in city, county, and State government agencies for low-income youth. Students, school dropouts. or graduates entering the labor market who are between 16 and 21 years of age are eligible. In addition, the Job Corps, with more than 100 centers throughout the United States, helps young people learn skills or obtain education.

Service centers also refer applicants to opportunities available under the Job Training Partnership Act (JTPA) of 1982, JTPA prepares economically disadvantaged persons and those facing barriers to employment for jobs.

Federal job information. For information about employment with the U.S. Government, call the Federal Job Information Center, operated by the Office of Personnel Management. The phone number is (202) 606-2700, or write to Federal Job Information Center, 1900 E St. NW., Room 1416, Washington. DC 20415.

Private employment agencies. These agencies can be very helpful, but don't forget that they are in business to make money. Most agencies operate on a commission basis, with the fee dependent upon a successful match. You or the hiring company will have to pay a fee for the matching service. Find out the exact cost and who is responsible for paying it before using the service.

While employment agencies can help you save time and contact employers who otherwise may be difficult to locate, in some cases, your costs may outweigh the benefits. Consider any guarantee they offer when figuring the cost.

College career planning and placement offices. College placement offices facilitate matching job openings with suitable jobseekers. You can set up schedules and use available facilities for interviews with recruiters or scan lists of part-time, temporary, and summer jobs maintained in many of these offices. You also can get counseling, testing, and job search advice and take advantage of their career resource library. Here you also will be able to identify and evaluate your interests, work values, and skills; attend workshops on such topics as job search strategy, resume writing, letter writing, and effective interviewing; critique drafts of resumes and videotapes of mock interviews; explore files of resumes and references; and attend job fairs conducted by the office.

Community agencies. Many nonprofit organizations offer counseling, career development, and job placement services, generally targeted to a particular group, such as women, youth, minorities, ex-offenders, or older workers.

Many communities have career counseling, training, placement, and support services for employment. These programs are sponsored by a variety of organizations, including churches and synagogues, nonprofit organizations, social service agencies, the State employment service, and vocational rehabilitation agencies. Many cities have commissions that provide services for these special groups.

Evaluating a Job Offer

Once you receive a job offer, you are faced with a difficult decision. Fortunately, most organizations will not expect you to accept or reject an offer on the spot. You probably will be given at least a week to make up your mind. Although there is no way to remove all risks from this career decision, you will increase your chances of making the right choice by thoroughly evaluating each offer—weighing all the advantages against all the disadvantages of taking the job.

There are many issues to consider when assessing a job offer. Will the organization be a good place to

---

Job Interview Tips

Preparation:
- Learn about the organization.
- Have a specific job or jobs in mind.
- Review your qualifications for the job.
- Prepare answers to broad questions about yourself.
- Review your resume.
- Practice an interview with a friend or relative.
- Arrive before the scheduled time of your interview.

Personal Appearance:
- Be well groomed.
- Dress appropriately.
- Do not chew gum or smoke.

The Interview:
- Answer each question concisely.
- Respond promptly.
- Use good manners. Learn the name of your interviewer and shake hands as you meet.
- Use proper English and avoid slang.
- Be cooperative and enthusiastic.

- Ask questions about the position and the organization.
- Thank the interviewer, and follow up with a letter.

Test (if employer gives one):
- Listen closely to instructions.
- Read each question carefully.
- Write legibly and clearly.
- Budget your time wisely and don't dwell on one question.

Information to Bring to an Interview:
- Social Security number.
- Driver's license number.
- Resume. Although not all employers require applicants to bring a resume, you should be able to furnish the interviewer with information about your education, training, and previous employment.
- Usually an employer requires three references. Get permission from people before using their names, and make sure they will give you a good reference. Try to avoid using relatives. For each reference, provide the following information: Name, address, telephone number, and job title.

work? Will the job be interesting? How are opportunities for advancement? Is the salary fair? Does the employer offer good benefits? If you have not already figured out exactly what you want, the following discussion may help you develop a set of criteria for judging job offers, whether you are starting a career, reentering the labor force after a long absence, or planning a career change.

The Organization. Background information on the organization—be it a company, government agency, or nonprofit concern—can help you decide whether it is a good place for you to work. Factors to consider include the organization's business or activity, financial condition, age, size, and location. Information on growth prospects for the industry or industries that the company represents also is important. Here are some questions to ask.

Is the organization's business or activity in keeping with your own interests and beliefs? It will be easier to apply yourself to the work if you are enthusiastic about what the organization does.

How will the size of the organization affect you? Large firms generally offer a greater variety of training programs and career paths, more managerial levels for advancement, and better employee benefits than small firms. Large employers also have more advanced technologies in their laboratories, offices, and factories. However, jobs in large firms tend to be highly specialized—workers are assigned relatively narrow responsibilities. On the other hand, jobs in small firms may offer broader authority and responsibility, a closer working relationship with top management, and a chance to clearly see your contribution to the success of the organization.

Should you work for a fledgling organization or one that is well established? New businesses have a high failure rate, but for many people, the excitement of helping create a company and the potential for sharing in its success more than offset the risk of job loss. It may be almost as exciting and rewarding, however, to work for a young firm which already has a foothold on success.

Does it make any difference to you whether the company is private or public? A private company may be controlled by an individual or a family, which can mean that key jobs are reserved for relatives and friends. A public

company is controlled by a board of directors responsible to the stockholders. Key jobs are open to anyone with talent.

Is the organization in an industry with favorable long-term prospects? The most successful firms tend to be in industries that are growing rapidly.

Where is the job located? If it is in another city, you need to consider the cost of living, the availability of housing and transportation, and the quality of educational and recreational facilities in the new location. Even if the place of work is in your area, consider the time and expense of commuting and whether it can be done by public transportation.

Where are the firm's headquarters and branches located? Although a move may not be required now, future opportunities could depend on your willingness to move to these places.

It frequently is easy to get background information on an organization simply by telephoning its public relations office. A public company's annual report to the stockholders tells about its corporate philosophy, history, products or services, goals, and financial status. Most government agencies can furnish reports that describe their programs and missions. Press releases, company newsletters or magazines, and recruitment brochures also can be useful. Ask the organization for any other items that might interest a prospective employee.

Background information on the organization also may be available at your public or school library. If you cannot get an annual report, check the library for reference directories that provide basic facts about the company, such as earnings, products and services, and number of employees. Some directories widely available in libraries include the following: *Dun & Bradstreet's Million Dollar Directory; Standard and Poor's Register of Corporations, Directors and Executives; Moody's Industrial Manual; Thomas' Register of American Manufacturers; and Ward's Business Directory.* If you plan to continue your job search, these directories also will list the names and addresses of other firms that might hire you.

Stories about an organization in magazines and newspapers can tell a great deal about its successes, failures, and plans for the future. You can identify articles on a company by looking under its name in

OCCUPATIONAL OUTLOOK HANDBOOK

periodical or computerized indexes—such as the *Business Periodicals Index, Reader's Guide to Periodical Literature, Newspaper Index, Wall Street Journal Index,* and *New York Times Index.* It probably will not be useful to look back more than 2 or 3 years.

The library also may have government publications that present projections of growth for the industry in which the organization is classified. Long-term projections of employment and output for more than 200 industries, covering the entire economy, are developed by the Bureau of Labor Statistics and revised every other year—see the November 1993 Monthly Labor Review for the most recent projections. The *U.S. Industrial Outlook,* published annually by the U.S. Department of Commerce, presents detailed analyses of growth prospects for a large number of industries. Trade magazines also have frequent articles on the trends for specific industries.

Career centers at colleges and universities often have information on employers that is not available in libraries. Ask the career center librarian how to find out about a particular organization. The career center may have an entire file of information on the company.

The Nature of the Work. Even if everything else about the job is good, you will be unhappy if you dislike the day-to-day work. Determining in advance whether you will like the work may be difficult. However, the more you find out about it before accepting or rejecting the job offer, the more likely you are to make the right choice. Ask yourself questions like the following.

Does the work match your interests and make good use of your skills? The duties and responsibilities of the job should be explained in enough detail to answer this question.

How important is the job in this company? An explanation of where you fit in the organization and how you are supposed to contribute to its overall objectives should give an idea of the job's importance.

Are you comfortable with the supervisor?

Do the other employees seem friendly and cooperative?

Does the work require travel?

Does the job call for irregular hours?

How long do most people who enter this job stay with the company? High turnover can mean dissatisfaction with the nature of the work or something else about the job.

The Opportunities. A good job offers you opportunities to grow and move up. It gives you chances to learn new skills, increase your earnings, and rise to positions of greater authority, responsibility, and prestige. A lack of opportunities can dampen interest in the work and result in frustration and boredom.

The company should have a training plan for you. You know what your abilities are now. What valuable new skills does the company plan to teach you?

The employer should give you some idea of promotion possibilities within the organization. What is the next step on the career ladder? If you have to wait for a job to became vacant before you can be promoted, how long does this usually take? Employers differ on their policies regarding promotion from within the organization. When opportunities for advancement do arise, will you compete with applicants from outside the company? Can you apply for jobs for which you qualify elsewhere within the organization or is mobility within the firm limited?

The Salary and Benefits. Wait for the employer to introduce these subjects. Most companies will not talk about pay until they have decided to hire you. In order to know if their offer is reasonable, you need a rough estimate of what the job should pay. You may have to go to several sources for this information. Talk to friends who recently were hired in similar jobs. Ask your teachers and the staff in the college placement office about starting pay for graduates with your qualifications. Scan the help-wanted ads in newspapers. Check the library or your school's career center for salary surveys, such as the College Placement Council Salary Survey and Bureau of Labor Statistics occupational wage surveys. If you are considering the salary and benefits for a job in another geographic area, make allowances for differences in the cost of living, which may be significantly higher in a large metropolitan area than in a smaller city, town, or rural area. Use the research to come up with a base salary range for yourself, the top being the best you can hope to get and the bottom being the least you will take. An employer cannot be specific about the amount of pay if it includes commissions and bonuses. The way the plan works, however, should be explained. The employer also should be able to tell you what most people in the job earn.

You also should learn the organization's policy regarding overtime. Depending on the job, you may or may not be exempt from laws requiring the employer to compensate you for overtime. Find out how many hours you will be expected to work each week and whether you receive overtime pay or compensatory time off for working more than the specified number of hours in a week.

Also take into account that the starting salary is just that, the start. Your salary should be reviewed on a regular basis—many organizations do it every 12 months. If the employer is pleased with your performance, how much can you expect to earn after 1, 2, or 3 or more years?

Don't think of your salary as the only compensation you will receive—consider benefits. Benefits can add a lot to your base pay. Health insurance and pension plans are among the most important benefits. Other common benefits include life insurance, paid vacations and holidays, and sick leave. Benefits vary widely among smaller and larger firms, among full-time and part-time workers, and between the public and private sectors. Find out exactly what the benefit package includes and how much of the costs you must bear.

When you evaluate a job offer, you have many things to consider. Only you will be able to weigh the advantages of a job that is more compatible with your interests and skills against a job that offers a higher salary and more promising advancement opportunities, or weigh the advantages of a job that offers better benefits against a job that is much closer to your home. Asking yourself these kinds of questions won't guarantee that you make the best career decision—only hindsight could do that—but you probably will make a better choice than if you act on impulse.

Detailed data on wages and benefits is available from the Bureau of Labor Statistics, Office of Compensation and Working Conditions, Division of Occupational Pay and Employee Benefit Levels, 2 Massachusetts Ave. NE., Room 4160, Washington, DC 20212-0001. Phone: (202) 606-6225. Data on weekly earnings, based on the Current Population Survey, is available from the Bureau of Labor Statistics, Office of Employment and Unemployment Statistics, 2 Massachusetts Ave. NE., Room 4945, Washington, DC 20212-0001. Phone: (202) 606-6400.

Organizations for Specific Groups

The organizations listed below provide information on career planning, training, or public policy support for specific groups.

Disabled: President's Committee on Employment of People with Disabilities, 1331 F St. NW., 3rd Floor, Washington, DC 20004. Phone: (202) 376-6200.

The blind: Information on the free national reference and referral service provided by the Federation of the Blind can be obtained by contacting Job Opportunities for the Blind (JOB), National Federation of the Blind, 1800 Johnson St., Baltimore, MD 21230. Phone: toll-free, 1-800-638-7518, or locally (410) 659-9314.

Minorities: National Association for the Advancement of Colored People (NAACP), 4805 Mount Hope Dr., Baltimore, MD 21215-3297. Phone: (410) 358-8900.

The National Urban League is a nonprofit community-based social service and civil rights organization that assists African-Americans in the achievement of social and economic equality. There are 113 local affiliates throughout the country that provide services related to employment and job training, and education and career development. Contact the affiliate nearest you for information.

Older workers: National Association of Older Workers Employment Services, c/o National Council on the Aging, 409 3rd St. SW., Suite 200, Washington, DC 20024. Phone: (202) 479-1200.

For publications on job opportunities, contact the American Association of Retired Persons, Workforce Program Department, 601 E St. NW., Floor A5, Washington, DC 20049. Phone: (202) 434-2040.

Asociacion Nacional Por Personas Mayores (National Association for Hispanic Elderly), 2727 W. 6th St., Suite 270, Los Angeles, CA 90057. Phone: (213) 487-1922. This organization specifically serves low-income, minority persons who are 55 years of age and older.

National Caucus/Center on Black Aged, Inc., 1424 K St NW., Suite 500, Washington, DC 20005. Phone: (202) 637-8400.

OCCUPATIONAL OUTLOOK HANDBOOK

Veterans: Contact the nearest regional office of the Department of Veterans Affairs.

Veterans' Employment and Training Service (VETS), 200 Constitution Ave. NW., Room S-1313, Washington, DC 20210. Phone: (202) 219-9116.

Women: U.S. Department of Labor, Women's Bureau, 200 Constitution Ave. NW., Washington, DC 20210. Phone: (202) 219-6652.

Catalyst, 250 Park Ave. South, 5th floor, New York, NY 10003. Phone: (212) 777-8900.

Wider Opportunities for Women, 1325 G St. NW., Lower Level, Washington, DC 20005. Phone: (202) 638-3143.

Federal laws, executive orders, and selected Federal grant programs bar discrimination in employment based on race, color, religion, sex, national origin, age, and handicap. Information on how to file a charge of discrimination is available from U.S. Equal Employment Opportunity Commission offices around the country. Their addresses and telephone numbers are listed in telephone directories under U.S. Government, EEOC, or are available from the Equal Employment Opportunity Commission, 1801 L St. NW., Washington, DC 20507. Phone: (202) 663-4264.

Information on Federal laws concerning fair labor standards such as the minimum wage and equal employment opportunity can be obtained from the Office of Information and Consumer Affairs, Employment Standards Administration, U.S. Department of Labor, Room C-4331, 200 Constitution Ave. NW., Washington, DC 20210. Phone:(202)523-8743.

Other Career Resources

The resources described in this chapter are good places to begin your exploration. Any career center should have many other resources that can provide such information, including:

Dictionary of Occupational Titles

Chronicle Occupational Briefs

Occupational Information Overview (R. Sharf)

Vocational Biographies

Military Career Guide

Chronicle Career Index

Additional information on these sources and others may be found in the Bibliography at the end of this book. The next chapter will show you how to use the key resources you've reviewed in a step-by-step career search process.

Quiz 3

*P*lease answer the following questions. Continue answers on reverse side if additional space is needed.

1. Where is the most likely local location for you to find the career information resources discussed in this chapter?

2. Of the kinds of information that can be gathered from these sources, which do you think will be most useful for you to research further?

3. Why is it important to gather information about occupations you are considering?

4. What kind of information are you *not* likely to find in the resources listed in this chapter? How can you get this kind of information?

5. What is the most important thing that you learned about yourself by working through this chapter?

6. What topic covered in this chapter would you like to explore further?

To Consider . . .

1. Written sources of career information have some obvious limitations.
    What are the most significant limitations?
    How can these limitations be minimized?

2. If you were researching an occupation and found conflicting information in two different sources, what would you do?

3. What would you do if the occupation you are researching is not listed in any of the resources presented in this chapter?

Suggested Activities

1. Locate the closest career center available for your use. Where is it? What are its hours of operation? How up-to-date are its resources? Is there any staff to assist you? Does it charge a fee for services?

2. Locate a copy of the *Occupational Outlook Handbook*. Familiarize yourself with its contents.

3. Review other resources in your local career center. Which ones look as if they may be helpful?

The Parable of the Solitary

*I*t was a cold and clear winter day. The air was still as death itself, as if frozen in place. The naked trees, ice hanging from their bony-fingered branches, reached silently toward the sky. Zara sat alone on a rock, deep within the sleeping forest.

Zara thought to himself: "How utterly alone we are in our heart of hearts. We are born alone and we die alone. And in between, we must ultimately live alone. We may have friends and find comfort in their company. We may have companions and find solace in our sharing. We may find a kindred spirit or two and rejoice in the recognition we find in their eyes. We may even find our connection to the Creative Force of this universe. But, those of us who seek our Way must be willing to walk alone.

"To be alone with oneself is a trial of one's well-being. Those who cannot be alone without flight or fantasy or depression are afraid to face the emptiness of being from which we all emerge. At the first touch of this void they run or fall into dreams or lament their existence. Because of their lack of courage, they will never know the fullness of the void, nor the still comfort of the emptiness. Only the brave dare to endure this first touch. Only the brave can learn to be alone in the presence of the creation of all things."

Zara sat in silence for a moment. He then continued his reflection: "Only those who have reconciled themselves to their aloneness are delivered from loneliness. Many men and women have lost themselves in the herd because of their deep loneliness. The herd animals move together and the herd animals rub against each other to make themselves feel safe and secure. But loneliness has set up camp within their souls and gnaws at them from within. At the slightest threat, they bolt and run, trampling each other and all that stands in their path.

"The alone ones, the seekers of truth and true calling, must beware of herds. The herd animals sense that these seekers are somehow different. The herd animals can smell the scent of deep silence and lack of fear that resides within the soul of those reconciled to their aloneness. In the presence of such a one, the herd becomes restless and uneasy. At the slightest provocation, the herd will stampede and trample underfoot all those who do not run with them in frenzy and fear.

"The alone ones can no longer be part of the herd. They must follow their own Way rather than the herd-traveled trails. A great distance of being separates the alone ones from the herd."

Zara sank into a deep silence for many hours. He was stirred from this silence by the sound of his eagle landing on a rock next to him. Zara spoke: "Greetings, my kindred spirit! Were you called from your heights by the sinking sound of my depths? Sink your claws into my back and help me overcome the Gravity that would crush this alone one. Lift me into the sky so that I may look at these heavy thoughts from far above and laugh rather than cry . . . . Far-above laughter shatters the gravity of such thoughts. Let us fly and laugh together!"

Zara arose and started walking out of the woods, singing and laughing as he went. His eagle soared high above him, in a clear sky, now warmed by the winter sun.

CHAPTER 4

Exploring Career Territory

Preview

*. . . be a Columbus to whole new continents and worlds within you,
opening new channels, not of trade, but of thought.*

HENRY DAVID THOREAU

Seeking your Way through the unfamiliar territory of career possibilities is a formidable expedition to undertake. But, even though this territory may be unfamiliar, it is not uncharted. In this chapter you will find a great deal of valuable information about occupations you may want to explore. The main sections of this chapter are described as follows.

- **Three-Step Career Search** suggests a simple strategy to get some basic information about occupations that may interest you.

- **Exploration Summary Sheets** provide forms that you can use to guide your exploration and to record important information about occupations you explore.

- **Worker Interview** suggests another method to get valuable occupational information that may not be found in print references. It also provides forms with suggested questions that you may use to structure this experience.

- **Other Methods to Explore** outlines various other strategies that may be employed to obtain useful occupational information.

When you have finished this chapter, you should have a lot of specific information about occupations that are compatible with your personal characteristics.

Information can help you open new channels of thought. As you explore the occupations you have decided to consider, you will be gathering puzzle pieces that will eventually reveal the shape of your Way.

You have completed some basic self-assessment and are familiar with a few primary information resources. You are now ready to translate your results into a list of specific occupations to consider. Once you have such a list, the resources covered in the previous chapter will provide you with information that will make your decision an easier one.

As you will see, there are many places to look for occupational information. Some are easier to come by than others, but the easiest will not necessarily provide you with the most valuable data. You might have to work a little harder to find the type of information that could make a critical difference in your career decision. By following a simple step-by-step procedure, you can get started with this process.

Three-Step Career Search

To do some further career exploration, follow the steps outlined in this section. If you have any questions as you go along, you may want to seek counseling assistance.

Step 1

Use the Occupational Listing. Select a Worker Trait Group to explore (listed at the end of Chapter Two). Locate this group in the Occupational Listing section of Chapter Three. (Note: groups are listed in numerical order.) Read the general description for that group and determine if it describes the kind of work you want to explore.

For example: If you listed *1.01 Literary Arts* as a Worker Trait Group you wanted to explore, you would find "1.01 Literary Arts" in the Occupational Listing and read the following entry:

1.01 Literary Arts

GOE Worker Trait Group Description
Workers in this group write, edit, or direct the publication of prose or poetry. They find employment on newspapers or magazines, in radio and television studios, and in the theater and motion picture industries. Some writers are self-employed and sell stories, plays, and other forms of literary composition to publishers.

Step 2

Review Specific Occupations. Just below the description you will find a list of occupational titles related to the occupational group you want to explore. Circle those occupations you want to explore. If you are uncertain, you may want to refer to the job-matching information in Appendix B before making up your mind.

For example: The occupational titles listed under 1.01 Literary Arts are:

Related OOH Listings

Reporters and correspondents
Writers and editors

If you weren't sure about "Reporters and correspondents," you would refer to Appendix B (in the Communications Occupations section), where you would find out that these jobs:

Usually require a college degree
Involve Data/Information tasks such as researching and
  compiling, analyzing and evaluating, and artistic expression
Involve People tasks such as persuading and public contact
Involve working conditions of mobility and irregular hours

Based on this information, you could now make a better-informed decision about including this occupational group in your career exploration.

Step 3

Use the OOH. Locate the *Occupational Outlook Handbook* (*OOH*). Using the index in the back of the *OOH*, find the page number for the occupation you are exploring. Use a photocopy of the Exploration Summary Sheet in Travelog #14 to summarize the most important information as you read (this sheet is organized to follow the main categories used in the *OOH*). Pay particular attention to the listing of related occupations; it may contain other possibilities worth exploring. When you are finished reading, write your personal evaluation of this occupation in the space provided on the Exploration Summary Sheet.

For example: If you circled "Writers and editors," *you would find this occupational group listed word-for-word in the OOH index, along with the relevant page number. You would complete the top of an Exploration Summary Sheet (provided on the following pages) with the Worker Trait Group number (1.01) and* occupation (Writers and editors), and then start taking notes as you read through the first information category: the nature of the work. You would then continue with each such section, taking notes as you go.

Repeat these three steps for each Worker Trait Group you want to explore.

Some of the resources that you may be using will organize occupations differently than those you have worked with thus far. The information in Appendix A and Appendix B, for example, groups occupations by categories related to those used in the contents of the *Occupational Outlook Handbook* (*OOH*). The following table is not a comprehensive cross-index, but it may be a useful starting point for translating from one system to another.

CTG CLUSTER	APPENDIX RESOURCES and *OOH* CATEGORIES
Mechanical	Agricultural, Forestry, Fishing, and Related
	Construction Trades, and Extractive Occupations
	Mechanics, Installers, and Repairers
	Production Occupations
	Service—Protective
	Transportation and Material Moving
Analytical	Professional Specialty—Computer, Mathematical and Operations Research
	Professional Specialty—Life Scientists
	Professional Specialty—Physical Scientists
	Professional Specialty—Social Scientists and Urban Planners
	Professional Specialty—Health Diagnosing Practitioners
Technical	Professional Specialty—Engineers
	Technicians and Related Support Occupations
	Professional Specialty—Health Assessment and Treating
Expressive	Professional Specialty—Communications
	Professional Specialty—Visual Arts
	Professional Specialty—Performing Arts
Empathic	Professional Specialty—Social and Recreation Workers
	Professional Specialty—Religious Workers
	Professional Specialty—Teachers, Librarians, and Counselors
	Service Occupations—Health Service Occupations
	Service Occupations—Personal Service
Persuasive	Executive, Administrative, and Managerial Occupations
	Marketing and Sales Occupations
Clerical	Administrative Support Occupations, Including Clerical

Travelog #14

*T*he following summary sheet is provided to help you gather information during your occupational exploration. Make copies as needed, and complete a summary sheet for each occupation you explore as you read through the *OOH*.

Exploration Summary Sheet

Worker Trait Group #_____   Occupation_____

■ Nature of the work

■ Working conditions

■ Employment

■ Training/education/qualifications required

Exploration Summary Sheet (continued)

■ Job outlook

■ Earnings

■ Related occupations

■ Sources of additional information

■ Personal evaluation of this occupation

Another excellent method to explore occupations is to interview people who are already working in the fields that interest you.

Worker Interview

*B*y interviewing people about their occupations, you will discover things that cannot be found in even the best reference books. Studs Terkel used interviews as the basis for his book *Working: People Talk About What They Do All Day and How They Feel About What They Do*. You might want to review this book to get some insight into the value of this information-gathering technique.

One of the best ways to find someone to interview is to ask friends, family, teachers, and counselors if they know people working in the fields you want to explore. If they do, they can provide an introduction. If this doesn't work, the Yellow Pages in the telephone book provide a place to start. If you have to call some people "cold" after using this source, simply explain that you are doing some career exploration and would appreciate about 20 to 30 minutes of their time to ask them some things about the kind of work they do. Most people enjoy talking about their work and would be happy to spend a few minutes helping you decide on an occupation; if this is not the case, thank them anyway and try the next person on your list.

Once you have located someone willing to talk to you about his or her work, set up an interview and explore the issues that interest you. Use photocopies of the Worker Interview Form to guide your interview and to record the responses to your questions. It would be helpful if you could provide the questions to the person in advance of the interview; you are more likely to get quality information if he or she is allowed time to reflect on your concerns.

Interview the person in the setting and at a time he or she prefers. Request permission to take notes, so you have a record of what is said. Feel free to ask for clarification of responses, but do not push for answers if the person seems hesitant or resistant. When you are finished, thank the person for the kindness he or she has extended to you. A thank-you note might be another manner of expressing your appreciation.

Travelog #15

Complete three (3) interviews with people currently working in occupations that interest you. Make copies and fill out a Worker Interview Form for each.

Worker Interview Form

Person interviewed _____ Date _____

Occupation _____

Years experience _____

- What are the typical tasks that you perform on the job? What equipment do you use? Where do you do most of your work?

- Are there things about your job that would not be obvious to someone outside your field? If so, what?

- What kinds of skills are important to succeeding in your kind of work?

Worker Interview Form *(continued)*

■ How do people usually advance in your line of work? What factors are the most important for promotions?

■ What do you enjoy most about your work?

■ What would you change about your job if you could?

■ How would you advise someone who wanted to prepare for your line of work? What's the best kind of training to obtain?

■ Are job opportunities in your field increasing, decreasing, or staying about the same?

Worker Interview Form (continued)

■ How difficult is it to obtain an entry-level position in your line of work? How is this best accomplished?

■ What kind of employment benefits are typical for your kind of work?

■ Are there "hidden" benefits or drawbacks in your job—factors that may not be obvious at first glance?

■ What kind of people do you work around? How much personal contact is involved in your work?

■ Are there opportunities for volunteer or part-time work for someone interested in the field?

Worker Interview Form (continued)

- How stable are the employment opportunities for this kind of work? What factors affect this?

- What other kinds of jobs are available in your line of work?

- What is a typical starting salary in your line of work? What is the earning potential for an experienced worker?

- What advice would you give someone just starting out in your line of work?

- Do you have any other comments about your work or advice to someone considering it as an occupation?

- Where can I get further information about this occupation?

Travelog #16

N ow that you have taken the time to find out more about some career options, it might be useful to consider the following questions.

■ What was the most surprising thing that you found concerning one of the occupations you explored?

■ What kind of information did you find to be most useful in evaluating the potential of different occupations?

■ Did you change your mind about one or more of the occupations as a result of your research? If so, which one(s) and why?

■ Do you have any experience related to the occupations you have chosen to explore? If so, briefly describe this experience.

■ What other kinds of information might you need to help you make up your mind?

■ What are the most important things you have learned as a result of this exploration process?

Other Methods to Explore

Always confirm what you have found in written sources by gathering reality-based information as well. The worker interviews you have completed are an example of a way to gather this kind of information. There are a number of other excellent methods that may prove fruitful.

- **Obtain related work experience** through an internship, volunteer work, or cooperative education. There is no substitute for "hands-on" experience. This can also be helpful when seeking positions in the future; many people find opportunities for advancement once they get their foot in the door. Also, work experience is an important factor in any hiring decision; having such experience will put you a step ahead of someone without it. Most important, it will give you the experience upon which to base a realistic career decision.

- **"Shadow" workers through a typical work day.** Observe what they do, what they do *not* do, and their interaction with others. There are many elements of any occupation that are not written in a reference book, and that may not correspond to the stereotype for that kind of work. By carefully observing someone doing the kind of work you want to explore, you will gain valuable insight into the nature of that work.

- **Think about what excites you.** What kinds of activities add to your energy? What kind of activities leave you feeling depleted? When you read about different occupations, try to determine how the tasks involved affect your level of energy. For example, if working with detail is tiring for you, you would want to think twice before you went into a field like accounting.

- **Take related course work.** If you want to work in a field that requires math and science, your experience in related courses can provide valuable data for your consideration. One of the advantages of the college experience is that it serves as a reality test. If you think you want to be a brain surgeon but faint dead away when you dissect an earthworm in Biology 101, you may want to reconsider. By the same token, if you find that you do much better than you expected in a course, it may lead to your consideration of occupational fields that you had previously overlooked. Do not place too much emphasis on your performance in any given course. Look for subject-related trends and patterns that may mean something in terms of your occupational options.

- **Read a related textbook.** If you think you might want to be a psychologist, go to the library or bookstore and browse through textbooks in the field of psychology. Does the content interest you? Does it seem to be an area that you want to study in depth?

- **Visit work sites.** Find out where you would be working and take a look at a typical work site. How does the environment feel to you? Would you be comfortable working in such an environment all day? How do people interact in this setting? What kind of people would you work with in this setting? What is the work pace?

- **Watch television documentaries** related to specific occupations. Although the picture presented is often incomplete, it can provide some insight into the work. Public television documentaries are usually more objective and complete in their presentation.

The following Travelog exercises will ask you to focus on some specific occupations. This will be helpful as you consider job outlook information in Chapter Five.

Travelog #17

*P*lease answer the following questions.

■ Which "other method" of exploring seems most promising for you? Why?

■ How would you go about arranging for this experience?

■ Close your eyes and imagine an ideal work day sometime in the future when you are well established in your occupation of choice.

What are you wearing?

Where are you working?

What are you doing?

Who are you working with?

What kind of expression do you see on your face?

How do you feel after a typical day of such work?

Travelog #18

You have collected all the data you can find related to occupations of interest. You have reviewed and compared this information. Based on your analysis, you should be ready to make a tentative decision. List your tentative occupational selection, including a second and third choice. For each of these choices, also list two related occupations that might merit further consideration.

RELATED OCCUPATIONS

First choice _____   _____

                                      _____

Second choice _____   _____

                                      _____

Third choice _____   _____

                                      _____

Career counselors can assist you through this career decision-making process. If you are attending school, guidance professionals or your instructor should be available to assist you. If you are not presently attending school, counselors in private practice can often be quite helpful. If you choose to seek assistance, it is a good idea to ask the counselor for references and to inquire whether he or she has a special interest in career guidance.

■ Do you feel that you could use some assistance at this point in the career planning process? Why, or why not?

If so, what kind of help would you like?

If so, who would you prefer to help you?

Quiz 4

*P*lease answer the following questions. Use a separate sheet if additional space is needed.

1. What are the three (3) most significant things that you found out as a result of your exploration?

    a.

    b.

    c.

2. What information resource or method was most helpful in your research? Why?

3. What types of information provided by these resources are most likely to be affected by the passage of time? Why?

4. What types of information provided by these resources are least likely to be affected by the passage of time? Why?

5. What is the most important thing that you learned about yourself by working through this chapter?

6. What topic covered in this chapter would you like to explore further?

To Consider . . .

1. Sometimes the information you gather from a written source may be different from that you gather in an interview.

   What might be some reasons for this?

   What could you do to resolve this discrepancy?

2. A student's parent may have strong feelings about what occupation is right for a son or daughter.

   To what extent should parents have a say in occupational choice?

   Does the fact that they may be paying for the required education make a difference?

   Why might some parents try to influence this choice?

3. Some people consider things like ecological impact and principles of nonviolence when choosing an occupation.

   Are there some occupations you would not consider on principle?

Suggested Activities

1. Talk to friends and relatives about how they ended up in their occupations. Was it through a careful planning process? Did chance play a role?

2. Interview two or more people doing the same job. How do their perceptions about their work differ?

The Parable of "Thou Shalt"

Zara awoke with a start and sat straight up in his bed. His disciple stood at the door and asked him: "Zara, I heard you call out. Can I help you?"

Zara's glazed eyes slowly came into focus and he spoke: "I have just awakened from a most curious dream. In this dream, I was in a room with many doors, all of them closed. The room was becoming smaller and smaller, as were the doors. On each of the doors was a sign, each one inscribed with the same words: 'Thou Shalt.' "

Zara paused for a moment and then continued: "I sensed the time was short before I would be crushed by the collapsing walls; even sooner, the doors would be too small for me to pass through them. I must choose, I thought to myself. But, which door? And what lies in wait behind the doors labelled 'Thou Shalt'? I grabbed the doorknob of the closest door and yanked it open. . . ."

Zara sat in his bed for almost an hour, without moving a muscle, lost in a kind of trance. His disciple had seen this before and knew he was in a far-beyond realm of thought.

Zara took a deep breath and looked his disciple straight in the eye. He spoke: "I yanked it open . . . and there stood before me a most horrible monster! The monster spoke to me. It said: 'I am Thou Shalt! Behold me and tremble, Zara! I will burn your heart with my breath. I will eat your liver and your brain. Your life is mine to consume. Prepare to die a slow and painful death!' "

Zara continued: "Behind each door a monster, I thought to myself. Behind each 'Thou Shalt,' a monster ready to consume our lives. The monster's eyes were red with fury. Its body was armored with scales. Its foul breath withered everything around me. I stood firm, drew my sword, and addressed the beast: 'This steel has been forged upon the anvil of my will, by the fire of my passion for meaning and truth. It will slice open your belly and send you back to the void from which you came.' The monster then fell silent and, after a moment, slowly slithered back into its darkness."

Zara looked deeply into the eyes of his disciple and spoke: "From the very day of your birth, these monsters began to gather behind the doors of your life. They feed upon fear, ignorance, illusion, commandment, and coercion. They grow until they block the Way behind every door of your life.

"However, you do have a weapon against them. Such monsters have a soft underbelly and they fear the sharpened sword of 'I will.' 'Thou Shalt' can only harm those who are unarmed. The unarmed often fool themselves into thinking they are safe, but it is the false safety of a room becoming ever smaller."

Zara put his arm on his disciple's shoulder and spoke sternly to her: "Arm yourself, my friend! Arm yourself, or every door you enter will lead to beastly darkness and slow death. Arm yourself, or you shall surely be consumed by the monster Thou Shalt! Forge your will to razor sharpness and become fearless in its use."

Zara turned his gaze upward and raised his arms as he spoke: "Monsters beware! Your soft bellies will soon know the taste of our sharpened steel!"

PART TWO

Decisions

Now that you have a tentative list of occupational options, it's time to take a look at two other factors that will help you narrow this list. Chapter Five provides information on employment trends and projections. Chapter Six covers a number of important factors related to decision-making skills.

CHAPTER FIVE

Down the Road

Preview

Only that day dawns to which we are awake.

HENRY DAVID THOREAU

The opportunities you have to work in the occupation of your choice are directly influenced by societal, economic, technological, and political trends. An awareness of these trends can facilitate career decision making by helping you determine relative opportunity within different fields of interest. The sections of this chapter cover some of the best available information related to such projections. Main sections of this chapter are as follows.

- **The Future** explains the benefits and pitfalls associated with predicting the future.
- **Economic Trends** takes a look at the forces that are likely to influence the United States economy—the engine that produces job opportunity.
- **Projections: Tomorrow's Jobs** provides specific projections of job outlook in a variety of occupational fields.
- **25 Fastest Growing Occupations** is a list of occupations with the highest percentage increase in positions predicted for 1990 to 2005.
- **25 Occupations with Largest Numerical Increases** is a list of occupations with the most positions added over the period 1990 to 2005.
- **25 Slowest Growing Occupations** is a list of occupations that are either in decline or growing very slowly.
- **Preparing for the Future** suggests a number of strategies to cope with the workplace of the future.
- **Challenges of Diversity** explores the implications of workforce trends and the concept of equity in the workplace.

By the end of this chapter, you will have a better idea of trends that may influence your future job opportunities.

Prediction of the future is based upon a careful analysis of the past and the present. Trends are an extrapolation of what is known (the past and the present) into what is unknown (the future). This chapter presents a number of such extrapolations—predictions of what is to come in terms of job outlook and opportunity.

The Future

As you look down the road toward an occupation of your choice, you can only see so far ahead. You might be able to see as far as the education required. You have already seen some of the directional signs in terms of personal and job characteristics. But you won't be able to see what is just over the hill, around the bend, or over the horizon.

What is just beyond your vision can have a very real effect on you. If you select an occupation without regard to predicted outlook, you run the chance of expending a great deal of time and money to prepare yourself for an occupation that may have very limited job opportunity. Though job outlook should not be the only (or even the primary) factor in your career decision, it makes good sense to include this kind of information somewhere in the decision equation.

Fortunately, the U.S. Department of Labor does extensive, ongoing research related to employment trends. This research takes many things into consideration: economic changes, world trade trends, labor force changes, technological developments, and the like. The projections put out by this agency are updated every two years, and are available in publications like the *Occupational Outlook Handbook*. The information from these sources has been summarized in this chapter to provide you with a resource to be used in your decision-making process.

Predicting the future is not without risk. The best predictions are often affected by factors that could not have been anticipated. Political, economic, and technological developments are in constant flux and defy precise prediction.

A healthy respect for the unpredictability of life will serve you well. Nonetheless, an educated prediction is better than no prediction at all. Prediction allows anticipation. Anticipation allows planning. Planning allows preparation. And preparation helps assure success. As an old Chinese proverb says: "It is better to light one candle than curse the darkness." The following Travelog exercise, which asks you to look at prediction in terms of your personal life, is an illustration of this principle.

Travelog #19

Prediction is as much an art as it is a science. It may be useful to think about what is predictable in your own life. Imagine yourself as you were five years ago. Try to remember what you were like back then: what you were wearing, who you were running around with, how you were spending your time, the things you were interested in or concerned about.

■ How were you different then than you are now?

■ Five years ago, would you have been able to predict how you have changed? Why, or why not?

■ How have your life circumstances changed over the last five years?

■ Five years ago, would you have been able to foresee the changes in your life circumstances? Why, or why not?

■ How do you think you will be different five years from now? Why?

■ How do you think your life circumstances will be different five years from now? Why?

■ If you had difficulty answering the last two questions, to what do you attribute this difficulty?

■ What can you do to prepare for the changes that you anticipate?

Job trends and predictions are based on the factors that influence such future directions. Economic indicators are the most obvious of such factors.

Economic Trends

*T*he economy of today will not be the economy of tomorrow. There are powerful forces at work that will change the shape of the American economy, with resulting changes in the nature of work within this economy. Some of the factors the U.S. Department of Labor expects to drive such changes are summarized as follows (adapted from the *Occupational Outlook Handbook*).

Factor 1

The world economy will become more intertwined. World trade has created an interdependence among nations. The United States, for example, depends on imported oil for most of its energy. Therefore, what affects oil-producing nations, their production, and their trade policies has an immediate impact upon the U.S. economy. And when the U.S. economy is affected, repercussions are felt by our trading partners around the world. In one manner or another, this same principle applies to most nations; there are no truly independent national economies.

Factor 2

Manufacturing done in the United States will continue to decline. This is a continuing trend that shows no sign of reversal. Since 1989, over 1.6 million manufacturing jobs have been lost (*Harper's*, September 1993). So-called postindustrial (information and service-based) industries are taking the place of manufacturing-based industries. Many manufacturing industries have moved to other countries in order to reduce labor and manufacturing costs.

Factor 3

Services will continue to expand. This is the fastest growing sector of the economy and, by all signs, will continue to be so.

Factor 4

Technological advances will affect every sector of the economy. The application of technology is a trend that will continue to expand in its scope. Once limited primarily to industry, technology is now being applied to medical science, consumer products, education, information retrieval, and business operations in a manner that is having a major impact on productivity, efficiency, and effectiveness. The pervasive utilization of increasingly powerful microcomputers is one obvious factor in this trend.

Factor 5

There will be increased competition for existing markets. The competition for world and national markets will become fiercer as developing nations enhance their industrial capabilities. Such nations have the advantage of cheap labor and use this to undercut prices and lure more industrial investment. Implementation of free trade agreements such as NAFTA (the North American Free Trade Agreement) will also have the effect of increasing competition.

Factor 6

Productivity will determine business survival. As competition is increased, productivity becomes more critical. Those businesses that can effectively deliver the best-quality products at the lowest cost will be the survivors in a free-market economy.

Factor 7

Ecological considerations will play a key role. There is a growing awareness of a worldwide ecological responsibility. Scientific evidence of global warming and depletion of the atmosphere's ozone layer have made it clear that a disregard of ecological considerations can result in severe repercussions for all people. Industrial practices and existing technologies will be modified, and new technologies developed in response to this awareness.

The following Travelog asks you to consider how such trends might influence occupations in the future. Then we will turn our attention to another important factor—how the United States' population, workforce, and job market are changing.

Travelog #20

Select one of the trends identified in the previous section and answer the following questions related to it.

- Selected trend:_____

- Why is this a significant trend?

- List two possible *negative* consequences of this trend.

- List two possible *positive* consequences of this trend.

- How are the occupations you are considering likely to be affected by this trend?

- What can you do to anticipate possible changes resulting from this trend, to minimize its negative affect or to turn it to your advantage?

Projections: Tomorrow's Jobs

*T*he U.S. Bureau of Labor Statistics develops employment projections for 10 to 15 years into the future. These projections are updated every two years and are printed in summary form within the *Occupational Outlook Handbook*. The following information is reproduced from this source and presented for your information. These projections cover the period between 1990 and 2005.

A reprint of "The Job Outlook in Brief" is provided in **Appendix A**. This reprint provides more specific job outlook information for hundreds of occupations.

OCCUPATIONAL OUTLOOK HANDBOOK

Tomorrow's Jobs

Every 2 years, the Bureau of Labor Statistics develops projections of the labor force, economic growth, industry output and employment, and occupational employment under three sets of alternative assumptions—low, moderate, and high. These projections cover a 10- to 15-year period and provide a framework for the discussion of job outlook in each occupational statement in the *Handbook*. All of the approximately 250 statements in this edition of the *Handbook* identify the principal factors affecting job prospects, then discuss how these factors are expected to affect the occupation. This chapter uses the moderate alternative of each projection to provide a framework for the individual job outlook discussions. For more information on the alternative assumptions, see page 464.

Population Trends

Employment opportunities are affected by population trends in several ways. Changes in the size and composition of the population between 1992 and 2005 will influence the demand for goods and services. For example, the population aged 85 and over will grow about four times as fast as the total population, increasing the demand for health services. Population changes also produce corresponding changes in the size and characteristics of the labor force.

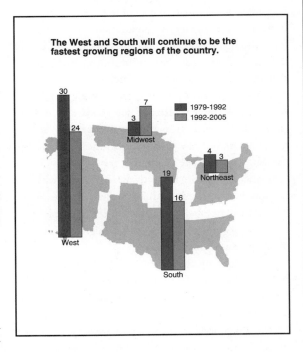

The West and South will continue to be the fastest growing regions of the country.

Legend: 1979-1992 / 1992-2005

West: 30, 24
Midwest: 3, 7
Northeast: 4, 3
South: 19, 16

The U.S. civilian noninstitutional population, aged 16 and over, is expected to increase from about 192 to 219 million over the 1992–2005 period—growing more slowly than it did during the previous 13-year period, 1979–92. However, even slower population growth will increase the demand for goods and services, as well as the demand for workers in many occupations and industries.

The age distribution will shift toward relatively fewer children and teenagers and a growing proportion of middle-aged and older people into the 21st century. The decline in the proportion of teenagers reflects the lower birth rates that prevailed during the 1980's; the impending large increase in the middle-aged population reflects the aging of the "baby boom" generation born between 1946 and 1964; and the very rapid growth in the number of old people is attributable to high birth rates prior to the 1930's, together with improvements in medical technology that have allowed most Americans to live longer.

Minorities and immigrants will constitute a larger share of the U.S. population in 2005 than they do today. Substantial increases in the number of Hispanics, Asians, and Blacks are anticipated, reflecting immigration, and higher birth rates among Blacks and Hispanics. Substantial inflows of immigrants will continue to have significant implications for the labor force. Immigrants tend to be of working age but of different educational and occupational backgrounds than the U.S. population as a whole.

Population growth varies greatly among geographic regions, affecting the demand for goods and services and, in turn, workers in various occupations and industries. Between 1979 and 1992, the population of the Midwest and the Northeast grew by only 3 percent and 4 percent, respectively, compared with 19 percent in the South and 30 percent in the West. These differences reflect the movement of people seeking new jobs or retiring, as well as higher birth rates in some areas than in others.

Projections by the Bureau of the Census indicate that the West and South will continue to be the fastest growing regions, increasing 24 percent and 16 percent, respectively, between 1992 and 2005. The Midwest population is expected to grow by 7 percent, while the number of people in the Northeast is projected to increase by only 3 percent.

Geographic shifts in the population alter the demand for and the supply of workers in local job markets. Moreover, in areas dominated by one or two industries, local job markets may be extremely sensitive to the economic conditions of those industries.

For these and other reasons, local employment opportunities may differ substantially from the projections for the Nation as a whole presented in the *Handbook*. Sources of information on State and local employment prospects are identified on page 465.

Labor Force Trends

Population is the single most important factor governing the size and composition of the labor force, which includes people who are working, or looking for work. The civilian labor force, 127 million in 1992, is expected to reach 151 million by 2005. This projected 19-percent increase represents a slight slowdown in the rate of labor force growth, largely due to slower population growth (chart 2).

America's workers will be an increasingly diverse group as we move toward 2005. White non-Hispanic men will make up a slightly smaller proportion of the labor force, and women and minority group members will comprise a larger share than in 1992. White non-Hispanics have historically been the largest component of the labor force, but their share has been dropping, and is expected to fall from 78 percent in 1992 to 73 percent by 2005. Whites are projected to grow more slowly than Blacks, Asians, and others, but

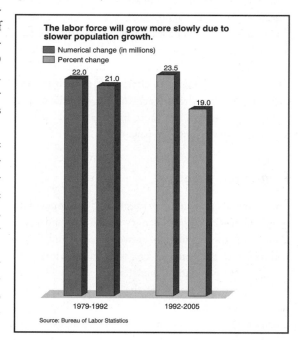

The labor force will grow more slowly due to slower population growth.

■ Numerical change (in millions)
■ Percent change

22.0   21.0   23.5

                              19.0

1979-1992   1992-2005

Source: Bureau of Labor Statistics

because of their size, whites will experience the largest numerical increase. Hispanics will add about 6.5 million workers to the labor force from 1992 to 2005, increasing by 64 percent. Despite this dramatic growth, Hispanics' share of the labor force will only increase from 8 percent to 11 percent, as shown in chart 3. Blacks, Hispanics, and Asians and other racial groups will account for roughly 35 percent of all labor force entrants between 1992 and 2005.

Women will continue to join the labor force in growing numbers. The percentage increase of women in the labor force between 1992 and 2005 will be larger than the percentage increase in the total labor force, but smaller than the percentage increase for women in the previous 13-year period. In the late 1980's, the labor force participation of women under age 40 began to increase more slowly than in the past. Women were only 42 percent of the labor force in 1979; by 2005, they are expected to constitute 48 percent.

The changing age structure of the population will directly affect tomorrow's labor force. Compared to young workers, the pool of experienced workers will increase. In 1992, the median age of the labor force was 37.2 years; by 2005, it will be 40.5 years.

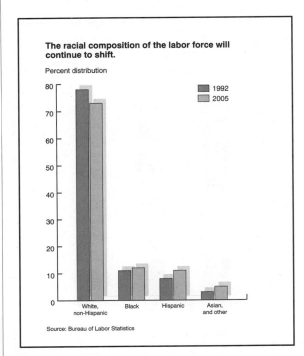

The racial composition of the labor force will continue to shift.

Percent distribution

■ 1992
■ 2005

White, non-Hispanic — Black — Hispanic — Asian, and other

Source: Bureau of Labor Statistics

Between 1979 and 1992, the youth labor force (16 to 24 years of age) dropped by 5 million, a 20-percent decline. In contrast, the number of youths in the labor force will increase by 3.7 million over the 1992–2005 period, reflecting an increase of 18 percent, compared to 19 percent growth for the total labor force. As a result, young people are expected to comprise roughly the same percentage of the labor force in 2005 as in 1992. Among youths, the teenage labor force (16 to 19 years of age) will increase by 31 percent over the 1992–2005 period, a numerical increase of 2.1 million. The labor force 20 to 24 years of age is projected to increase by 12 percent, a numerical increase of 1.6 million. The total youth labor force accounted for 24 percent of the entire labor force in 1979, fell to 16 percent in 1992, and should stay about the same through 2005.

The scenario should be somewhat different for prime-age workers (25 to 54 years of age). The baby boom generation will continue to add members to the labor force, but their share of the labor force peaked in 1985. These workers accounted for 62 percent of the labor force in 1979, and rose significantly to 72 percent in 1992, but should decline slightly to 70 percent by 2005. The proportion of workers in the 25–34 age range will decline dramatically, from 28 percent to 21 percent in 2005. On the other hand, the growing proportion of workers between the ages of 45 and 54 is equally striking. These workers should account for 24 percent of the labor force by the year 2005, up from 18 percent in 1992. Because workers in their mid-forties to mid-fifties usually have substantial work experience and tend to be more stable than younger workers, this could result in improved productivity and a larger pool of experienced applicants from which employers may choose.

The number of older workers, aged 55 and above, is projected to grow about twice as fast as the total labor force between 1992 and 2005, and about 15 times as fast as the number of workers aged 55 and above grew between 1979 and 1992. As the baby boomers grow older, the number of workers aged 55 to 64 will increase; they exhibit higher labor force participation than their older counterparts. By 2005, workers aged 55 and over will comprise 14 percent of the labor force, up from 12 percent in 1992.

In recent years, the level of educational attainment of the labor force has risen dramatically. In 1992, 27 percent of all workers aged 25 and over had a bachelor's degree or higher, while only 12 percent did not possess a high school diploma. The trend toward higher educational attainment is expected to continue. Projected rates of employment growth are faster for occupations requiring higher levels of education or training than for those requiring less.

Three out of the 4 fastest growing occupational groups will be executive, administrative, and managerial; professional specialty; and technicians and related support occupations. These occupations generally require the highest levels of education and skill, and will make up an increasing proportion of new jobs. Office and factory automation, changes in consumer demand, and movement of production facilities to offshore locations are expected to cause employment to stagnate or decline in many occupations that require little formal education—apparel workers and textile machinery operators, for example. Opportunities for those who do not finish high school will be increasingly limited, and workers who are not literate may not even be considered for most jobs.

Those who do not complete high school and are employed are more likely to have low paying jobs with little advancement potential, while workers in occupations requiring higher levels of education have higher incomes. In addition, many of the occupations projected to grow most rapidly between 1992 and 2005 are among those with higher earnings.

Nevertheless, even slower growing occupations that have a large number of workers will provide many job openings, because the need to replace workers who leave the labor force or transfer to other occupations account for most job openings. Consequently, workers with all levels of education and training will continue to be in demand, although advancement opportunities generally will be best for those with the most education and training.

Employment Change

Total employment is expected to increase from 121.1 million in 1992 to 147.5 million in 2005, or by 22 percent. The 26.4 million jobs that will be added to the U.S. economy by 2005 will not be evenly distrib-

uted across major industrial and occupational groups, causing some restructuring of employment. Continued faster than average employment growth among occupations that require relatively high levels of education or training is expected. The following two sections examine projected employment change from both industrial and occupational perspectives. The industrial profile is discussed in terms of wage and salary employment, except for agriculture, forestry, and fishing, which includes self-employed and unpaid family workers. The occupational profile is viewed in terms of total employment (wage and salary, self-employed, and unpaid family workers).

Industrial Profile

The long-term shift from goods-producing to service-producing employment is expected to continue (chart 5). For example, service-producing industries, including transportation, communications, and utilities; retail and wholesale trade; services; government; and finance, insurance, and real estate are expected to account for approximately 24.5 million of the 26.4 million job growth over the 1992–2005 period. In addition, the services division within this sector—which includes health, business, and educational services—contains

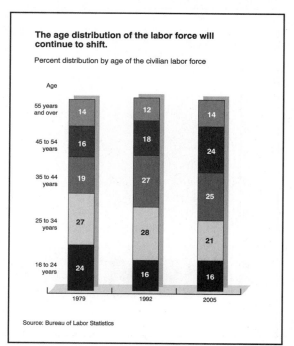

The age distribution of the labor force will continue to shift.

Percent distribution by age of the civilian labor force

Age	1979	1992	2005
55 years and over	14	12	14
45 to 54 years	16	18	24
35 to 44 years	19	27	25
25 to 34 years	27	28	21
16 to 24 years	24	16	16

Source: Bureau of Labor Statistics

OCCUPATIONAL OUTLOOK HANDBOOK

15 of the 20 fastest growing industries. Expansion of service sector employment is linked to a number of factors, including changes in consumer tastes and preferences, legal and regulatory changes, advances in science and technology, and changes in the way businesses are organized and managed. Specific factors responsible for varying growth prospects in major industry divisions are discussed below.

Service-Producing Industries

Services. Services is both the largest and the fastest growing division within the service-producing sector (chart 6). This division provided 38.6 million jobs in 1992; employment is expected to rise 40 percent to 54.2 million by 2005, accounting for almost two-thirds of all new jobs. Jobs will be found in small firms and in large corporations, and in industries as diverse as hospitals, data processing, and management consulting. Health services and business services are projected to continue to grow very fast. In addition, social, legal, and engineering and management services industries further illustrate this division's strong growth.

Health services will continue to be one of the fastest growing industries in the economy with employment increasing from 9.6 to 13.8 million. Improvements in

medical technology, and a growing and aging population will increase the demand for health services. Employment in home health care services—the second fastest growing industry in the economy—nursing homes, and offices and clinics of physicians and other health practitioners is projected to increase rapidly. However, not all health industries will grow at the same rate. Despite being the largest health care industry, hospitals will grow more slowly than most other health services industries.

Business services industries also will generate many jobs. Employment is expected to grow from 5.3 million in 1992 to 8.3 million in 2005. Personnel supply services, made up primarily of temporary help agencies, is the largest sector in this group and will increase by 57 percent, from 1.6 to 2.6 million jobs. However, due to the slowdown in labor force participation by young women, and the proliferation of personnel supply firms in recent years, this industry will grow more slowly than during the 1979–92 period. Business services also includes one of the fastest growing industries in the economy, computer and data processing services. This industry's rapid growth stems from advances in technology, world wide trends toward office and factory automation, and increases in demand from business firms, government agencies, and individuals.

Education is expected to add 2.8 million jobs to the 9.7 million in 1992. This increase reflects population growth and, in turn, rising enrollments projected for elementary, secondary, and postsecondary schools. The elementary school age population (ages 5–13) will rise by 2.8 million between 1992 and 2005, the secondary school age (14–17) by 3.4 million, and the traditional postsecondary school age (18–24) by 2.2 million. In addition, continued rising enrollments of older, foreign, and part-time students are expected to enhance employment in postsecondary education. Not all of the increase in employment in education, however, will be for teachers; teacher aides, counselors, and administrative staff are projected to increase.

Employment in social services is expected to increase by 1.7 million, bringing the total to 3.7 million by 2005, reflecting the growing elderly population. For example, residential care institutions, which provide around-the-clock assistance to older persons and

Service-producing industries will continue to account for virtually all job growth.

Total

Service-producing

Goods-producing

1979   1992   2005

Non-farm wage and salary employment

others who have limited ability for self-care, is projected to be the fastest growing industry in the U.S. economy. Other social services industries that are projected to grow rapidly include child daycare services and individual and miscellaneous social services, which includes elderly daycare and family social services.

Wholesale and retail trade. Employment in wholesale and retail trade is expected to rise by 19 and 23 percent, respectively; from 6 to 7.2 million in wholesale trade and from 19.3 to 23.8 million in retail trade. Spurred by higher levels of personal income, the fastest projected job growth in retail trade is in apparel and accessory stores, and appliance, radio, television, and music stores. Substantial numerical increases in retail employment are anticipated in large industries, including eating and drinking places, food stores, automotive dealers and service stations, and general merchandise stores.

Finance, insurance, and real estate. Employment is expected to increase by 21 percent—adding 1.4 million jobs to the 1992 level of 6.6 million. The strong demand for financial services is expected to continue. Bank mergers, consolidations, and closings—resulting from overexpansion and competition from nonbank corporations that offer bank-like services—are expected to limit job growth among commercial banks and savings and loan associations. The fastest growing industries within this sector are expected to be holding and investment offices and mortgage bankers and brokers. Insurance agents, brokers, and services is expected to register the largest numerical increase in jobs.

Transportation, communications, and public utilities. Overall employment will increase by 14 percent. Employment in the transportation sector is expected to increase by 24 percent, from 3.5 to 4.3 million jobs. Truck transportation will account for 50 percent of all new jobs; air transportation will account for 29 percent. The projected gains in transportation jobs reflect the continued shift from rail to road freight transportation, rising personal incomes, and growth in foreign trade. In addition, deregulation in the transportation industry has increased personal and business travel options, spurring strong job growth in the passenger transportation arrangement industry, which includes travel agencies. Reflecting laborsaving technology and industry competition, employment in communications

is projected to decline by 12 percent. Employment in utilities, however, is expected to grow, adding 117,000 new jobs, highlighted by strong growth in water supply and sanitary services.

Government. Between 1992 and 2005, government employment, excluding public education and public hospitals, is expected to increase 10 percent, from 9.5 million to 10.5 million jobs. Growth will be driven by State and local government. Employment in the Federal Government and U.S. Postal Service is expected to decline by 113,000 and 41,000 jobs, respectively.

Goods-Producing Industries

Employment in this sector has not recovered from the recessionary period of the early 1980's and the trade imbalances that began in the mid-1980's. Although overall employment in goods-producing industries is expected to show little change, growth prospects within the sector vary considerably.

Construction. Construction is expected to increase by 26 percent from 4.5 to 5.6 million. The need to improve the Nation's infrastructure, resulting in increases in road, bridge, and tunnel construction, will offset the slowdown in demand for new housing, reflecting

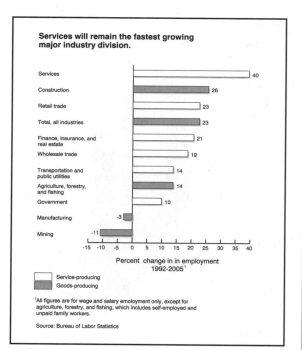

Services will remain the fastest growing major industry division.

Percent change in in employment 1992-2005[1]

☐ Service-producing
▨ Goods-producing

[1]All figures are for wage and salary employment only, except for agriculture, forestry, and fishing, which includes self-employed and unpaid family workers.

Source: Bureau of Labor Statistics

the slowdown in population growth and the overexpansion of office building construction in recent years.

Agriculture, forestry, and fishing. After declining for many decades, overall employment in agriculture, forestry, and fishing is projected to grow by 14 percent, from 1.7 million to 2 million jobs. Strong growth in agricultural services will more than offset an expected continued decline in crops, livestock and livestock products.

Manufacturing. Manufacturing employment is expected to decline by 3 percent from the 1992 level of 18 million. The projected loss of manufacturing jobs reflects productivity gains achieved from increased investment in manufacturing technologies.

The composition of manufacturing employment is expected to shift since most of the jobs that will disappear are production jobs. On the other hand, the number of professional positions in manufacturing firms will increase.

Mining. Mining employment is expected to decline 11 percent from 631,000 to 562,000. Underlying this projection is the assumption that domestic oil production will drop and oil imports will rise, reducing employment in the crude petroleum industry. In addition, employment in coal mining should continue to

decline sharply due to the expanded use of laborsaving machinery.

Occupational Profile

Continued expansion of the service-producing sector conjures up an image of a work force dominated by cashiers, retail sales workers, and waiters. Although service sector growth will generate millions of these jobs, it also will create jobs for financial managers, engineers, nurses, electrical and electronics technicians, and many other managerial, professional, and technical workers. As indicated earlier, the fastest growing occupations will be those that require the most formal education and training.

This section furnishes an overview of projected employment in 12 categories or "clusters" of occupations based an the Standard Occupational Classification (SOC). The SOC is used by all Federal agencies that collect occupational employment data, and is the organizational framework for grouping statements in the *Handbook*.

In the discussion that follows, projected employment change is described as growing faster, slower, or the same as the average for all occupations. (These phrases are explained on page 2.) While occupations that are growing fast generally offer good opportunities, the numerical change in employment also is important because large occupations, such as retail sales workers, may offer many more new jobs than a small, fast-growing occupation, such as paralegals (chart 7). For a more detailed discussion of occupational growth, see the discussion of job outlook in an earlier chapter, Keys to Understanding What's in the *Handbook*.

Professional specialty occupations. Workers in these occupations perform a wide variety of duties, and are employed in almost every industry. Employment in this cluster is expected to grow by 37 percent, from 16.6 to 22.8 million jobs, making it the fastest growing occupational cluster in the economy (chart 8). Human services workers, computer scientists and systems analysts, physical therapists, special education teachers, and operations research analysts are among the fastest growing professional specialty occupations.

Service occupations. This group includes a wide range of workers in protective services, food and beverage preparation, health services, and cleaning and

Employment change will vary widely by broad occupational group.

Occupational group	Percent
Professional specialty	37
Service	33
Technicians and related support	32
Executive, administrative, and managerial	26
Transportation and material moving	22
Total, all occupations	22
Construction trades and extractive	21
Marketing and sales	21
Helpers, laborers, and material movers	17
Mechanics, installers, and repairers	16
Administrative support, including clerical	14
Agriculture, forestry, fishing, and related	3
Production	1

Percent change in in employment 1992-2005

Source: Bureau of Labor Statistics

OCCUPATIONAL OUTLOOK HANDBOOK

personal services. Employment in these occupations is expected to grow by 33 percent, faster than average, from 19.4 to 25.8 million. Service occupations that are expected to experience both fast growth and large job growth include homemaker-home health aides, nursing aides, child care workers, guards, and correction officers.

Technicians and related support occupations. Workers in this group provide technical assistance to engineers, scientists, physicians, and other professional workers, as well as operate and program technical equipment. Employment in this cluster is expected to increase 32 percent, faster than average, from 4.3 to 5.7 million. Employment of paralegals is expected to increase much faster than average as use of these workers in the rapidly expanding legal services industry increases. Health technicians and technologists, such as licensed practical nurses and radiological technologists, will add large numbers of jobs. Growth in other occupations, such as broadcast technicians, will be limited by laborsaving technological advances.

Executive, administrative, and managerial occupations. Workers in this cluster establish policies, make plans, determine staffing requirements, and direct the activities of businesses, government agencies, and other organizations. Employment in this cluster is expected to increase by 26 percent, from 12.1 to 15.2 million, reflecting average growth. Growth will be spurred by the increasing number and complexity of business operations and result in large employment gains, especially in the service industry division. However, many businesses will streamline operations by employing fewer managers, thus offsetting increases in employment.

Like other occupations, changes in managerial and administrative employment reflect industry growth, and utilization of managers and administrators. For example, employment of health services managers will grow much faster than average, while wholesale and retail buyers are expected to grow more slowly than average.

Hiring requirements in many managerial and administrative jobs are becoming more stringent. Work experience, specialized training, or graduate study will be increasingly necessary. Familiarity with computers will continue to be important as a growing number of firms rely on computerized management information systems.

Transportation and material moving occupations. Workers in this cluster operate the equipment used to move people and equipment. Employment in this group is expected to increase by 22 percent, from 4.7 to 5.7 million jobs. Average growth is expected for bus drivers, reflecting rising school enrollments. Similar growth is expected for truck drivers and railroad transportation workers due to growing demand for transportation services. Technological improvements and automation should result in material moving equipment operators increasing more slowly than the average. Water transportation workers are projected to show little change in employment as technological advances increase productivity.

Construction trades and extractive occupations. Workers in this group construct, alter, and maintain buildings and other structures, and operate drilling and mining equipment. Overall employment in this group is expected to increase 21 percent, about as fast as average, from 3.7 to 4.5 million. Virtually all of the new jobs will be in construction. Spurred by new projects and alterations to existing structures, average employment growth is expected in construction. On the other hand, increased automation, continued stagnation in the oil and gas industries, and slow growth in

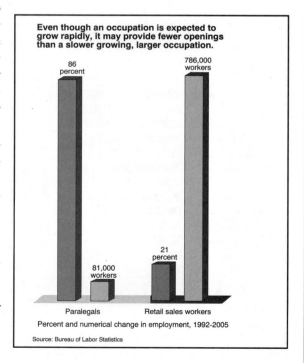

Even though an occupation is expected to grow rapidly, it may provide fewer openings than a slower growing, larger occupation.

86 percent — Paralegals — 81,000 workers

786,000 workers — Retail sales workers — 21 percent

Percent and numerical change in employment, 1992-2005

Source: Bureau of Labor Statistics

OCCUPATIONAL OUTLOOK HANDBOOK

demand for coal, metal, and other materials will result in a decline in employment of extractive workers.

Marketing and sales occupations. Workers in this cluster sell goods and services, purchase commodities and property for resale, and stimulate consumer interest. Employment in this cluster is projected to increase by 21 percent, from 13 to 15.7 million jobs, about as fast as average. Demand for travel agents is expected to grow much faster than average. Due to strong growth in the industries that employ them, services sales representatives, securities and financial services sales workers, and real estate appraisers will experience faster than average growth. Many part- and full-time job openings are expected for retail sales workers and cashiers due to the large size and high turnover associated with these occupations. Opportunities for higher paying sales jobs, however, will tend to be more competitive.

Helpers, laborers, and material movers. Workers in this group assist skilled workers and perform routine, unskilled tasks. Overall employment is expected to increase by 17 percent, about as fast as average, from 4.5 to 5.2 million jobs. Some routine tasks will become increasingly automated, limiting employment growth among machine feeders and offbearers. Employment of

service station attendants will decline, reflecting the trend toward self-service gas stations. Employment of construction laborers, however, is expected to increase about as fast as average, reflecting growth in the construction industry.

Mechanics, installers, and repairers. These workers adjust, maintain, and repair automobiles, industrial equipment, computers, and many other types of equipment. Overall employment in these occupations is expected to grow by 16 percent, from 4.8 to 5.6 million, due to increased use of mechanical and electronic equipment. The fastest growing occupation in this group is expected to be data processing equipment repairers, reflecting the increased use of these types of machines. Communications equipment mechanics, installers, and repairers, and telephone and cable television line installers and repairers, in sharp contrast, are expected to record a decline in employment due to laborsaving advances.

Administrative support occupations, including clerical. Workers in this largest major occupational group perform a wide variety of administrative tasks necessary to keep organizations functioning smoothly. The group as a whole is expected to grow by 14 percent, from 22.3 to 25.4 million jobs, about as fast as the average. Technological advances are projected to slow employment growth for stenographers and typists and word processors. Receptionists and information clerks will grow faster than average, spurred by rapidly expanding industries such as business services. Because of their large size and substantial turnover, clerical occupations will offer abundant opportunities for qualified jobseekers in the years ahead.

Agriculture, forestry, fishing, and related occupations. Workers in these occupations cultivate plants, breed and raise livestock, and catch animals. Although demand for food, fiber, and wood is expected to increase as the world's population grows, the use of more productive farming and forestry methods and the consolidation of smaller farms are expected to result in only a 3-percent increase in employment, from 3.5 to 3.6 million jobs. Employment of farm operators and farm workers is expected to rapidly decline, reflecting greater productivity; the need for skilled farm managers, on the other hand, should result in average employment growth in that occupation.

Job openings arise from both occupational replacement needs and occupational growth.

Percent distribution of job openings, 1992-2005

■ Growth
■ Replacements

Production occupations: 22 percent (Growth), 78 percent (Replacements)

Professional specialty occupations: 62 percent (Growth), 38 percent (Replacements)

Source: Bureau of Labor Statistics

Production occupations. Workers in these occupations set up, install, adjust, operate, and tend machinery and equipment and use hand tools to fabricate and assemble products. Little change in the 1992 employment level of 12.2 million is expected due to increases in imports, overseas production, and automation. Relative to other occupations, employment in many production occupations is more sensitive to the business cycle and competition from imports.

Replacement Needs

Most jobs through the year 2005 will become available as a result of replacement needs. Thus, even occupations with little or no employment growth or slower than average employment growth still may offer many job openings.

Replacement openings occur as people leave occupations. Some transfer to other occupations as a step up the career ladder or change careers. Others stop working in order to return to school, assume household responsibilities, or retire.

The number of replacement openings and the proportion of job openings made up by replacement needs varies by occupation. Occupations with the most replacement openings generally are large, with low pay and status, low training requirements, and a high pro-

portion of young and part-time workers. Occupations with relatively few replacement openings tend to be associated with high pay and status, lengthy training requirements, and a high proportion of prime working age, full-time workers. Workers in these occupations generally acquire education or training that often is not applicable to other occupations. For example, among professional specialty occupations, only 38 percent of total job opportunities result from replacement needs, as opposed to 78 percent among production occupations (chart 9).

Interested in More Detail?

Readers interested in more information about projections and detail on the labor force, economic growth, industry and occupational employment, or methods and assumptions should consult the November 1993 *Monthly Labor Review* or *The American Work Force: 1992–2005*, BLS Bulletin 2452. Information on the limitations inherent in economic projections also can be found in either of these two publications. For additional occupational data, as well as statistics on educational and training completions, see the 1994 edition of *Occupational Projections and Training Data*, BLS Bulletin 2451.

It should be noted that all of the figures provided in this section are *projections*. Although based on the best available information, variation from these figures is to be expected as unforeseen factors affect the economy.

This section has given you an idea of the employment trends for many different sectors of the economy. The following three sections will provide a summary of more specific job opportunity information.

25 Fastest Growing Occupations

The following figures are based on U.S. Department of Labor projections of *percentage increase* of openings between 1990 and 2005.

% Increase	Occupation
88	Home health aides
85	Paralegals
79	Computer systems analysts
76	Physical therapists
74	Medical assistants
73	Operations research analysts
71	Human services workers
70	Radiologic technologists
64	Psychologists
62	Travel agents
61	Corrections officers
59	Flight attendants
57	EEG technologists
56	Computer programmers
55	Services sales representatives
55	Occupational therapists
55	Surgical technologists
54	Medical record technicians
53	Nuclear medicine technologists
52	Managers, analysts, and consultants
52	Respiratory therapists
49	Preschool workers
47	Receptionists and information clerks
47	Marketing, advertising, and public relations managers
46	Podiatrists

Percentage increase is a good indicator of what fields are growing in demand in the job market. You should note that job opportunity must also take into account the number of positions available as well as the percentage increase (a high percentage increase in a very small occupational field may be misleading). Refer to the section that follows this one (showing occupations with greatest numerical increases) and to the full text of the article from the *Occupational Outlook Quarterly* (found in **Appendix A**) for further information.

25 Occupations with Largest Numerical Increases

The following figures are based on U.S. Department of Labor projections of the increase in the number of openings between 1990 and 2005.

No. Increase	Occupation
1,381,000	Retail sales workers
1,223,000	Food and beverage service workers
1,035,000	Chefs, cooks, and kitchen workers
767,000	Registered nurses
685,000	Cashiers
670,000	General office clerks
659,000	Truck drivers
587,000	Nursing aides
555,000	Janitors and cleaners
540,000	Secretaries
437,000	Secondary school teachers
366,000	Computer systems analysts
350,000	Kindergarten and elementary teachers
348,000	Gardeners and groundskeepers
343,000	Home health aides
340,000	Accountants and auditors
325,000	Services sales representatives
317,000	Computer programmers
298,000	Guards
284,000	Manufacturers sales representatives
278,000	Teachers aides
269,000	Licensed practical nurses
264,000	Adjusters, investigators, and collectors
263,000	Clerical supervisors and managers
257,000	Stock clerks

You will note that a few of the occupations on this list are also on the list of the fastest growing occupations, while many others are not. Generally, occupations on this list are those that employ a large workforce. The greatest job opportunities will be in fields that employ a large workforce *and* show a significant projected percentage increase. In contrast to this, the next section lists those occupations that are projected by the U.S. Department of Labor to be the slowest growing.

Slowest Growing Occupations

The following occupations represent those with the slowest percentage increase in positions between 1990 and 2005, based on U.S. Department of Labor projections. Generally, job opportunities in these positions would be limited by automation, manufacturing decline, and other business and economic trends.

% Increase	Occupation
−38	Communication equipment mechanics
−33	Precision assemblers
−32	Telephone operators
−20	Armed services occupations
−19	Shoe and leather workers
−14	Line installers and cable splicers
−13	Water transportation occupations
−8	Apparel workers
−8	Machine operators
−6	Bookkeeping, accounting, and auditing clerks
−5	Stenographers and court reporters
−5	Bank tellers
−5	EKG technicians
−4	Rail transportation workers
−3	Typists, word processors, and data entry keyers
−1	Small appliance repairers
−1	Inspectors, testers, and graders
−1	Vending machine repairers
0	Nuclear engineers
1	Petroleum engineers
1	Electronic equipment repairers
1	Stationary engineers
3	Order clerks
3	Payroll and timekeeping clerks
3	Boilermakers

This list represents employment sectors in decline. This is often due to technological changes, foreign trade competition, or changing government policies.

Travelog #21

*R*efer to the projections in the previous sections and those provided in **Appendix A**. Answer the following questions.

- List three general trends that are likely to affect your work situation in the future.

    1.

    2.

    3.

- Describe how each of these trends might affect you.

    Trend 1 effect:

    Trend 2 effect:

    Trend 3 effect:

■ What is the employment outlook for the occupation you are most strongly considering at this time?

■ Does the outlook for your possible occupational choice have any affect on your choice? Why, or why not?

Preparing for the Future

*I*n the November 22, 1993, issue of *Time* magazine, an article on "America's Frightening New World of Work" suggests a number of strategies workers could use to prepare for the future job market. According to *Time*, workers should "forget any idea of career-long employment with a big company." Between 1979 and 1992, over 4.4 million employees have been removed from the payrolls of Fortune 500 companies (*Harper's*, September 1993). In a cover story in its February 22, 1993, issue, *Business Week* concluded: "Corporate America has developed a deep, and perhaps abiding, reluctance to hire." This magazine article identified at least seven factors that have contributed to this situation:

1. the rising cost of providing benefits for fulltime employees (particularly health care)

2. rising productivity levels among employees

3. a trend toward downsizing staff to increase profits and competitive position

4. lagging output as measured by real gross domestic product

5. increasing exposure to global competition

6. employment costs that are rising faster than capital costs

7. increasing use of labor-saving technology

These are not, by and large, temporary factors. Many of these factors are trends that are likely to remain in effect even after output measures have risen.

Such corporations are quickly becoming "contracting centers" that use smaller subcontractors to meet their needs. These small and medium-size companies offer greater opportunity for future workers. Workers should also be prepared to work for foreign companies, many of which (for example, Nissan, Toyota, Honda) have already built factories within the United States. *Fortune* magazine (January 24, 1994) describes a trend toward a "contingency work force"—part-time, temporary, and self-employed contract staff that fulfill defined needs for a limited period of time. Such workers already compose over 25% of the workforce and, given the benefits accruing to employers (increased flexibility, lowered payroll, decreased benefit costs), the percentage is likely to increase.

The authors of the 1993 *Time* article also advise workers to obtain as much education as possible since " . . . the future belongs to the knowledge worker. . . ." In a related recommendation, workers are told to constantly upgrade their skills to prepare themselves " . . . to change [occupations]—not just jobs, [occupations]—three or four times during their working lives."

Futurist author Alvin Toffler describes "The Future of Work" in his book *Previews and Premises*. He approaches this future in terms of "great waves of change." The *First Wave* was the agricultural revolution that occurred over thousands of years, forming the basis for organized society. The *Second Wave* was the rise of industrialization within the last few hundred years—the "smokestack" world in which we have grown up. The *Third Wave* is a postindustrial trend—led by high-technology, information-based services, and more flexible and responsive management practices—that radically affects the foundations of industrial society, and thus personal and social life based upon these foundations. The Third Wave is just now emerging and will significantly change the world within the span of a few decades. Readers who are interested in Toffler's view of the future are referred to his books listed in the "Career Planning" section of the **Bibliography**.

As a result of this accelerating move into the Third Wave, **Toffler foresees a "radical reorganization" of the economy and of employment trends:**

- **Old-style manufacturing jobs that depended upon routine, repetitive, and fragmented tasks will be automated** for greater efficiency (this is already happening). Robotics will play a much greater role in manufacturing.

- **New occupations will be created.** Toffler predicts opportunities ranging ". . . from PET-scan technicians, to resource recyclers, to speech-recognition repair people . . . to materials designers, to solar photovoltaic panel installers, to space lab architects . . . to video trainers, and teleconference consultants." As some traditional opportunities disappear, new ones will arise. Another futurist, John Naisbitt, wrote that "The information economy is producing an extraordinary number of well-paying, challenging jobs." According to Naisbitt, during the four years between March 1985 and March 1989, ". . . 73 percent of the new jobs created fell into the top three upper-paying Department of Labor categories: professional administration, sales and technical, and precision crafts."

- **Job enrichment will be more important.** In what Toffler calls "Third Wave industries," there is increased employer concern for employee well-being, opportunity, participation in work decisions, flex-time arrangements, quality enhancement, and the encouragement of creativity. Total Quality Management (TQM) is a currently popular approach within many major U.S. companies. TQM includes most of these job-enrichment elements within its structure.

- **There will be more emphasis upon working "smarter" instead of working harder.** Where muscle-power was once the source of increased productivity, in the modern workplace *mind-power* will be the source. Widespread and instantaneous access to huge stores of information, the development of technology to manipulate this information, and the skills needed to master the technology and utilize the resulting output are all elements dependent upon efficient use of the mind. Third Wave industries will be knowledge-based ventures. In *Re-inventing the Corporation*, Naisbitt observes that "In the new information society, the key resource has shifted [from capital] to information, knowledge, creativity. And there is only one place where the corporation can mine this valuable, new resource—in its employees." Naisbitt also sees a trend toward "self-management" among knowledge workers, eliminating the need for layers of administrative managers. He also makes the point that "Self-management presumes independence, self-confidence, and competence, values which are increasingly important in the new worker. . . ."

- **Many more workers in the future will be "mind-workers."** In *The Age of Unreason*, Charles Handy projects that by the year 2000, 80% of U.S. jobs will require primarily thinking skills rather than manual skills. These workers will have specialized skills and knowledge. Toffler describes these workers as " . . . more independent, more resourceful . . . better educated . . . used to change, ambiguity, flexible organization." He also sees the need for many workers with "people skills" to meet the need for training, retraining, employee relations, management, organizing, negotiating, and communicating. In *Megatrends 2000*, Naisbitt looks at the situation of those without such skills, concluding that " . . . the unskilled, the undereducated will command salaries that match their economic value in an information society—not very high."

- **Unemployment will be caused by more diverse factors.** Toffler foresees at least seven variables that will result in unemployment in the future. *Structural* unemployment results from the changing mix of industries that compose the economy. *Trade-related* unemployment will come from dislocations related to changed world trade policies. *Technological* unemployment will result from automation and the resulting increase in worker productivity. *"Normal"* unemployment will continue to come from factors like over-production, altered consumer tastes, and mergers. *Frictional* unemployment will also continue to come from people who are between jobs as they change from one job to another. *Informational* unemployment will come from the increasing complexity of jobs and the problems of matching job requirements to worker skills. *Iatrogenic* unemployment is unintended dislocation of workers due to "stupid government policies." It's clear that unemployment cannot be treated as a unitary problem.

- **Training and retraining will become much more important.** Many workers who lose their jobs will never regain the positions they lost. They will be in the position of requiring significant retraining in order to qualify for other skilled employment. Many major corporations have recognized this trend, and have developed effective in-house retraining programs that allow displaced workers to move to different positions within the corporation. Even those workers who are not displaced will have to participate in ongoing training programs to maintain their skills in the fast-paced Third Wave industries. One study of this trend, *Schools of the Future*, states that "In the future, worker's jobs will change dramatically every 5 to 10 years." This same study foresees a partnership between business and education, aimed at increasing the relevance and responsiveness of education to the ever-changing demands of the workplace. Training is even more important for those with marginal employability.

Eric Hoffer also describes the "skill-healing" effect of training people to enhance their mastery of work skills. He suggests that this kind of healing is particularly useful in the " . . . human renewal of the chronically poor, the unemployable, and people who can't cope with life." Hoffer observes that "The acquisition of a skill generates confidence, and, since people enjoy doing what they are good at, it may have an energizing effect." The movement away from welfare, toward "workfare," is a trend that reflects such an emphasis upon skill development and self-reliance.

■ **New entrepreneurial forces will become an important factor.** Naisbitt identifies the shift toward information as a strategic resource, less job security in large corporations, new opportunities emerging from an information age, and the wide availability of venture capital as factors that have strengthened entrepreneurial opportunities. To document this trend, he found that "Nearly 11 million Americans work for themselves. . . . People are starting new businesses at a rate of 700,000 per year—double what it was a decade ago and eight times what it was in the 1950's. . . ."

As you have seen, the world of work is a dynamic environment, influenced by many factors in constant flux. This results in many challenges for workers and employers alike. One of the most significant challenges has to do with the growing diversity of the population and the workforce of the United States, which is the focus of the next section.

Challenges of Diversity

A s the trends indicate, major changes in the composition of the workforce will take place within the next 10 to 15 years. As business and government are forced to accommodate these changes, they will deal with a number of issues that are not new, but will become more significant influences. In a study of these issues by The Conference Board, *Workforce Diversity: Corporate Challenges, Corporate Responses*, there is an emphasis on the importance of " . . . creating a work environment in which all employees feel valued." In relation to the growing emphasis on Total Quality Management, the authors of this work also observe that "We can't value diversity in customers unless we value diversity in the employees who serve them."

In the report cited above, companies taking the initiative in this area talk of "managing diversity" in a manner that would facilitate resolution of concerns and increase competitive advantage by " . . . helping our people interact with and understand others in a way that will draw the best from the richness of these differences." **The Conference Board identifies six areas of emphasis in this effort:**

- **Communication** is extremely important. Speeches by the company's chief executive officer, executive forums, a clearly formulated diversity policy, an employee handbook, and new employee orientations are methods used to influence peoples' attitudes and behaviors.

- **Education and training** is an obvious focus of those promoting the management of diversity. Classes, lectures, seminars, briefings, awareness training, diversity skills training, and cross-race/gender training teams have been used as effective tools.

- **Employee involvement** is an element that cannot be overlooked in trying to establish positive attitudes toward diversity. Employees may be involved by forming task forces, focus groups, advisory committees, a steering committee, and networking groups to deal with diversity issues and concerns.

- **Career development and planning** is equally vital. Programs that encourage mentoring, career ladders, individual career plans, developmental assignments, internships, and educational opportunities provide a framework to assure progress related to diversity.

- **Performance and accountability** measures are also important. In order to be effectively implemented, diversity priorities may be linked to corporate goals, included in performance measures, monitored, reported, and tied to compensation and other rewards.

- **Culture change** is the sixth area of focus. Diversity goals can be facilitated by implementing internal diagnostic studies, conducting employee attitude surveys, encouraging flexibility in management styles, and revising policies and benefits to support diversity needs.

The companies that have instituted such measures are in the forefront of dealing with diversity issues, which we will now examine in more detail. The following issues were originally presented in *Opportunity 2000*, a publication of the U.S. Department of Labor.

Women in the Workforce

Work and families will be more closely tied together than ever before. By the year 2000, every group of 100 new employees will include 50 women. In *Megatrends 2000*, John Naisbitt wrote: "The days of women as some sort of minority in the work force are over." Many of these women workers will have families; some will be single mothers. As women become a more significant part of the labor force, the issues that affect them in the workplace will become more pressing.

The greater proportion of women tend to be concentrated in lower-paying clerical, teaching, health care, and housekeeping positions—jobs traditionally considered to be "women's work." As a result, the average woman worker earns only 70 cents for every dollar earned by the average male worker. Also, the concept of a "glass ceiling" that invisibly limits the upward mobility of women is used to explain the low percentage of women in high-paying executive and professional positions. One book that examined such issues, *Womanpower*, observed that "The number of women managers doubled [between 1979 and 1989], but . . . 40% of women managers do not even have any staff to manage." This obviously calls into question the validity of the progress claimed by some.

There is also some evidence that women within the same fields as their male counterparts earn considerably less. In *Womanpower*, authors Sekaran and Leong state that " . . . on an average, women at the V.P. level and above make 42% less money annually than men in the same positions." Some employers have attributed this discrepancy to differences in seniority, merit, or productivity.

Women have been traditionally hindered by a lack of consideration for the issues that they must deal with in order to participate in the workforce. The authors of *Breaking the Glass Ceiling*, Morrison, White, and Van Velsor, observe that working women " . . . are still expected to take major responsibility for maintaining a household, raising children, even nurturing an intimate relationship." Only within recent history have some companies taken a more active role in providing maternity or family leave and child care services. Many women's unwillingness to change geographical location frequently (owing to a desire not to uproot children or out of consideration for the impact on their spouse's career) have limited their success in companies where promotion is tied to a willingness to accept frequent transfer. Sexual harassment of women in the workplace frequently goes unreported because of the economic vulnerability of those who are the victims of such abuse.

In one study of the pressures affecting women executives, *Women at Work*, by Firth-Cozens and West, three primary types of pressure and stress were identified. Pressure associated with the job itself, its responsibilities and its pace, was one factor. The second factor was the "pioneering role" in which many such women find themselves, often being the first female fulfilling a high-level management function; this adds significant pressures. The third source of pressure, family obligations, often affects women more significantly than it does men.

Another interesting piece of research, done by the authors of *Breaking the Glass Ceiling*, calls into question many of the stereotypes that affect women executives. Their research shows that there is *no significant difference* between female executives and their male counterparts on a wide range of variables, including:

impulsivity	ability to reduce interpersonal conflict	humanitarianism
flexibility	concern for self-presentation	self-confidence
adaptability	dominance in leadership situations	suspiciousness
insightfulness	ability to define and achieve goals	rationality
sociability	ability to cope with stress	self-discipline
intelligence	optimism about being successful	even-temperedness

Futurist John Naisbitt projects that "As the nineties progress, conventional wisdom will concede that women and men function equally well as business leaders, and women will achieve leadership positions denied them in years past."

Social equity and human dignity will be bolstered by economic necessity as women's concerns are addressed. The family leave legislation passed by the federal government in 1993 was a major step toward protecting the careers of parents who leave their occupations in order to have and care for children. Company policies related to day care, flexible work schedules, part-time work, job-sharing, promotional opportunities, and sensitivity to issues of sexual harassment are beginning to reflect a concern for issues that affect women more directly than men. Though far from resolved, awareness of these issues, and action based upon this awareness, is more prevalent than in the past.

Minorities and the Economically Disadvantaged

Minorities and the economically disadvantaged will compose a much larger proportion of the workforce of the future. According to *Opportunity 2000*, nonwhites comprised less than 15% of the labor force in 1988; by 1998, this will increase to over 40%. In *Future Vision: The 189 Most Important Trends of the 1990s*, the authors wrote that " . . . by the year 2088, 'minority' populations will become the U.S. majority. This is already true in major cities such as New York and Los Angeles [and Miami]."

The factors that have traditionally disadvantaged these groups in the workplace will become major issues that must be more effectively addressed. The impact of equal opportunity laws, increasing labor shortages, and a larger proportion of minority workers all suggest an enhanced opportunity for such workers to achieve economic equity. The evidence, however, does not always support this kind of conclusion.

The unemployment rate for African Americans is commonly twice as high as it is for European Americans. The percentage of young African American males participating in the workforce has actually declined since 1965. Minorities are disproportionately concentrated in occupations (and within urban areas) that will decline in job opportunity over the next ten years. At the same time, the editors of Research Alert found that " . . . more than a third of all African Americans live at middle-class income levels or above, and in these households, educational and income attainments continue to increase at a faster than average rate."

Racial discrimination remains a factor in American society, though arguably less so than in the past. Affirmative action and equal employment opportunity legislation have provided a legal basis for addressing some of these problems and recognizing the human rights issues involved. Title VII of the Civil Rights Act of 1964 prohibits discrimination on the basis of race, color, religion, sex, and national origin. But sometimes there is a gap between legislation and reality.

For minorities, as with women, economic necessity will also be a more dominant factor in the future. The American economic machine runs on human capital—the skills and energy of those in the workforce. As this workforce changes, any lack of resolve in dealing with issues of opportunity and mutual respect would result in most unfortunate economic as well as social consequences.

For years now, business has sounded the alarm over the lack of adequate basic skills among job applicants, a situation disproportionately affecting minority and disadvantaged applicants. Even the most basic jobs of the future require a level of literacy not currently found in a significant number of applicants. The desire for increased accountability in education has led to some reforms: assessment of skills is more prevalent, social promotion less likely, and developmental course work more readily available. But the gap between the need and the solutions is growing rather than shrinking.

Many large businesses spend a significant part of their own funds providing in-service education to their employees, focusing on literacy skills as well as job skills. Cooperative educational ventures between business and education are becoming more common. Some reformers are proposing radical national changes that will reshape the kind of education available to the American public. Some of the suggested changes might result in a network of private schools that directly compete with public schools for students. There is a growing realization that new solutions are needed to improve the effectiveness of education.

Corporate acculturation is another factor that affects the success of minorities and the economically disadvantaged. People from different backgrounds often have expectations, manners of communication, and social customs that vary from the dominant (that is, white middle-class) norm. An exposure to, and a sensitivity to, such differences can be beneficial for everyone involved. Some companies are using methods of pre-employment exposure (such as cooperative education), mentoring, and in-service training to address these differences. An increased understanding and acceptance of such differences is a necessity in a global economy with rapidly changing workforce characteristics.

Disabled Workers

Individuals with disabilities have often made significant contributions in spite of the challenges they faced. President Franklin Roosevelt, inventor Thomas Edison, musician Ray Charles, and physicist Stephen Hawking are examples of outstanding individuals who also happened to have disabilities. Of the 13 million developmentally and physically challenged persons of working age, over 66% are unemployed, and two-thirds of these express a desire to obtain gainful employment. Stereotypes and ignorance have often led to discrimination, which has limited the job opportunities of those outside the mainstream.

Fortunately, increased public awareness, legislation, and modern technology are working in favor of increased opportunity for challenged individuals. There is a growing recognition that a disability may be experienced by anyone at any time—it is not something that only affects "those" people. Laws that mandate access to public buildings, accommodations for physical limitations, and nondiscriminatory hiring practices are steps toward opportunity for this underutilized segment of the population. The Americans with Disabilities Act of 1991 was a milestone in this regard, prohibiting discrimination against challenged individuals who are otherwise qualified to perform essential job functions, given reasonable accommodations. Also, technology is providing an ever-expanding array of devices that minimize the effect of physical limitations, as well as increasing the potential for such individuals to work from their home (for example, telecommuting).

Increasing exposure to the capabilities of individuals who are challenged is also changing the attitudes of employers. Surveys of employers who have hired such people report consistently positive job performance ratings. Reports that have compared job performance and safety records of workers with and without disabilities have found no significant difference between the groups.

Barriers to effective participation in the workforce by persons with disabilities are also being addressed by more effective career and academic counseling, by employer involvement in training, and by workplace modification. As these approaches become more widespread, an increasing number of these individuals will take their place in the labor market.

Older Workers

Older workers will constitute a larger proportion of the workforce of the future. As the swell of baby boomers moves into middle and old age, it will affect the demographics of the workforce. Advances in medical science promise to keep extending the life expectancy of older adults, making retirement at a later age a possibility. Also, the decline of the availability of younger workers will place increased importance upon the retention and retraining of older workers. Many companies that now encourage early retirement as a means of downsizing will have to rethink this policy in the future. Such companies must also consider the Age Discrimination in Employment Act of 1967, which prohibits discrimination against individuals age 40 or older.

Companies wanting to retain an older workforce will do so by making continued employment more attractive through providing work incentives and alternatives to retirement. Increased vacation time, enhanced insurance and pension benefits, and a phased-in retirement option are steps in this direction.

Employers who wish to hang on to older workers will also be more flexible in adapting jobs to this part of their workforce. Opportunity for part-time work, transfer to less stressful or demanding positions, and flex-time scheduling are elements that address the needs and preferences of older workers.

Training and retraining becomes more important for companies trying to maintain their older workforce. Employees who stay with the same company can expect to be retrained three or four times during their career. Rapid changes in technology make such training a necessity for everyone. Children in elementary school now use computers as a matter of course, but many older workers have never touched such a device. Technology training for older workers must take this lack of exposure and experience into account. As the benefits of maintaining the employment of older workers become evident, more employers will move in the directions described. As a result, people will continue to make significant contributions to the workforce into old age.

Diversity issues may be discussed in the abstract, but they affect real people in real ways. The next Travelog asks you to relate your personal experience to such issues.

As you will see, there is a great deal of information to be considered when including job outlook as an element of your occupational decision. Collecting this kind of information is an important part of the decision-making process, and it is the focus of the next chapter.

Travelog #22

*E*veryone has been affected either directly or indirectly by issues of diversity. Please consider and answer the following questions.

- Think of a situation when you felt that someone discriminated against you (or someone you know) because of sex, race, age, religion, disability, or some other factor. Describe the people, circumstances, and the issues involved.

- How did this situation make you feel?

- How did you react at the time? Why?

- Would you react differently if it happened to you today? Why?

- Why do you think you were treated in such a manner?

- What can be done to make such situations less likely to occur?

Quiz 5

*P*lease answer the following questions. Use the reverse side if additional space is needed.

1. Give two (2) reasons why it is important to consider future economic trends as a part of your career planning.

   a.

   b.

2. Why should even the best projections be considered as tentative?

3. Provide two (2) reasons why it is important to educate people about issues of diversity.

   a.

   b.

4. Has the information in this chapter influenced your tentative occupational choice? Why, or why not?

5. What is the most important thing that you learned about yourself by working through this chapter?

6. What topic covered in this chapter would you like to explore further?

To Consider . . .

1. In some cases, employment outlook projections may turn out to be completely wrong. With this in mind:

   How should projections be used in career planning?

   How could the validity of the information be verified?

   If you know what you want to do, should such projections matter to you?

2. Some people might argue that a more diverse workforce has many potential advantages. Others may feel that it has some potential disadvantages.

   What are some of the possible advantages?

   What are some of the possible disadvantages?

   Will it be more difficult for some people to adjust to the changes than for others? Why?

   What can be done to facilitate a positive approach to such changes?

Suggested Activities

1. Talk to someone you think is prejudiced against others because of their race, age, sex, or some other such factor. How did he or she develop this attitude? How resistant to change is this attitude? What could be done to facilitate such a change?

2. Select one challenge of diversity and do some further research on the subject. What are the origins of the problem? How has it been addressed in the past? To what extent is it still a problem?

The Parable of the Anvil

Zara and his disciple entered the city and were walking down the street when, all of a sudden, Zara stopped in front of a blacksmith shop. Within the shop, the blacksmith, a large woman of powerful build, was forming a knife upon her anvil. The metal she was working was red hot, and each time the hammer struck, sparks flew in every direction. Zara stood silently watching the blacksmith as she formed a finely shaped blade out of a blank of ordinary metal.

Then Zara turned to the townspeople in the street and spoke: "Do you see the sparks fly toward the heavens? Such sparks are the glory of creation, the celebration of the forming of a spirit, strong and sharp. But do not become mesmerized by the sparks of creation. It is the anvil and the hammer that create the form of the blade. Do you hear the hardness and the heaviness of the anvil? Can you stand the ferocity of the hammer?

"Your spirit is the blade, the scimitar, that will divine your Way. It comes to you as a blank of metal, as dull as the earth from which it came. It must be submitted to the blast furnace of life before it is ready for the anvil. When your spirit is red hot with desire for the height of life, then the anvil of your being will be ready to stand solid beneath you. And the anvil will call forth the hammer—the terrible, most glorious hammer!

"It is the hammer of a clear and powerful mind that shapes the nature of your spirit. The fire is always present, but the choice to lie upon the anvil must be your own. And the hammer called forth by the anvil must also be your own. The hammer must be hard but not brittle, heavy but well-balanced, ready to obey the forces of existence but willing to sends sparks of creation into the heavens themselves."

The people began to murmur among themselves: "Who is this madman talking of hammers and fire and the spirit? What does this have to do with us? Who needs a hammer when the blacksmith can do such work for us? How dare he call us dull blanks!"

Hearing this talk, Zara sat in the street and dropped his head. He remained slumped over for hours, until it was dark and the crowd had dispersed.

Zara arose slowly, raised his head, and spoke to his disciple: "Heavy and dull are the spirits in this city. They descend upon me and would smother the fireball of truth I bring them. These people run from the fire and flee from the sparks. They know nothing of the hammer that would shape their spirit. They know nothing of the calling of the anvil. Their mettle remains dull and shapeless, without reflection or purpose. We are too early, my friend! Their Blacksmith is yet to come!"

Then Zara fell into silence again. He turned from the city and slowly walked away.

CHAPTER SIX

Navigation Aids

Preview

If you stand . . . face to face to a fact, you will see the sun glimmer on both its surfaces, as if it were a cimeter, and feel its sweet edge dividing you through the heart and marrow . . .

HENRY DAVID THOREAU

After you have collected facts about yourself and a variety of potentially satisfying occupations, you must face another task: a career decision. This chapter provides a number of hints and suggestions that may enhance the effectiveness of such a decision. The main sections of this chapter are described as follows.

- **Steps to Decision Readiness** will help you determine if you have the basic prerequisites for career decision making.

- **How to Avoid Decision Hazards** explains a number of the more common roadblocks that can sidetrack effective decision making.

- **Decision Strategies** suggests a number of methods to use as you approach decision making, thus increasing the likelihood that you will be satisfied with the outcome of this process.

- **Seven-Step Decision Making** presents a step-by-step model of decision making.

- **Intuitive Decision Making** presents an approach that may be used to supplement the logical model of decision making.

- **How to Improve Your Thinking** summarizes a variety of critical thinking strategies that can contribute to more effective thinking and decision making.

- **Creativity Tips** describes how you can enhance your creative thinking ability.

When you finish this chapter, you will know a number of methods for improving your ability to make decisions.

Decisions are the turning points in the journey of life that will determine where you end up. Making decisions is not always easy. Rollo May expressed this when he wrote that " . . . a man or a woman becomes fully human only by his or her choices and his or her commitment to them. . . . These decisions require courage." It is now time for you to gather your courage and make a tentative occupational decision. This chapter will suggest a number of strategies that may make this decision somewhat easier. Our first consideration has to do with your readiness to make a decision.

Steps to Decision Readiness

You might have all the information in the world, but if you aren't ready or able to make a decision, it does you little good. Decision making is a skill that must be developed—it is not an inborn talent. It is a skill that inevitably involves some risk, since the future must always remain unknown. But decide you must.

The following Travelog will provide a starting point for discussing factors related to decision readiness.

Travelog #23

*I*n order to explore career decision making, please take a few moments to consider the following questions. Circle the response of your choice.

Do you have some possible occupational options, or a tentative choice?	Yes No
Are important decisions generally easy for you to make?	Yes No
Do you usually go through a systematic process of exploring alternatives and consequences when making an important decision?	Yes No
Have you developed confidence in your ability to make wise decisions about important things in your life?	Yes No
Is it important to have a general career goal at this point in your life?	Yes No
Do you feel that you are ready to make a career decision if you have the right information?	Yes No

If you answered no to more than one of these questions, you may have a decision-making concern that needs to be addressed before you can make a wise career choice.

One manner of considering decision readiness is to think in terms of decision status and decision satisfaction. Consider where you think you fall on the following three continua (in terms of a career decision) and mark a representative spot along each:

Where are you in terms of selecting an occupation to pursue?

DECIDED   UNDECIDED

How do you feel about your decision status?

SATISFIED   DISSATISFIED

How would you characterize your overall approach to difficult decisions?

DECISIVE   INDECISIVE

Descriptions are now provided for several possible combinations that emerge from this model. Check the one you think best describes your situation.

☐ **Decided and satisfied** people have made a career decision and are happy with that decision. They have no real motivation for career decision making.

☐ **Decided and dissatisfied** people have made a decision but are no longer happy with that choice. Many mid-life career changers fall into this category. These people must realize that another decision is necessary before they can get on with career planning.

☐ **Undecided and satisfied** people have not made a career decision yet but feel no real need to do so. Some college freshmen are in this situation.

☐ **Undecided and dissatisfied** people have not made a decision and are uncomfortable with this status. They are good candidates for career planning.

☐ **Indecisive and satisfied** people have difficulty making a career decision but are not concerned about this. They will have little motivation to pursue career planning until it becomes a concern for them.

☐ **Indecisive and dissatisfied** people have difficulty making a career decision and feel frustrated with this difficulty. They are good candidates for career planning that is focused initially upon decision-making skills.

As you can see, dissatisfaction is often a key to decision readiness. Most people will not undertake the effort involved in career planning until they are pressured into it by discomfort. This is not always true; some people actually plan ahead and conduct their career planning as part of a step-by-step process of career decision making (believe it or not!). In any case, readiness to undertake productive career planning is necessary for any real progress to be made.

In order for your career exploration to be productive, you need to take the following steps:

- **Be willing to make a tentative decision.** Few decisions that you make are "final." Generally, you make the best decision you can, given the information you have at the time. If the considerations that influenced this decision change, then it is your prerogative to modify your decision. Decision making is not as scary if you look at it in this manner. You may be more willing to make a tentative decision if you understand that such a decision can be reconsidered.

- **Be motivated to make a career choice.** You are probably at a point in your life where you are motivated to make a career decision. Why else would you be reading this book? However, not everyone gets to this point at the same time or in the same manner. Even if you are not ready to make a career decision, an understanding of the process of career planning can be a valuable asset when you do become ready. College is often a factor that contributes to decision readiness. When you are putting forth the time, money, and effort required to succeed in college, it becomes more important to have a goal in mind. External pressures are often a factor. For instance, the demands of a family can cause one to face tough decisions in a timely manner.

- **Have confidence in your decision skills.** Confidence in your own decision-making skills is something that is developed as a result of experience. If your parent(s) allowed you to make decisions for yourself in some matters, you started gaining this experience at an early age. If you have depended on others to make many of your important decisions, you may not have developed very much confidence in your own ability to do so.

- **Have effective decision-making skills.** Confidence is also a function of how effectively you make decisions. If your decisions are flawed by sloppy thinking, poor information, or improper timing, your decision confidence will be undermined by the unfortunate consequences of such flaws.

The next few sections of this chapter explore some of the issues that affect the decision-making process and suggest some strategies that may be helpful to you as you deal with this process.

Travelog #24

*T*hink of a time when you had difficulty making a career-related, or school-related, decision.

■ What was the decision?

■ What were the circumstances and other factors that complicated your decision?

■ How long did it take you finally to make a decision? How difficult was it to come to this point?

■ Were you satisfied with the outcome of the decision? Why, or why not?

■ What would be different if you were faced with the same decision now?

■ How would you classify your career decision status: decided, undecided, or indecisive?

■ How would you classify your satisfaction with your decision status: satisfied or dissatisfied?

■ List two methods that you can use to better prepare yourself for these kinds of difficult decisions.

1.

2.

Even when you have come this far down the road, making a decision about your career direction is not as easy as it may seem; there are a variety of hazards that can delay or complicate your journey.

How to Avoid Decision Hazards

We will be looking at two different kinds of decision obstacles: personal and social. **Personal hazards can seriously hamper effective decision making.** Typical decision problems and their considerations follow.

Problem 1

You may overemphasize the finality of a decision.

Consideration 1

Very few decisions in life are irreversible. Most can be considered to be tentative, pending a change in circumstances, provision of additional information, or conclusions drawn from actual experience.

Problem 2

You may fear making the "wrong" decision. You may think that every decision has a "right" and a "wrong" resolution and that being wrong is a terrible thing.

Consideration 2

Everyone makes decisions that sometime lead to less than desirable consequences. You cannot avoid making decisions. (Avoidance is a decision in itself.) Sometimes these decisions will not turn out for the best. If you were infallible, rather than human, this would not happen; but, it is part of the human condition that you will make mistakes. Accept the inevitability. It is one thing to make a mistake; it is another to keep making the same mistake. It can help if you think of mistakes as learning experiences. If you try to learn something from every mistake, it is less likely that you will make exactly the same mistake (variations will occur!).

It might also be helpful to notice whether you tend to look at decision making in a dichotomous manner. If you see all of your decisions as either right or wrong, with no shadings of a middle ground, you might be setting yourself up to experience problems. Many decisions end up being partially correct or somewhat mistaken—approximations of perfection rather than perfection itself. Once you recognize this tendency, you can take some of the pressure off your decision making.

Problem 3

You may fear either failure or success. You might avoid decisions because you think the outcome will result in negative consequences.

Consideration 3

Indecision seems, on the surface, to postpone consequences. If you fear that failure may be such a consequence, you may think that you have a good reason not to make a decision. Even success can be threatening if it involves some kind of change or increasing responsibility. If you decide not to decide, you may think that you are avoiding the possibility of painful consequences. In truth, however, this is about as effective as the ostrich's technique of sticking its head in a hole when under attack. The ostrich figures that if it cannot see the attacker, the attacker cannot see it. Wrong!

Problem 4

You may fear change. You may avoid decisions that might involve change because of the disruption and disorientation of such change, and because of the unknown consequences of such change.

Consideration 4

Most people are threatened by change, however inevitable it may be. Change disrupts your routines, expectations, and comfort. Change is also the fundamental nature of life. Ideally, you learn to cope with change in a constructive manner, so that it is not so threatening. You may even come to see opportunity within change. Chapter Ten will deal with change issues and strategies in greater detail.

Problem 5

You may have ambivalent or conflicting feelings. You may feel lost, or torn by feelings that often change.

Consideration 5

Ambivalent feelings can often be resolved by reviewing your values and deciding accordingly. It helps to have a clear sense of what is most important to you. In a previous chapter you completed a values inventory. The results of this inventory may help you sort out what kinds of things are most important to you. Once this sorting of values is done, you will still have to make difficult decisions, but doing so will not be quite as trying. Decisions often involve giving up something to obtain something else. Values clarification can help assure that what you give up is less important to you than what you gain, but feelings of loss and ambivalence may remain. There are also other tests and books available on values clarification, if you want to pursue this in more depth.

Such fears and feelings are not unusual when facing an important decision.

Nonetheless, it is important to confront yourself honestly, recognize what you are dealing with, and then do what it takes to overcome these hazards. If you recognize that some of these hazards may be affecting your career decision making, talking with a friend, parent, or a counselor can often help.

Social hazards may be a concern as well. Some of the more common decision problems of this kind are presented below, along with considerations that address such problems.

Problem 6

You may have to deal with significant family expectations and responsibilities. You may have other forces in your life that complicate your decision making.

Consideration 6

Family expectations and responsibilities vary from one individual to another; they may present more of a problem, for example, to a student still living at home as a dependent or to a single parent who is trying to work and raise children at the same time. Such factors may place limitations on what is feasible or practical. These limitations may introduce difficulties that complicate the decision-making process. For example, a single parent who is working has more to take into consideration when committing to a career change that involves years of further education.

Problem 7

You may be affected by age, race, or sex stereotypes. You may be dealing with unfair perceptions of others that seem to limit your options.

Consideration 7

Stereotypes are often simplistic views of things that distort the characteristics of a given segment of the population. Stereotypes about sex, race, and age have all worked against various groups in terms of job opportunity in this country. You may want to explore your legal options if this is the case.

Problem 8

You may be unduly bound by common social expectations. You may have some preconception or expectation about what you are "supposed to do" that is affecting your decisions.

Consideration 8

Common social expectations can distort your own value system and make a sound and satisfying career decision less likely. Pressures to gain prestige, success, and financial well-being may influence you in a manner that inhibits effective decision making. Some people are more vulnerable to social or peer pressure than others. The factors related to this vulnerability will be discussed in later chapters that deal with key elements of personal and career development.

The following Travelog asks you to think about how such hazards may have affected your decision making in the past. Later in the chapter we will move on to consider a step-by-step model of decision making that suggests some methods for improving the outcomes of your decisions.

Travelog #25

■ List two (2) decision hazards or problems (either personal or social) that have caused you problems in the past. Do not necessarily limit yourself to those covered in the previous sections.

1.

2.

■ For each of the two decision hazards you have selected, describe how such a factor could influence your ability to make an effective career decision.

Hazard 1:

Hazard 2:

■ For each hazard, describe how the situation mentioned above might be resolved.

Hazard 1:

Hazard 2:

It's nice to have an understanding of the hazards involved in decision making, but this is rarely enough to solve decision difficulties. The next section will suggest some strategies that may help you unravel such difficulties.

Decision Strategies

There are a number of strategies that you can employ to improve your decision making. It may be helpful to:

- **Clarify decision difficulties**. List the things that make your career decision a difficult one. Once you clearly define the problems, the solutions are often easier to see. After you have your list, you may want to try to categorize your difficulties. You can separate those that you can do something about from those that you can have little affect upon. Or you may want to look at short-term versus long-term problems. However you are able to clarify the nature and differences of your difficulties may be helpful.

- **List how you can obtain support**. You may underestimate the help available from friends, relatives, counselors, and others. If you feel that you must carry the entire burden of such difficulties, you will have a heavy load indeed! Nonetheless, self-reliance is an important characteristic to nurture when it comes to decision making. Ultimately, the decision must be yours.

- **Consider whether a deeper issue may be complicating things**. In Chapter Nine, you will be reviewing a number of life issues that can influence your ability to make wise decisions. Such developmental issues have a direct affect upon many parts of your life. If an issue such as identity is not successfully resolved at the appropriate time in your development as an adult, there may be significant repercussions related to your ability to make wise decisions.

- **Use the step-by-step decision-making process**. This involves a conscious plan of action—and perhaps setting a realistic decision deadline for yourself. The model presented in the next section is an excellent place to start.

- **Cultivate your intuition**. Intuitive decision making can be a useful supplement to the logical model of decision making. As you will see, intuition is particularly useful under certain conditions and can widen the range of your alternatives.

- **Consider a full range of alternatives**. There are usually alternatives that you may not see at first glance. Talking to others is one of the best methods to explore such alternatives. Reading can also reveal alternatives you haven't considered. Counselors are trained to help you generate alternatives that you may not see because you are "stuck" in a the same old way of looking at something. The suggestions provided in a later section on creativity may be useful in this generation of alternatives.

- **Gain some confidence.** This can be approached by making decisions about less important issues in your life. Once you make a series of smaller decisions, you may find it easier to make more important ones. Start with something you are sure you can decide on without too much difficulty.

- **Spend time clarifying your goals.** Decisions should be put within a larger context. If you do not have a clear goal for making a decision, you will find it difficult to make a wise one. Once your goal is clear, the best choice between alternatives often becomes more evident. As David Campbell reminds us, "If you don't know where you're going, you'll probably end up somewhere else."

- **Consider if you have a clear priority of personal values.** If not, spend some time clarifying what is most important to you. You may want to spend more time considering some of the philosophical issues introduced in Chapter One.

- **Make sure that you have a realistic view of the consequences.** It is common to overestimate the negative consequences of a decision. It may help to think about what is the worst that might happen, and how likely this outcome may be. Likewise, be sure that you don't overestimate the possible positive outcomes. The key to this process is to be as objective as possible in your analysis of the possible outcomes of your decision options.

- **Adopt a "power perspective."** If you are like most people, your view of things is sometimes colored by your state of mind. A given situation can look very different when you feel strong and confident, compared to when you may be feeling insecure or stressed-out. Faced with a difficult decision, it can be helpful to ask yourself how you would approach the decision if you were feeling at your best, even if you are not feeling like that right at the moment. This perspective, though sometimes difficult to adopt, can help you overcome the influence of temporary emotions that may cloud your vision. This is not to say that you should disregard how you feel; but, rather that you should not let such feeling exert undue influence on your decisions. After all, your feelings can change; sometimes it is difficult to change decisions that you have made.

- **Base your decisions upon clear principles.** If you have established clear principles in your life, such principles will guide your decisions. Although emotions constantly change, carefully chosen guiding principles are a point of personal stability. Clear values, a consistent commitment to dealing with reality, and the formulation of a personal philosophy are important elements that contribute to this decision resource. Just as in navigation of unfamiliar territory, when you are approaching decisions it is important to have a compass to orient yourself. Principles serve just such a function.

There are many approaches to any given decision. However, many people find the following model of decision making to be a good place to start.

Seven-Step Decision Making

Most people find that following a simple step-by-step model of decision making can improve the quality of their decisions. This is a general model that can be applied to almost any kind of decision. As you read through these steps, you will recognize some of the things you have already done as a result of being this far along in this book. You should also be alert for things that you have *not* done that might prove beneficial in your career planning.

As part of the Decision Sheet exercises that follow, you will be asked to generate two questions. Here are a few examples of the kinds of questions you might consider:

1. What occupation is best suited to my interests?

2. What occupation is best suited to my skills?

3. What occupation is best suited to my values?

4. What kind of Way might be meaningful to me?

5. Is it more important for me to enter the job market quickly or to continue my education as far as possible?

6. Do I need to go through a critical examination of my values before I make a career decision?

7. Would I benefit from some time spent thinking about my philosophy of life?

Feel free to use any of these questions or to compose ones that better reflect your important issues at this point in the career planning process. On the following pages there are Decision Sheets for each of the seven decision steps. Carefully read the explanation of the step presented on the sheet, and then answer the related questions before you go on to the next Decision Sheet.

Decision Sheet: Step 1

Clarify the Decision

First of all, you have to understand that you have a decision to make. If you do not recognize this need, you will often experience tension, anxiety, boredom, moodiness, irritation, and frustration. Once you recognize the need to make a decision, it's important to have a clear idea what you are trying to decide. In addition, there needs to be a commitment to making a decision and a clear goal or outcome for the decision. Sometimes it helps to write down what needs to be decided and what you expect to be the outcome of such a decision.

In the space provided below, write down the two (2) most important questions you need to answer before your career planning is complete.

■ Question 1:

■ Question 2:

Do you feel that you need to talk to someone in order to clarify any of these questions? If so, who might be helpful?

Decision Sheet: Step 2

Do Your Research

Gathering information is the next step. You will need to gather data about yourself, possible alternatives, and the feelings of significant others. The research on yourself should include an evaluation of how the decision relates to your personal values and goals. The data on alternatives should focus on a list of all possible options. Considerations related to significant others should include who is likely to be affected and how their feelings could affect your decision.

Try to identify as many sources of information as possible (reading, interviewing others, talking with friends and family, meeting with a counselor). As you gather this information, note possible complications and difficulties that may affect your decision. Gathering information will continue throughout the decision process.

For each of the questions you listed on Decision Sheet: Step 1, describe the information gathering you have done (or will do) that will contribute to answering these questions.

■ Question 1 Research:

■ Question 2 Research:

Decision Sheet: Step 3

Identify Your Options

Now it is time to narrow down your list of options to those you consider most viable. Consider which alternatives are most realistic and are most likely to lead to a satisfying outcome.

For each of the two questions you have identified, write down two (2) alternative answers.

■ *Question 1 Alternatives*

Alternative Answer A:

Alternative Answer B:

■ *Question 2 Alternatives*

Alternative Answer A:

Alternative Answer B:

Do you feel that you might need some help generating alternatives? Who might be able to help you?

Decision Sheet: Step 4

Consider Pros and Cons

Once you have narrowed the alternatives, you can consider the advantages and disadvantages of each. This may involve additional information gathering. Think in terms of what is most important to you (your values) and the probability of successful outcomes for each option.

For each of the alternatives you generated on Decision Sheet: Step 3, write down one possible advantage and one possible disadvantage.

- *Question 1 Alternative A*
  Advantage:

  Disadvantage:

- *Question 1 Alternative B*
  Advantage:

  Disadvantage:

■ *Question 2 Alternative A*
Advantage:

Disadvantage:

■ *Question 2 Alternative B*
Advantage:

Disadvantage:

Decision Sheet: Step 5

Choose among the Options

Ideally, you will be able to select from among the options the one with the greatest number of positive and highly probable outcomes. Closely monitor your emotions and intuition at this point. Does your decision feel right to you? Do you have a positive sense about this possibility? This is the point in the process where you must assume the most responsibility; a choice must be made and you are the only one who can make it. If you have difficulty at this point, try to determine what is holding you back. It may help to visualize yourself in terms of each option and to note how you respond.

For each of the two questions you have identified, write down the alternative that you think is the best solution for now. Give a brief rationale.

- *Question 1*

    Alternative Chosen:

    Rationale for Choice:

- *Question 2*

    Alternative Chosen:

    Rationale for Choice:

Decision Sheet: Step 6

Take Some Action

Once a decision is made, you can plan how you want to implement the decision. It is often helpful to write down the steps you must go through and to set up a timetable for the completion of each such step.

For each of the solutions you have chosen, identify two (2) specific steps you can take to implement your decision. Write down a target date by which you plan to have each step completed.

- *Question 1 Solution*

    Step 1 (Date:):

    Step 2 (Date:):

- *Question 2 Solution*

    Step 1 (Date:):

    Step 2 (Date:):

Decision Sheet: Step 7

Review Your Decision

Continue to gather information after a decision is made and revise your decision as necessary. Very often, additional information will become available that may change your perspective on the decision or introduce other options. Don't expect everything to come out as you may have predicted, and be flexible enough to modify your decision when this is to your benefit.

For each of the two career decisions you have made, write down two (2) questions that you could use to review the effectiveness of these decisions at some time in the future. Focus on how you will know if the decision was a good one.

- *Question 1 Solution*

  Review Question A:

  Review Question B:

- *Question 2 Solution*

  Review Question A:

  Review Question B:

The following Travelog will help you review your experience with the decision-making suggestions of this chapter.

Travelog #26

*L*ist two (2) decision strategies that you think will be most helpful. Explain how or why you think so.

■ Decision strategy:

■ How or why helpful?

■ Decision strategy:

■ How or why helpful?

Review the seven steps of the decision-making procedure covered in this chapter.

■ Which step was the most difficult for you to complete?

■ Why?

■ What can you do to strengthen this skill?

■ Which step was the easiest for you to complete?

■ Why?

■ What advice would you give a friend who is having trouble with this step?

■ Do you feel that you have the decision-making skills you need to make a wise occupational choice? Why, or why not?

So far we have been discussing decision making as if it was a special kind of mental process. Actually, making an effective choice is critically dependent upon the clarity of your thinking. The next section will explore another approach to decision making that, under certain conditions, can contribute to such clarity.

Intuitive Decision Making

*T*he logical model of step-by-step decision making can be applied to most situations, most of the time. However, under certain conditions, a supplemental approach—intuitive decision making—can provide a valuable tool that will enhance your decision-making ability. As you will see, logical and intuitive processes interact in a complex manner and can be used to supplement and strengthen one another. Weston Agor, in his book *The Logic of Intuitive Decision Making*, proposes this tool as a logical choice under the following conditions:

- **High levels of uncertainty** can undermine a decision process based solely on the prediction of various alternative outcomes. By using a rational process to reduce uncertainty to a minimum, you will increase the reliability of your intuition.

- **Little or no precedent** is another factor that presents problems in a purely logical analysis of probabilities. If there is some precedent, this can be used to help predict possibilities and outcomes. If such precedents are lacking (as is often the case in highly speculative scientific exploration), intuition can be used as a guide.

- **Unpredictable variables** that cannot be taken into account present their own special kind of problem. To increase decision reliability, it is important to know something about the variables you are dealing with. Experimentation is a logical means to gain such information. In the beginning of such experimentation, when data are lacking, intuition can play an important role in determining experimental focus and design.

- **Limited availability of facts** makes it very difficult to gather the information necessary for a logical analysis of decision outcomes. Intuition is based on a level of knowing that is not independent of facts, but may precede their conscious formulation.

- **Time constraints** do not always allow for a step-by-step process of decision making. This is an important factor in certain human performance situations. A test pilot, for example, has carefully practiced and consciously learned a wide variety of reactions to possible flying situations. This pilot, however, may not have time during an emergency to think about his response—he must depend on his conditioning and his intuition for his very survival. The most outstanding athletes do the same thing. They consciously hone their skills to the point where they can operate on "feel" rather than conscious thought.

- **Rationale stalemate** can occur if the probable outcomes and associated values are roughly equivalent. A logical process of decision making does not always lead to a clear choice. Sometimes, all things considered, the alternatives may seem to be equally attractive (or distasteful). Intuition can play an important role in resolving such an impasse.

The last factor is the one most likely to play a role in your career decision making. It is entirely possible that you may end up with two or more occupational alternatives that are equally appealing possibilities. How do you make a decision among them? Intuition may be the key.

Based upon his study, Agor cites several factors that promote intuitive decision making:

- **Intent to develop your intuitive ability** is the first step toward using this technique. You have to commit yourself to this as a goal.
- **Practice** is equally important. You have to devote some time to this effort.
- **Physical and emotional relaxation** is a precondition to the use of intuition. Meditation or other relaxation exercises can increase your sensitivity to intuitive cues.
- **Quiet time** is also important. If you are constantly busy, rushing around, you won't be able to tune into the "small, still voice" of your intuition.
- **Openness to internal cues** provides an avenue for information coming from your subconscious mind. Intuitive information is often communicated through feelings, dreams, or daydreams.
- **Trust in yourself and your intuitive capacity** is fundamental. If you don't believe you can be intuitive or if you don't trust your intuition, this ability will remain dormant.
- **Courage** is necessary, because intuition involves facing the unknown and the unfamiliar in a manner to which you may not be accustomed.

Some of the techniques used to develop intuitive abilities include meditation, mental imagery, humor, sleeping on a problem, total immersion in a concern, discussions with others with divergent points of view, and the use of a "creative pause" that allows you to back away from the immediate situation and establish a different perspective. Many of the techniques suggested later in the chapter in relation to fostering creative thinking are closely allied to intuitive processes. You may want to read that section closely. Agor's book is a useful resource for those who want to explore this process.

The following Travelog will help you explore the relevance of intuitive decision making.

Travelog #27

■ If you were to estimate where your most natural decision-making process would fall on a continuum such as the one below, where would you place yourself?

PURELY LOGICAL   PURELY INTUITIVE

On what basis do you make such an estimate?

■ Do any of the conditions cited as appropriate for intuitive decision making apply to your career decision making? Why, or why not? If so, which ones?

■ List at least three techniques that you think might increase your intuitive abilities.

1.

2.

3.

■ Try to remember a time when you made a decision based primarily on your intuition. Describe the decision, how you made it, and the resulting outcome.

Decision:

Process:

Outcome:

■ Do you think that intuitive decision making might be useful in your career decision making? Why, or why not?

Both intuitive and logical decision making are based upon the bedrock of effective thinking skills. The next section suggests some strategies to assure that your thinking forms a firm foundation for your career decisions.

How to Improve Your Thinking

*I*f your thinking is fuzzy or flawed, your decisions may lead to less than desirable consequences. Thinking skills are easily taken for granted. "Surely I can think!" you say to yourself. The question is: How *well* do you think?

Critical thinking is the practical skill of reflective reasoning, used to examine your beliefs, actions, and thinking itself. It is not a new development; its application can be traced back to the philosopher Socrates in 400 B.C. if not earlier. Critical thinking is strengthened by a love of ideas. Eric Hoffer, one of the best social critics of our time, wrote: "I love ideas as much as I love women. I derive a sensuous pleasure from playing with ideas. Genuine ideas . . . titillate the mind, kindle the imagination, and warm the heart." A passion for ideas and an appreciation for their power is a reflection of respect for the power of your mind.

There are many methods you can use to enhance the quality and reliability of your thinking. A few of these methods follow:

■ **Value objective reality**. Your thinking can only be effective if it is based on reality. Reality is objective—it exists independently of your desires, wishes, whims, and objectives. Your thinking will be productive to the extent that you are able to accurately perceive and interpret this reality. This ability requires a quality of objectivity on your part—that you are able to separate "what is" from what you might want or from what might be more comforting to believe.

■ **Keep an open mind**. A closed mind is cut off from reality. The closed-mind thinker can easily be recognized; he or she has a rigid set of opinions and attitudes that are not open to discussion. Such a thinker cannot be reasoned with, since this process involves processing new input. If you feel as if you are talking to a brick wall, you are probably dealing with a closed-mind thinker. However, being open-minded does *not* mean that you should not stand by the truth as you know it, or that you must accept every point of view. Truth will withstand questioning; only illusion fears the exchange of thought.

■ **Do not tolerate ongoing ambiguity**. Most decisions that you face involve a degree of ambiguity, a "gray" area between the obvious black or white alternatives. This is *not* an argument for the tolerance of uncertainty; it is the motivation to exercise the power of thought to establish clarity. Ambiguity is often a symptom of sloppy, incomplete, or irrational thinking. When you experience such a state, it is time carefully to examine your premises, your principles, your knowledge, and the efficacy of your thinking process. Knowledge is the progressive retrieval of clarity from uncertainty and confusion.

- **Avoid the bandwagon.** When a notion becomes popular, many people will jump on the bandwagon to embrace it. This is usually more a function of conformity than it is of critical thought. Look (and think) before you leap.

- **Withhold judgment until you are sure you have adequate information.** It may be tempting to jump to conclusions, but you may end up in a hole you didn't see! On the other hand, once you have adequate information, do not hesitate to make judgments based upon it. Judgment is part of the process of thinking, the application of your ability to come to conclusions about reality.

- **Maintain a sense of humor.** You can't think straight if everything seems like a matter of life and death to you. The ability to laugh at yourself and to see the humor in situations can often help you maintain clarity of thought and perspective. However, beware of laughter used as a weapon to denigrate what you value or as a psychological defense; such uses require a serious response.

- **Cultivate intellectual curiosity.** The world is full of things you don't yet know about. Curiosity is the sign of a mind that is free and open to the wonders of reality, unafraid to face the unknown in order to grasp new knowledge. A curious thinker will explore new manners of looking at things and doing things. Learning can be an adventure of constant and exciting discovery if you cultivate a curious mind.

- **Don't take things at face value.** At an early age, most of us learn not to believe everything we hear. Imagine how disappointed you would be if you believed all the claims you hear in television advertising! This same principle applies to much of the information that comes through the media. It is meant to be chewed (and sometimes spit out), not swallowed whole! Beware of packaging that hides the truth. Sometimes a big box with a fancy picture on the front bears little relationship to what is hidden inside. Open it up and take a look for yourself!

- **Challenge "conventional wisdom."** Every culture is based upon certain assumptions that go largely unquestioned. Galileo Galilei, the Italian astronomer and mathematician, was brought before the Inquisition because he dared to question the "truth" that the Earth is the center of the universe. Even today, members of the Flat Earth Society are said to believe that the world is as flat as a pancake! You cannot assume that what is commonly accepted as truth is indeed true. Truth is established by rational thought and scientific investigation, not by a public-opinion poll or past practice.

- **Resist appeals to emotion.** Emotion can sometimes cloud your reason. If you are angry or ecstatic, your thought process will not be exactly the same as when you are in a more dispassionate mood. Beware of situations in which your emotions are being intentionally stimulated (by flattery, fear, or anticipation) while you are being asked to make a decision. It may be a strategy to manipulate the outcome.

- **Do not automatically accept authority.** The "appeal to authority" is a favorite advertising gimmick: Hollywood stars, sports figures, and popular culture heroes are used to promote everything from breakfast cereal to underwear and underarm deodorant. We are encouraged to think that "if he (or she) says this is great stuff, it must be!" As the Bo Jackson commercial says: "Bo Knows!" The fact that Bo is getting paid millions of dollars for his endorsement might be enough to make you question him as an objective authority. It is not always easy or safe to question authority. A certain amount of courage and judgment are required to do so effectively.

- **Beware others' ego-pleasing behavior.** Flattery is a time-honored method of persuasion. If someone starts with flattery, they often intend to end with your thinking or your money in their pocket. It's not always easy to tell the difference between a sincere compliment and a statement designed to manipulate you. It's a good idea to program yourself so that a "mental buzzer" goes off when you are being flattered. It will warn you to look for the hook that the worm is wrapped around!

- **Be aware of your own ego-enhancing behavior.** Decisions can often be influenced by how you want to appear to yourself or to others. If you are overly concerned about maintaining a given image, you may find yourself doing and saying things that are not really in your own best interest. As you achieve authentic self-esteem, behavior based on appearances often loses its appeal.

- **Maintain a sense of perspective.** When you are in the midst of an important matter, it is easy to lose a balanced view of the situation. It can often be a good practice to "zoom out" and view the matter in a larger context. One method to establish perspective: On a scale of 1 to 10, with "1" being the death of a blade of grass and "10" being worldwide nuclear annihilation, what does your situation rate? Is it truly as critical as it seems at the moment?

- **Be aware of unspoken rules.** Sometimes how we behave is dictated by hidden rules. If you are not aware of such unspoken rules, you won't have the knowledge you need to make a wise decision. If you are in a familiar situation, chances are you know the rules (for example: don't rock the boat, don't question the boss, don't interrupt the professor). If you are in an unfamiliar situation (or a foreign culture), it may pay to be unusually observant and to question those more familiar with the situation. This is not to say that you should be limited by such rules—only that an awareness of them is advisable.

- **Be aware of nonverbal behavior clues.** The impact of verbal communication is less than half of the message you receive from others. The rest of the message is communicated by nonverbal behavior. You will be influenced by both. If someone is acting friendly while painfully squeezing your hand in a handshake, you may have reason to question what they are saying! The same would apply if someone is stretched back in his chair and yawning while telling you how interested he is in your ideas. The clearer your perception of the facts of the situation, the clearer your thinking will be.

- **When under pressure, stop and think.** Impulsive decision making often results in poor decisions. As the pressure for a decision increases, the temptation to make an impulsive decision also increases. You may rationalize this by thinking that any decision is better than indecision; this is rarely true. Indecision is often the result of poor decision-making skills. Impulsiveness only assures that you'll reap the consequences of poor decisions that much sooner!

- **See beyond labels and stereotypes.** Labels and stereotypes are a type of "mental shorthand" that can facilitate thinking and communication. If you are in need of a four-legged piece of furniture designed for sitting, it is easier to ask for a "chair" and to ignore the many possible variations of design and materials. However, if you are investigating a possible career choice, you should not be satisfied with a stereotypical description of the occupations involved—you want to know exactly what it really means to be a police officer, brain surgeon, or financial analyst. Likewise, dealing with people from different backgrounds or cultures is seriously hampered by prejudicial stereotypes that obscure the truth.

- **Weed out negative self-talk.** Much of what passes for thinking is really self-talk, subvocal conversations we constantly hold with ourselves. This self-talk often takes the form of judgments and attitudes about ourselves. Your thinking skills may be undermined by self-talk that conveys negative messages over and over again, reinforcing a negative self-image ("I can't do anything right," "I'm just not as smart as everyone else") or attitudes ("I better not trust anyone," "School is a waste of time"). Unless this kind of negative thinking is challenged and replaced by more positive self-talk, it will tend to influence your decisions in an undesirable manner. The fundamental element in such change is the cultivation of self-esteem. Counseling is a good solution to this kind of problem.

- **Look for consistency.** Ralph Waldo Emerson once said that consistency was "the hobgoblin of little minds." However, consistency of thought is the hallmark of careful and thorough thinking. Consistency and logic are criteria that should be applied to whatever you consider. Inconsistency or illogic are often used to obscure the truth.

- **Practice empathy.** There's an Indian saying that you should walk a mile in another person's moccasins before passing judgment. In other words, you should not judge others until you fully understand their situation. By practicing this type of empathy, you will decrease the likelihood of making snap judgments that you may later regret. You may also find that a little understanding facilitates a deeper insight into other people and their behavior. And the deeper your insight into yourself and others, the wiser your decisions will be.

■ **Take time to check the facts**. If you don't have the facts straight, your decisions are likely to be skewed. In important matters, you should try to obtain firsthand access to the relevant facts. If you are trying to make a career decision and want to know something about your occupational skills, it is better to take an aptitude test than to ask your buddies what they think "you're good at." Likewise, it is better to find out the nature of work for a given occupation, based on accepted references and worker interviews, than to rely on stereotypes that may be full of partial truths and significant omissions. Check the reliability of your information. Did it come from a reliable source? Can you find another source that confirms your information? If you can answer yes to these questions, you can be more confident about the facts you use as a basis for your decisions.

■ **Check the validity of your information**. Information may be reliable but not valid. Validity has to do with the relevance of the information to the context in which it is being applied. It may be a reliable fact that when you strike a match, fire will result—unless you are underwater or in outer space! Context is important!

■ **Cultivate listening skills**. When it comes to conversation, what you hear is what you get. Listening is another skill we tend to take for granted, but it is rarely utilized as effectively as we think. How many times have you been in the middle of a conversation and suddenly realized that the other person had asked you a question that you didn't even hear? How often are you so preoccupied with your own thoughts in class that you tune out the instructor? It happens to us all, which illustrates the difficulty of practicing this seemingly simple skill. The better you listen, the more correct information you will obtain; the more correct information you have, the better decisions you will make.

■ **Be aware of illogical thinking**. There are entire philosophy books devoted to logic and the manner in which it can be distorted. Stereotypes are often based on illogical thinking—applying specific characteristics in a universal manner without verifiable basis in fact, or assuming a causal connection between two unrelated events. Advertising commonly encourages illogical associations: beef is touted as "food for real people" (What do "unreal" people eat?), and white teeth or the right deodorant seem to guarantee a bevy of babes (or hunks) at your feet (Where's the Crest?). It may seem obvious that such claims are ridiculous, but someone is paying big bucks for these commercials for a reason!

■ **Listen to your intuition**. All of us have "hunches" about things at one time or another. These hunches are often the result of information that registers at a level other than conscious awareness. It's like when you "sense" someone staring at you, only to look up and find it is true. There was no logical reason to believe someone was looking at you; but it somehow registered nevertheless. Intuition cannot take the place of logical thought, but it can be developed as a valuable supplement. By trying to be more aware of your intuitions, you can increase your sensitivity to this kind of information. As you learn to test it and to trust it, it can enhance your decision-making skills.

A little critical thinking may suggest occupations that you have never considered or may help you solve problems that have kept you from realizing your true potential. As you begin to think more effectively, you may find that you are able to turn problems into possibilities.

Travelog #28

■ List the four (4) thinking strategies that you think have the most potential for your use.

1.

2.

3.

4.

■ Describe how you would use each of the four strategies you have selected to improve your career decision making.

Statement of Career Decision Concern:

Applying Strategy 1:

Applying Strategy 2:

Applying Strategy 3:

Applying Strategy 4:

Critical thinking skills can help you make sure that your thinking is logical, consistent, and thorough. When supplemented by a focus on creative thinking, your mind becomes a powerful tool in the service of your Way and your everyday life.

Creativity Tips

Creative thinking skills are closely aligned to the critical thinking skills you just finished considering. Both types of thinking will allow you to process information more effectively and productively. Creative thought is built upon a foundation of critical thought; if flawed or fuzzy thinking is the basis for creative efforts, these efforts will rarely be fruitful.

Creative thinking is a thought process that generates something from nothing; or, to be more exact, it is capable of generating something not yet known from that which is known. It is a birth of sorts—generating new thought from existing thought, as life generates new life from existing life. Research indicates that creative thinking is strongly correlated to intelligence up to an IQ of about 120; beyond this point, the correlation is much weaker. Often this can be due to the narrowing of focus that at times accompanies high intelligence. Such a narrowing can restrict the creative process.

There are a number of simple guidelines that can increase your creative potential:

- **Value creativity.** Creativity will not grow from barren ground. Creative achievement springs from ground that has been enriched by knowledge, desire, devotion, and concentrated effort. Creativity is not evenly distributed among people, any more than intelligence or honesty are universal constants. Some people are more creative than others. This being said, however, it is important to note that most people have not even come close to realizing their creative potential. The first step to this realization is to value creativity, to think of it as a possibility worthy of cultivation.

- **Focus your energy.** Creativity requires significant mental resources of energy. If your energy is scattered among many competing projects, you may not have enough energy focused at any one time and place to realize your creative potential. Highly creative people are able to focus their energy on their efforts. Sometimes this may mean that they deliberately disengage themselves from other situations or responsibilities that might serve to drain this energy. A kind of single-mindedness seems to facilitate creativity.

- **Don't limit yourself.** To a significant degree, how you think about your creative ability will determine its presence. If you generate self-talk that insists that "I'm just not a creative person" or that "creativity is the province of genius," then you are limiting your own ability to exercise your inborn creative talents. Everyone has the ability to be creative. It is true that some people have this ability in greater measure than others, just as some people can run faster than others. But just like running, with a little training, you'll be better able to realize the talent you do possess.

■ **Avoid premature evaluation.** Judging an idea at too early a stage in its development is much like closing a door on an infant who can't reach the doorknob—it blocks further progress. New ideas need a chance to wander around for awhile, to learn to walk and develop their potential. All of us have had the experience of someone's passing judgment on an idea of ours ("That's stupid . . . or impractical . . . or unrealistic . . . or naive . . . or too idealistic . . . "). Such comments can stunt an idea's growth, whether it comes from others or from your own self-talk. Give new ideas some room to grow!

■ **Don't be afraid to make a mistake.** Most of us are programmed to fear making a mistake. We take such an error as a reflection on our worth as a person or our basic capability. The fact is, we all make mistakes and will do so until the day we die. Mistakes are a part of life—an important part. Learning often comes as a result of mistakes that provided an opportunity to understand something we may have previously overlooked. The more creative you are, the more likely you are to make mistakes—you are stretching the limits of the known into unknown territory. The key is to try to not make the same mistakes over and over again, and to learn something from the mistakes that you do make.

■ **Expect the unexpected.** Expectations can shape reality. There is a psychological principle called the *self-fulfilling prophesy* that describes how the expectation that something will happen actually makes its occurrence more likely. For example, if you expect to be in a car accident, this will make you tense and overreactive and will inhibit your ability to avoid potential accident situations. In a similar manner, if you expect to confront novelty and potentiality, you will be more likely to run into it! The unexpected is grist for the mill of creativity; it disrupts the routine and established manner of doing things and presents the possibility of change.

■ **Break out of established patterns.** Are you a creature of habit? Do you go through the same routine every morning when you get out of bed? Do you brush your teeth in the exact same sequence every time? Do you eat the food on your plate in the same manner and sequence every time? Do you find yourself espousing the exact same opinions over and over again? All of us have a tendency to settle into a comfortable routine; our minds have this same tendency. If you want to enhance your creativity, it is important to disrupt your habitual manner of thinking and acting, to create new pathways across your life and your brain. Eat something that you've never eaten before. Shower before you brush your teeth. Try on a new opinion for a change.

- **Check out your assumptions**. Thinking is often limited by the assumptions it is based upon. If you are trying to design a new chair and assume that it must have four legs, this assumption will limit the scope of your design; it would eliminate a three-legged chair, a five-legged chair, a chair with no legs, and so forth. If you make certain assumptions about what you are capable of, you will be unduly limiting your career possibilities. Such assumptions are often hidden in our thinking—so taken for granted that we do not recognize their influence. Take the time to examine the basic parameters you draw around a problem and extend them if you can.

- **Try brainstorming**. *Brainstorming* is a tried-and-true method of generating creative ideas. This process involves freely generating as many ideas as possible and totally holding any evaluation of them in reserve. No idea is too outlandish to suggest. All ideas are recorded without editing of any kind. Only once the "idea pool" is exhausted does the evaluation process take place; ideas are sorted into similar categories, combined, contrasted, defined, explored, and evaluated in terms of possible constraints. This process works best with a small group of people, taking advantage of a stimulating cross-fertilization of ideas. You may want to try some career possibility brainstorming with a group of your friends.

- **Expand your associations**. We tend to fall into patterned ways of (uncreative) thinking by unconsciously limiting how we associate things. If you think of college only as a means of obtaining a better job, you will be unduly limiting your educational possibilities. The college experience can also be associated with personal growth, social networking, mentoring by professors, exploration of different values, appreciation of differing cultures, expansion of artistic appreciation and expression, athletic development, leadership opportunities, development of a philosophy of life, spiritual practice, intimate relationships, scientific exploration, travel—you get the idea. Expand your associations and you will expand your experience; expand your experience and you will expand your knowledge and your life.

- **Look for order in chaos**. Sometimes what appears to be chaos is actually order just waiting to happen. When you began the process, career planning and decision making may have seemed like chaos to you; by now you probably have a sense that some order is possibly emerging. Chaos or disorder can be viewed as a puzzle with all the pieces mixed up. As you begin to see how things fit together, the puzzle will begin to make some sense. So don't let disorder scare you; begin by looking for the pieces that seem to go together and a pattern will often appear. As the patterns come together, the entire picture becomes clear.

- **Look for chaos in order**. All order harbors within itself an element of chaos. If the element of disorder within your life is ignored, it grows in darkness and may one day provide you with an unwelcome surprise. However, if you recognize this element of disorder, you can use it to enrich your life. For example, once you are settled into a given job, there will always be an element of dissatisfaction, something about your work that is troublesome or unpleasant. If you recognize this factor, you will have the opportunity to develop new skills to deal with it, to use your ingenuity to get someone else to do it, to develop an alternative more to your liking, or to otherwise exercise a creative solution to address the concern. On the other hand, if you try to ignore such a problem, it may fester and grow to poison your attitude about your work in general.

■ **Utilize thinking stimulators**. Different things stimulate creative openness for different people. Some people prefer silence and solitude; others want the stimulation that interaction with others can provide. Classical music suits some; hard rock or country music works for others. Some people are early-morning creators while others do their best work late at night. Take the time to observe the conditions that seem to foster your most creative work. You can then consciously use these conditions to increase your creative susceptibility.

■ **Don't be limited by compartmentalization**. The most creative accomplishments, by definition, do not fit into pre-established categories. The advent of the airplane created a whole new category of transportation; one that would not have developed within the categories of ground and sea transport. Similarly, the categories of occupations you have been working with will be different in 10 or 20 years; whole new categories will have developed as new occupations are generated by future discoveries. Categories are important intellectual tools that organize thinking, but a lack of openness to new categories and concepts will unduly limit your creative ability.

■ **Avoid premature conclusion**. There is a natural movement toward closure in any problem-solving process. If you want this process to be a creative one, it is important to forestall such closure. Creativity requires a certain amount of room to move. It is not a linear process of a given duration; creativity is more like wandering about. This principle is especially important when it comes to career choice. If you force yourself to a conclusion, you may be eliminating better possibilities that might have emerged, given a little more time and consideration. A time for a decision will come; don't rush the process.

■ **Get silly every now and then**. Humor is a powerful creative stimulus. If you insist on being dead serious about everything, your ideas are likely to be seriously "dead." Creativity should be more like play than work. A playful attitude can open up new avenues of thinking and interacting with others, often leading to a kind of synergistic teamwork that fosters creativity and novelty.

■ **Foster creative inspiration**. As you explore your creative potential, you will discover the conditions that facilitate this potential. Different people find different strategies to enhance their creativity. Some people find that solitude or meditation enriches their imagination. Others stimulate creativity by exposing themselves to novel situations or unfamiliar surroundings, forcing themselves to deal with reality in a nonhabitual manner. The creation of a stable environment might be important to some people, enabling them to focus their energy and attention on a creative endeavor. Music and art or nature are often used as sources of inspiration. The point is to experiment with different conditions, environments, and states of mind. Pay close attention to how such variables affect your creative capacities. Over time, you will discover your own unique mixture of elements that enhance your creativity.

- **Strengthen your independence.** Creativity is a product of individual minds. Although it may be stimulated by interaction with others, it may also be inhibited by others who do not value it. The ability to maintain a personal commitment to creative effort and to sustain such effort in the face of opposition and discouragement is a key characteristic of highly creative individuals. Successful creators stand by their vision even when it is not seen or appreciated by others around them. In *The Fountainhead*, one of Ayn Rand's characters (Howard Roark, an architect) speaks of this characteristic: "The basic need of the creator is independence. The [creative] mind cannot work under any form of compulsion. . . . The creators were . . . self-sufficient, self-motivated, self-generated. A first cause, a fount of energy, a life force, a Prime Mover."

Roger von Oech, in his book *A Kick in the Seat of the Pants*, describes another view of the creative process, focused in terms of different creative roles. Von Oech suggests that the creative process can be facilitated by assuming four different roles or perspectives at different stages in the creative process.

- **The Explorer role is used to gather resources,** search for information, and scan the environment for creative suggestions. Creativity does not emerge from a void. There is often a conscious and unconscious gathering of force, information, impressions, understanding, experience, and energy that precedes creative expression.

- **The Artist role facilitates the generation of ideas** from the resources and information gathered. At a certain point in the creative process, the resources gathered by the Explorer will coalesce in the form of a creative idea. The Artist is receptive to this process and encourages it. The emergence of a creative idea is often a fragile process, something like the emergence of a newborn bird from its shell. The drive of an idea to be born is insistent, but it does require a certain degree of warmth and care provided by the "parent."

- **The Judge role is used to critically examine the ideas generated** in order to determine viability, practicality, and purpose. Not all creative ideas are born equal. Some ideas will prove to be mundane, impractical, or otherwise without merit; others have the potential to impact reality in a significant manner. It is the role of the Judge to examine the creative ideas from a dispassionate perspective in order to sort out those ideas that are worth pursuing from those that are not.

- **The Warrior role is used to implement the creation**, to counter opposition, and to champion its achievement. Creativity must often face odds stacked in favor of inertia and the status quo. The greater the potential impact of a creation, the more vehemently it has been opposed by those threatened by the possibility of change. Ayn Rand expressed this in her book *For the New Intellectual*: "The great creators—the thinkers, the artists, the scientists, the inventors—stood alone against the men of their time. Every great new thought was opposed. Every great new invention was denounced. . . . But the men of unborrowed vision went ahead." The Warrior's role is to brave this opposition and to fight to bring creation into reality.

If you want a thorough and entertaining presentation of this model, refer to von Oech's book, listed in the Bibliography.

The Travelog that follows will ask you to apply some of what you have learned about creative thinking. As you move into the next chapter, you will focus on another kind of tool that will probably be an important part of your journey—further education and training.

Travelog #29

■ List the four (4) creativity tips that you think have the most potential for your use.

1.

2.

3.

4.

■ Select a personal career planning concern that you would like to approach in a more creative manner. Using the four creativity roles proposed by Von Oech, describe how you would apply each role to this concern.

Statement of career planning concern:

Applying Explorer strategies:

Applying Artist strategies:

Applying Judge strategies:

Applying Warrior strategies:

Quiz 6

*P*lease answer the following questions.

1. Name two (2) typical concerns that may disrupt or otherwise negatively influence the decision-making process.

   a.

   b.

2. For each of the two problems listed in your answer to question 1, suggest a solution or strategy that will help solve the problem.

   a.

   b.

3. Why are thinking skills important to the decision-making process?

4. Why are creativity skills important to the decision-making process?

5. Has the information in this chapter influenced your tentative occupational choice? Why, or why not?

6. What is the most important thing that you learned about yourself by working through this chapter?

7. What topic covered in this chapter would you like to explore further?

To Consider . . .

1. Some may argue that most people's careers are guided more by fate than reason and planning.

   What role does fate play in career planning?

   If fate plays a role, what impact does this have on the need for planning?

2. The application of critical thinking skills may lead to the questioning of authority.

   When is such questioning a legitimate right?

   Are there conditions under which authority should not be questioned?

   Why does questioning of authority so often lead to conflict?

3. Creative activity is often perceived as unconventional, even strange by normal standards.

   How is creative expression different from simple unconventionality?

   Why is modern art so often perceived as "strange"?

Suggested Activities

1. Interview two of the most creative people you know. How are they different from others? What stimulates their creativity? What kinds of things do they value?

2. Choose an *appropriate* situation and manner in which to challenge something that is said by an authority figure in a group setting. Carefully observe and then analyze the reactions of everyone to the ensuing interaction.

The Parable of the Deepening

Zara was awakened by the wind, howling outside his cabin. He roused his disciple and both of them walked into the forest. The winter-naked trees were swaying in the wind and the clouds were racing across the bright morning sky.

Zara stopped and addressed his disciple: "Like trees we stand before the winds of change. We are swayed but hold our ground. And when the season comes, we lose all our leaves to the wind. We must then stand naked, without the protective covering of our traditions and our commonplace beliefs. We must sink our roots deeper into the earth, deeper into our being, when our leaves are blown away. And from the nourishment of this sinking and deepening, new leaves will, in due time, grow."

Zara stopped for a moment and turned his head, as if listening to the wind. Then he spoke once again: "This wind speaks of things to come. Shallow-rooted beings, beware! The winds of change will test your roots! You cannot hold to your leaves; perhaps you will even loose your grasp of the earth. The shallow will be uprooted and tumbled across the plain of the future—trees become tumbleweeds! Only those with deep roots will withstand the howling winds that are coming.

"Deep roots come from longing. If you are satisfied with surface water, you will not seek the deeper springs that can nourish the spirit. Truly it is the thirsty, the seeking, and the dissatisfied who sink their roots ever deeper. The spirit's thirst cannot be quenched with surface water. But the shallow ones think they thirst for what can be found in the muddy puddles. Their roots spread across the surface in search of puddles of purpose and meaning. But puddles contain only muddy intoxicants that mask the thirst without satisfying it. The more intoxicated these shallow beings become, the more they seek the puddles that can never satisfy them. Eventually, their roots wither and their souls shrivel. Lost in their pain, they await the howling wind for their tumbleweed deliverance. Only the deep-rooted ones will withstand the winds of the new millenium."

Zara turned to his disciple and spoke: "Stay away from muddy puddles, my friend! Sink your roots deep within your fathomless, clear being. Seek the nourishment of your Way. Let your longing for meaning live within you and drive you deeper into thought."

Zara then braced himself against the wind and raised his voice: "Truly a great howling wind of change is coming. Listen to my howling wind! Rejoice, shallow ones—your deliverance is near! Beware, all tumbleweeds of thought and being, you will be blown and tumbled across the desert of your future. The deep ones will watch your tumbling with compassion; but roots cannot be shared!"

PART THREE

Education

Further education will be a part of the career development of most people. Chapter Seven shows how education relates to career goals and will provide useful information for those who choose (or have chosen) to further their education by attending college. Chapter Eight focuses on the importance of academic advisement and provides a number of practical suggestions related to college success.

CHAPTER SEVEN

Getting There from Here

SCHOOL

Preview

The intellect is a cleaver; it discerns and rifts its way into the secret of things.

HENRY DAVID THOREAU

For most people, some kind of education or training is necessary to prepare for the occupation of their choice—a means to sharpen the cleaver of thought and skill that discerns their Way in life. As we saw in Chapter Five, education will be required for more jobs in the future, especially for those with the fastest growing opportunities. College is one of the surest paths to these opportunities. This chapter describes some of the most important factors involved in college decisions. The main sections of this chapter are as follows.

- **Training Levels** describes the different levels of training that can lead to jobs within a given occupational area.

- **College Education** is a section that outlines the kinds of educational programs and degrees commonly available at community colleges, four-year colleges, and universities.

- **Educational Directory** is a chart that relates different levels of occupations to different levels of training.

- **Questions for College Decisions** suggests some factors to be considered when you are facing a decision about which college to attend.

- **Testing Tips** makes a number of recommendations to help you prepare for any kind of testing situation.

- **Benefits of College Orientation** explains the purpose of the orientation session for new college students.

- **Things to Find in Your Catalog** points out some key items with which college students need to be familiar, and which are commonly found in a college's catalog.

- **Credit by Exam** provides some information on obtaining college credit through the CLEP (College-Level Examination Program).

- **Other Kinds of Training** explains some of the training options, other than college, that may be available to you.

By the end of this chapter, you should have a better idea of what you need to do to obtain the training and education required for your chosen occupation.

Learning requires a kind of readiness in order to fulfill its purpose. For some people, a love of learning for its own sake creates this readiness. For others, the clarification of a goal that can be accomplished through learning serves this function. If your career goal involves further education for its realization, learning may take on a new and powerful meaning in your life.

Higher education is a good investment in your future. Data clearly show that advancing your education enhances your earning power and your job security. In the Spring 1992 issue of the *Occupational Outlook Quarterly*, the following figures were published (based upon 1990 salary and unemployment figures):

Years of Education	Average Salary	Unemployment Rate
Less than 12	$19,168	8.5%
12	$24,308	4.9%
1–3 years college	$29,454	3.7%
4 years college	$38,620	2.4%
5+ years college	$49,153	1.9%

The evidence is clear: the more education you have, the greater your earning power and the less you'll have to worry about being unemployed.

Now that you have a tentative occupational choice, the next step is to figure out how to translate your choice into a plan of action. The process of career planning has, thus far, been one of self-examination, reflection, information gathering, and decision making. You have probably found that some kind of further training or education is going to be required for you to reach your career goal. It's time to start thinking of concrete action you can take to obtain this education. Such action involves making some additional decisions about occupational level and program of study.

Training Levels

M any career fields may be entered at a variety of levels, depending on the level of education and training you attain. If you wanted a career in Health Care, for example, you could enter the field of nursing at any of these occupational levels:

- With less than one year of noncredit training, you could become a **Licensed Practical Nurse** (L.P.N.).
- With an A.S. degree, you could become a **Registered Nurse** (R.N.).

- If you wanted to pursue further training at the Bachelor's level, you could get a **Bachelor of Science in Nursing** (B.S.N.).

- If you wanted to teach other nurses, you could obtain a **graduate degree in Nursing**.

The Educational Directory presented later in this chapter provides many other examples of occupational levels for related kinds of work. Generally, with more education, you are able to enter a job at a higher level, with increased pay, and with greater opportunities for advancement. These advantages must be balanced against other factors, such as:

- **How much do you enjoy going to school?** If you are not oriented toward academics, you may want to choose a program of study that emphasizes job skills rather than general education. This route will get you into the job market faster, but it also may limit your future opportunities. In general, the more education you have, the greater your opportunities and earnings will be in the future.

- **What are your general academic abilities?** It is important to have an accurate gauge of your academic skills. Most high schools and colleges administer academic tests that give you an idea of your potential for academic study. If you score high on a test such as the SAT or the ACT, this can be a good indication of potential success in college (though many factors other than academic potential contribute to such success). If, on the other hand, your scores are low, you may need to take certain college preparatory classes that will strengthen your abilities. Your actual performance in college will be a valuable clue. The easier you find it to succeed in college, the more you should consider furthering your education.

- **What are the costs involved?** Obviously, the longer you spend in school, the higher your cost of education. Also, costs vary widely between public and private institutions. The financial aid office of the institution you are considering can provide information on eligibility for financial assistance and typical costs of attendance. If you want to attend an out-of-state institution, tuition may be considerably higher until you can establish residency in that state.

- **What level of responsibility do you want to assume in your occupation?** As the example of nursing training demonstrated, there are often several levels of positions within a given occupational area. The level you choose will determine the minimum training required.

- **What other responsibilities compete for your time and energy?** Many people must balance the responsibilities of school with work and/or family obligations. Such reality factors can often influence the kind of education you pursue. Keep in mind, however, that you should not necessarily scale down your goals; you may just have to take a little longer to achieve your objectives.

■ **How quickly do you want to enter the job market?** The faster you can complete your training, the sooner you can enter the job market. If you are anxious to get started in an occupation, you may want to focus on programs that emphasis job preparation skills and that have minimal general education requirements. If you are not in a hurry, or are willing to put it off for awhile, additional education can be to your benefit.

As you can see, there are many options. It's important to find what works for you—what is needed for you to reach your career and life goals. You might also consider the range of your goals. Short-term goals, such as getting a job to "bring home the bacon," may dictate that you pursue a program of study that will satisfy your more immediate needs. With some planning, immediate needs can often be satisfied while leaving the door open for long-range goals that involve further training and education. There's a good chance that this will include some kind of college education.

College Education

Community colleges, four-year colleges, and universities typically offer several kinds of training and degree programs. These training options will vary widely in terms of duration, cost, and depth of instruction.

■ **The Job Training programs are nondegree studies that focus on entry-level job skills in trade, technical, and service occupations.** The training for these programs often varies from 100 to 1500 or more hours and is usually found in community colleges and private trade or technical schools. Descriptions of these programs may be found in the college's catalog.

■ **The Technical Certificate programs focus almost exclusively on job-related skills and require less than two years of full-time study.** Some of these programs can be an intermediate step toward related A.S. degree programs.

■ **The Associate in Science (A.S.) degree is designed for students who want training that provides academic as well as skills training.** Most A.S. programs require two years of full-time study at the community college, longer for part-time students. Some general education courses are required, but significantly fewer than the A.A. degree; emphasis is on obtaining job-related skills.

■ **The Associate in Arts (A.A.) program is designed for those students who want to complete at least a bachelor's degree.** It is an academically oriented program, typically with general-education requirements in English, mathematics, humanities, natural sciences, social sciences, and electives related to your choice of a university major. An A.A. degree may usually be completed at either a community college or a four-year college or university.

A full-time student can usually complete the A.A. in two years; a part-time student will take longer.

- **The bachelor's degree (B.A. or B.S.) can only be obtained at a four-year college or university.** It usually involves at least two years of full-time study beyond the A.A. degree level, and focuses on course work closely related to the chosen major. For some majors, a bachelor's degree is considered adequate for entry into the job market; others require a graduate degree to qualify for a job in the field.

- **Graduate and professional degrees are offered at the university level and require from one to five or more years of specialized full-time study.** The Master's, Doctorate, Juris Doctor, and Medical Doctor degrees are examples of different kinds of graduate and professional training.

There are a number of useful books that can help you sort out the educational opportunities available to you. Books such as the following should be available in your local career center or public library:

- *College Blue Book*
- *Chronicle Two-Year College Databook*
- *Chronicle Four-Year College Databook*
- *Chronicle Vocational School Manual*

You have seen how you may enter an occupational field at a variety of levels, each requiring a different level of training and education. The following Educational Directory (ED) divides the seven occupational clusters you have been working with into three different levels of training and lists many related programs of study. The ED can be used to translate occupational choices into decisions about educational programs of study.

Educational Directory (ED)

*T*his directory is organized in terms of three levels of educational preparation:

- **Typical university and four-year college majors** (for those seeking a bachelor's degree or higher)
- **Typical Associate in Science programs** (usually offered in community colleges)
- **Typical job training (and certificate) programs** (requiring job-oriented training)

This listing is not exhaustive, but it represents the type of training related to each occupational cluster. No given institution will have all of the listed programs. *The College Blue Book*, and various publications by Chronicle Guidance (listed in the

Bibliography), are good references for locating those institutions that offer programs of study of interest to you.

Usually (but not always), the more time spent in training, the greater the benefit in terms of financial reward, opportunities for advancement, and occupational status. A little research in the *Occupational Outlook Handbook* can help you evaluate these factors.

Mechanical Cluster

Typical University Majors	Typical A.S. Degree Programs	Typical Job Training Programs
Agriculture	Air Conditioning Technology	Air Conditioning Service
Agronomy	Air Traffic Control	Aircraft Airframe Mechanics
Animal Science	Architectural Technology	Animal Caretaking
Construction Technology	Automotive Service	Architectural Drafting
Criminology	Aviation Technology	Automotive Mechanics
Forestry	Conservation Technology	Automotive Machine Shop
Industrial Technology	Construction Technology	Automotive Body Repair
Industrial Arts Education	Criminal Justice Technology	Bricklaying
Vocational Education	Culinary Arts	Building Maintenance
	Fire Science	Carpentry
	Forestry Technology	Catering
	Horticulture	Construction Electricity
	Landscape Technology	Correctional Officer
	Police Science	Dog Training
	Radio & TV Broadcasting	Drafting
	Surveying	Firefighting
	Veterinary Technology	Food Service
		Gas Engine Mechanics
		Gunsmithing
		Landscaping
		Locksmithing
		Machining
		Marine Mechanics
		Meatcutting
		Pipefitting
		Plumbing
		Printing
		Roofing
		Sewing
		Tailoring
		Truck Driving
		Watch Repair
		Welding

Analytical Cluster

Typical University Majors	Typical A.S. Degree Programs	Typical Job Training Programs
Anthropology	Business Data Processing	Business Software Applications
Astronomy	Computer Programming	
Biology	Computer Systems Analysis	
Chemistry	Integrated Systems Specialist	
Computer Science		
Dentistry		
Ecology		
Economics		
Entomology		
Geology		
History		
Information Systems		
Mathematics		
Medicine		
Oceanography		
Pharmacy		
Physics		
Psychology		
Sociology		
Statistics		
Veterinary Medicine		
Zoology		

Technical Cluster

Typical University Majors	Typical A.S. Degree Programs	Typical Job Training Programs
Architecture	Architectural Technology	Auto Appraiser
Electronics Technology	Biomedical Engineering Tech.	Claims Adjuster
Engineering, Mechanical	Cardiopulmonary Technology	Claims Examiner
Engineering, Nuclear	Computer Engineering Tech.	Communications Electronics
Engineering, Civil	Computer-Aided Design	Contractor
Engineering, Environmental	Drafting & Design Technology	EEG Technology
Engineering, Biomedical	Electronics Engineering Tech.	EKG Technology
Engineering, Electrical	Environmental Studies	Fire Inspection
Quality Control	Histologic Technology	Fire Alarm Technology
	Laser Technology	Industrial Electronics
	Medical Lab Technology	Private Investigation
	Medical Sonography	Quality Control Inspector
	Nuclear Medicine Technology	Safety Inspection
	Quality Control Technology	Surgical Technician
	Radiologic Technology	
	Robotics	
	Telecommunications Tech.	
	Video Technology	

Expressive Cluster

Typical University Majors	Typical A.S. Degree Programs	Typical Job Training Programs
Animation	Cinematography	Animation
Art	Commercial Art	Ceramics
Art Education	Commercial Photography	Fashion Illustration
Art History	Computer Graphics & Design	Graphic Reproduction
Broadcasting	Dance	Modeling
Classics	Desktop Publishing	Radio Announcing
Communications	Fashion Design	Set Design
Drama	Graphic Arts Technology	
English	Interior Design Technology	
Film		
Graphic Design		
Industrial Design		
Journalism		
Literature		
Music		
Painting		
Photography		
Speech		
Theater		

Empathic Cluster

Typical University Majors	Typical A.S. Degree Programs	Typical Job Training Programs
Child Development	Audiology Technology	Ambulance Attendant
Community Health	Child Care Management	Audiometrist
Counseling	Coronary Care Technology	Bartending
Education, Vocational	Dental Hygiene	Customer Services
Education, Special	Dietetic Technician	Dental Assistant
Education, Elementary	Emergency Medical Services	EEG Technology
Education, Secondary	Geriatric Care	EKG Technology
Gerontology	Human Services	Emergency Medical Technician
Library Science	Medical Technology	Home Health Aide
Nursing (BSN)	Mental Health Technology	Massage Therapist
Nutrition	Nursing (RN)	Medical Assistant
Occupational Therapy	Occupational Therapy Assistant	Nursing Assistant
Physical Therapy	Ophthalmic Technology	Nutrition Aide
Physician Assistant	Paramedic Technology	Orderly
Psychology	Physical Therapy Assistant	Paramedic
Rehabilitation Counseling	Recreational Therapy	Patient Care Assistant
Social Work	Respiratory Care	Practical Nursing (LPN)
Sociology		Psychiatric Aide
Speech Pathology		
Theology		
Women's Studies		

Persuasive Cluster

Typical University Majors	Typical A.S. Degree Programs	Typical Job Training Programs
Advertising	Aviation Administration	Barbering
Banking	Business Administration	Child Care Center Operations
Business, Accounting	Child Care Management	Cosmetology
Business, Marketing	Fashion Marketing	Dietetic Management
Business, Economics	Financial Services	Fashion Merchandising
Business, Finance	Golf Course Management	Fast-Food Management
Business, Management	Hospitality Management	Floral Design & Marketing
Insurance	Industrial Management	Insurance Marketing
International Relations	Insurance Management	Merchandising
Law	Management Development	Real Estate Marketing
Public Administration	Marketing Management	Retail Merchandising
Public Relations	Medical Office Management	Telemarketing
Recreation Management	Postal Service Management	Travel Agency Operations
Sports Administration	Public Relations Specialist	
Transportation & Logistics	Real Estate Management	
Urban Land Development	Restaurant Management	
Urban Planning	Retail Management	
	Sales & Marketing	

Clerical Cluster

Typical University Majors	Typical A.S. Degree Programs	Typical Job Training Programs
Accounting	Accounting Technology	Administrative Assistant
Business Education	Court Reporting	Bookkeeping
	Executive Secretary	Cashiering
	Legal Assistant	Claim Adjusting
	Legal Secretary	Computer Operation
	Medical Records Technology	Data Entry Operations
	Medical Secretary	Executive Receptionist
	Office Systems Specialist	General Office Clerk
	Office Management Tech.	Medical Office Assistant
	Secretarial Science	Medical Transcription
		Office Assistant
		Office Automation
		Stenography
		Teller Operations
		Typing
		Word Processing

Travelog #30

■ What are your most important considerations as you decide on the occupational level that is right for you?

■ Take your top two (2) occupational options and, for each one, list related jobs available at various levels of training.

Occupation 1:_____

Education Required   **Related Job**

Little or none   _____

A.S. Degree   _____

B.A. or higher   _____

Occupation 2:_____

Education Required   **Related Job**

Little or none   _____

A.S. Degree   _____

B.A. or higher   _____

■ Returning to your answer to the previous question, circle the (related) jobs you prefer at this time.

■ What will you have to change in your life in order to achieve the level of education required for the jobs you prefer?

Once you have decided upon the kind of training you want to pursue, it's time to do something about it! This means actually doing what it takes to get started in the college (or other training institution) of your choice.

If you are thinking about attending college, the questions in the following section might help you decide where to attend. If you are already attending college, it might be interesting to see how these questions reflect things you considered when you made your decision about college.

Questions for College Decisions

Narrowing down the choice of what institution to attend will usually be considerably easier than deciding upon an occupation. In making this choice, you should consider the following questions.

- **Is training provided at the occupational level you have selected?** If you are looking for job skills training of minimum duration, the community college may be your best bet. If you plan to complete a bachelor's degree or higher, a four-year college or a university may be a logical choice.

- **Is accessibility and location important?** Would there be a social or emotional benefit to staying close to home and friends? Is there a financial benefit to staying close to home? If so, local options might be given first consideration.

- **What is the cost of instruction (tuition, fees, etc.)?** This can vary widely among institutions. Tuition and fees are generally listed in the college's catalog. The financial aid office of the college should also be able to supply you with an estimated budget, detailing typical costs related to attendance.

- **Is it accredited by official agencies?** It is important to know if the institution you will be attending is accredited by the regional accrediting agency. State colleges and universities must meet stringent standards to maintain their accreditation. Some private training institutions are not accredited, and the credit you earn will *not* usually be transferable to an accredited institution if you decide to further your education at a later date. The college's registrar would be a good source for this kind of information.

- **Does it have a local reputation for quality training?** A reputation for quality training is important if you plan to join the local job market. It may be worthwhile to talk to local employers and to current students concerning this factor.

- **Does it offer flexibility in training programs and class scheduling?** The more training options offered, the greater flexibility you will have if you change your mind about your objective. Also, class scheduling may be important to you if you are working or otherwise have time limitations that affect your ability to schedule classes.

- **What resources are available to you as a student (advising, library, learning labs, tutors, financial aid, computer labs, etc.)?** The services and resources offered by a college should be listed in the college catalog or the student handbook. You can usually obtain a copy of one or both of these publications from the admissions or advising office.

- **Is assistance offered with job placement and/or cooperative education?** Most institutions have job placement offices that assist their students with part-time work, as well as with job placement after graduation. Job placement statistics may also be available from the office of institutional research. Such statistics can give you a good idea of how graduates fare in the job market.

- **What are the admissions criteria and policies?** Some institutions are very selective in their admissions and only take a fraction of the students who apply for admission. Others are less restrictive, and some have an "open door" policy—admitting anyone who applies and who meets minimum requirements. Community colleges are typically open-door institutions and have been instrumental in offering educational opportunities to many students who could not otherwise have attended college.

- **What are the qualifications of the faculty?** The instruction that you receive will only be as good as the instructors who deliver it. You can evaluate this factor by looking at the type and level of the faculty's degrees (bachelor's, master's, doctorate), institutions from which the degrees were obtained (well-respected?), and the percentage of full-time (versus part-time) faculty. In general, a high percentage of full-time faculty with advanced degrees from respected universities would be most desirable.

- **What is the student-to-faculty ratio?** Class size is an important measure of educational quality. The fewer students in a class, the more personal attention can be given to each student. A class size of less than 25 students is desirable.

- **Are the facilities and equipment up to date?** This is particularly important if your program of study involves the use of such equipment. Scientific, technical, trade-related, and health care programs require equipment that is state-of-the-art if effective training is to be delivered.

- **What kind of financial assistance is available?** Most institutions offer a package of financial assistance to students with demonstrated financial need. This package usually consists of a combination of scholarships, grants, part-time work, and loans. Additional information can be obtained from the financial aid office of any educational institution.

- **What is the attrition rate for entering students?** The percentage of students who drop out after one year is often a useful piece of information. This can indicate the difficulty of course work, the effectiveness of support services, institutional retention policies, and/or the dedication of the school's students.

- **What is the primary method of instruction?** Is instruction typically delivered through lectures? Classroom discussion? Independent study? Computer-assisted instruction? Field experience? Laboratory work? This may vary from one instructor or course to another.

To enroll in college, you will be required to complete an official admissions application and submit official transcripts from any other schools you have attended. It's a good idea to inquire regarding financial assistance as soon as you decide to apply, since the process to determine your eligibility almost always requires additional paperwork, documentation of income, and often a month or longer in processing time. The following sections will help prepare you for some of the stages you must pass through to get started in college.

Testing Tips

*I*f you are applying for a training or educational program that involves academic course work, you will usually be required either to submit the results of a standardized college admissions test (such as the SAT or ACT) or to take another exam that measures your basic English, reading, and mathematics skills. Some schools use the results for purposes of screening applicants, while others (such as community colleges) often use them only to advise students as to the proper level of academic skill courses.

To score your best on such exams, you may wish to:

- **Seek assistance** with tutoring or otherwise brush up on your academic skills. This is particularly important in regard to mathematics skills that you may not have used in some time. This kind of assistance is typically offered by educational institutions and by private organizations conducting preparation sessions for a fee.

- **Obtain some information in advance** about exactly what kinds of skills will evaluated by the test. This will focus your study efforts.

- **The day before testing, spend 15 to 20 minutes in a relaxed state** and imagine yourself in the testing situation; picture yourself as relaxed and confident while you take the exam.

- **Eat a *light* meal before the session.** This will give you energy that can only help the old brain! A mixture of carbohydrate and protein is usually best. Beware eating too much; it could make you mentally sluggish or even sleepy.

- **Get to the testing session on time and well rested.** If you are late, you may not be admitted; even if you do gain entry, you are likely to be frazzled before you begin.

- **Make sure you bring with you any materials that may be required** (#2 pencils with erasers, scratch paper, picture identification, reading glasses, etc.).

- **Do not bring children with you.** Leave them at home with a sitter or with a friend or relative. They will not be allowed into the testing room, and the last thing you want to worry about is what they are getting into while you are trying to remember how to work quadratic equations!

- **Ask questions** to clarify instructions before the test begins. Once testing has begun, questions are not usually permitted.

- **Find out if there is a penalty for guessing** on multiple-choice questions; if not, try to mark an answer for every item.

- **If you can't answer a question** within a reasonable period of time, it is better to move on to the next item. This makes it more likely that you will have the opportunity to answer all the questions to which you know the answer. If time remains when you have finished those you can easily answer, go back to those you skipped and give them another try.

- **Write down the answer** to a multiple-choice item *before* you look at the alternatives. If the answer you write down matches one of the alternatives, you can be more confident about its being the correct answer.

- **Wear a watch** and keep track of the time limits allowed for each test. This will help you to pace yourself.

- **Focus on the problems one at a time.** Don't worry about your total score, your previous answers, or the problems to come. Your total concentration should be on that one problem until you have solved it or until you decide to skip it.

- **Suspend self-critical thought.** Don't scold yourself or second-guess yourself as you go through the test. Remain as relaxed and confident as possible.

- **Look for clues** in a question that may provide information related to other questions. Sometimes an answer to a question will trigger your memory and help you remember something about another question.

■ **Read the answers first on multiple-choice reading tests.** If you know the questions you will have to answer, you can focus your attention more effectively as you read the passage.

These suggestions are only some of the methods you can use to improve your test-taking performance. If you suffer from test anxiety, you may want to seek counseling assistance.

SCHOOL

Travelog #31

*D*o you experience undue anxiety when you have to take a test?

■ If so, what are the symptoms?

■ If so, when do you first remember experiencing these symptoms?

■ If so, what do you currently do to try to control this anxiety?

■ Do you feel that the results of tests you take truly reflect what you know? If not, what kind of evaluation do you prefer?

■ List three (3) things you can do that might improve your ability to perform in testing situations.

1.

2.

3.

Many schools will require that you attend an orientation. If you take an institutional entrance exam, this session is sometimes used to review your test results.

Benefits of College Orientation

A new-student orientation can range from a few hours to a few days and is designed to provide you with important information. Some of the objectives of this session are:

- **You will feel more at home on campus.** You will usually receive a map of the campus and may even be offered a tour of the facilities.

- **You will be familiar with resources on campus.** You'll be introduced to learning labs, the library, computer labs, the counseling and advising offices, and other important resources.

- **You might get to meet key staff.** You will usually be introduced to some of the college staff who can be most helpful to you—counselors and advisors. Often, the dean or another administrative officer will welcome you to campus.

- **You will be alerted to important policies and procedures.** The college catalog contains a lot of valuable information. Key sections of the catalog are usually covered during orientation. You may also receive a student handbook that summarizes the information that is most important to new students.

- **You will be provided with information about registering for classes.** Registration policies and procedures are covered in detail. There may be a mock registration or, in some cases, you may even be allowed to register as part of the orientation process. Some initial course advisement is commonly provided at this point to make sure you register for the right classes.

- **You will get a chance to ask questions.** The staff who run the orientation expect you to have many questions and are prepared to provide you with the answers you need. Ask away!

- **You will get a chance to meet other new students.** You will find out that you are not alone in whatever apprehensions you may have. It can also help to have a few familiar faces on campus when you begin to attend classes.

The orientation session can be a valuable source for the information you need to get started. Another way to get some of this information is to review the college catalog thoroughly.

Things to Find in Your Catalog

You should ask for whatever literature is available to new students. The college catalog is usually a storehouse of information, providing details about:

- **Important dates and deadlines.** A college calendar is commonly included in the catalog. This calendar provides beginning and ending dates for each term, application deadlines, withdrawal deadlines, graduation application deadlines, and other important dates.

- **Descriptions of various programs of study.** A description of the college's training and degree programs should be in the catalog. The requirements for each type of program will either be listed or you will be told how to obtain this information.

- **Specific course descriptions.** A short description of the content of a course will help you select from among course options. Typically, the description will also note any *prerequisites* (a course that must be taken beforehand) or *corequisites* (a course that must be taken simultaneously) that apply.

- **Descriptions of services available to students.** The college's academic and counseling services are described briefly. The counseling or advising office on campus is usually a good place to begin if you have questions about these services.

- **Explanation of student rights and responsibilities.** As a student, you have certain rights with which you should be familiar. You are also responsible for maintaining legal and ethical behavior while on campus and are subject to penalties for infractions. Be sure to read this section of the catalog. Ignorance is no excuse!

- **Names and position titles of faculty and administrative staff.** Full-time faculty and administrative staff are usually listed in the back of the catalog, along with an indication of their degrees and the institutions that granted these degrees.

- **Grading policies and standards.** The college will present its standard grading scale in the catalog. Individual instructors may have specific grading policies that apply to their particular courses, and these are typically described in a course syllabus handed out the first day of class.

■ **Graduation requirements.** Requirements for graduation are spelled out in the catalog. You should not, however, rely solely on this information. There are often graduation requirements that are not listed in the catalog. Also, be aware that such requirements sometimes change, owing to legislation or curricular revisions. Often this kind of updated information may be obtained only by meeting with a counselor or advisor.

The catalog is one document that you should read from cover to cover, paying special attention to the topics listed in the preceding checklist. Sometimes a student handbook may be available that provides supplemental information of special interest to students. Student newspapers may also supply valuable information.

SCHOOL ▸ Travelog #32

U sing a college catalog of the institution you attend, or plan to attend, locate the following items and record the page numbers where you found them.

ITEM	PAGE #
Beginning and ending dates for each term	_____
Admissions requirements	_____
Graduation requirements	_____
Course descriptions	_____
Course withdrawal policy and/or deadlines	_____
Degrees offered	_____
Student rights and responsibilities	_____
Grading scale	_____
Student support services	_____
College costs (tuition and fees)	_____
Financial aid information	_____
Student activities	_____
Career counseling services	_____
Names of faculty and administrators	_____

Another thing you may want to find in the catalog is the institutional policy regarding acceptance of credit-by-exam. The College-Level Examination Program (CLEP) is a national program that allows you to earn college credit based on your knowledge of a subject, rather than by attending a traditional class.

Credit by Exam

*B*y scoring at a certain level on a national exam, you can actually be awarded college credit that counts toward completion of your program of study. CLEP credit is accepted by over 2800 accredited educational institutions. There are five General Examinations and 30 Subject Examinations available. All exams are 90 minutes in duration and cost $40 each at the time of this writing. The price is subject to change; some institutions also charge an additional administration fee.

The **General Examinations** cover the following topics:

- **English Composition** tests a variety of writing skills and the ability to apply rules of standard written English. **English Composition with Essay** requires that a 45-minute essay be written in addition to a multiple-choice section covering college-level writing skills. A college will usually only accept one of the two English exams; be sure to find out which one is approved for credit by your institution.

- **Humanities** covers a variety of topics typically covered in humanities, literature, and fine arts courses. Questions focus on poetry, fiction, drama, painting, music, sculpture, architecture, and dance.

- **Mathematics** covers topics usually taught in beginning college courses. Skills that are tested include arithmetic, algebra, geometry, logic, functions, and statistics.

- **Natural Sciences** deals with topics covered in basic biological and physical science courses. Questions cover subjects such as classification of organisms, genetics, evolution, cell structure, ecology, atomic structure, chemical elements, electricity, astronomy, and geology.

- **Social Sciences and History** covers material related to subjects like psychology, sociology, anthropology, U.S. history, Western civilization, economics, and political science.

CLEP **Subject Exams** are grouped into five general categories.

- **History and Social Science exams** cover the following subjects:

American Government	American History
Human Growth and Development	Educational Psychology
Macroeconomics	Microeconomics
General Psychology	Introductory Sociology
Western Civilization	

- **Foreign Language exams** cover two different levels of French, German, and Spanish.

- **Composition and Literature exams** cover topics related to:

American Literature	College Composition
Analysis and Interpretation of Literature	English Literature
Freshman English	

- **Science and Mathematics exams** cover subjects related to:

College Algebra	Trigonometry
Calculus	Biology
Chemistry	

- **Business exams** are offered in areas such as:

Information Systems	Management
Accounting	Business Law
Marketing	

Specific exam titles are listed in the CLEP "Information for Candidates and Registration Form." It is important to note that this information is subject to change. Also, each institution establishes its own policies concerning which CLEP tests to accept and which of their courses CLEP credit may apply to. You can contact your college's counseling or testing office to receive a list of CLEP exams approved for credit. This information should also indicate the minimum cut-off scores required for acceptance of credit and the amount of credit awarded.

CLEP examinations provide the opportunity to earn credit for the knowledge you have acquired, regardless of how you have done so. CLEP credit can save you time, money, and effort as you move toward your educational and career goals. If you are interested in obtaining more information about CLEP, talk to an educational counselor and/or write CLEP, P.O. Box 6600, Princeton, NJ 08541-6600 (telephone: 609-951-1026).

Other Kinds of Training

Not every occupation requires a college education, nor can everyone take advantage of a traditional college education. Fortunately, there are a number of other options available.

- **Correspondence courses** can be a viable option for people who are highly motivated students, good readers, and independent learners. These courses may be delivered by mail, television, radio, telephone, or even computers. They are available from, or sponsored by, colleges, universities, the military, professional business organizations, private schools, and the government. If you want further information about this kind of training, contact the National Home Study Council, 1601 18th St. N.W., Washington, DC 20009; and the National University Extension Association, Suite 360, One Dupont Circle, Washington, DC 20036.

- **External degree programs** provide a means for individuals to obtain a college degree with minimal time in the classroom. These programs are designed for people who work full-time or who, for some other reason, choose not to attend regular college classes. Typically, each student is assigned an educational coordinator who assists with the design and supervision of a flexible program of study. Some residence on campus is usually required, but most of the work is done through field work, self-study, library research, or on-the-job assignments. A good source for further information is University Without Walls, 35 Richmond St., Providence, RI 02903.

- **Private trade, technical, and business schools** are another alternative. Such schools can often provide nondegree occupational training for entry-level positions. The training is usually focused on specific job skills and does not require general education courses beyond those directly related to the occupational requirements. Classes are often small, and the training period is of short duration. On the downside, course work may not be transferrable and the cost is usually several times that of comparable training in a public institution. For further information, contact the National Association of Trade and Technical Schools, 2021 L Street N.W., Washington, DC 20009.

- **Apprenticeship** is a time-honored method of training in the skilled trades. Classroom learning is combined with on-the-job training by a master craftsperson. The apprentice is paid while learning, with pay increasing as training progresses (usually requiring up to four years). There is tough competition for entrance into apprenticeship programs, and such programs are often physically demanding. For more information, contact your State Employment Service or look under "Labor Organizations" in the Yellow Pages of your phone book.

- **Industry training programs** are usually sponsored by large corporations, serving the company's new or existing employees. Such training is used to prepare new employees, upgrade the skills of existing employees, assist employees in qualifying for promotions, introduce new product lines, and so forth. It is offered only to company employees, usually on work time, and is focused on the needs of the company. Check with your employer's Human Resources office for more information.

- **Government training** programs are designed to address problems related to unemployment, lack of job opportunity, and social inequity. These programs usually provide subsidized training and special counseling services to individuals who qualify based on income, education, or other barriers to employment. Contact your local State Employment Service office for further information.

- **Military training** is provided for active duty personnel in the armed forces. Course work and on-the-job training are used to prepare military personnel for their duties. State-of-the-art training is provided in a great variety of areas, but military job skills are not always directly transferrable to civilian positions. The military is also affiliated with a number of colleges and universities offering correspondence courses for credit. This credit can be directly applied to degree programs at colleges and universities throughout the nation. In addition, the military offers a number of benefits you can use to save money to further your education after your military duty is concluded. For more information, contact a military recruiter.

Although multiple options for training exist, many jobs require a college education, and most people choose to go the traditional route for such an education. The next chapter will focus on strategies to increase your chances of success in higher education.

Quiz 7

*P*lease answer the following questions.

1. Why is it important to consider the different levels at which you can enter an occupation?

2. List two (2) key factors that contributed, or will contribute, to your choice of a college.

   a.

   b.

3. Describe at least one "testing tip" that is not listed in this chapter. Why do you think it would be helpful?

4. List two (2) benefits of obtaining credit by exam.

   a.

   b.

5. Has the information in this chapter influenced your tentative occupational choice? Why, or why not?

6. What is the most important thing that you learned about yourself by working through this chapter?

7. What topic covered in this chapter would you like to explore further?

To Consider . . .

1. Having a college degree often bestows a certain degree of status on the recipient. Certain occupations are often held in higher esteem than others.

   How important is this status in the world of work?

   How important is this status to you?

   Why is someone with a college degree often considered better qualified for a job than someone without one?

   Why do some jobs have a higher status than others?

   Why does job status often vary in different cultures?

2. External degree programs and correspondence courses require little or no on-campus instruction.

   What are the advantages of these kinds of programs?

   What are the possible disadvantages in terms of college life experience?

Suggested Activities

1. Interview several people who seem to be fearless when it comes to taking tests. How do they think about the testing situation? How do they prepare themselves?

2. Visit a college campus. Stop by the Admissions office and pick up a college catalog and an application for admissions. Review these materials.

The Parable of the Groundlings

*Z*ara and his disciple decided to sleep under the stars, beneath the overhanging branches of a tall oak tree. In the middle of the night they were awakened by a frightful storm, full of lightning and fury. They ran for the shelter of a nearby barn. Reaching the barn, they looked back toward the tree, only to see the oak struck by a surging bolt of lightning that lit the night sky. The air was shattered by a deafening blast of thunder that shook the barn and the ground on which it stood.

The next day, Zara took his disciple back to the great oak tree. Though scarred the length of its trunk, the tree was intact. Zara spoke: "What a grand tree is this! Alone in this meadow it reaches for the stars, grasping deep within the earth to steady its reach.

"Great are those who reach beyond themselves, who seek to extend their reach into the unknown. And dangerous is their reaching. The ground beneath such beings attracts fire from the skies. And many such Reachers have been struck by the vengeance that burns within the hearts of the timid and the fearful."

"The fearful lie close to the ground and hate those who dare to tower above them with their reaching. 'There is nothing worth reaching. A dangerous folly! Man was born of earth and was meant to stay close to it. Reaching is antisocial—some can reach higher than others—all must be the same!' So scream the groundlings. But those who dare to reach toward the sky hear this screaming as a distant whine and pay it no heed.

"Your mind naturally seeks the light of truth. Your reason is the sap that nourishes your seeking. Your imagination and vision draw strength from the earth as you reach toward the stars. Hard the Reachers must be, as hard as this great oak."

Zara turned to his disciple and spoke: "You must harden yourself if you wish to reach your destiny. Steady yourself by sending roots deep into life. And ready yourself for the lightning! And for the vengeful chattering of the groundlings."

CHAPTER EIGHT

On-the-Road Assistance

Preview

I know of no more encouraging fact than the unquestionable ability of [people] to elevate [their] life by conscious endeavor . . .
HENRY DAVID THOREAU

Once you are enrolled in the college of your choice, your success will be determined by many factors, not least of which is the advice you can obtain from others. There is no shame in becoming lost in a city you have never before visited, but this can often be avoided by seeking directions from those more familiar with the territory. This chapter suggests some road maps and some tour guides who can help point you toward your destination. The main sections of this chapter are described below.

- **How to Prepare for Advising** suggests some steps you can take, before you meet with an academic advisor, that will make this meeting more productive.
- **Advising Guidelines** will help you understand what to expect from your advisor and how to get the most from your advising session.
- **Secrets to College Success** is a list of commonsense strategies that can increase your chance of success in college.
- **Vital Study Skills** is a short survey of important academic skills that also provides suggested resources for further study.

By the end of this chapter, you should be able to identify a number of important methods that can increase your chances of realizing your educational and career goals.

Guidance is an important part of any journey. A few words from someone who has been down the road ahead of you can often save you a great deal of trouble. Once you've decided to return to school, academic planning becomes an important element. Any school you attend will have staff designated as academic advisors. These advisors are trained to assist you in translating your training needs into a program of study that will meet these needs. This chapter will cover a few of the more important things you should know about working with an advisor.

How to Prepare for Advising

*I*f you have completed the exercises in the *Career Guide* and followed the suggested guidelines, you and your counselor or advisor should be able to work out a program plan that will show you what courses you must take to achieve your career goal. Once you have this information, it is up to you to follow this program of study.

If you change your mind, it is no problem; simply make another appointment with your counselor or advisor. You should be aware, however, that a change of major may involve a significant change in the course work involved, sometimes requiring additional course work in order to meet the requirements.

Also, catalog requirements do change, and the requirements within a given catalog may only be honored for a given period of time. If you are, or plan to be, attending school part-time, you may want to ask an educational counselor how you might be affected by such changes.

Here are a few things that you can do to prepare for your advising appointment:

■ **Have a tentative career goal (or some options) in mind.** Up to a point, it really doesn't matter too much what your major may be; there are certain requirements that everyone must satisfy (for example, certain English and mathematics courses). If you focus on these general requirements initially, you can buy yourself some time to make a decision about your specific program of study. But, once you have taken most of these general requirements, further selection of course work may be difficult if you have no specific major in mind, particularly if you plan to continue your education to a bachelor's degree or higher. Until you have an idea where you are headed, it will be impossible to provide you with a detailed list of all the courses you will need as part of your program of study. One reason for this is that different majors require specific prerequisites as a part of your lower-division program of study. For example, if you plan to be a Business major, the Business School will probably require that you take a number of specific accounting, economics, mathematics, and computer courses before you will be admitted. Obviously, the sooner you know about these requirements, the easier it will be to work them into your program of study.

- **Have an idea what occupational level you desire.** There are often a number of options within a given field of study. If you are interested in accounting, for example, you may have a choice between an Associate in Science degree in Accounting Technology and an Associate in Arts degree leading to a bachelor's degree in accounting. If you want to become a Certified Public Accountant (CPA), additional requirements apply. The clearer you are concerning your goal, the easier it will be for an advisor to assist you.

- **If you plan to transfer, have a major and a college or university in mind.** Most colleges and universities have their own specific admissions requirements, and these requirements often carry additional stipulations related to the major you select. It is important that you have the specific requirements for the major at the institution you plan to attend, and that you assume this may change if your plans change. Your advisor is your best source for this information.

- **Read the information in the college catalog.** This is the single best source for general (and some specific) information about the college, its programs, services, policies, and procedures. Read it carefully! This will also assure that your advisor doesn't have to spend valuable time explaining what is already written in the catalog.

- **Write down any specific questions you have.** Give some thought to what you want to cover during the advising session and write down the topics. This will help ensure that you will get all of the information you need and it will free up your memory for other things.

- **Bring along any documentation of previous education or training.** If you have attended any other colleges and your transcripts are not yet on file, an unofficial copy will be very helpful for advising purposes. If you don't have an unofficial transcript, grade reports can serve the same function.

Do not worry if you can't satisfy all of these suggestions, especially when it comes to having a clear career goal; such concerns can be dealt with at the advising session itself. This session can be a valuable experience if you will follow a few simple guidelines.

Advising Guidelines

When you meet with your counselor or advisor, you will want to make the most of this opportunity. The following guidelines are suggested for your consideration:

- **Be prepared to share your concerns, doubts, thoughts, and feelings.** The advisor cannot read your mind. You should be candid and straightforward about any questions and concerns.

- **Ask questions** to clarify anything you do not understand. This is usually the most direct way to find out what you want to know. Also, letting something pass that you do not understand can often cause problems down the road.

- **Listen carefully and take notes** of things you want to remember. This will provide a written record of what was said in the session and you won't have to rely on your memory for details.

- **Ask for a written copy of advising recommendations** for your own records. You should receive a copy of any forms that are completed as part of the advising process. Then you are protected in case the original is misplaced.

- **Keep a file of all the advising information you receive.** Your own personal advising folder can be very important. If you keep a record of everything you receive, you will have the documentation you need if a question ever arises about the accuracy of the information you received.

- **Bring along your program advising sheet** (if you already have one) and ask questions about anything you don't understand. If you are seeing a new advisor, it's a good idea to bring along your last advising sheet or, better yet, your entire personal advising file. Your new advisor should have access to the previous advisor's records, but this is not always the case.

- **See your advisor whenever your program of study changes,** and also when you think you are within two terms of graduation. Changes in a major can cause changes in course requirements; check out requirements as soon as you begin to consider a change of major. The closer you get to graduation, the more critical it becomes that you have regular advising sessions to make sure you stay on track. Some colleges require advising at certain points of your academic program; others leave it up to you to initiate contact when assistance is desired. If you are not required to attend regular advising sessions, it's a good idea to check with your advisor every couple of terms or whenever you have any doubt about what you are doing.

- **Start checking on university admissions** 9 to 12 months before you plan to graduate (if you are a community college A.A. student). Some limited-access programs have early application deadlines (which can be up to a year in advance of entry) and may require additional application materials, an interview, an audition, or other special documentation. You might also note that you are usually required to have a *complete* application package turned in by the deadline; it's a good idea to start early in case any questions arise about the materials you submit.

- **Don't expect the advisor to make decisions for you.** Your advisor can provide you many kinds of useful information and can make recommendations with regard to certain issues; but, he or she cannot assume responsibility for making the decisions you alone can make. He or she can help clarify requirements, alternatives, and consequences, but the decisions (and the responsibility) will always be your own.

■ **Don't expect the advisor to comment on or recommend instructors.** This is a matter of professional courtesy and political realism on the part of the advisor. Much of the information advisors receive about professors is in the form of secondhand comments from students that cannot be easily verified. Advisors will not convey this kind of information to other students. If you want to know what other students think about a given professor, ask students who have taken a class from that professor and take what you receive with a grain (or a dash!) of salt.

■ **Ask your advisor to help you determine an appropriate course load.** Especially when you are just beginning, it is difficult to predict how much work will be required by a given number of classes. This decision may be affected by the nature of the courses you take, your other commitments, your academic history, how long you have been out of school, your level of academic confidence, and other such factors.

Travelog #33

■ Have you ever met with an educational advisor?

If so, was the experience helpful? How so?

If not, why not?

■ List three (3) benefits of meeting with an educational advisor.
   1.

   2.

   3.

■ List three (3) questions that you would ask an advisor, given the opportunity.

1.

2.

3.

Advising is an important step down the road to your educational goal. The next section will provide you with some of the "secrets" that can help you make sure your educational journey is a pleasant one.

Secrets to College Success

Success in your college studies is the result of many factors. The following list attempts to summarize some practical things you can do to increase your chances of success. None of these suggestions are really "secret"; they are time-tested methods that have been used by many successful students.

- **Have a clear goal in mind.** Such clarity of purpose will make it easier to maintain your motivational level. Without a clear goal, you may have a tendency to wander and to become frustrated by requirements that seem to have no purpose. Requirements that are steppingstones to a goal of your own choosing are often easier to accept. If you do *not* have a clear goal, take action to help yourself formulate one. The career planning you are doing should help you develop a concrete goal for attending college. You might also think in terms of short-term goals (for example, maintaining a high grade-point average) while you are in the process of clarifying long-term goals.

- **Have an academic plan.** With such a plan, you know what classes are required by your program of study. Refer to this plan at regular intervals. This plan should clearly indicate courses that have prerequisites or involve a given sequence of completion. If your academic goals change, be sure to see an advisor and have your plan revised to reflect this change.

- **Set clear priorities.** Allocate your time in accordance with these priorities. Sometimes it helps actually to complete a schedule of how you currently spend your time during a typical week. Then examine this schedule to see if it really reflects what is most important to you. If not, make some changes.

- **Take a class load appropriate to your responsibilities.** It's often better to take a load that is too light (rather than too heavy) until you get a sense of what is workable for you. Too many people try to go to school full-time while they are also working full-time. More times than not, the result is poor school performance as well as reduced work efficiency and unhappy family members. Experiment and find the right balance for your particular situation.

- **Register as early as possible.** This helps to ensure a good selection of classes. Competition for some classes is fierce. If your school has a priority registration system, when you are able to register may be determined by factors such as how many credits you have on record. Make sure you know how your priority is determined.

- **Make use of the college resources.** Many resources are available to assist you with your academic and career progress: learning labs, computer resources, library assistance, and similar services. Such services should be listed in the college catalog. Counselors are also an excellent resource to use to access such services.

- **Be aware of college rules and regulations.** Abide by all such rules. Make sure you know about withdrawal deadlines, grade appeal procedures, and other academic regulations. Important deadlines will typically be listed in the college catalog or the student handbook.

- **Take advantage of learning/study skills classes.** Such classes will often count as an elective in your program of study and will benefit you in all the course work you must complete. If you cannot locate such a course, try to get hold of Ellis' *Becoming a Master Student*—a textbook commonly used for such a course. This book contains many helpful suggestions and is easily used as a self-study text.

- **Learn to use computer word processing.** This skill will increase your writing efficiency, will save you a great deal of time, and will enhance the quality of the work you submit to instructors—something that may affect your grades. The time that you spend learning a word-processing program will be repaid a hundred times over during your college years.

- **Take a course to increase your reading speed and comprehension.** By doubling your speed (a very realistic goal), you'll cut in half the time you spend on reading assignments. Time thus saved will allow more time for other assignments (or for some fun!).

- **Try never to miss a class, and come to class on time.** Attendance is a simple, but often overlooked, requirement for success. If you cannot avoid missing a class, let the instructor know ahead of time if at all possible. If this is not possible, get the notes from a fellow student as soon as possible, so you don't fall behind. Also, don't ask the professor if you will "miss anything" by not attending; your instructor will almost always think that you will be missing something and might be offended by such a question.

- **Be well prepared for every class.** Anticipate the class discussion and be prepared to participate actively in class. Some instructors use class participation as part of the assigned grade for the class. Even if this is not the case, you will learn more effectively if you are actively involved in the class. If you find it difficult to speak up in class, you should seek assistance from a counselor to address this concern; it can be a serious detriment to your academic progress.

- **Know all class requirements and grading policies.** Your instructor should provide you with a class syllabus the first day of class. This document usually covers the class requirements, attendance policy, reading assignments, exam schedule, and other important items of information. If you are not given a syllabus, make sure to ask enough questions to be absolutely clear about course requirements.

■ **Consult with your instructors.** Whenever you need assistance with a class, the first thing to do is to talk to your instructor. Instructors are almost always glad to help and often know about resources that may assist you. They are usually as concerned about your success as you are and will help you however they can. Most instructors have established office hours set aside to assist students with problems, concerns, special projects, and other class-related issues.

■ **Participate in a study group.** Share notes, discuss assignments, and quiz each other before exams. This kind of interaction can dramatically increase your retention of material and will make the class more enjoyable as well. If you can't join an established study group, form one of your own by approaching other students in your class who might be interested. Posting a notice in the student newspaper or on a board in the student center can also be effective strategy for starting a group.

■ **Never hesitate to ask a question.** Letting something go by without clarification only breeds confusion. Any professor who is concerned about your learning will take the time to answer your questions and will foster an environment where questioning is encouraged. This assumes, of course, that you have done what you should have done (read your assignments, for example) and that you are not asking something because you haven't taken the time to try to learn it yourself.

■ **Protect your intellectual rights.** Open-mindedness is a prerequisite for learning. Your best instructors will challenge your thinking in order to engage you in the intellectual process. However, there are times when you should assert your intellectual rights. If you feel that your instructor is abusing his or her power by intimidating, belittling, intentionally confusing, harassing, or otherwise undermining you or other students, you have the right, and responsibility, to question these practices. Most schools have a grievance policy to protect students against such rare occurrences.

■ **Review supplemental textbooks.** Other texts might clarify a topic that was not presented clearly in your text. Your librarian can help you find texts covering the same material in a different manner. You will often find that a different approach or different examples covering the same material can clarify something for you.

■ **Ask your fellow students to recommend instructors.** Don't look for easy instructors; rather try to find those who excel in their field, are helpful to students, and teach in a style compatible with your strengths. Take such advice judiciously—professors are sometimes judged unfairly by students who fail to take responsibility for their own failure.

- **Study, study, and study some more.** Simply put, if you don't study, you won't learn. Some subjects require more study than others; this is something that varies dramatically among students. You will have to study harder for those subjects that you don't particularly enjoy, but this too is part of the learning process.

As the last item indicates, studying is an important factor contributing to college success. It's not only important that you spend time studying, but also that you have learned to study effectively. After the following Travelog, you will evaluate your own study skills and consider if assistance with such skills might be helpful.

Travelog #34

■ List four (4) "secrets" that you think would be helpful to you.

1.

2.

3.

4.

■ Explain why each of the four "secrets" you listed would improve your academic success. Give specific examples from your own experience.

1.

2.

3.

4.

■ What is the one (1) most important thing you could do within the next week to improve your academic progress?

Vital Study Skills

*T*he effectiveness of your study skills directly affects your academic progress. The purpose of this section is to help you determine if you could benefit from study-skill development.

Read each item and circle either "Yes" or "No" in response. If you answer yes to one or more of the questions in a given area, you should strongly consider seeking assistance in that area. One of the best resources available for development of study skills is *Becoming a Master Student* by David Ellis; relevant chapters of this textbook are cited for each study skills area. Refer to the Bibliography for additional references that may be helpful.

Goals, Motivation, and Meaning

- Are you undecided about a major and/or an occupation?   Yes   No
- Do you lack a clear goal for attending school?   Yes   No
- Do you wish your life had more meaning or a clearer purpose?   Yes   No

If you answered "Yes" to a question above, these resources may be helpful:

- *Becoming a Master Student:* Chapter 1
- *For the New Intellectual*—Ayn Rand
- *Man's Search for Himself*—Rollo May
- *Man's Search for Meaning*—Viktor Frankl

See other listings under "Philosophy" in the Bibliography.

Academic Skills

- Do you have difficulty keeping up with reading assignments?   Yes   No
- Would you be more successful if you had stronger writing skills?   Yes   No
- Could you use some assistance with your mathematics skills?   Yes   No

If you answered "Yes" to a question above, these resources may be helpful:

- Learning Assistance Center (LAC) on campus
- Further assessment to decide proper course placement (see a counselor)
- Student tutors

- *Becoming a Master Student:* Chapter 4 (Reading)
- *Where There's a Will There's an "A"*—Claude Olney

Time Management

- Are you overwhelmed by too many commitments?   Yes   No
- Does it seem like you never have enough time?   Yes   No
- Are you always doing things at the last minute?   Yes   No

If you answered "Yes" to a question above, these resources may be helpful:

- *Becoming a Master Student:* Chapter 2
- Clarification of values to figure out priorities (see a counselor)
- *Get It All Done and Still Be Human*—Tony Fanning
- *Practical Time Management*—Marion Haynes
- *The Confident Student*—Carol Kanar
- *Eliminating Procrastination without Putting It Off*—Ross Van Ness
- *High Impact Time Management*—William Brooks and Terry Mullins
- *The Ninety-Minute Hour*—Jay Levinson
- *The Time Trap*—Alec Mackenzie

Memory

- Do you have trouble memorizing facts for exams?   Yes   No
- Do you often forget things that you want to remember?   Yes   No
- Do you wish you knew some more effective memory techniques?   Yes   No

If you answered "Yes" to a question above, these resources may be helpful:

- *Becoming a Master Student:* Chapter 3
- *Your Memory, a User's Guide*—Alan Baddeley
- *Use Your Perfect Memory*—Tony Buzan
- *Your Memory: How It Works and How to Improve It*—Kenneth Higbee
- *Remembering Made Easy*—Arthur Logan
- *Memory in the Real World*—Gillian Cohen
- *Super Memory, Super Student*—Harry Lorayne
- *Supermemory*—Douglas Herrman
- *Total Recall*—Joan Minninger

Note-Taking

- Do you have trouble understanding notes made in class? Yes No
- Do you have trouble knowing what to write down in your notes? Yes No
- Do your notes often leave out important points that you need to know? Yes No

If you answered "Yes" to a question above, these resources may be helpful:

- *Becoming a Master Student*: Chapter 5
- *Student Success Secrets*—Eric Jensen

Test-Taking

- Do you tend to panic during a test? Yes No
- Do you feel that testing doesn't reflect what you know? Yes No
- Are you often unpleasantly surprised by what is on a test? Yes No

If you answered "Yes" to a question above, these resources may be helpful:

- *Becoming a Master Student*: Chapter 6
- *How to Beat Test Anxiety*—James Divine
- *Help Is on the Way for Tests*—Marilyn Berry
- *Test-Taking Power*—Fred Orr
- *Test Taking Strategies*—Judi Kesselman-Turkel
- *Test Taking Techniques*—Mildred Manwarren

Once you have focused on the study skills that you need to polish, you will find the road to academic success becoming much smoother. The following Travelog relates your experience to these skills.

Travelog #35

■ List two (2) of the study skills that give you the most trouble. Describe how this difficulty affects your learning progress. Then list one resource you think might be helpful in addressing this difficulty.

1. _____

Affect:

Resource:

2. _____

Affect:

Resource:

■ List the two (2) study skills that you think are your strongest. Describe how you developed these skills and how you might improve them even further.

1. _____

Developed by:

Improved by:

2. _____

Developed by:

Improved by:

This book began with a discussion of issues that establish a framework for your career planning. The next chapter fulfills a similar function by addressing various stages of human development and the influence of philosophy upon your life and your Way.

Quiz 8

Please answer the following questions.

1. Name two (2) benefits of seeking academic advising.

   a.

   b.

2. Name two (2) things that an academic advisor *cannot* do for you.

   a.

   b.

3. List two (2) reasons why study skills can contribute to college success.

   a.

   b.

4. Why is it valuable to have a sense of your learning strengths and limitations?

5. Has the information in this chapter influenced your tentative occupational choice? Why, or why not?

6. What is the most important thing that you learned about yourself by working through this chapter?

7. What topic covered in this chapter would you like to explore further?

To Consider . . .

1. Students are sometimes reluctant to seek the assistance of a counselor.

   What factors might contribute to this reluctance?

   What might be some of the consequences of this reluctance?

   How would you convince a friend to seek such help?

2. To what degree do you think students are responsible for their own academic planning?

   Should academic planning sessions be required of everybody? Or only certain categories of students? Why, or why not?

Suggested Activities

1. Make a list of subjects that you would like to learn just for the sake of learning.

2. Make an appointment with an advisor to discuss your educational plan.

The Parable of Zara's Animals

*Z*ara sat in the woods with his two animals: an eagle and a serpent. He spoke to them: "My dear eagle, how high you fly! And with such power and silent grace. I envy your easy overcoming of Gravity; at times, I feel crushed by its weight. To defy Gravity is the task of all those who would have high thoughts and lofty callings.

"And my serpent, how easily you shed one skin for another! Your growth will not be stopped by the limits of your skin. So courageous and bold you are—to shed your skin before you would shed the possibility of further growth. I am feeling constrained by this old skin of who I was, being stretched thin by what I have become. To shed one's skin is the task of all those who would grow beyond themselves, into themselves."

Zara paused and took a deep and slow breath. He stared down at his animals for a long time. Then he spoke again: "Alas! I have no wings, and this skin will not molt. Am I to be crushed from without and from within?" He then lay down on the ground and fell into a deep sleep. He slept for two days and two nights, his animals staying close by his side, protecting him.

On the morning of the third day, Zara awoke and slowly got to his feet. He spoke: "My faithful animals, what a dream I had! A flying and molting dream! How strange are these animals called Man and Woman, and how powerful! They have no wings and yet they fly. They have but one skin and yet they molt and grow. At least some of them—the Flyers and the Molters."

Zara spoke to his eagle: "The Flyers take flight upon the wings of thought and laugh in the face of Gravity. The wings of a strong mind delight in defying Gravity. The Flyers have minds as deep and clear as the sky above. With powerful vision, they spot the truth and the meaning that hides upon the earth, diving with lightning speed and sinking their claws deep into that which they seek. They soar above the earth and view all things from above. How small are our miseries when viewed from above. How uplifting are the winds of change when we take wing!"

He then turned to his serpent: "The Molters risk their skin in order to change. They refuse to be bound by what they were. They are unafraid of changes that accompany growth. The Molters nourish themselves on wisdom and wash it down with the juice of courage. They defy those who would hold them to a skin that no longer fits. How empty is the skin we leave behind. How small, thin, scaly, and torn it is!

"This dream has given me a new vision of Man and Woman. These human creatures have a power that belies their lack of wings and molting skin. They have a mind that flies in defiance of Gravity. They have a being that transforms their identity as they grow. But these treasures are for naught without their greatest gift—the fire of their will! It is their will that teaches their mind to fly and their being to grow. Without a will of their own, they remain tied to the earth. Without a will of their own, they remain small and shriveled within. And yet, so many of them are without such a will . . . ."

Zara seemed saddened by this thought. He fell silent for awhile. But then he arose with great energy, looked down at his beloved animals and spoke: "Come, my animal friends. Let us return to the world. Let us call forth some lightning from the sky! Some lightning to scatter the herds of the soggy-spirited. Some lightning to ignite the wills of the Flyers and the Molters."

Further Exploration

Part Four broadens the scope of your career exploration journey. Chapter Nine will focus on how your career development is related to various stages of personal development and to the development of a personal philosophy. Chapter Ten explains how the process of change plays a part in your career and your life.

Life's Crossroads

YIELD

Preview

What was the meaning of the South-Sea Exploring Expedition, with all its parade and expense, but an indirect recognition of the fact that . . . it is easier to sail many thousand miles through cold and storm and cannibals, in a government ship, with five hundred [shipmates] to assist one, than it is to explore the private sea, the Atlantic and Pacific Ocean of one's being . . .

HENRY DAVID THOREAU

There are many turning points in life. These points involve basic issues that affect significant aspects of your personal well-being and have direct effects on your career planning. To the extent that you address such issues successfully, you will be able to chart a true course in the "Atlantic and Pacific Ocean" of your being. Resolving developmental issues is not always easy—you must often face "cold and storm and cannibals"—but the shape of your future depends on your ability to do so. Developmental issues that are unresolved, or that are resolved in a less than healthy manner, can delay or distort further development. The information in this chapter may contribute to a better understanding of some of these issues. The main sections of this chapter are as follows.

- **Developmental Principles** explains the basic assumptions underlying a discussion of personal development.
- **Developmental Crossroads** lists some of the key stages of adult development.
- **Confidence: Can I Do It?** describes a stage of development associated with a basic sense of being able to cope with life events.
- **Independence: My Way** explains a stage of development that involves the ability to establish individual autonomy in the context of healthy relationships with others.
- **Identity: Who Am I?** addresses the process of establishing a realistic and stable sense of self.
- **Direction: Where Am I Going?** describes the need to define a sense of direction in your life.
- **Meaning: Why Am I Here?** explains issues related to the search for a meaningful path in life that transcends personal desires.

- **Practical Philosophy** explains the importance and relevance of philosophy as the foundation of career planning and your search for meaning.

- **Guiding Signs** recommends a number of methods that address developmental issues and should be useful to those who want some ideas about how to seek further information and assistance.

By the time you finish this chapter, you should have a framework to help you understand developmental issues that may affect your career planning; also, you may have a better idea how to constructively confront basic developmental and philosophical issues in your life.

Life cannot be neatly compartmentalized. What happens in one part of your life will influence every other part of your life one way or another, at one time or another. This chapter deals with the context of your career search: *your life!*

You are reading this book because you want to make a realistic, rewarding, and satisfying career decision. You want a job that is compatible with your interests—that makes use of your skills and reflects your values. You want to live in adequate comfort and to look forward to going to work. You'd like to feel that you are doing something significant and personally fulfilling. You'd like for it all to fit into a meaningful Way of life.

The purpose of this chapter is to provide a structure that will help you take a look at how your career choice is embedded in the larger context of your life. The first step of this process is to understand some general developmental principles.

Developmental Principles

On the path to your career destination, you will cross many roads. These crossroads are a part of the journey as well; they provide bearings that help you find your Way. Each crossroad represents a significant issue in your growth and maturation that affects almost every other area of your life. Many outstanding researchers have studied how people change and grow throughout their lives. In general, they agree on five key principles:

- **Growth follows a pattern of stages.** Psychological growth follows a general pattern of development, just as physical growth does. It is no surprise to anyone that childhood is a definable stage of development with a given set of characteristics (learning to walk, feed oneself, control physical functions). Psychological growth is very much the same, in that there are stages people go through that involve a common set of developmental tasks. This does not mean, however, that everyone will progress lock-step through the process.

People progress at different rates, are delayed or stopped at different stages, and may even deal with issues in a different order.

- **Each stage is organized around a key life issue or task.** The developmental tasks identified in this chapter are significant crossroads in adult life. They involve your ability to cope with the world, to assume adult responsibilities, to establish your own identity, and to direct your life meaningfully.

- **Grappling with such issues will challenge you to grow** and often involves some anxiety, confusion, and sense of loss. As you grow, you will be forced to change. The fetus, comfortable in the warm and accommodating womb, is forced through a radical change as it is born into this world. Likewise, each of us must leave comfortable ways of thinking and acting if we are to live up to our true potential. We too must grow through many radical changes.

- **Successful resolution prepares you to address the next stage.** As you successfully grow through one stage, you develop the skills that will help you meet the next challenge. Psychological growth is an organic process that, given the right circumstances, happens naturally.

- **Lack of resolution will hinder and/or distort further development.** Unfortunately, the circumstances for natural development are rarely ideal. Lack of proper nurturance, trust, support, or other important elements can inhibit or complicate the growth process. When this delays or distorts the resolution of key issues, further development can be negatively affected, or even arrested. Then a person may try to deal with the world in a manner that was suitable to an earlier stage of development. Since this behavior is no longer appropriate, it usually causes personal, interpersonal, and career difficulties. You may know people who act "immature for their age" or seem as if they "never grew up"—this is the result of arrested development.

The first principle suggests that developmental growth occurs in stages. The next section presents several stages that have particular relevance to the career planning process.

Developmental Crossroads

*T*his growth process becomes very important when you are considering something as complex as the choice of an occupation. Such a choice will be directly influenced by the resolution (or lack of resolution) of basic life issues.

Such life crossroads must be negotiated carefully. Each crossing demands your attention, thought, and consideration to particular issues. You must be willing to confront difficult issues and to take risks in order to grow.

The next five sections are based on a few of the growth issues commonly recognized by those who study adult development. Erik Erikson and Arthur Chickering deserve much credit for the groundbreaking work they have done in this area. Chickering expanded the ideas of Erikson and proposed seven "vectors of student development": Developing Competence, Managing Emotions, Developing Autonomy, Establishing Identity, Freeing Interpersonal Relationships, Developing Purpose, and Developing Integrity. If you want to review some research that has a conceptual relationship to what is presented in this chapter, refer to Chickering's classic textbook, which is listed in the Bibliography.

This chapter's sections present an outline of the following key developmental crossroads:

- **Confidence.** A basic sense of being adequate to the task of dealing with the world.

- **Independence.** The ability to establish autonomy within the context of meaningful social relationships.

- **Identity.** The ability to define and establish yourself as a unique human being.

- **Direction.** To have clear goals in your life and a sense of how to move toward these goals.

- **Meaning.** To have a sense of purpose, destiny, and significance in your life.

As you pass through each of these intersections, you will be gathering information important to your career decision making. These developmental issues have an obvious connection to your career planning. Unless you have **Confidence**, you are not likely to realize your true potential in the world of work. Without appropriate **Independence**, you will risk confronting either isolation or a lack of personal integrity. **Identity** is the foundation of the kind of self-analysis vital to determining career plans. **Direction** is one of the obvious outcomes of an effective career planning process. **Meaning** is the underlying force that motivates career planning, as well as its hoped-for result. Each of these developmental factors is separately addressed in the following sections.

It is worth noting that these developmental characteristics are "culture-bound" to some degree. Individuals in different cultures may have different conceptions about the significance of independence or identity, for example. Some cultures do not stress personal autonomy and individualism as they have been emphasized in the United States. Such cultural variations are not completely understood by developmental researchers at this point, but keep in mind that people from other cultural backgrounds may not follow the developmental pattern described in this chapter. Their developmental pattern (and they have one) is determined, to some extent, by the characteristic world view of their culture and the values and expectations that derive from such a view.

Confidence: Can I Do It?

All of us strive for a sense of personal capability—a feeling of confidence in our ability to meet the challenges of life (such as succeeding in the occupation you choose). Confidence is something that is developed as a result of experience, by learning to use your primary tool of survival—your mind. Humans have climbed to the top of the food chain, *not* because of their claws, teeth, sense of smell, strength, speed, or visual acuity; many other animals have advantages when it comes to such mechanisms of survival. Human beings have succeeded as a species primarily because of their ability to think, reason, and create. Your confidence is fundamentally based on your mind's ability to deal with reality. Fear, confusion, irrationality, dependence, and illusion will undermine this ability. Confidence requires clear thinking, based on a firm grasp of objective reality.

Confidence also requires courage. Each time you face a challenge and are able to deal with it effectively, this sense of confidence is strengthened. Each time you back away from, or otherwise fail to deal with, a challenge, this confidence is weakened. As Robert de Ropp wrote in *Warrior's Way*: "Strength exerted equals greater strength; weakness indulged equals greater weakness."

Genuine confidence has little to do with arrogance or egotistical self-inflation. Indeed, arrogance can often be a compensation for a *lack* of confidence. True confidence is a balanced feeling and an expression of personal security.

Please answer the following questions by circling the answer of your choice.

- Do you welcome situations that involve learning   Yes   No
  new skills?

- Do you assume you have the ability to succeed in a job?   Yes   No

- Do you want a position in life that challenges you?   Yes   No

- Do you assume that you will usually succeed at things   Yes   No
  you try?

- Do you keep trying when faced with a lack of success?   Yes   No

If you answered "No" to any of the items above, confidence may be an area in which you might not have yet fully realized your potential. **The following paragraphs provide an explanation of the characteristics you would have upon successful resolution of this stage of development.** Reasons for a lack of such success are also suggested. *Check the descriptions that apply to you.*

☐ **You welcome situations that call upon you to learn new skills.** Learning involves facing the unknown and unfamiliar—a challenge to your intellectual capability. Confidence is something that is developed as a result of experience. Ideally, we are challenged by the tasks of growing up in proportion to our ability to deal with them—we may have to stretch a bit, but we have been provided with enough support to maintain our footing while doing so. If you were somehow challenged out of proportion to the support available to you, you may have been taught that learning is a painful and frustrating experience that often ends in failure. This conclusion can be "untaught," given proper support and enough experience of success, but it often requires significant effort, guidance, and understanding.

☐ **You are confident of your ability to achieve in an occupation.** If you have confidence in your own basic capabilities, this should generalize to your work. Prior work experience can contribute (or detract) from this level of confidence. If you have no significant work experience at this point in your life, you can make some judgment of your ability to succeed in an occupation based on related course work taken in college (for example, accounting course work for an accounting major). If you also have previous work experience, you might have a sense of how you fare in terms of the many factors (knowledge, attitude, motivation, work ethic, interpersonal skills) that contribute to career success.

☐ **You desire an occupation that will challenge you.** People who are confident are usually avid learners; they are always looking for a new method of working or a new skill to learn that might help them on the job. People who complain of being in dead-end jobs are often there because they have not sought challenges, made commitments, or taken risks that would have led them out of it. This lack of initiative may sometimes be due to fear—either fear of failure or fear of success. Fear of failure is common among individuals whose confidence has somehow been undermined. Fear of success can be just as debilitating and has the same root cause; success is seen as a prelude to failure—a threat to self rather than a reinforcement. To some extent, the mind is like a muscle—it must be challenged (exercised) in order for it to grow in flexibility and strength. Fear of any kind is debilitating.

☐ **You assume that you can usually succeed at things you try.** Expectations can alter the shape of reality. If you approach a task expecting to succeed, your own confidence, poise, and positive attitude will work to make success more likely. On the other hand, if you approach a task expecting to fail, you generate a number of real forces (anxiety, hopelessness, lack of motivation) that make success less likely. Such expectations are largely shaped by prior experience, and once a pattern is set, it is usually resistant to change. Whether your experience has resulted in either positive or negative expectations, these expectations will tend to generate a reinforcing cycle of similar results. Those results that do not meet expectations are usually filtered out of your perception or explained away. If you expect to fail, this is likely to generate continued failure experiences; and if a success does occur, it will be discounted or ignored. This is a tough cycle to break! On the other hand, expecting success makes success more likely.

☐ **You take appropriate responsibility for any lack of success.** A person who expects success will not always succeed. Like anyone else, he or she will have to contend with failure on occasion. When this happens, the failure is approached as an opportunity for learning. Such a person will ask questions like: What went wrong? To what extent am I responsible for what went wrong? What could I have done differently that might have led to a more desirable outcome? As you might notice, there is no blaming of self or others. A person whose sense of capability is not fully realized will tend to blame others and to rationalize failure—never really approaching the cause of failure or its remedy. The inevitable result of this negative approach is the repetition of the same mistakes over and over again.

If you feel that you have a solid sense of confidence, you are ready to move to the next crossroad. If not, confidence in your own capabilities is something that can be developed, given the willingness to approach the concern directly and to seek assistance and support.

Please complete the following Travelog in order to explore the personal significance of this developmental crossroad.

Travelog #36

■ Which of the characteristics of achieving confidence apply to you?

■ Which of the characteristics of achieving confidence do not apply to you?

■ To what degree do you think you have achieved confidence? Why?

■ If you have any "unfinished business" in this developmental area, what would it be? What can you do about it?

■ Think of someone you know who has not fully resolved the issues of this stage of development. How is his or her behavior affected by lack of resolution? How has it affected his or her career development?

Independence: My Way

As you progress from childhood, through adolescence, and into adulthood, there is a movement away from environmental support and toward self-support. This movement is reflected by your assuming responsibility for more and more aspects of your life (for example, your career choices). You learn to think for yourself and to come to your own conclusions, based on your own reasoning. As you become more independent, you also learn to balance your needs and rights with those of others. You also learn that relationships with others can be rewarding, within the context of personal autonomy and mutual respect—a learning that forms the basis for healthy adult-to-adult relationships.

Please answer the following questions by circling the answer of your choice.

- Do you feel responsible for fulfilling your own obligations?   Yes   No
- Do you stand up for your own beliefs while respecting others'?   Yes   No
- Do you seek appropriate help from others as needed?   Yes   No
- Do you offer appropriate help to others as they need it?   Yes   No
- Do you make your own decisions?   Yes   No
- Do you have "adult–adult" relationships with authority figures?   Yes   No
- Do you have your own source of income?   Yes   No

If you answered "No" to any of the items above, independence may be an area in which you might not have yet fully realized your potential. **The following paragraphs provide an explanation of the characteristics you would have upon** *successful* **resolution of this stage of development.** Reasons for a lack of such success are also suggested. *Check the descriptions that apply to you.*

☐ **You fulfill your obligations in a responsible manner.** Assuming responsibility for yourself is one of the most obvious signposts of adulthood. The transition from dependence on others to independent functioning is most effective if it is achieved relatively early in life and in a gradual manner measured to the child's true capabilities. Such a transition serves to reinforce self-reliance as an achievable and desirable end. However, if the demands for this transition were made too early, were beyond your capability at that time, or were delayed due to an overprotective attitude on your caretaker's part, you may have experienced independence as a burden or as beyond your ability—leading to a dependent personality that excessively relies upon others to meet needs. This kind of dependency on others inhibits movement toward true independence and undermines the process of independent thought that leads to personal identity, direction, and meaning.

☐ **You stand up for your own beliefs.** As a child, you were exposed to the opinions, attitudes, and values of others at a time when you could do little else than absorb them. Parents, peers, teachers, and television are powerful forces in shaping the belief system of the child. Only from adolescence into adulthood does there emerge the capacity critically to analyze these beliefs—to start thinking for oneself. This is often a point in life where a serious re-evaluation of values and beliefs occurs. Such an evaluation may initially take the form of rebellion—a rejection of what was once believed. The mature person will go beyond this stage and sort out his or her own values and beliefs through a process of critical thought and analysis. This process usually results in maintaining some values from the past and discarding others. Once this re-evaluation is completed, a new belief system emerges. Establishing a belief system of your own is one thing; standing up for what you believe is another. This is especially true if what you believe is unpopular or unconventional. The willingness to back up what you believe with what you say and do, while respecting the rights of others to do the same, is a sign of independence.

☐ **You usually try to solve problems yourself before seeking assistance from others.** Independence involves a balance between self-sufficiency and a willingness to seek assistance appropriately from others. An independent person will usually take care of most things, but is not afraid to ask others for appropriate assistance. Assistance from others is requested—not demanded—and is appreciated. If your balance is tilted too far toward self-sufficiency, you will feel that you must do everything for yourself, and that you either have no right to ask for help or cannot depend upon others. If your balance is tilted too far toward dependence, you will seek to have others meet needs you could easily meet yourself and may impose upon others in a demanding or manipulative manner. Either situation can lead to problems.

☐ **You offer assistance to others.** Just as they are not afraid to ask for help, independent people offer assistance when to do so is consistent with their values. They will not impose their assistance on others; nor will they assume responsibility for things that other people can and should assume for themselves. Independent people will not usually do something simply out of a sense of social obligation or expectation; their actions are an expression of their values and their goals.

☐ **You depend upon others for input but make important decisions for yourself.** Decision making is rarely a process best conducted in isolation. When collecting information upon which to base a decision, it is important to seek the ideas and opinions of others. But when it comes down to making a decision about important personal concerns, independent people assume the responsibility. They will not ask (or allow) others to make a decision for them. Decisions are the mechanism by which independent people choose their destiny. Because of the importance of decisions, it is essential that the internal compass (your values and the process of rational thinking) used to evaluate alternatives be aligned with life-enhancing and reality-based standards. If your thinking is flawed by superstition or irrationality, or if your values subvert your ability to guide your own life, your destiny will be shrouded in darkness.

☐ **You maintain "adult–adult" relationships with authority figures.** People who have not yet established their independence will often have trouble dealing with authority figures. This trouble can often arise from a "child–parent" form of interaction that is carried over from childhood. The individual may be stuck in the role of the "rebellious child," casting the authority figure in the role of "critical parent." Someone who falls into the role of an "adaptive child" may be overly concerned about pleasing and impressing authority figures. In both cases, the result is a predictable and dysfunctional interaction. Once a person is more secure in his or her identity and has established a balanced independence, "adult–adult" interactions become more likely with authority figures (and everyone else as well), resulting in much more productive and satisfying outcomes. Independence also serves to immunize people against the influence of harmful mass movements and cults. Eric Hoffer wrote that "All mass movements rank obedience with the highest virtues." He also was one of the first to recognize that "A mass movement attracts and holds a following . . . because it can satisfy the passion for self-renunciation . . . [and] freedom from the intolerable burden of autonomous existence." To the extent that you are capable of independent thought and action, you will find yourself at odds with any person or group preaching self-sacrifice, unquestioning obedience to incomprehensible doctrine, and devaluation of individual creativity and achievement.

☐ **You are able to ensure your own economic security.** Economic security is an important part of independence. If you are unable to secure your own financial security, it may be difficult for you to maintain true independence. Even in a situation where one person in a marriage works outside the home, it is important for the person who works within the home to have the capacity for economic independence. Divorce, disability, or death of one's spouse are real possibilities that make this capacity particularly important. Part-time work and continued education can help maintain this economic capacity.

Issues of independence directly influence your ability to make the kind of decisions that lead to a rewarding and satisfying career. Such issues, when not successfully resolved, cause problems in any social environment, college and the workplace included.

Please complete the following Travelog in order to explore the personal significance of this developmental crossroad.

Travelog #37

■ Which of the characteristics of achieving independence apply to you?

■ Which of the characteristics of achieving independence do not apply to you?

■ To what degree do you think you have achieved independence? Why?

■ If you have any "unfinished business" in this developmental area, what would it be? What can you do about it?

■ Think of someone you know who has not fully resolved the issues involved in this stage of development. How is his or her behavior affected by this lack of resolution? How has it affected his or her career development?

Identity: Who Am I?

Achieving a sense of personal identity, or self-definition, is a complex task. It involves the integration of self-understanding, personal and career goals, opinions and viewpoints, philosophy, and the ability to be objective about yourself. It may be argued that a sense of identity is one of the most pressing of human needs, particularly within a society, such as ours, that values individualism so highly.

Identity is a key developmental issue that forms the foundation of wise career choices. It is important to have a stable and realistic sense of "who you are" before you make a definitive decision about your career direction.

Please answer the following questions by circling the answer of your choice.

- Do you have a sense of inner stability?   Yes   No
- Do you have a strong sense of "who you are"?   Yes   No
- Do you have a sense of goals that might direct your   Yes   No
  efforts?
- Have you critically examined the values you were taught?   Yes   No
- Have you experienced and resolved an "identity crisis"?   Yes   No
- Can you realistically accept your strengths and limitations?   Yes   No

If you answered "No" to any of the items above, identity may be an area in which you might not have yet fully realized your potential. **The following paragraphs provide an explanation of the characteristics you would have upon** *successful* **resolution of this stage of development.** Reasons for a lack of such success are also suggested. *Check the descriptions that apply to you.*

☐ **You feel that you have a stable sense of who you are.** Once you have achieved a sense of identity, you are operating from a relatively stable "center." One method of understanding where this center comes from is to see it as a process of awareness, understanding, healing, and commitment. Self-examination born of awareness is the starting place; without it, you are little more than an organic robot programmed by your environment and experience to react in a certain manner. And if you are always reacting according to how you have been "programmed" by your past, you won't be able to develop any inner stability—your life will seem like a whirlwind of mysterious changes over which you have little control.

Awareness requires the ability to step back from your own experience and the willingness to explore the nature of this experience. Life without self-awareness may be compared to watching a movie and getting so involved that you forget you are sitting in a dark room watching light images being projected onto a screen. As long as you are "lost" in the movie, you will be reacting (with real fear, excitement, joy, horror, or sadness) to what *seems* to be happening on the screen. Only when you become aware that you are watching a movie do you have a choice about what you are experiencing. Life is *not* a movie, but it is subject to illusion!

Understanding requires critical thinking, and tolerance of the pain that sometimes comes from facing the truth about ourselves. As self-awareness grows, some things you notice will not be very pleasant. Sometimes, abuse or a traumatic loss of one kind or another have been factors in our lives. The underlying pain can contribute to inappropriate behavior, obsessive-compulsive disorders, thrill-seeking, depression, hyperactivity, drug abuse, and a variety of other symptoms. These are but a few of the strategies that human beings employ as they try to quell inner pain they do not understand.

Understanding can lead to *healing*, but it is not easy. Becoming more aware of your "inner workings" is the first step toward understanding. It often helps to have a model of human behavior as a framework for self-understanding. Philosophy and psychology provide many such models. Part of your growth involves finding a model that provides a personally meaningful and objectively realistic view of yourself and the world. This is a process that many people undertake with the assistance of a guide or counselor—someone who has an understanding of human development, its issues and its challenges.

Commitment comes from healing. As you heal, new truths about yourself and your life emerge, and you move toward your potential for health and well-being. This movement must be assisted if it is to succeed against the tide of habit and inertia that acts to resist such change. Commitment to new attitudes, beliefs, values, and behaviors will assist this movement as you change your life to reflect the new truths you have discovered. This commitment is based on something we discussed at the very beginning of this book—your *will*—the power of rational choice to change your life.

The result of this continuous cycle of awareness, understanding, healing, and commitment is the development of an inner stability that transcends the changes that must be a part of such growth—a stable (yet flexible and changing) sense of identity. Once this is achieved, you have a platform from which to generate appropriate goals. This cycle may be familiar to you, though you may think of it in different terms. Many excellent books on this process are available in your local bookstore, usually categorized as "personal growth," "psychology," or "philosophy."

☐ **You are not preoccupied with "finding yourself."** Before you are involved in conscious identity development, there is no concern about "finding yourself"—it will be a phrase that has little meaning to you. As you begin to become more self-aware, it is not unusual to become preoccupied with the process of self-discovery. It may seem like a new world of possibilities is opening before you and that nothing else is as important as learning "who you are." As you develop a stable sense of identity, this preoccupation recedes. The cycle of growth becomes a natural part of yourself and your energy is released for other uses. It's a little like when you lose your car keys—until you find them, all of your attention and energy is focused on the search. Once the keys are found, you use them to start the car and then forget about them.

☐ **You have carefully examined your values.** What you believe to be important is a defining part of who you are. Your values determine how you decide important matters and how you spend your time, energy, and money. If these values have been inherited from others and never seriously examined, you may be living your life in a manner that is not very satisfying; that is, you may be doing everything that you are "supposed" to do but remain unhappy or unsatisfied. Fortunately, you have the ability to clarify and reorder your values at any time. The *identity crisis* that comes from this kind of clarification and re-evaluation can be rather unsettling—it may call into question many of your most fundamental beliefs and commitments. But it will help ensure that your values reflect your own nature and the nature of reality.

☐ **You have learned to accept yourself.** May Sarton has written that "We have to dare to be ourselves, however frightening or strange that self may prove to be." As you learn more about yourself, you will come to face your limitations as well as your assets. As a human being, you are not (nor are you likely to become) perfect. You have failings, disappointments, and flaws that will complicate your life, mar your self-image, and delay your goals. As you attempt to overcome these failings, it is important to accept them. It is a paradox of life that whatever you wish to change must be accepted before it can be altered. If you are failing a class, you may blame your instructor, criticize the school, or make resolutions to study more; but nothing you do will have any effect until you squarely face the fact that you are failing. You must accept this fact and let it soak into your consciousness. The same principle applies in cases of addictive disorders such as obesity and drug abuse—until the affected person hits the wall of reality and self-responsibility, there is little hope of real change. The first step an alcoholic must take is to admit that "I am an alcoholic."

Acceptance is *not* an ending place, it is a beginning. Change can only be successful if it is based on an acceptance of reality. You cannot really change something that you deny exists, or that you have distorted out of the need to protect yourself. In fact, this is a good guideline to apply in your use of self-acceptance: If it is employed to protect yourself or to excuse some behavior, it is probably being misused. True self-acceptance is based on facing hard facts about yourself in a compassionate manner and opening yourself to change. Acceptance does *not* mean that you like or approve of any given behavior, but rather that you *acknowledge* the reality of its presence.

Identity is also one of the keys to understanding some people's attraction to cults and other such mass movements. In his book *The True Believer*, Eric Hoffer wrote that "...the freedom the masses crave is not freedom of self-expression and self-realization, but freedom from the intolerable burden of an autonomous existence." This surrender of self can lead one to cling desperately to the movement's creed and mission. Hoffer also points out the consequences of such a surrender: "The urge to escape our real self is also an urge to escape the rational and the obvious. The refusal to see ourselves as we are develops a distaste for facts and cold logic." And, of course, without a taste for such tools of the mind, the true believer also surrenders the only mechanism of his or her recovery. It is in the interest of such movements, says Hoffer, to strip " . . . each human entity of its distinctness and autonomy . . . turning it into an anonymous particle with no will and no judgment of its own." Then, the true believer becomes fodder for the cannon of the movement.

☐ **You have a realistic sense of your strengths and limitations.** A stable sense of identity must be based on a realistic evaluation of your assets and liabilities. If you overestimate your strengths, you will undertake tasks that are beyond your capability. On the other hand, if you underestimate your assets, you may never realize your true potential. Either error can lead to frustration, self-doubt, and hopelessness. It is difficult to find the proper balance, but it will become easier as you gain more experience and understanding.

James Marcia did some research into identity status back in the 1960s that resulted in the suggestion of four classifications of identity achievement. Check the one that you think best describes your own identity status.

☐ **Identity Achieved** represents someone who has experienced an identity crisis and has resolved it by formulating definite goals and values.

☐ **Identity Moratorium** describes someone who has experienced (or is experiencing) an identity crisis, but has yet to formulate and commit to definite goals and values.

☐ **Identity Foreclosure** describes the status of someone who has firmly established goals and values (usually accepted from significant others and not questioned) and who has not experienced any kind of identity crisis.

☐ **Identity Diffusion** represents the situation of someone who has not experienced an identity crisis and who has not yet formulated definite goals and values.

Marcia's original research is cited in the Bibliography if you care to explore this model of identity development.

Identity is not something you develop automatically or once and for all. Identity is something that may be called into question by changes in your life (loss of a job, death of parents, divorce) and, more important, something that is influenced by the integrity of your thinking. The stability and coherence of your identity are directly related to the quality of thought that you invest in your life and your decisions. Sloppy, irrational, or wishful thinking can only result in an insecure and inconsistent sense of identity, often unconnected to basic personal values. Clear and honest thinking, on the other hand, results in a secure and consistent sense of identity that reflects personal values. The choice is yours to make.

If you want to work on identity issues, counseling can often be helpful. Identity is an issue that usually must be successfully resolved before you can develop a true direction for your life.

Please complete the following Travelog in order to explore the personal significance of this developmental crossroad.

Travelog #38

- Which of the characteristics of achieving identity apply to you?

- Which of the characteristics of achieving identity do not apply to you?

- How would you evaluate your identity status according to Marcia's categories? Why?

- If you have any "unfinished business" in this developmental area, what would it be? What can you do about it?

■ Think of someone you know who has not fully resolved the issues involved in this stage of development. How is his or her behavior affected by this lack of resolution? How has it affected his or her career development?

Direction: Where Am I Going?

As you get older, the pressure increases for a sense of direction in your life. The determination of a career direction is the life stage most obviously related to your career planning efforts. Until you have a sense of direction, you will likely flounder from one thing to another and you may have difficulty maintaining the motivation required to achieve academically. A meaningful goal can integrate many elements of your life into a meaningful venture—an opportunity to direct your energy more forcefully than when your energies are scattered and your goals unclear.

Please answer the following questions by circling the answer of your choice.

- Do you have specific goals for your life?   Yes   No
- Are you able to do some long-range planning?   Yes   No
- Do you have a clear sense of what you want in an occupation?   Yes   No
- Have you clarified what you value in an occupation ?   Yes   No
- Do you know how to establish a sense of direction in your life?   Yes   No

If you answered "No" to any of the items above, direction may be an area in which you might not have yet fully realized your potential. **The following paragraphs provide an explanation of the characteristics you would have upon *successful* resolution of this stage of development.** Reasons for a lack of such success are also suggested. *Check the descriptions that apply to you.*

☐ **You are not wandering from one thing to another.** A clear goal can serve as directional marker for your life. It allows you to plot a direct course toward your objectives and to avoid dead ends. Wandering has its place, but it can be comforting to have a sense of where you are going and how to get there. It's not unusual for people to switch from one college major, or from one occupation, to another; this is often part of the exploration that is essential to learning. However, carried too far, wandering can result in a lack of success at anything. With a clear goal in mind, you may *choose* to wander, but it is a choice rather than a consequence, and it is done within a larger context. Career planning is a systematic method of establishing a meaningful direction for your life. Such planning is like a compass that allows you to get your bearings. The choice of direction is always your own; but planning helps you make this choice a realistic and satisfying one.

☐ **You are able to make long-range plans.** One result of deciding upon a direction for your life is that you are able to make plans toward the realization of your goals. Planning is an important process that allows you to foresee future requirements and possible obstacles. Planning is a creative act that extends the power of your mind into the future, allowing you to increase the scope of your actions and, thus, the chance of achieving your goals.

☐ **You are clear about what you want and don't want in an occupation.** Different people will take different approaches to making a career choices. Some people have a clear sense of what they do not like and can eliminate many alternatives very quickly. Others have a difficult time eliminating any option and avoid a career choice because they feel it will somehow limit their horizons. A few have a strong sense of where they want to go and only need to clarify how to get there.

If you have been able to eliminate many occupations from consideration, you still may have a dilemma on your hands. At some point you have to switch gears and start looking for things that are viable possibilities. This may be more difficult for you. Remember that no occupation is going to be 100% compatible with all your interests, skills, values, and other preferences—some compromise may be necessary. The key to success is taking a realistic view of an occupation and trying to select an alternative on knowledge and experience.

☐ **You accept the fact that an occupational choice will limit your future options.** No person can realize all his or her potentials. Mapping out a path in life calls your attention to "paths not taken" and though this may be painful, it is a reality that must be accepted. You may feel a sense of loss, but it will pass as you focus on the many possibilities along the path you have chosen. Though commitment is necessary to move along a given career path, this does not mean you will be limited to one path forever. In fact, most people will travel several different career paths during their lifetime. The thing to remember is that commitment leads to alternatives, while *indecision* truly limits your options.

If you have a strong career direction, take the time to confirm your chosen path. Decisions made at one point in your development may be limiting if they are not updated as you grow. Many people who begin college thinking they have a clear direction change their minds before they graduate. Be open-minded about other alternatives. If you end up where you began, nothing is lost and a strengthened resolve is gained. If you discover a new direction that is even more meaningful, you have gained even more.

☐ **You know how your values relate to your occupational choice.** Choosing a career without reference to your values would be like plotting a course without a compass. If you take the time to clarify your values and apply them to your occupational choice, you are much more likely to be satisfied with the result. It is even more important to have carefully examined and re-evaluated your values. Are your values derived from a carefully reasoned philosophy? Do you understand the importance of clear perception, life-enhancing principles based in reality, and reasoned judgment?

☐ **You are not unduly disturbed if you temporarily lose your sense of direction.** Achieving direction is not something you do once and for all. There will be points in your life where a change in course is called for. This may make you feel disoriented. Rollo May wrote that "To live . . . means to leap into the unknown, and this requires a degree of courage for which there is no immediate precedent . . . ." It does take courage, but, when you have found your direction once, the next time it will be easier. You will remember the process you went through before. You will know what tools are helpful and what hazards to avoid. You will have confidence in your mind's ability to reorient yourself and to master the challenges that confront you.

The process you are going through as you work through this book is teaching you how to establish direction in your life. This step-by-step process of thoughtful consideration, gathering information, exploration, understanding, and decision making may be useful in dealing with issues other than career direction.

Please complete the following Travelog in order to explore the personal significance of this developmental crossroad.

Travelog #39

■ Which of the characteristics of achieving direction apply to you?

■ Which of the characteristics of achieving direction do not apply to you?

■ To what degree do you think you have achieved direction? Why?

■ If you have any "unfinished business" in this developmental area, what would it be? What can you do about it?

- Think of someone you know who has not fully resolved the issues involved in this stage of development. How is his or her behavior affected by this lack of resolution? How has it affected his or her career development?

Meaning: Why Am I Here?

This book started with a brief discussion of the search for meaning as an existential foundation of career planning. You are not simply choosing a job. Nora Watson (one of the people Studs Terkel interviewed in his book *Working*) said it well when she observes that "Jobs are not big enough for people." If you just settle for a job, without reference to a larger Way, sooner or later you will probably find that the job is not "big enough" for you—that it is limiting at best, or crippling at worst.

It's one thing to know *where* you are going; it's another to know *why*. A sense of meaning and destiny have always been important to people's well-being. Spiritual and philosophical concerns often come to the fore in the search for meaning. When you realize you will not live forever, it suddenly becomes important to know *why* you are living and how to achieve meaning within the framework of your own mortality.

Please answer the following questions by circling the answer of your choice.

- Do you have a sense of meaning and purpose in your life?   Yes   No
- Is your career direction related to a larger purpose in life?   Yes   No
- Do you have a clear sense of what is most important in life?   Yes   No
- Are you committed to something beyond your own well-being?   Yes   No
- Do you have an understanding of the spiritual aspects of life?   Yes   No

If you answered "No" to any of the items above, meaning may be an area in which you might not have yet fully realized your potential. **The following paragraphs provide an explanation of the characteristics you would have upon *successful* resolution of this stage of development.** Reasons for a lack of such success are also suggested. *Check the descriptions that apply to you.*

☐ **You have a sense of your own destiny.** It is one thing to establish a direction in your life; it is another to feel this direction to be your Way—a purpose that defines your existence—a personally meaningful reason for your all-too-brief presence on this third planet from the sun. A few people have a sense of their destiny at an early age, while others never have it clearly defined. For those who have a calling, life takes on a different perspective; everything else is placed within the context of this overriding purpose.

This kind of integration brings with it a feeling of power and purpose that is the hallmark of life lived to its potential. If you have a sense of your destiny, you are indeed fortunate. If not, it is a goal that is most worthwhile. Such a goal can usually be achieved only when preceding developmental issues have been resolved. The first step toward your destiny is to resolve the earlier developmental stages in your life: confidence, independence, identity, and direction.

☐ **You are moving toward a career that has meaning to you.** A meaningful career is often central to a sense of purpose in life. For most people, a career is a major focus of their energies and talents and offers the potential for some degree of personal meaning. If your career offers you meaning above and beyond financial reward, then your everyday duties take on larger significance. Few people are truly satisfied by a job that has no value other than a paycheck. This is one reason why your examination of values is so important. The more fully a job coincides with your basic values, the more satisfying it will be. To the extent that your values reflect an affirmation of life and the creative power of your mind, such rewards will contribute to a sense of achieving your destiny.

☐ **You have committed yourself to what is most important.** You may be able to identify what you value most in your life, but this will have little meaning until your life truly reflects these values. This is an issue of personal integrity. Unless your behavior, decisions, and attitudes reflect your basic values (and, therefore, your philosophy of life), you will feel empty and devoid of power. It is important to note that your values will be influenced by the type of developmental issues you are addressing. If you are trying to achieve the ability to cope with the demands of life, confidence will be a priority. If you have not yet found a direction in life, this will be a defining value. Each time you progress from one developmental issue to another, your values are likely to shift. New developmental challenges bring forth new commitments, and new commitments result in further development. Note that fundamental values, if grounded in a well-considered philosophical framework, should not be affected by developmental change. Such basic values (honesty, liberty, clarity of thought, affirmation of life, self-esteem, creativity, autonomy) form the foundation for your growth and change.

☐ **You are not totally absorbed in meeting your own immediate needs.** One characteristic of the achievement of meaning is a kind of self-overcoming. As you advance from one developmental crossroad to another, you will notice that you have come to feel and think of yourself differently. Your view of self changes as a result of your response to the challenges of life. At the stage of meaning, an extraordinary thing begins to happen. The self that, up until this point, has been adding to itself in terms of capability, defining values, and personal achievement, now begins to focus on other values. At this stage, people devote their lives to their ultimate values and capabilities—those that are so important they transcend lesser (sometimes more immediate) needs.

Though this involves giving up some things, it is not a sacrifice (sacrifice is the surrender of a higher value to a lower one). George Washington, Abraham Lincoln, Martin Luther King, Jr., Marie Curie, and Thomas Edison are examples of outstanding individuals who devoted themselves to the realization of their highest values: national independence, human freedom and dignity, scientific discovery, and creative invention. Their Ways became an expression of (and a fulfillment of) their highest values.

When your development reaches this stage, something else sometimes occurs. Some people, at this point in their lives, begin to feel a deep connection with all things, a sense of oneness with the universe. Psychologists have described this sense of oneness as a "peak experience" or a "transcendent experience." It is an element of what Abraham Maslow calls "self-actualization." Those of a spiritual orientation may experience it as a "oneness with God," "spiritual awakening," or "satori." Whatever the interpretation, the common experience is a deep feeling of peace, fulfillment, and destiny achieved.

☐ **You have a clear sense of your place in the universe.** The search for meaning in life is a journey that will bring you face-to-face with difficult questions —questions about the origin and meaning of your life, your relationship to the universe, and your inevitable death—the kind of philosophical questions you will review in the following section of this chapter. The achievement of meaning requires a context that provides concepts and understandings suited to such inquiry. It requires a philosophy that truly reflects the nature of reality, your human nature, and the values that promote your well-being and further development.

Please complete the following Travelog in order to explore the personal significance of meaning as a developmental crossroad.

Travelog #40

■ Which of the characteristics of achieving meaning apply to you?

■ Which of the characteristics of achieving meaning do not apply to you?

■ To what degree do you think you have achieved meaning? Why?

■ If you have any "unfinished business" in this developmental area, what would it be? What can you do about it?

■ Think of someone you know who has not fully resolved the issues involved in this stage of development. How is his or her behavior affected by this lack of resolution? How has it affected his or her career development?

Developmental concerns are embedded within the framework of philosophy—the discipline devoted to the study of reality, the nature of human beings, and the relationships between the two. The next section provides a brief introduction to basic philosophical terms and explains why your philosophy has a very practical effect on your career planning and your life.

Practical Philosophy

*P*hilosophy provides a foundation for individual living and social experience. Depending on its premises, philosophy can either support meaningful life within a healthy society, or it can lead to the crumbling of all that is built upon it. The formulation of a meaningful philosophy, when firmly grounded in clear thinking and life-enhancing values, can lead to self-esteem, creativity, autonomy, productivity, personal and social responsibility, emotional balance, reasoned judgment, and the achievement of fulfilling goals. These kinds of values and outcomes can serve as a foundation for a vibrant and healthy life within a society that reflects the same values.

This section is *not* an introduction to philosophy, but a very brief definition of some of the most important elements of a philosophical system that may help you understand the nature of the task before you. We will focus on three such elements:

- Questions about the fundamental nature of reality and life: why you are here, where you came from, your capacity to influence reality (*metaphysics*).
- Concerns about the nature of truth and knowledge: how you come to know truth and how you know the difference between what is true and what is not (*epistemology*).
- Issues dealing with the conduct of life: the standards upon which you base judgments of "right and wrong" and "good and evil" (*ethics*).

These are high-sounding terms for basic considerations about life. Because it deals with life concerns that affect everyone, philosophy is both abstract and imminently practical. Your "world view" is a combination of the philosophical premises you have adopted and formulated.

Whether you know it or not, you are directly influenced by a view of reality, truth, and moral standards—by metaphysics, epistemology, and ethics—by philosophy.

You may not think you have a philosophy of life. Indeed, you may *not* have consciously formulated a consistent world view. Nonetheless, your life *is* being guided by basic premises concerning the nature of the world and reality. Ayn Rand observed that " . . . you have no choice about the fact that you need a philosophy . . . an integrated view of existence." According to Rand, the choice you *do* have to make is to " . . . define your philosophy by a conscious, rational, disciplined process of thought . . . or let your subconscious accumulate . . . unwarranted conclusions, false generalizations, undefined contradictions, undigested slogans, unidentified wishes, doubts and fears, thrown together by chance . . . ."

To the extent that your philosophy is consciously and consistently formulated in accordance with reality and the requirements of your true nature, you will find the world open to your quest for knowledge, direction, and meaning. However, if your philosophy is based upon precepts that you have accepted without questioning or that distort reality and your true nature, the world will remain a mysterious place, directed by forces beyond your comprehension that silently lead you toward resignation and despair. Such is the fundamental importance and practicality of a consciously developed philosophy.

The following two Travelogs will ask you to think about your own philosophy. There are no right or wrong answers to the questions in these exercises.

Travelog #41

O ne of the methods you can use to start exploring your world view is to review your current thinking on a number of philosophical issues. Answer the questions on this and the next Travelog as thoughtfully as you can. Don't be concerned if you don't have a "good" answer to a question—many philosophers throughout history have been in the same boat! The purpose of this exercise is to explore your opinions on some fundamental philosophical issues.

■ What are two (2) elements of your life that provide you with a sense of meaning, purpose, or fulfillment? Briefly describe why each is so meaningful to you.

1.

Why meaningful?

2.

Why meaningful?

- Do you have a philosophy of life (an understanding of reality that guides your life)? If you do, what are one or two of the basic principles or ideas that express this philosophy? If you don't think you have a philosophy, do you think it is important to develop one? Why, or why not?

- Do you believe that you have a Way in life (even if you don't know what it is yet)? Why, or why not? Do you have any idea what it might be?

Travelog #42

■ How do you view your basic human nature? Is it fundamentally good or evil, or neither, or both? How much control do you have over your human nature and natural tendencies? Why do you think this?

■ When it comes to the overall direction of your life, do you believe that you have freedom of choice or that your fate is predetermined? To what extent? On what do you base your opinion?

■ To what extent do you think you are capable of understanding the true nature of reality and the universe (where it came from, how it works, and how you may influence it)? What tools, practices, or resources could you use to gain such understanding?

■ How do you personally determine what is "good or bad" and "right or wrong"? What do you use as a standard for such decisions? What is your single most important standard or principle of morality?

Your answers to the questions on the preceding Travelogs may provide some clues to your personal philosophy and the manner in which it may affect your career planning:

■ **If you feel that you have a Way in life,** you will examine your career options in a different light. A sense of purpose and significance related to your work will greatly enrich your life. Without such a sense, work can become drudgery—a "necessary evil" rather than a source of meaning and personal fulfillment. In his book *Reinventing the Corporation,* John Naisbitt cites some research that indicates that "Some 40 percent of the work force has adopted (at least in part) the notion that work should be personally satisfying . . . ." He concludes: " . . . there is a widespread expectation that work should be fulfilling . . . ." Although this expectation has been hampered by the social and economic factors we identified earlier and by what Naisbitt identifies as a workplace " . . . still organized to fit the industrial society of thirty years ago," many people hang onto the hope for "daily meaning as well as daily bread." Those who have relinquished this hope have lost a significant potential for personal fulfillment.

■ **Your view of human nature** may determine the basis of your interaction with others and may influence the kinds of occupations you choose to explore. If you take an optimistic stance, you are probably more open and trusting with others, and perhaps more likely to consider occupations that involve close interpersonal contact. Your view of human nature also influences how you feel about yourself and, therefore, your level of self-esteem. If you think you are a creature with a natural inclination toward the positive, the productive, and the moral elements of life, you will see other kinds of inclinations (in yourself and others) as aberrations that must be addressed and changed. However, if you believe yourself to be somehow fundamentally flawed by an attraction to the negative and the immoral in life, you will be in a state of constant warfare within yourself and with others.

■ **Beliefs about your relationship to reality** determine how much influence you feel you have in your life and over your career. Such beliefs will understandably influence your commitment to personal initiative, decision making, and planning—elements of career planning that make sense only if we have a significant degree of personal and social freedom. Personal responsibility is only possible in a world of objective reality that responds in a predictable and understandable manner to choices and actions initiated by thinking human beings. How can you be held responsible for your actions in a world that is unresponsive to your actions and that unfolds in an unpredictable manner, according to a plan not merely unknown, but unknowable?

■ **Fundamental views about the openness of reality to rational inquiry** will color the depth and energy of your seeking. Also, the tools you choose to use to seek knowledge (logic, critical and creative thinking, faith, intuition, revelation) determine the effectiveness and reliability of this search. If you are to find your Way in this world, you must exercise the power of your mind to find intelligible answers in the realm of objective reality.

■ **Principles that underlie your judgments and decisions** will form the basis of your personal and professional ethics. Whether you realize it or not, the conduct of your life and your career is guided by a set of ethical elements. These elements may vary widely in their conscious selection, consistency, strength, relationship to reality, and facilitation of life. To the extent that your ethical standards are consciously chosen, consistent, stable, grounded in reality, and promote life-enhancing values, your decisions will have a solid foundation. However, if your choose to violate such standards, or if your standards tend to be unconscious, inconsistent, unstable, grounded in illusion or in negative values, your decisions will lack integrity. Only a conscious effort to examine such elements will foster a foundation for wise decision making. Only a commitment to *apply* this ethical foundation to your every act will foster your integrity.

You are encouraged to explore the significance of these philosophical issues as a part of the career exploration you are undertaking. This kind of basic inquiry will enrich your career planning and your life. Several references are provided in the "Philosophy" section of the Bibliography that may be used to follow up these concerns.

As you consider the importance of developmental changes and your personal philosophy, you might notice some issues with which you could use some further assistance. The next section presents signposts toward such assistance.

Guiding Signs

Developmental (and related philosophical) issues are often difficult to resolve. Resolution may take years of dedicated struggle and growth. Some guidelines for addressing such issues follow.

■ **Strengthen the primary tool of your growth and development—your mind.** Exercise your capacity for clear and creative thinking. The quality of your life will ultimately be a reflection of the quality of your thinking. Poorly considered decisions and unclear or inconsistent principles can only lead to confusion and other unfortunate results. Clear thinking is a straight path toward your goals.

■ **Expand your understanding of the issues you are dealing with.** A commitment to understanding is a powerful first step as you face any issue. Philosophy and psychology are imminently practical disciplines in that they address many fundamental issues of human development. The clearer your understanding of such issues, the easier it will be for you to face the challenges of career and life.

- **Develop a clear set of life-promoting values.** Your value system is the navigation system for your life. If your values are formulated in accordance with rational principles and an understanding of the nature of reality, you will be able to guide your life toward your chosen goals. If, however, your values are unclear or based on confused premises, you will not be able to depend on your decisions to promote your well-being and the goals you choose for yourself. A value system *not* calibrated by a commitment to life and a thinking process that promotes the values of life is like a compass that does not show true North—it will inevitably lead you astray.

- **Develop and maintain your self-esteem.** Self-esteem was defined by psychologist Nathaniel Branden as " . . . the integrated sum of self-confidence and self-respect." To the extent you have achieved self-esteem, you feel confident about your ability to deal with reality and you have a sense of personal worth. Branden also quoted the German philosopher Goethe: "The greatest evil that can befall a man is that he should come to think ill of himself."

- **Do not let yourself be stopped by fear.** Fear is a natural human emotion in the face of the unknown. It is a signal that you have some work to do, not that you should stop dead in your tracks. Courage is as important as thoughtful understanding. As Nietzsche said: "Even the bravest of us rarely has the courage for what he [or she] really *knows* . . . ."

- **Consider seeking counseling assistance** from a professional counselor. Counselors are familiar with developmental issues and can help clarify problems, alternatives, consequences, and solutions.

- **Scan the shelves of local bookstores** for titles that relate to the issue(s) you want to focus on. You might start with categories related to philosophy, psychology, and self-help. "Bibliotherapy" can help you learn more about such issues and to begin to understand the nature of the concerns you must face. You are not the first person to deal with such issues, and you can benefit from the experience of others who have been down the road ahead of you. Some of the references listed under Adult Development and Philosophy in the Bibliography might be helpful as well.

- **Discuss the issue(s) with friends or family members** who you feel can be trusted and who can relate to your concerns. A candid opinion from someone who knows you well can be an important piece of information. Sometimes it is difficult to be truly objective about yourself; someone who cares enough to be honest with you can be a great asset to your development.

- **Take a self-development course** at your local college or university. Look for course titles like "Life Skills," "Dynamics of Behavior," "Adult Transitions,"

"Personal Development," and the like. A course with an experiential approach can often be more beneficial than one that uses a purely academic or theoretical format; personal involvement is a key factor in the developmental potential of such learning experiences.

■ **Seek the advice of people who exemplify what you want for yourself.** Find out how they achieved resolution of key developmental issues for themselves. Experience is a powerful teacher. If you include the experience of others as an element of your own experience, you have the opportunity to distill the wisdom they have gained and use it to your own benefit. This does not absolve you from the need to find your own solutions to your own concerns, but it may serve as a compass to help you find your bearings in unfamiliar territory. Some people find that literature can serve a function in this regard—providing models of character and behavior that reflect or challenge their own values and goals.

■ **Spend some time in reflection.** Every now and then it is important to back away from your life and take a look at it from a different perspective. Ask yourself where you are in terms of achieving your most important goals. Consider whether your life truly reflects a carefully formulated philosophy. Think about the nature of your Way and what stands between you and its realization. It is often best to do this kind of thing in a "retreat" environment, away from the day-to-day responsibilities, activities, and interruptions that usually absorb your attention. Many people come away from this kind of reflection with a renewed sense of purpose and direction.

■ **Beware of mass movements that pander to insecurity, dependence, a lack of purpose or meaning, and that emphasize self-sacrifice.** Eric Hoffer concluded that " . . . the chief preoccupation of an active mass movement is to instill in its followers a facility for . . . self-sacrifice . . ." The call for self-sacrifice is a warning siren for those who would realize life-sustaining values. In *For the New Intellectual*, Ayn Rand explained one of the reasons for such a siren: "It stands to reason that where there's sacrifice, there's someone collecting sacrificial offerings. Where there's service, there's someone being served. The man [or woman] who speaks to you of sacrifice, speaks of slaves and masters. And intends to be the master."

This chapter has provided a rudimentary introduction to some very important life issues. Though it may seem as if we have traveled far afield from step-by-step career exploration, a little thought will reveal the importance of such issues as you are considering your career in the larger context of your life experience. As you pass through the developmental stages we have discussed, transition will be your constant companion. The next chapter will explain the process of transition and suggest how you can facilitate this process.

Quiz 9

*P*lease answer the following questions.

1. What are the five (5) major principles of human development?

    1.

    2.

    3.

    4.

    5.

2. Fill in the blank with the developmental issue most closely related to each description provided below:

_____ A person who is afraid to return to school.

_____ A person who is afraid to make his own decisions.

_____ A person who has never questioned her values.

_____ A person who cannot decide on a career path.

_____ A person who is seeking some philosophical understanding.

3. Has the information in this chapter influenced your tentative occupational choice? Why, or why not?

4. What is the most important thing that you learned about yourself by working through this chapter?

5. What topic that was covered in this chapter would you like to know more about?

To Consider . . .

1. An evaluation of your own developmental status (in relationship to key developmental issues) requires considerable insight and understanding.

   Why is it sometimes so difficult to understand an issue when you are in the midst of it?

   Do you have a responsibility to point out developmental problems to those you care about?

   What happens to people who become stuck at a given developmental stage?

   Why do some people deal with developmental issues more adeptly than others?

   How can an understanding of the developmental process contribute to growth?

   What social or cultural factors might influence the developmental process?

   Would developmental issues vary significantly across different cultures?

   What role does philosophy play in the developmental process?

   What role does philosophy play in the career planning process?

Suggested Activities

1. Interview someone who exemplifies a developmental goal of yours. How did they deal with the concerns involved? What would they recommend as helpful?

2. Talk to someone you trust and respect about your spiritual or philosophical beliefs and concerns. How have these changed over the years? Are you satisfied with where you stand on this aspect of your life?

3. Try to summarize your basic philosophical beliefs in writing. Analyze where these beliefs came from and their effects on your decisions and your life.

The Parable of the Creator

Zara and his disciple were walking through town when they came upon a construction site. Workers were tearing down an old ruin of a building to make room for a new one. In front of the site, a sign with an illustration of the new building depicted a tall and elegant structure with many windows—a thing of beauty. Zara sat down and watched the construction for a long time.

He turned to his disciple and spoke: "See how the old must be torn down to make room for the new. Out of the rubble, a thing of beauty will arise. Out of the destruction, a new creation will come forth. So it is with the ideas that drive people's lives. Most people live within ideas that are ancient and falling apart. These ideas have sheltered many people before them, but now the shelter is becoming dangerous—as many people are hit on the head by falling bricks as are sheltered. When the bricks of one's ideas begin to fall, it is time for a new creation, new ideas.

"But, before a new structure can be built, the old one must be taken apart and removed. The wrecking ball of life is up to this task. But people often fear its swinging and the shake and shudder of its striking. They hide in the rubble and lament the destruction.

"The Creator, on the other hand, welcomes, even wields, the wrecking ball. The Creator knows that destruction is a necessary part of creation, that the old must be leveled to make room for the new. The Creator rejoices in the falling away of the old because it announces the coming of creation."

Zara turned to his disciple and spoke: "Woe to those who fear the wrecking ball of the world! It swings in a mighty arc and destroys everything in its path. The fearful will scatter at its approach and huddle in the remains and the ruins. They will curse those who do not share their fear. They will throw stones at those who watch the passing of the old without remorse. The fearful see only the crumbling of what they have known; their eyes are not keen enough to see the vision of what is coming.

"Only the fearless and the far-sighted can see what is coming. They can read the signs of the future. They see the towering possibilities that will be built upon the leveled ruins. They live for the day when the wrecking ball has finished its work.

"The short-sighted and the fearful herd have always been threatened by the Creator. The Creator threatens the structures of the old and the known. In the eyes of the herd, the Creator is a malefactor, a devil, a dreamer, a corrupter of youth, a sacrilegious renegade, a prophet of destruction. 'Better trample this devil underfoot!'—so thinks the herd.

"The Creators are driven by their far-sighted vision of the future, of the possible. They do not rely on the comforts and consolations of the herd; creators stand alone with their vision. Creators never destroy for the sake of destruction; they merely push aside the ruins of the past to make room for the coming of the future. Only the herd is capable of destruction for its own sake, driven as it is by fear, self-loathing, and loneliness."

Zara turned to his disciple and spoke: "Can you hear the singing of the wrecking ball of creation as it approaches? Can you sense the rush of air that precedes it in its arc? Dare you stand in its path? Are you strong enough and fearless enough to create your meaning and your possibilities out of your own tumbling ruins? Do you dare to question and shake even the very foundations of your thought? Do you dare to re-evaluate even your most solidly constructed values? Are you creative enough to make a new beginning out of every ending?"

Zara paused and held his hand to his ear, and then spoke: "Listen carefully, my friend . . . I hear the singing of creation . . . and it's swinging this way!"

CHAPTER TEN

Transitions

Preview

This is the only way, we say; but there are as many ways as there can be drawn radii from one center. All change is a miracle to contemplate; but it is a miracle that is taking place every instant.

HENRY DAVID THOREAU

This chapter focuses on the changes that are a part of life and how better to understand the process of change itself. The main sections of this chapter are as follows.

- **Inevitable Changes** discusses the many different kinds of change that may affect your life.

- **Approaches to Change** describes how different people respond to change.

- **Stages of Transition** outlines the stages people usually go through when they confront a significant change in their lives.

- **Transition Hazards** explains why some transitions may be more difficult to handle than others.

- **Transition Tips** suggests strategies to minimize the trauma of changes in your life.

By the time you finish this chapter, you should have a better understanding of how change occurs and how you can approach change in a constructive manner.

Change is something that influences everyone. Many people have a natural inclina-tion to resist change. They may be heavily invested in the status quo and quite satisfied with things just as they are. They may fear the unknown element of change or may not want to cope with the anxiety and stress that accompanies change. On the other hand, some people love change. These people will actively seek it out and often view change as exciting or as a great adventure.

This chapter explains that change cannot be avoided and that there are con-structive approaches to such change. Much of what is known about change and the transition process is founded on the pioneering work of people like Alvin Toffler, William Bridges, and Elizabeth Kübler-Ross; references to their work are listed in the Bibliography.

Learning to deal with change is important for someone on a career planning journey. You are likely to change occupations several times during your career. Even if you do not, there will many changes in your work (and personal) life that will affect your career. The more effectively you address these inevitable changes, the more successful and less traumatic they will be.

Inevitable Changes

As you move through your career and your life, you will address many issues and tasks. The developmental issues covered in the previous chapter are only a few of the changes that will directly affect your career decision making and your life. What all of these life issues have in common is the element of change. As long as you are alive, you will be faced with change.

- **Changing technology** affects everyone. Technology changes at an accelerat-ing pace, bringing forth new products and enhancements to existing products. Some of these products can have far-reaching affects upon occupational oppor-tunity, making some jobs obsolete while they create others that never before existed.

- **Changing jobs** is a reality that almost everyone will face more than once dur-ing their career. Sometimes this may be a necessity (due to a layoff or down-sizing, for example); or it may be a matter of choice, in order to secure a more desirable job.

- **Changing working conditions** are common. Even if you stay in the same position, you will be subject to many kinds of change. Your supervisor may change, your co-workers may change, new duties may be assigned, new sys-tems may be introduced, or procedures may change.

- **Changing interests and activities** are a natural part of continuing to develop as an adult. New interests will emerge and activities will change as you pursue these interests. Old interests will fade and perhaps be renewed after awhile. This kind of change is a sign of being actively involved and interested in life.

- **Changing relationships** are also inevitable. As people go through changes in their lives, their relationships will change as well. If the relationship is a close one, the changes that can occur contribute to this closeness. Sometimes, the changes are so significant that a rift in the relationship occurs; the effect of the changes outweigh the strength of the relationship. Death, a most radical change, is another reality that we must all experience. Sooner or later, most people have to deal with the death of parents, a change that may have far-reaching effects.

- **Changing goals** can be expected throughout your life. As we have seen, the goals within each stage of development vary as a function of the issues that must be faced. Once you have resolved meaning issues, chances are that your most significant goals will not dramatically change, though corollary goals will do so.

- **Changing geographical location** is a fact of life in a mobile industrial economy. Very often, a person just starting out with a large company will be expected to transfer to another company location regularly. At times, promotion is predicated on a willingness to relocate. A major geographical move is an undertaking that will tax anyone's resources, especially if children are involved.

- **Changing economic conditions** have a major effect on job stability. The recession of the early 1990s put millions of people out of work. Some industries are more vulnerable to economic decline than others (retail enterprises, for example). Economic cycles are a reality that produce constant change in the job market.

- **Changing political and social policies** often have a direct impact upon people's lives. Decisions about taxes, trade policies, employment practices, individual and civil rights, and national defense introduce dramatic changes into society.

- **Changing personality characteristics** must also be dealt with. Such changes are usually evolutionary among adults, but occasionally a major shift in personality may occur over a relatively short period of time. In a healthy adult, such changes are primarily in the direction of increasing confidence and capability, mutually satisfying interdependence, identity definition, directional clarity, and realization of meaning. Unfortunately, this is not always the case. In fact, if developmental issues have not been successfully addressed, psychological problems can be expected to occur.

- **Changing physical condition** is something we all face as we grow older. Thinning hair, reduced muscular tone and strength, wrinkled skin, and weakening vision are part of growing older. With proper nutrition, reasonable physical activity, and good medical care, the effects of such changes can be minimized.

Change implies a transition from one circumstance to another. Even positive change usually involves some anxiety, uncertainty, and resulting stress. It is to your benefit to understand this process of change and transition, since understanding often relieves some of the stress involved. The next section discusses how people approach change from a variety of perspectives.

Approaches to Change

There are many responses to change. In her book *The Aquarian Conspiracy*, Marilyn Ferguson suggests four basic approaches people take when they process new information. The following is based on Ferguson's concepts. **Check the one that best describes how you approach change.**

☐ **The Reluctant approach is taken by people who resist change.** The Reluctants are basically conservative in their approach and like to stay with traditional, tried-and-true methods of doing things. They find change to be frightening, unsettling, and unnecessary. "If it ain't broke, don't fix it" is their motto. In career development terms, the Reluctant is exemplified by the person who is satisfied to stay in the same job until retirement. Reluctants have to change like everyone else, but they go kicking and screaming. On a positive note, this approach can provide a valuable element of stability in an otherwise rapidly changing environment.

☐ **The Step-by-Step approach is taken by those who are open to change but want it to happen slowly and predictably.** The Steppers like to have things planned and sequenced. They usually have an ideal toward which they move in predictable steps. "A little better every day" is their motto. In career development terms, the Stepper is exemplified by the person who methodically works from one position to another, seeking promotion, status, autonomy, or some other social or personal value. Steppers accept change but want it to be gradual and according to their own plan.

☐ **The Polar approach is taken by those who tend to go from one extreme to another.** The Polars tend to look at things in terms of black and white, with little room for gray areas. If they are going to change, they want a sweeping change, with no middle ground. Polars often totally reject one way of thinking and adopt a diametrically opposed one. "Out with the old, in with the new" might be their motto. In career development terms, the Polar is exemplified by the well-paid urban stockbroker who decides to drop out and buy 40 acres in the country in order to live off the land. Polars react to change by making reactive decisions.

☐ **The *Contextual* approach is taken by those who seek to understand and live in accordance with change.** The Contextuals take change for granted. They tend to think in relativistic terms, seeing things flexibly, from many different perspectives. For them, change comes about as an organic process—it grows out of existing conditions as naturally as a plant grows from a seed in the ground. Contextuals often make radical changes, but the changes are within the context of transformation. This transformation is not the reactive approach of the Polar, but a move into change itself. In career development terms, the Contextual is exemplified by the high school English teacher who has been successful in freelance writing and who decides to become a writer instead of teaching—a significant change that has grown out of experience. The Contextuals move into change in a proactive manner. Because of this readiness to change, Contextuals may appear unstable or unprincipled to others not comfortable with this approach.

No one approach to change is inherently better than another—they all have a place in the grand scheme of things. Also, many people do not fall clearly into any given category, but are a blend of approaches. However, if you wish to live more harmoniously with the change you encounter in life, you might want to study the approach of the Contextuals. People who approach change in a contextual manner have a number of characteristics in common:

■ **They accept the inevitability of change.** They take change for granted as part of life. They do not avoid, resist, try to control, or react to, change. Instead, they learn to merge with the change in their lives, much like a surfer merges with the wave. Just as surfers use the power of waves to sustain them toward the shore, you can use the energy behind change to sustain you as you move toward your goals.

■ **They are open-minded.** They are not stuck in any given way of thinking. They are open to new ideas and perspectives. At the same time, they are solidly grounded by clearly established principles and values. They are confident in their ability to discover truth and to apply their thinking skills to new situations.

■ **They do not fear insecurity.** They accept the inherent insecurity of change and life. They learn to re-establish a sense of security and to develop resources that support them when they are challenged by change.

■ **They are careful and creative thinkers.** They develop and use the critical and creative thinking techniques described in Chapter Six. They have a firm grasp on the reality of any given situation and do not cloud this perception with fuzzy, distorted, or wishful thinking.

■ **They are quick to see the potential hidden in change.** They focus on the positive aspects of change. They do not deny the pain involved in transitions, but it is not their focus. Where others see problems, they see opportunities.

- **They value personal growth.** They desire change as an opportunity to develop their personal strength, integrity, purpose, and meaning. They reflect upon the changes in their lives and seek to understand the lessons these changes so often contain.

- **They study the nature of change.** They are curious about how things change and have spent time observing and studying change. They are concerned about making change a constructive part of their understanding of life. This understanding provides a conceptual framework within which they can use change to their advantage.

The following Travelog exercise will help you apply this model of change to your own experience.

Travelog #43

- List one advantage of each approach to change.

    Reluctant

    Step-by-Step

    Polar

    Contextual

- For each of the four approaches, describe a situation in your life that you approached in the described manner. Describe it in enough detail to justify your selection.

    Reluctant

Step-by-Step

Polar

Contextual

It is important to recognize how you approach change situations. It is also valuable to have an idea of the stages you pass through as a part of the transition process.

Stages of Transition

William Bridges, author of *Transitions*, proposed three basic stages of transition: an ending, the neutral zone, and a new beginning. Elisabeth Kübler-Ross, in her pioneering work with the transition of death, proposed five stages of dealing with the ultimate transition: denial and isolation, anger, bargaining, depression, and acceptance. The model presented in this section is a conceptual hybrid of the Bridges and the Kübler-Ross models and suggests that major life transitions may be described in terms of six stages:

- **The experience of disintegration** is usually the first clue to an impending change. This may be experienced as old and familiar ideas, associations, or sources of meaning begin to fall apart or end. There is a sense that what once was, will be no more. Leaving a job could lead to this sense of disintegration. Some part of your life is coming to an end.

- **A period of shock** is often the first reaction to such a disintegration. The degree of shock will be determined by how prepared you are for the change, the shock being less severe when the change was expected or anticipated. For example, leaving a job would be less of a shock if you had some forewarning and had started looking for other opportunities. Denial—a refusal to accept what is happening—may also be an important element of this stage.

- **A period of anger** is not unusual once the shock wears off. When you lose something that was a familiar and important part of your life, anger is natural. If you were fired, or forced out of a job, anger is a natural reaction that will pass with time and understanding.

- **A period of sadness and emptiness** may follow as your anger dissipates. This sadness and emptiness is part of a natural period of adjustment to loss. This can be a very difficult stage of the transition process, and it varies in duration from one individual or situation to another.

- **Acceptance of change** will naturally occur as you allow yourself to pass through each stage of transition. The typical emotional reactions have passed and healing begins to take place. A clearer sense of the present reality sets the stage to move ahead with your life. If you lost your job, this would be the stage at which you fully recognize the need to move toward new opportunities.

- **Reintegration** comes out of this acceptance. The past is set aside and new opportunities emerge and come together. Both excitement and some anxiety may often be a part of this stage. This is a stage of creative risk-taking, and of formulating new meaning and direction. A new start in college or a new job could be examples of this last stage of transition.

As with the developmental stage theory explained in Chapter Nine, it is important to note that individual variations are common. Not everyone will start at the same stage, go through every stage, progress in the same order, or stop at the same place. This model simply provides a framework for understanding. It should not be taken as absolute.

The following Travelog asks you to apply these stages to a real-life transition.

Travelog #44

■ List two (2) major transitions that you have been through in the last few years.

1.

2.

■ For one of the transitions you listed above, describe how each of the stages of transition were evident. Give examples where possible.

Transition: _____

1. Disintegration

2. Shock

3. Anger

4. Sadness and emptiness

5. Acceptance

6. Reintegration

You know from your own experience that some transitions are more difficult to handle than others. There are identifiable reasons for this, some of which will be explored in the following section.

Transition Hazards

Not every change will lead to all six stages of transition, nor will the stages be of equal impact. The amount of trauma resulting from a transition depends, to a significant degree, upon the nature of the change. **A transition will likely be more difficult if the following characteristics are present (check those that apply to your career decision):**

☐ **If the change is unexpected**, it will hit you harder than if you are able to anticipate it to some degree. A sudden change in employment status is harder to deal with than a similar change that comes with adequate notice. Anticipation gives you time to process the natural reactions you will have and to prepare for the repercussions of the change.

☐ **If you did not have any choice in the matter**, you are more likely to feel like a victim and to harbor ill will toward those responsible. This lack of involvement can be especially difficult for people with a strong internal locus of control who want to feel responsible for the changes in their lives. If you have some degree of choice in a matter of change, you are much more likely to accept what is happening and to approach it from a more positive attitude.

☐ **If there are other sources of stress present in your life**, the cumulative effect of the stress of change can result in repercussions out of proportion to the change itself. It's like "the straw that broke the camel's back"—a seemingly small change can temporarily overwhelm your ability to cope. This is because you have been taxed by other stressors that depleted your capacity to buffer yourself against the debilitating effects of such stress.

☐ **If you have never dealt with this kind of change before**, the novelty of a change makes it more difficult to deal with. If you have experienced a similar event, you know what to expect and have an idea of what must be done. A change that is completely novel demands that you cope with the unexpected and the unknown, which is always challenging.

☐ **If the change conflicts with your goals or values in some manner**, it will have a greater impact. Change that furthers your goals, or that is aligned with your values, may still involve stress, but the cost is offset by the value gained. However, if you are dealing with a change that also impacts on what you value, you must deal with this as well.

☐ **If you have limited support from others**, you are obliged to call more exclusively upon your own resources. The comfort that comes from friends or family in a time of trouble is often invaluable. This kind of support can diffuse the impact of change. If such support is absent for some reason, the burden must be carried alone. The negative impact is more focused, and therefore has greater possibility for harm.

☐ **If the change involves a larger life issue** that you have not fully resolved, you are not as likely to have the required resources at your disposal. At each stage of adult development, you acquire coping skills that increase your ability to cope with life in a positive and productive manner. If you have unresolved developmental issues, you will be handicapped in dealing with change. Unresolved developmental issues can also contribute to a distortion of reality that needlessly complicates the situation.

With a better understanding of what affects the impact of change, you will be able to exercise some control over the transition process. This control will allow you to handle changes in a more constructive manner and to minimize the stress involved.

Transition Tips

*I*mproperly handled, transitions can have many negative effects: increased self-absorption, loss of energy and motivation, debilitating anxiety, loss of self-esteem, increased defensiveness, and even illness or injury due to the associated stress. These negative effects become less likely as you take an active role in understanding and managing the transition process. **There are a number of strategies you can use to better prepare yourself for the inevitable changes in your life:**

■ **Anticipate changes and plan for them.** Whenever possible, plan for the changes that are likely to impact your life. You will never be able to foresee all the changes that will affect you, but a "look-forward" posture will at least give you some warning in advance of many things that are headed in your direction.

■ **Allow yourself to experience the natural stages of transition.** It is one thing to be slightly "freaked out" by change; it is a needless mental complication to get freaked out about being freaked out! Accept that what you are going through may not be pleasant, but is a natural response to what you have experienced. If you have any doubts about the "normality" of what you are experiencing, it can be helpful to consult with a trusted friend, family member, or mental health professional.

- **Control the things you can influence.** Obviously, you will not be able to control all the variables involved in a transition. Too often, however, you may underestimate the amount of control you can assume over a situation. If you are realistic about your situation and have cultivated strength of mind and spirit, few changes will be beyond some possibility of influence.

- **Change your perspective.** One of the things you can control is the manner in which you view things. Changing your perspective can have a dramatic effect on how you think and feel. It helps to put your situation into a different context or to throw new light on it. Viktor Frankl argued that one important difference between those who survived in the Nazi death camps during World War II and those who did not was the ability to ascribe meaning in the face of horror.

- **Let go of those things you cannot control.** It is a waste of precious life energy to try to change things over which you have no influence. It is best to accept the inevitability of the situation and focus your energies on those things you can influence.

- **Keep in mind that each stage of transition will pass.** You will not feel anger or sadness forever, even though it may seem so at the time. Emotions are, by their very nature, constantly changing. Paradoxically, if you resist an emotion, it is more likely to persist and recur. By accepting and experiencing an emotion, you allow your mind and body to go through a natural process of healing and resolution.

- **Seek help if you seem to get "stuck."** A period of sadness is natural; if this turns into prolonged depression, counseling assistance might be indicated. Just sharing your experience with someone you can trust and who cares about you is a powerful tool of healing.

- **Try to discover if a change is related to a developmental issue.** If you can understand such a change in terms of the larger issue involved (for example, identity or direction), you will have a better chance of dealing with it in a constructive manner. For example, you may change majors every two months until you have a sense of identity and direction in your life. Dealing with this kind of change without dealing with the larger issue cannot be truly effective.

- **Beware of too much "change for the sake of change."** It may be an unconscious attempt to distract yourself from other more serious issues and concerns. There may be times when you should *not* change. Too much change may even lead to stress-related illnesses. Consciously limiting change can be used to bring stability to your life at a time when this could be very beneficial.

- **Learn how to relieve stress.** Make time to do the things you find relaxing. Physical exercise is often a constructive and effective outlet for stress. You may want to consider a class on stress-reduction techniques or meditation (often available through community schools). Never use unprescribed drugs (including alcohol) as a method of coping with stress. Drug use will inevitably add to the stress in your life, rather than reliev it. Such abuse also short-circuits your own natural healing process and retards your progress through the transition.

- **Resolve unfinished psychological business.** We have already discussed how unresolved developmental issues can complicate the transition process. This kind of "unfinished business" is like dead weight that you carry around with you all the time. You may not even notice it any more, but it affects you nonetheless. Most people can benefit from some kind of psychological counseling during key points in their life. A competent counselor can help you heal old hurts, let go of old resentments, bury old anger, and otherwise loosen the rope that hangs the burden of the past around your neck.

- **Enhance your psychological flexibility.** Most people are creatures of habit and fixed expectations. By consciously changing some of your habitual behavior and altering your expectations, you can cultivate greater flexibility in the face of change. It is best to do this during a time of relative stability in your life, not when you are going through an important transition.

- **Accept change as an inevitable part of life.** Resisting or fighting change makes the process more difficult. Change will affect your life—you have no choice about this. However, you *do* have a choice about how to approach change.

- **Spend some time alone.** Use this time for reflection and to allow yourself free expression of your emotions. If you have trouble spending time alone, you might want to explore the developmental area of independence as described in the previous chapter.

If you are able to do the kinds of things just mentioned, the road ahead will be straighter and smoother. The following Travelog asks you to consider elements of some of the transitions you have experienced.

Travelog #45

■ Think of a major life transition you had difficulty dealing with. List at least three (3) characteristics of this transition that made it difficult for you.

1.

2.

3.

■ Think of a major life transition that you handled easily. List at least three (3) characteristics of this transition that made it easy for you.

1.

2.

3.

■ List at least three (3) transition strategies that would make life and career transitions easier for you to handle.

1.

2.

3.

Quiz 10

*P*lease answer the following questions.

1. Read the following quotes and write (in the blank) the stage of transition each one best represents. There is one example for each stage.

   "I just feel numb. I can't believe this is happening."   _____

   "I feel as if I'm entering another phase of my life."   _____

   "There is no way that I'll let this happen!"   _____

   "I can see that this happened for a reason."   _____

   "It seems that the old behaviors no longer work."   _____

   "I just want to pull the covers over my head and cry."   _____

2. Read the following quotes and write (in the blank) the *approach to change* each one best represents. There is one example for each approach.

   "Viewed from this perspective, it looks very different."   _____

   "Things are fine just as they are."   _____

   "The old tradition needs to be turned on its head."   _____

   "We are gradually moving toward our goal."   _____

3. Has the information in this chapter influenced your tentative occupational choice? Why, or why not?

4. What is the most important thing that you learned about yourself by working through this chapter?

5. What topic covered in this chapter would you like to know more about?

To Consider . . .

In the United States and other advanced industrial nations, technological change is occurring at an ever-accelerating pace. Such changes have an impact that reverberates throughout the society.

Should a society be classified as "advanced" based solely on its technological progress?

Are there certain kinds of technology (for example, genetic research, new weapons development) that should not be pursued even if progress is possible?

Should the human cost of change be a consideration in pursuing new technology?

Should environmental impact be a major factor in the implementation of new technologies?

What can be done to assist people who have trouble adjusting to rapid technological changes?

From what perspective is this society still relatively primitive?

Why is it easier for some people to adjust to change than others?

Suggested Activities

1. Observe someone you know who is going through a major transition. Can you identify the stages they go through?

2. Interview several people who represent approaches to change (described in this chapter) that differ from your own. How do they view change? How do they approach the necessity to handle change in their life?

The Parable of Endings

Zara walked alone in the woods. Surrounded by the quiet he loved, only the crush of leaves underfoot announced his presence. He stopped and thought to himself: "The spirit is nourished by such silence and by the fresh air passed through the lungs of the virgin forest. The busy sounds of the city drown out the small voice within us that so softly calls us toward our Way."

He sat down upon a fallen log. Watching the airborne leaves, he thought: "Such a glorious, twirling death! When their time has come, these leaves, full in the glory of their autumn colors, fall gently and fearlessly from the tree of life to adorn the earth in a cover of wonderful hues. Their calling is complete. They go in peace. Such a death I would want for myself and my fellow spirits.

"But enough of these ending thoughts! I am here to speak of new beginnings!" With this, he stood up and walked out of the woods, back to the cabin where he and his disciple had spent the night. As he approached the cabin, he heard a great commotion. His disciple was running toward him, waving her arms, and screaming "Zara! Zara! Come quickly! The mayor is ill and asks for you!"

Zara went into town, to the bedside of the mayor, who was grievously ill. The mayor opened her eyes and spoke to Zara. "Zara, is that you? I have need of your counsel. I am dying. I know my end is near and I have made all the proper arrangements. Everything is ready for my passing except me! I fear this specter of death that is now approaching me. I have lived a good life. I have tried to follow my Way. But this encroaching darkness is so frightful!"

Zara took the hand of the mayor and looked into her eyes. Zara spoke to her: "Dear mayor, have you never before considered your ending? Did you think yourself immortal? Death stands beside the living at every instant, only a footstep away."

Zara thought for a moment and then said: "You have served this city well, my friend. Your Way is now complete. Do not struggle against the wind that calls you back to the earth from which you came. Let the wind take you with no fear in your heart. Like a falling leaf, let yourself twirl to a glorious ending, to the tranquil Ground of Being from which you came." The mayor nodded with understanding, smiled at Zara, relaxed her grip on his hand, and peacefully exhaled her last breath.

When Zara returned to the cabin, he spoke to his disciple: "Be glad you are not cursed with immortality! Live every instant of your life with the knowledge of your inevitable ending. Death stalks you upon this earth and will one day claim you as its prey. Use this knowledge to adjust your attitude and your values. Use this aware-ness to quicken the search for truth and meaning. Only those who have found their Way can fulfill their lives. Only those who have found their Way can die in peace!"

Conclusion

Do you possess courage . . .? [The courageous one] knows fear but mas-
ters fear . . . [and] grasps the abyss with an eagle's claws . . .
FREIDRICH NIETZSCHE

Pulling Things Together

You started this journey with a consideration of the *search for meaning* in your life. As you worked through this text, you have collected a lot of information about yourself, your career options, and the other factors that affect your career development.

As you conclude this book, it might be helpful to review the work you have done. Look over the results of your assessment and of the career exploration you did. Read through the Travelogs you completed. Consider what you have learned about decision making, critical and creative thinking, and developmental change. After you have done so, complete the following final Travelog in order to summarize your current career development status.

Travelog #46

1. What was the most *surprising* thing that you learned through your career planning? Why was it surprising?

2. What was the most *important* thing that you learned about yourself? Why do you consider this important?

3. What was the most *important* thing that you learned about the career planning process? Why do you consider this important?

4. List three (3) reasons you feel better prepared to make a career decision now than when you began this book.

   a.

   b.

   c.

5. Taking into consideration everything you have learned, what occupation do you plan to pursue? Why do you think this is a wise choice? How sure are you of this choice?

6. What additional resources do you need at this point to complete this phase of your career planning? How can you obtain these resources?

Wherever you may be along the path of career planning, you now have at your disposal a variety of skills and resources that can help you continue your journey. You need to continue to develop your skills and to make use of the resources you find most helpful. You have a framework of understanding that will serve you well when you revisit your career goals and objectives in the future.

Before the days of Columbus, mapmakers drew a line at the edge of the then-known world and labeled it: "Beware! Beyond this line, there be monsters!" The *Career Guide* has directed you toward the edge of your possibilities—toward a career decision that will, to some extent, influence your destiny. We hope you haven't run into too many "monsters" and that you have discovered something meaningful about yourself . . . and your Way.

The Parable of the Cipher

Zara and his disciple were awakened by a howling wind and a terrible crashing noise. The shutters on the windows were banging against the side of the cabin like the wings of a startled bird flushed from the underbrush.

Zara turned to his disciple and spoke: "The world awakens with such fury this morning . . . it is a dangerously opportune day for those who would fly . . . . Let us depart before this cabin itself takes flight!" They dressed and moved toward the daybreak, the wind at their backs pushing them deeper and deeper into the forest.

The trees were twisting violently in the wind, their leaves screaming a wild, enchanting hymn. Without a word, the two small figures made their way into the woods, following a straight path amid a swirling, writhing world. They reached a clearing, from which they could clearly see the birth of day. As the sun rose, the wind suddenly subsided and an eerie calm descended upon the surrounding forest. In the clearing just before them was a black stone marker, inscribed with strange symbols, planted in the earth like a signpost.

Zara knelt beside the marker and passed his fingers over the inscriptions. He then turned to his disciple and spoke: "I have seen this marker before! In a dream, I was lost when I came upon this same marker. But, in this dream, the marker's inscription was clear to me, not an unfamiliar code like this . . . ."

Zara grew quiet again. He sat in front of the stone and stared at the inscription. After a long while, he arose and spoke: "The way of the world is written in such a strange code. Even the few markers we find are themselves puzzles! Must we spend our entire lives in search of the cipher? It must be hidden deep within the world! The cipher must lie within the seed of all existence. Are we damned to forever bite the shell of this seed and never taste its germ?"

Zara's disciple approached the marker and spoke: "But master, the inscription is clear to me. It is written in my native tongue!" Zara jumped in amazement, his eyes wide with excitement. "What does it say?" he exclaimed.

The disciple carefully studied the inscription, softly touching and following each mark with her fingers. Then she spoke: "Zara, it is but one sentence and makes no sense to me . . . ."

Zara shouted at the top of his voice: "What? Can it be that those who know the meaning cannot read the markers, and those who can read the markers know nothing of their meaning? This world is full of surprises! Read the words to me, my friend!"

She looked once more at the black surface of the stone and spoke: "It says 'Those who would fly must surrender their wings.' " Zara gasped and backed away from the stone. "This is but a cipher to another terrible mystery," he said in a low, troubled voice.

Zara walked around the marker. Then he stopped and spoke to his disciple: "You have indeed found a marker! A signpost to oblivion! Our arch enemy, Gravity, has planted this stone upon the earth. Gravity: Enemy of all who would fly! Adversary of all seekers! Foe of those who would find their Way! Gravity would have you surrender your wings and crawl upon the earth for the rest of your days. Gravity would crush your spirit and leave you to die a slow, lingering death.

"Gravity whispers in your ear: 'You were not meant to fly. Why fight against my pull? It is so much easier to rest your belly upon the earth and mingle with those who are contented to crawl. Why climb the precipice? Why struggle against the wind? Why face the fearful abyss of life in the air?' So speaks Gravity."

Zara paused and looked into the sky far above him. Suddenly his eagle came into view, diving with unearthly speed, straight toward the marker. Making a deafening shriek as it swooped to the ground, Zara's eagle seized the marker with its powerful claws and ripped it easily from the ground. The mighty bird carried the stone far above the forest and let it fall upon the rocky mountain ledge, shattering the marker into a thousand jagged pieces.

Zara laughed aloud and exclaimed to his companion: "My eagle understands the cipher and the curse of Gravity! My eagle understands what must be done! Strengthen your wings, my friend. Sharpen your claws! Gravity can be overcome and broken by its own weight. The abyss only frightens those who dare not fly!"

The Job Outlook in Brief: 1990–2005

Source: *Occupational Outlook Quarterly*, Spring, 1992

Reprinted from the Occupational Outlook Quarterly/Spring 1992

OCCUPATIONAL OUTLOOK QUARTERLY

The Job Outlook in Brief

by Jay M. Berman and Theresa A. Cosca

> *"If you do not think about the future, you can not have one."*
> —JOHN GALSWORTHY

Galsworthy's warning about planning for the future applies to more than Saturday night dates, crucial though that may be. It also points to the importance of considering the kind of work you want to do for a living. In today's competitive marketplace, people who have not thought about their future may not have one, or at least not a very bright one. Job seekers must be able to match their skills to the jobs available. You'll stand a better chance of having the right skills if you know which ones will be in demand. And, in order to know which skills will be demanded, you must know which occupations will be providing the most jobs. You can begin to find the answers on the following pages.

The United States economy is projected to provide 24 million more jobs in 2005 than it did in 1990, an increase of 20 percent. But the labor force will change in more ways than just its size. Changing technology and business practices, increased foreign competition, and shifts in the demand for goods and services will reshape tomorrow's workforce—creating employment opportunities for workers in hundreds of occupations and displacing workers in others.

The Bureau of Labor Statistics analyzes the interplay of demographic, economic, social, and technological trends in order to develop projections of future demand in hundreds of industries and occupations. This article, which is revised every 2 years when the projections are updated, summarizes the 1990–2005 job outlook for about 250 occupations.

Information in the "Brief"

"The Job Outlook in Brief" provides thumbnail sketches of employment data for each occupation in the *Occupational Outlook Handbook*, 1992–93 edition, on which it is based. Each entry presents the occupation's title, its 1990 employment, the percent change projected in employment between 1990 and 2005, the projected numerical change, and a summary of job prospects. The occupations are grouped in the following 12 clusters:

- Executive, administrative, and managerial occupations
- Professional specialty occupations
- Technicians and related support occupations
- Marketing and sales occupations
- Administrative support occupations, including clerical
- Service occupations
- Agriculture, forestry, fishing, and related occupations
- Mechanics, installers, and repairers
- Construction trades and extractive occupations
- Production occupations
- Transportation and material moving occupations
- Handlers, equipment cleaners, helpers, and laborers.

Before turning to the occupations that interest you, look over the next few pages. They discuss factors that affect employment in an occupation—such as the demand for goods and services—describe the assumptions used in making the projections, and give an overview of the employment outlook for each of the 12 groups.

Jay M. Berman and Theresa A. Cosca are economists in the Office of Employment Projections, BLS

Why Employment Changes

The number of workers employed in any occupation depends in part on the demand for the goods or services provided by those workers. Over the last decade or so, for example, increased use of computers by businesses, schools, scientific organizations, and government agencies has contributed to large increases in the number of systems analysts, programmers, and computer repairers. Even if the demand for goods and services provided by a group of workers rises, however, employment may not increase or may increase more slowly than demand because of changes in the ways goods are produced and services are provided. In fact, some changes in technology and business practices cause employment to decline. For example, even though the volume of paperwork to process is expected to increase rapidly, employment of typists and word processors will fall; this reflects the growing use of word processing equipment that increases the productivity of these workers and permits other office workers to do more of their own typing.

Using information on the demand for goods and services, advances in technology, changes in business practices, and the occupational composition of industries, economists at BLS have developed three sets of projections of the economy in 2005. Each projection was developed in the light of a series of assumptions about the future. By varying the assumptions about such factors as growth of the labor force, output, productivity, inflation, and unemployment, the Bureau developed three different views of the economy. Referred to as the low-, moderate-, and high-growth scenarios, each provides a different employment estimate for most occupations. All the data in the "Brief" come from the moderate-growth projections.

Future employment growth is clouded by uncertainty. The different scenarios represent only three of many possible courses for the economy; different assumptions would lead to other projections. For this reason, the scenarios should not be viewed as the bounds of employment growth; rather, they illustrate what might happen under different conditions. For example, unforeseen changes in technology or the balance of trade could radically alter future employment for individual occupations.

More information about the assumptions underlying the projections and the methods used to develop them—along with some of the actual projections—is presented in "Outlook 1990–2005: Major Trends and Issues," the first article in this issue. The fall 1991 issue of *Occupational Outlook Quarterly* contains numerous charts that illustrate these projections; a series of articles in the November 1991 issue of the *Monthly Labor Review* presents detailed projections for the labor force, gross national product (GNP), industries, and occupations. "The 1990–2005 Outlook for College Graduates," which will be published in the summer 1992 issue of the *Quarterly*, will also be based on this set of projections.

Employment through the Year 2005

Between 1990 and 2005, employment will rise from 123 million to 147 million. This section gives an overview of projected employment change, focusing on the 12 occupational clusters. Keep in mind that a particular occupation may not follow the trend projected for its group. Therefore, you should refer to the table on pages 431 to 458 for the outlook in a specific occupation.

Throughout this article, employment growth rates are compared to the average for all occupations; the box, "Key Phrases in the Brief," explains the terms used. The box also explains the phrases used to describe the amount of competition jobseekers are likely to encounter. Assessing the degree of competition is difficult, although for occupations with lengthy training and strict entry requirements, it can be done with some accuracy. However, since most occupations have several methods of entry and flexible requirements, the potential supply of workers is difficult to measure and talk about shortages or surpluses is not meaningful.

One final factor to remember when checking the outlook for an occupation is that growth in employment is only one source of job openings. In fact, most openings arise because of the need to replace workers who transfer to other occupations or leave the labor force. As a result, even occupations with slower than average growth may offer many jobs for new workers, especially if large numbers of people work in them.

OCCUPATIONAL OUTLOOK QUARTERLY

Executive, administrative, and managerial occupations. Workers in executive, administrative, and managerial occupations establish policies, make plans, determine staffing requirements, and direct the activities of businesses, government agencies, another organizations. Workers in management support occupations, such as employment interviewers or cost estimators, provide technical assistance to managers.

The increasing complexity of organizational activities and continuing expansion of the economy are expected to contribute to faster than average growth for these workers. Because these workers are employed throughout the economy, differences in the rate of expansion for individual industries will produce varying rates of employment change for particular kinds of managers and support workers. For example, managers and administrators should experience faster than average growth in the services industry division, especially business services and engineering and management services. In contrast, those working in government are likely to face average or slower than average growth. Also, many businesses will restructure operations to reduce administrative costs and employ fewer managerial workers.

Due to growth in the number of people seeking these positions and increasingly technical requirements, jobseekers with work experience, specialized training, or graduate study will have an advantage in competition for jobs. Familiarity with computers will continue to be helpful as more managers rely on computerized information systems to help direct their organizations.

Professional specialty occupations. This group includes engineers; architects and surveyors; computer, mathematical, and operations research occupations; life, physical, and social scientists; lawyers and judges; social, recreational, and religious workers; teachers, librarians, and counselors; health diagnosing, assessment, and treating occupations; and communications, visual arts, and performing arts occupations. Professional workers may provide services or conduct research. They are employed in almost every industry.

This major group as a whole is expected to continue to grow faster than average and to increase its share of total employment significantly by 2005. However, growth rates for individual occupations are as diverse as the jobs these workers perform. For example, physical therapists, human services workers, operations research analysts, and computer systems analysts are expected to grow much faster than average. On the other hand, physicists and astronomers; mining, nuclear, and petroleum engineers; librarians; and musicians should grow more slowly than average. Most new jobs will be in education and health services.

Technicians and related support occupations. This major group includes health technologists and technicians, engineering and science technicians, computer programmers, tool programmers, aircraft pilots, air traffic controllers, paralegals, broadcast technicians, and library technicians. Workers in this group operate and program technical equipment and assist engineers, scientists, health practitioners, and other professional workers.

Changes in technology, demographics, and ways of conducting business will contribute to faster employment growth in some of these occupations than in others. Overall employment is expected to grow faster than for any other major occupational group. This group contains one of the fastest growing occupations—paralegals; its growth will result in part from the increasing reliance of lawyers on these workers. Increased demand for health services from a growing and aging population will spur employment growth for radiologic technologists, medical record technicians, surgical technologists, and electroencephalographic technologists. In fact, jobs for health technologists and technicians are expected to account for almost half of all the jobs in this group. The employment of computer programmers will also continue to grow rapidly, as more organizations use computers and the number of computer applications increases.

Employment growth in other occupations in this group will be limited. For example, because of labor-saving technological advances, employment of broadcast technicians should show little change and employment of air traffic controllers should grow more slowly than average. Similarly, library technicians will grow more slowly than average, following the growth pattern of other library workers.

Marketing and sales occupations. Workers in this group sell goods and services, purchase commodities and property for resale, and stimulate consumer interest.

Employment is expected to grow as fast as average because of the increased demand for financial, travel, and other services. However, the rate of growth should be slower than over the previous 15 years because these workers are concentrated in wholesale and retail trade, industries which will grow more slowly than in the past.

A large number of part-time and full-time positions are expected to be available for cashiers and retail trade sales workers due to the large size of these occupations and high turnover, as well as employment growth. Higher paying sales occupations, such as securities and financial services sales workers, tend to be more competitive than retail sales occupations. Job opportunities will be best for well-trained, personable, and ambitious people who enjoy selling.

Administrative support occupations, including clerical. Workers in this group prepare and record memos, letters, and reports; collect accounts; gather and distribute information; operate office machines; and handle other administrative tasks.

This occupational group will continue to employ the largest number of workers, but overall employment growth is expected to be slower than average. As a result, these occupations will decline as a proportion of total employment by 2005. Despite the tremendous increase expected in the volume of clerical tasks to be done, increased automation and other technological changes will limit employment growth in many clerical occupations, such as typists, word processors, and data entry keyers; bookkeeping, accounting, and auditing clerks; and telephone operators. In contrast, teacher aides and hotel desk clerks should grow faster than average, and receptionists and information clerks is expected to experience much faster than average growth, because these occupations are concentrated in rapidly growing industries.

Because many administrative support occupations are large and have relatively high turnover, opportunities should be plentiful for full- and part-time jobs, even in slow growing occupations.

Service occupations. This group includes a wide range of workers in protective services, food and beverage preparation, health services, and personal and cleaning services. These occupations are expected to grow faster than average because a growing population and economy, com-bined with higher personal incomes and increased leisure time, will spur demand for many different types of services. This group is projected to add the largest number of jobs of any occupational group by 2005.

Among protective service occupations, guards is expected to increase faster than average because of growing concern over crime and vandalism. As the number of prisoners and correctional facilities increases, more correction officers will also be needed. However, the anticipated slow growth of local government spending is expected to produce only average employment growth for police officers and fire fighters.

Employment growth will also be faster than average for food and beverage preparation and service occupations. Due to the large size, high turnover, and fast growth of many food service occupations—such as chefs, cooks, and other kitchen workers—both full- and part-time jobs will be plentiful.

Growth in personal service and cleaning occupations will vary widely. For example, while homemaker–home health aides should be the fastest growing occupation—in part because of the substantial increase in the elderly population—private household workers will grow slowly due to the shift from home to institutional child care.

Among health services occupations, medical assistants—one of the fastest growing occupations in the economy—and nursing and psychiatric aides will grow much faster than average, in response to the aging population and expanding health care industry.

Agriculture, forestry, fishing, and related occupations. Workers in these occupations cultivate plants, breed and raise animals, and catch fish. Although demand for food, fiber, and wood is expected to increase as the world's population grows, the use of more productive farming and forestry methods and the consolidation of small farms are expected to result in little or no employment change in most of these occupations. The employment of farm operators and farm workers is expected to decline rapidly, reflecting greater productivity; the need for skilled farm managers, on the other hand, should result in employment growth about as fast as average for that occupation.

Mechanics, installers, and repairers. Workers in this group adjust, maintain, and repair automobiles, industrial equipment, computers, and many other types of machinery. Average overall growth is expected due to the continued importance of mechanical and electronic equipment throughout the economy, but projections vary by occupation. For example, computer and office machine repairers is expected to be one of the fastest growing occupations in this group, reflecting the increased use of these types of machines. In sharp contrast, communications equipment mechanics, installers, and repairers and telephone installers and repairers are expected to decline in employment due to laborsaving advances.

Construction trades and extractive occupations. Workers in this group construct, alter, and maintain buildings and other structures or operate drilling and mining equipment. Virtually all of the new jobs will be in construction. An increase in the number of households and industrial plants, the desire to alter or modernize existing structures, and the need to maintain and repair highways, dams, and bridges will result in average employment growth in construction. In contrast, continued stagnation in the oil and gas industries and low growth in demand for coal, metal, and other minerals will result in little change in the employment of extractive workers.

Because the construction industry is sensitive to changes in the Nation's economy, employment in construction occupations fluctuates from year to year. Many construction workers become unemployed during downturns in construction activity.

Production occupations. These workers set up, adjust, operate, and tend machinery and use handtools and hand-held power tools to make goods and assemble products. Increases in imports, overseas production, and automation—including robotics and advanced computer techniques—will result in little change or slight declines in overall employment. For a few occupations, however, employment growth is expected. Plastics-working machine operators, for example, is projected to grow as fast as the average because plastics are increasingly substituted for metal in many goods. Also, expansion of the printing and publishing industry will create average growth for prepress workers and printing press operators.

Many production occupations are sensitive to fluc-

tuations in the business cycle and competition from imports. When factory orders decline, workers face shortened workweeks, layoffs, and plant closings.

Transportation and material moving occupations. Workers in this group operate the equipment used to move people and materials. Although overall employment is expected to grow about as fast as average, prospects vary by occupation. Faster than average growth is expected for busdrivers, and average growth is expected for truckdrivers. These projections reflect rising school enrollments and growing demand for transportation services. However, slower than average growth is expected in the employment of material moving equipment operators because of the increased use of automated material handling systems. Both the water and railroad transportation industries will experience a decline in employment as technological advances increase productivity.

Handlers, equipment cleaners, helpers, and laborers. Workers in these occupations assist skilled workers and perform routine tasks. Because more of these tasks are being automated, employment is expected to increase more slowly than average. Many opportunities will arise from the need to replace workers who leave these occupations, because turnover is very high. However, economic downturns may substantially lower the number of openings. This is particularly true for construction laborers and other occupations in industries that are highly sensitive to changes in the economy.

Beyond the "Brief"

"The Job Outlook in Brief" is only a starting point for your exploration of careers. Although it provides outlook information in a format that allows easy comparison of job prospects in different fields, employment prospects are not the only consideration when choosing a certain career. Matching your goals and abilities to the work done on the job and the education required is another important part of choosing a career. Where you want to live and how much money you want to earn also are important. Besides the information in the "Brief," therefore, you may want more detailed occupational information or information about other occupations.

A major source of career guidance information is the 1992–93 edition of the *Occupational Outlook Handbook;* it contains more detailed outlook information on each of the occupations presented in the "Brief," as well as information about the nature of the work qualifications, average earnings, and other subjects.

Occupational Projections and Training Data, 1992 edition, is a statistical supplement to the *Handbook;* it contains current and projected employment estimates for about 500 occupations. It also presents information on occupational separation rates, unemployment rates, and the demographic characteristics of workers when such information is available. Both are available from the Bureau of Labor Statistics Publication Sales Center, P.O. Box 2145, Chicago, IL 60690, or from New Orders, Superintendent of Documents, P.O. Box 371954, Pittsburgh, PA 15250–7954. The *Handbook* costs $23 with a paper cover, $26 with a hard cover. Payment by check, money order, VISA, Master-Card, or GPO deposit account must accompany your order. Make check or money order payable to the Superintendent of Documents. In addition, copies usually are available in libraries and the offices of school guidance counselors and employment counselors.

Additional information on job growth also is available from State Job Service offices. The outlook for many occupations varies considerably among local job markets. For example, sections of the country with slow population growth may have less need for ele-mentary school teachers than regions with high growth. State Job Service offices, listed in the State government section of local telephone directories, can provide information on local labor market conditions.

Key Phrases in the "Brief"

Changing employment between 1992 and 2005

If the statement reads...	Employment is projected to...
Grow much faster than average	Increase 35 percent or more
Grow faster than average	Increase 25 to 34 percent
Grow about as fast as average	Increase 14 to 24 percent
Grow more slowly than average	Increase 5 to 13 percent
Show little change	Increase or decrease 4 percent or less
Decline	Decrease 5 percent or more

Opportunities and competition for jobs

If the statement reads...	Job openings compared to jobseekers may be...
Excellent opportunities	Much more numerous
Very good opportunities	More numerous
Good or favorable opportunities	About the same
May face competition	Fewer
May face keen competition	Much fewer

The 30 fastest growing occupations and the 30 occupations with the largest job growth are identified by this symbol: Reprints of this article will be sold by the Superintendent of Documentation.

Executive-Administrative-Managerial

CLUSTER Subgroup Occupation	Estimated employment 1990[1]	Percent change in employment 1990-2005[1]	Numerical change in employment 1990–2005[1]	Employment prospects
EXECUTIVE, ADMINISTRATIVE, AND MANAGERIAL OCCUPATIONS				
Accountants and auditors	985,000	34	340,000	As the number of businesses increases and the complexity of the financial information required grows, more accountants and auditors will be needed to set up books, prepare taxes, and advise management. Faster than average job growth is expected, which should result in favorable opportunities for those with a bachelor's or higher degree in accounting.
Administrative services managers	221,000	23	52,000	Average employment growth is expected. Although demand should be spurred by the growing need for various administrative services—overseeing the implementation and operation of sophisticated office systems, for example—corporate attempts to reduce administrative costs by streamlining office and information handling procedures will offset the increase in demand. As with other managerial jobs, the ample supply of competent, experienced workers seeking advancement should result in competition for these jobs.
Budget analysts	64,000	22	14,000	Although the increasing use of automation may make budget analysts more productive, the growing complexity of business and increasing need for information will result in average employment growth. Keen competition for jobs is expected; prospects will be best for holders of a master's degree and college graduates with experience in finance and accounting.
Construction and building inspectors	60,000	19	11,000	Increases in the level and complexity of construction activity, rising concern for public safety, and growing desire for improvements in the quality of construction should result in average employment growth. Job prospects will be best for experienced craft workers who have some college education or are certified.
Construction contractors and managers	183,000	33	60,000	Increases in the size and complexity of construction projects and the proliferation of laws setting standards for buildings and construction materials, worker safety, energy efficiency, and pollution should result in faster than average growth. Completion of a bachelor's degree program in construction science with emphasis on construction management can greatly enhance one's opportunities in this field.
Cost estimators	173,000	24	42,000	Average growth is expected as more estimators are needed to predict the cost of the growing number of construction and manufacturing projects. In construction, job prospects will be best for those with construction experience or with a degree in construction management, engineering, or architectural drafting; in manufacturing, job prospects will be best for experienced people with computer expertise and a degree in engineering, science, math, business, or economics.
Education administrators	348,000	24	85,000	Employment is expected to grow as fast as average as school enrollments increase. Substantial competition is expected for principal, assistant principal, and central office jobs because many teachers and other staff meet the requirements for these jobs and seek promotion.

[1]Nearly all estimates are from the BLS industry-occupation matrix.

CLUSTER Subgroup Occupation	Estimated employment 1990[1]	Percent change in employment 1990-2005[1]	Numerical change in employment 1990–2005[1]	Employment prospects
Employment interviewers	83,000	23	19,000	Average growth is expected due to the expansion of employment agencies and temporary help firms. Opportunities should be excellent for articulate, outgoing people who enjoy public contact and a fast-paced work environment.
Engineering, science, and data processing managers	315,000	34	108,000	Faster than average employment growth is expected. Employment growth of each type of manager is expected to correspond closely with growth of the occupation supervised.
Financial managers	701,000	28	193,000	The need for sound financial advice should spur faster than average growth for several reasons: The increasing variety and complexity of financial services, increased interstate and international banking, growing competition, changing laws regarding taxes and other financial matters, and greater emphasis on the accuracy of financial data. As in other management occupations, applicants face competition for positions; opportunities will be best for those familiar with data processing and management information systems and a wide range of financial services.
General managers and top executives	3,086,000	19	598,000	Expansion in the size, number, and complexity of business firms should spur demand for general managers and top executives. However, many firms are improving operating efficiency by establishing a leaner corporate structure with fewer management positions, resulting in average employment growth. Substantial competition is expected for these high paying, prestigious jobs due to the number of lower level managers seeking advancement.
Government chief executives and legislators	71,000	4	3,100	Little change in employment is expected. Few, if any, new local governments will be formed, nor will existing governments change the number of chief executives and legislators. Slight growth may occur as expanding communities become independent and elect officials or as communities with unpaid, therefore uncounted, officials create salaried positions.
Health services managers	257,000	42	108,000	Much faster than average growth is expected as the health care industry expands and diversifies. Employment in home health care services and nursing care facilities will grow the fastest.
Hotel managers and assistants	102,000	44	45,000	The growing volume of business and vacation travel will increase demand for hotels and motels, spurring much faster than average employment growth. Opportunities should be best for people with college degrees in hotel or restaurant management.
Industrial production managers	210,000	20	41,000	Average employment growth will be fueled by increased production of consumer and industrial products. Prospects will be best for those who have a master's degree in business administration, especially if they also have an undergraduate degree in engineering.
Inspectors and compliance officers except construction	156,000	30	46,000	Faster than average employment growth will be spurred by expansion of regulatory and compliance programs in government, especially in local government, and by increasing self-enforcement of government regulations and company policies in private industry.

[1]Nearly all estimates are from the BLS industry-occupation matrix.

CLUSTER Subgroup Occupation	Estimated employment 1990[1]	Percent change in employment 1990-2005[1]	Numerical change in employment 1990–2005[1]	Employment prospects
Management analysts and consultants	151,000	52	79,000	Competitive pressures on organizations will contribute to much faster than average growth. Opportunities will be best for those with a graduate degree or industry expertise. Good organizational and marketing skills, plus several years of consulting experience, are essential for people interested in starting their own firm.
Marketing, advertising, and public relations managers	427,000	47	203,000	Intensifying domestic and foreign competition—requiring greater marketing, promotional, and public relations efforts—should result in much faster than average growth. However, these jobs will be sought by other managers and experienced professional and technical personnel, resulting in substantial competition. Job prospects will be best for experienced, creative college graduates who communicate well.
Personnel, training, and labor relations specialists and managers	456,000	32	144,000	Faster than average growth is expected as employers devote greater resources to training programs in response to the increasing complexity of many jobs, the aging of the work force, and advances in technology that can leave employees with obsolete skills. Also, legislation and court rulings setting standards in occupational safety and health, equal employment opportunity, employment benefits, and other areas has increased the amount of recordkeeping, analysis, and report writing required. However, the job market is likely to remain competitive in view of the abundant supply of college graduates and experienced workers with suitable qualifications.
Property and real estate managers	225,000	34	76,000	Faster than average job growth is expected to result from increases in the number of office buildings, retail properties, and apartment complexes requiring management. Overbuilding and the subsequent concern for profitable property management should also stimulate employment growth. People with a college degree in business administration or a related field should have the best job opportunities.
Purchasing agents and managers	300,000	23	69,000	The increased recognition of the importance of efficient purchasing procedures is expected to result in average growth. Those with a bachelor's or advanced degree should have the best opportunities.
Restaurant and food service managers	556,000	32	177,000	Growth in the number of eating and dining establishments will result in faster than average growth in employment. Opportunities are expected to be best for people with degrees in restaurant or institutional food service management.
Underwriters	105,000	24	25,000	Employment is expected to grow as fast as average. The expected rise in the volume, complexity, and variety of insurance products will be offset by the trend toward self insurance and the increased use of artificial intelligence. Underwriters with extensive computer knowledge should have the best opportunities.
Wholesale and retail buyers and merchandise managers	361,000	19	68,000	Although sales volume will continue to increase, the centralization of purchasing departments will result in only average growth. Because merchandising attracts many college graduates, applicants are likely to continue to be more numerous than openings. Job prospects will be best for those with previous wholesale or retail experience.

[1] Nearly all estimates are from the BLS industry-occupation matrix.

Professional Specialty Occupations

CLUSTER Subgroup Occupation	Estimated employment 1990[1]	Percent change in employment 1990-2005[1]	Numerical change in employment 1990–2005[1]	Employment prospects
PROFESSIONAL SPECIALTY OCCUPATIONS				
Engineers	1,519,000[2]	26	400,000	Opportunities for those with degrees in engineering have been good since the mid-1970's, and this trend is expected to continue. Employment of engineers is expected to increase faster than average. Much of the growth will stem from higher levels of investment in industrial plants and equipment to meet the demand for more goods and services and to increase productivity.
Aerospace engineers	73,000	20	15,000	Although defense expenditures for military aircraft, missiles, and other aerospace systems are expected to decline, employment is expected to increase about as fast as average because of growth in the civilian sector. Many commercial planes will be replaced with quieter, more fuel-efficient aircraft, and increased demand for spacecraft, helicopters, and business aircraft is expected.
Chemical engineers	48,000	12	5,600	Employment will grow more slowly than average—because little, if any, growth is expected in the chemical manufacturing industry, where many chemical engineers are employed. Industrial chemicals, biotechnology, and materials science may provide better opportunities than other portions of the chemical industry.
Civil engineers	198,000	30	59,000	A growing population and economy—and the resulting need to design, construct, and rebuild transportation systems, water resource and disposal systems, large buildings, and other structures—should result in faster than average growth.
Electrical and electronics	426,000	34	145,000	Increased demand for computers, electronic consumer goods, communications equipment, and other electrical and electronic products is expected to result in faster than average growth. Opportunities should be favorable.
Industrial engineers	135,000	19	26,000	Employment is expected to grow about as fast as average due to the increased complexity of business operations, increased interest in efficiency by businesses, and greater use of automation in factories and offices. Qualified applicants should find good job prospects.
Mechanical engineers	233,000	24	56,000	Average growth is expected as the demand for machinery and machine tools grows and as industrial machinery and processes become increasingly complex. Because mechanical engineering is the broadest engineering discipline, opportunities should be favorable in many industries.
Metallurgical, ceramic, and materials engineers	18,000	21	3,900	Employment should increase about as fast as average to meet the demands on metalworking and other industries to develop new materials and to adapt existing ones to new applications.
Mining engineers	4,200	4	([3])	Little change in employment is expected because demand for coal, metals, and other minerals is expected to grow slowly. Also, mining operations employ few engineers per site, so even a large expansion in demand may not result in substantially greater opportunities.

[1] Nearly all estimates are from the BLS industry-occupation matrix.
[2] Total exceeds the sum of the individual estimates because not all branches of engineering are covered separately.
[3] Less than 500.

CLUSTER Subgroup Occupation	Estimated employment 1990[1]	Percent change in employment 1990-2005[1]	Numerical change in employment 1990–2005[1]	Employment prospects
Nuclear engineers	18,000	0	([3])	Although little change in employment is expected, opportunities should be good because the number of nuclear engineering graduates is small and has been declining.
Petroleum engineers	17,000	1	([3])	Little change in employment is expected. Oil exploration and production have been curtailed by low oil prices. In the long run, however, the price of oil is likely to increase, stimulating exploration and production, which would improve employment prospects.
Architects and surveyors				
Architects	108,000	24	26,000	Good opportunities are expected because employment growth should be as fast as average and because the number of degrees granted in architecture is not expected to increase significantly. Competition will continue for jobs in the most prestigious firms, as well as during recessions or slowdowns in construction.
Landscape architects	20,000	31	6,200	Growth in new construction over the long run and a growing commitment to environmental planning and historic preservation will result in faster than average growth.
Surveyors	108,000	14	15,000	Increased real estate transactions and construction should contribute to average growth. However, employment fluctuates from year to year because construction is sensitive to changes in economic conditions. The best opportunities will be for those with at least a bachelor's degree.
Computer, mathematical, and operations research occupations				
Actuaries	13,000	34	4,400	Faster than average employment growth will be spurred by the increasing volume and complexity of insurance policies and health and pension plans and by the introduction of new forms of insurance. Actuaries may face competition for jobs because the number of workers entering the occupation has increased substantially in recent years. Opportunities will be best for college graduates who have passed at least two actuarial exams while still in school and have a strong background in mathematics and statistics.
Computer systems analysts	463,000	79	366,000	Employment is expected to grow much faster than average as organizations attempt to maximize efficiency by networking their computer systems for office and factory automation, communications capability, and scientific research. Job prospects will be very good for college graduates who combine courses in programming and systems analysis with training and experience in applied fields.
Mathematicians	22,000	9	2,000	Employment is expected to grow more slowly than average. However, the continuing shortage of Ph.D.'s will result in favorable opportunities for mathematicians, especially those with doctorates in applied mathematics. Those with a master's or bachelor's degree who have strong backgrounds in computer science, electrical or mechanical engineering, or operations research should also have good job opportunities.
Operations research analysts	57,000	73	42,000	As computer costs fall and competitive pressures grow, more organizations will turn to operations research to aid decision making, resulting in much faster than average growth. Opportunities will be especially favorable in manufacturing, trade, and service firms.

[1] Nearly all estimates are from the BLS industry-occupation matrix.
[3] Less than 500.

OCCUPATIONAL OUTLOOK QUARTERLY

CLUSTER Subgroup Occupation	Estimated employment 1990[1]	Percent change in employment 1990-2005[1]	Numerical change in employment 1990–2005[1]	Employment prospects
Statisticians	16,000	12	1,800	Although employment is expected to grow more slowly than average, job opportunities should remain favorable, especially for people with advanced degrees. Graduates with a bachelor's degree in statistics and a strong background in mathematics or computer science should have the best prospects of finding jobs related to their field of study.
Life scientists				
Agricultural scientists	25,000	27	6,600	Good employment prospects are expected because enrollments in agricultural science curriculums have dropped considerably over the last few years and because employment should grow faster than average. Animal and plant scientists with a background in molecular biology, microbiology, genetics, or biotechnology; soil scientists; and food technologists will probably have the best opportunities.
Biological scientists	62,000	34	21,000	Increased demand for genetic and biological research, in part because of efforts to preserve and clean up the environment, should result in faster than average growth. Most new jobs will be in the private sector; employment in government is expected to grow slowly.
Foresters and conservation scientists	29,000	12	3,600	Budgetary constraints in government, where employment is highly concentrated, will result in slower than average overall growth. However, State governments and private owners of timberland may employ more foresters due to increased interest in environmental protection and land management. Overall, job opportunities should be more favorable than in the past due to an expected wave of retirements and recent declines in the number of graduates in forestry and related fields.
Physical scientists				
Chemists	83,000	16	13,000	Very good employment opportunities are expected because the number of graduates with degrees in chemistry is not expected to increase enough to meet future demand. Employment should increase about as fast as average. Job opportunities will be best in pharmaceuticals and biotechnology, where Ph.D. chemists are expected to be in strong demand.
Geologists and geophysicists	48,000	22	11,000	Environmental protection and regulation are becoming important fields of work for those with the appropriate training. When oil and gas exploration activities increase, geologists and geophysicists should have excellent opportunities. Average growth is expected.
Meteorologists	5,500	30	1,600	The National Weather Service, which employs many meteorologists, plans to increase employment to improve its short-term and local forecasts. This should result in faster than average growth.
Physicists and astronomers	20,000	5	1,000	Although slower than average growth is expected, job opportunities for Ph.D.'s should be good in the late 1990's when many physics and astronomy professors become eligible for retirement.
Lawyers and judges	633,000	34	217,000	The demand for legal services caused by population growth and economic expansion will create faster than average employment growth. Competition is expected to ease somewhat for salaried attorney positions, but remain intense for judgeships.

[1]Nearly all estimates are from the BLS industry-occupation matrix.

CLUSTER Subgroup Occupation	Estimated employment 1990[1]	Percent change in employment 1990-2005[1]	Numerical change in employment 1990–2005[1]	Employment prospects
Social scientists and urban planners				
Economists and marketing research analysts	37,000	21	8,000	Employment is expected to increase as fast as average, reflecting increased reliance on quantitative methods to analyze business trends, forecast sales, and plan purchasing and production. For economists, master's and doctoral degree holders will have the best opportunities. Bachelor's degree holders face competition; those skilled in quantitative techniques have the best prospects. For marketing research positions, those with an advanced degree in marketing or a related field have the best prospects.
Psychologists	125,000	64	79,000	Much faster than average growth is anticipated due to increased attention being paid to the expanding elderly population, the maintenance of mental health, and the testing and counseling of children. Ph.D.'s with training in applied areas, such as clinical or counseling psychology, and in quantitative research methods have the best prospects. Among master's degree holders, specialists in school psychology should have the best prospects, while bachelor's degree holders will have very few opportunities in this field.
Sociologists	([4])	([4])	([4])	Opportunities will be best for Ph.D.'s and master's degree holders with strong quantitative research skills and training in applied areas such as clinical sociology, gerontology, criminology, or demography. Bachelor's degree holders have very few opportunities in this field.
Urban and regional planners	23,000	19	4,400	Increased demand for planning related to the environment, the economy, transportation, and energy production should result in average employment growth. Opportunities will be best in rapidly growing areas, older areas undergoing preservation and redevelopment, and States that have mandated planning. Graduates of institutions with accredited planning programs have the best prospects.
Social and recreation workers				
Human services workers	145,000	71	103,000	Employment is expected to grow much faster than average due to the expansion of facilities and programs for the elderly and disabled and greater services for families in crisis. Prospects are excellent for qualified applicants, who are avidly sought because of the demanding nature of the work, the relatively low pay, and the subsequent high turnover.
Social workers	438,000	34	150,000	Faster than average growth is expected in response to the needs of a growing and aging population, as well as increasing concern about services for the mentally ill, the mentally retarded, and families in crisis. Employment in hospitals is expected to grow due to greater emphasis on discharge planning. Employment prospects in private practice are favorable due to funding from health insurance.
Recreation Workers	194,000	24	47,000	Employment is expected to increase as fast as average. Programs for special groups and greater interest in fitness and health will underlie expansion. Competition is expected for full-time career positions. Opportunities for seasonal jobs will be excellent.

[1] Nearly all estimates are from the BLS industry-occupation matrix.
[4] Estimates not available.

CLUSTER Subgroup Occupation	Estimated employment 1990[1]	Percent change in employment 1990-2005[1]	Numerical change in employment 1990–2005[1]	Employment prospects
Religious workers				
Protestant ministers	255,000[5]	([4])	([4])	While the increasing cost of operating a church will moderate demand for ministers, slower growth in the number of ordained ministers will result in less competition. The most favorable opportunities are for rural and part-time positions, but opportunities vary by denomination.
Rabbis	2,700[5]	([4])	([4])	Opportunities are expected to be good, especially in small communities and nonmetropolitan areas since most rabbis prefer to serve in large, urban areas.
Roman Catholic priests	53,000[5]	([4])	([4])	The continuing decline in seminary enrollments coupled with an expected increase in retirements should intensify the shortage of ordained priests.
Teachers, librarians, and counselors				
Adult education teachers	517,000	29	152,000	Overall employment is expected to grow faster than average as demand for adult education programs continues to rise. Many openings will arise from the need to replace workers who leave the occupation, particularly given the large number of part-time workers and high turnover in the occupation.
Archivists and curators	17,000	21	3,700	Employment will increase as fast as average, continuing past trends. Competition for jobs will remain keen, however, given the small number of job openings and large supply of workers.
College and university faculty	712,000	19	134,000	Average employment growth is expected as enrollments increase. Beginning in the late 1990's, job opportunities should improve due to an expected wave of faculty retirements. Job prospects are best with business, engineering, computer, and science faculties because of the availability of high-paying jobs outside academe.
Counselors	144,000	34	49,000	Employment is expected to grow faster than average, due to increasing school enrollments, greater use of third party payments to counselors, and the expanded responsibility of counselors. Job openings should increase by the year 2005 as the large number of counselors now in their 40's and 50's reach retirement age.
Kindergarten and elementary school teachers	1,521,000	23	350,000	Average employment growth is expected as enrollments increase and class size declines. The number of job openings should increase substantially after the mid-1990's, as the large numbers of teachers now in their 40's and 50's reach retirement age.
Librarians	149,000	11	17,000	Employment is expected to grow more slowly than average, continuing the limited employment growth of librarians during the 1980's. The decline in the number of graduates of library science programs in the 1980's, however, should result in favorable job prospects for such graduates.
Secondary school teachers	1,280,000	34	437,000	Employment is expected to increase faster than average as enrollments grow and class size declines. Job openings will increase substantially after the mid-1990's as the large number of teachers now in their 40's and 50's reach retirement age.
Health diagnosing occupations				
Chiropractors	42,000	([4])	([4])	Employment is expected to rise because of the rapidly growing older population, with its greater likelihood of physiological problems, and as the awareness of chiropractic services grows.

[1] Nearly all estimates are from the BLS industry-occupation matrix.
[4] Estimates not available.
[5] Includes only those who served congregations.

OCCUPATIONAL OUTLOOK QUARTERLY

CLUSTER Subgroup Occupation	Estimated employment 1990[1]	Percent change in employment 1990-2005[1]	Numerical change in employment 1990–2005[1]	Employment prospects
Dentists	174,000	12	21,000	Job prospects should continue to improve because the number of dental school graduates has declined since the early 1980's and is not likely to increase much. Despite a growing demand for dental services, employment is projected to grow more slowly than average. Dentists should respond to growing demand by working more hours and relying on dental hygienists and assistants to provide more services.
Optometrists	37,000	20	7,600	Employment is expected to grow as fast as average in order to meet the needs of a population that is larger, older, and more aware of the need for proper eye care. Job opportunities should be good, even though replacement needs are low.
Physicians	580,000	34	196,000	Employment is expected to grow faster than average due to a growing and aging population and technological improvements that encourage expansion of the health industry. Job prospects should be better in internal medicine, family practice, geriatrics, and preventive medicine than in other specialties.
Podiatrists	16,000	46	7,300	Employment is expected to grow much faster than average due to the rising demand for podiatric services, in particular by older people and fitness enthusiasts. Establishing a new podiatric practice will be toughest in areas surrounding the seven colleges of podiatric medicine since podiatrists are concentrated in these locations.
Veterinarians	47,000	31	14,000	Employment is expected to grow faster than average due to growth in the animal population and the willingness of pet owners to pay for more intensive care than in the past. The outlook for specialists—such as toxicologists, laboratory veterinarians, and pathologists—will be extremely good.

Health assessment and treating occupations

Dietitians and nutritionists	45,000	24	11,000	Employment is expected to grow about as fast as average in order to meet the expanding needs of nursing homes, hospitals, and social service programs and the growing interest and emphasis on dietary education.
Occupational therapists	36,000	55	20,000	Much faster than average growth is expected, reflecting anticipated growth in demand for rehabilitation services due to the increased survival rate of accident victims and the rising number of people in their 40's, an age when the risk of heart disease and stroke increases. The rapidly growing aged population will also increase demand for long-term care services. In addition, therapists will be needed for disabled students.
Pharmacists	169,000	21	35,000	Spurred by the pharmaceutical needs of a larger and older population and by scientific advances that will bring more drugs onto the market, employment is expected to grow as fast as average. Excellent job prospects are anticipated in both community and clinical settings; if current trends continue, demand is likely to outstrip supply in some places.
Physical therapists	88,000	76	67,000	Much faster than average job growth is expected due to the expansion of services for those in need of rehabilitation and long-term care. The shortage of physical therapists should ease somewhat as the number of physical therapy education programs increases and more students graduate.

[1]Nearly all estimates are from the BLS industry-occupation matrix.

CLUSTER Subgroup Occupation	Estimated employment 1990[1]	Percent change in employment 1990-2005[1]	Numerical change in employment 1990-2005[1]	Employment prospects
Physician assistants	53,000	34	18,000	Employment is expected to grow faster than average due to the expansion of the health services industry and the increased emphasis on cost containment. Excellent prospects are anticipated, especially in areas that have difficulty attracting physicians.
Recreational therapists	32,000	39	13,000	Employment is expected to grow much faster than average, chiefly because of anticipated growth in the need for long-term care, rehabilitation, and services for the developmentally disabled. Job prospects should be favorable for those with a strong clinical background.
Registered nurses	1,727,000	44	767,000	Much faster than average growth is expected, due to the overall growth in health care and the number of complex medical technologies. Hospitals in many parts of the country report shortages of RN's. However, increasing enrollments in nursing programs may result in a balance between job seekers and openings.
Respiratory therapists	60,000	52	31,000	Much faster than average growth is expected because of the substantial growth of the middle-aged and elderly population, which is more likely to suffer from cardiopulmonary diseases. Hospitals will continue to be the primary employer, but employment will grow fastest in home health care services.
Speech-language pathologists and audiologists	68,000	34	23,000	Faster than average overall growth is expected, but the rate varies by industry. Much faster than average growth is likely in the health care industry because the number of older people will grow rapidly and the baby-boom generation will enter an age bracket when the possibility of stroke-induced hearing and speech loss increases. Average growth is expected in educational services.
Communications occupations				
Public relations specialists	109,000	19	21,000	Average growth is expected as organizations increasingly recognize the need for good internal and external relations. Keen competition for these jobs is likely to persist among recent college graduates with communications degrees: people without the appropriate education or experience will face the toughest obstacles in acquiring these jobs.
Radio and television announcers and newscasters	57,000	20	11,000	Average growth is expected as new radio and TV stations are licensed and the number of cable TV stations continues to grow. Competition for beginning jobs will be very strong because the broadcasting field attracts many more jobseekers than there are jobs. Jobs will be easier to find in radio than in television because more radio stations hire beginners.
Reporters and correspondents	67,000	20	14,000	Employment is expected to grow about as fast as average. Writers who can handle highly specialized scientific or technical subjects will be at an advantage in the job market. The best opportunities are likely to be found on newspapers and magazines in small towns and suburbs.
Writers and editors	232,000	26	60,000	Increased demand for salaried writers in publishing, public relations, communications, and advertising should cause employment to rise faster than average. Keen competition is expected to continue. Opportunities will be best with business, trade, and technical publications.

[1] Nearly all estimates are from the BLS industry-occupation matrix.

CLUSTER Subgroup Occupation	Estimated employment 1990[1]	Percent change in employment 1990-2005[1]	Numerical change in employment 1990–2005[1]	Employment prospects
Visual arts occupations				
Designers	339,000	26	89,000	Continued emphasis on the quality and visual appeal of products will prompt faster than average growth for designers, especially industrial designers. Designers in most specialties will face competition throughout their careers because of the abundant supply of talented, highly qualified people attracted to this field. Finding a job in floral design should be relatively easy due to the relatively low pay and limited advancement opportunities.
Photographers and camera operators	120,000	23	28,000	Average overall growth is expected in response to the growing importance of visual images in education, communications, and entertainment. Faster than average growth is expected for camera operators. Jobseekers may face competition or keen competition, especially in commercial photography and photojournalism.
Visual artists	230,000	32	73,000	Strong demand for art, illustration, and design by advertising agencies, publishing firms, and other businesses will stimulate faster than average growth for graphic artists. Competition for jobs among fine artists will continue to be keen.
Performing arts occupations				
Actors, directors, and producers	95,000	41	39,000	Employment is expected to grow much faster than average as cable television, home movie rentals, and television syndication fuel a growing demand for productions. Still, continued overcrowding in this field will cause keen competition for jobs.
Dancers and choreographers	8,600	38	3,300	Employment is expected to grow much faster than average. Nonetheless, dancers seeking professional careers will continue to exceed the number of job openings, causing keen competition.
Musicians	252,000	9	24,000	Employment is expected to grow more slowly than average, reflecting the increasing use of synthesizers instead of multi-piece bands and orchestras. Also, a growing number of small clubs and dining establishments are hiring smaller bands than they have in the past. Competition will be extremely keen.

[1]Nearly all estimates are from the BLS industry-occupation matrix.

OCCUPATIONAL OUTLOOK QUARTERLY

Technicians and Related Support Occupations

CLUSTER Subgroup Occupation	Estimated employment 1990[1]	Percent change in employment 1990-2005[1]	Numerical change in employment 1990–2005[1]	Employment prospects
TECHNICIANS AND RELATED SUPPORT OCCUPATIONS				
Health technologists and technicians				
Clinical laboratory technologists	258,000	24	63,000	Although the number of medical tests will greatly increase, advances in laboratory automation should boost productivity, resulting in average employment growth. Many jobs will be in hospitals, but the fastest growth will be in commercial laboratories and doctors' offices due to changes in technology and business strategy. Job prospects are favorable.
Dental hygienists	97,000	41	40,000	Employment should grow much faster than average. Stimulating demand will be population growth, the tendency for middle-aged and elderly people to retain their teeth, and greater awareness of the importance of dental care along with the ability to pay for it. Also, dentists are expected to rely on hygienists to provide more services. Dental hygienists should have little trouble finding jobs.
Dispensing opticians	64,000	37	24,000	Employment is expected to grow much faster than average in response to rising demand for corrective lenses as the population ages. Opportunities should be very good for graduates of formal training programs.
EEG technologists	6,700	57	3,800	Much faster than average growth is expected, reflecting the increased numbers of neurodiagnostic tests performed. Job prospects should be excellent for formally trained technologists.
EKG technicians	16,000	-5	-800	Employment is expected to decline, despite the anticipated rise in the number of cardiology tests performed. Advances in technology have substantially raised EKG technicians' productivity and also have allowed registered nurses and other health personnel to perform the test.
Emergency medical technicians	89,000	30	26,000	Faster than average job growth is projected. Opportunities should be excellent in hospitals and private ambulance services, where pay and benefits generally are low. Competition will be keen in fire, police, and rescue squads because of attractive pay and benefits and good job security.
Licensed practical nurses	644,000	42	269,000	Employment is expected to grow much faster than average in response to the long-term care needs of a rapidly growing aged population and growth in health care in general. The job outlook should remain good unless the number of people completing L.P.N. training increases substantially.
Medical record technicians	52,000	54	28,000	Greater use of medical records for financial management and quality control will produce much faster than average job growth with excellent job prospects for graduates of accredited programs in medical record technology.

[1] Nearly all estimates are from the BLS industry-occupation matrix.

OCCUPATIONAL OUTLOOK QUARTERLY

CLUSTER Subgroup Occupation	Estimated employment 1990[1]	Percent change in employment 1990-2005[1]	Numerical change in employment 1990–2005[1]	Employment prospects
Nuclear medicine technologists	10,000	53	5,500	Employment is expected to grow much faster than average to meet the health care needs of a growing and aging population. Technological innovations will also increase the diagnostic use of nuclear medicine. Job prospects are excellent.
Radiologic technologists	149,000	70	103,000	Employment is expected to grow much faster than average due to the growth and aging of the population and the greater role radiologic technologies are playing in the diagnosis and treatment of disease. Job prospects for graduates of accredited programs are excellent.
Surgical technologists	38,000	55	21,000	Much faster than average growth is expected as a growing population and technological advances increase the number of surgical procedures performed. Growth will be fastest in clinics and offices of physicians due to increases in outpatient surgery; however, most jobs will be in hospitals.
Technicians except health				
Aircraft pilots	90,000	34	31,000	Due to an expected shortage of qualified applicants, opportunities should be excellent in the coming years. Faster than average employment growth and the large number of expected retirements will provide many job openings. Job prospects with major airlines are best for college graduates who have a commercial pilot's license or a flight engineer's license and experience flying jets.
Air traffic controllers	32,000	7	2,200	Despite growth in the number of aircraft in service, productivity gains stemming from laborsaving air traffic control equipment will result in slower than average employment growth. Keen competition for job openings is expected because the occupation's relatively high pay and liberal retirement program attract many applicants.
Broadcast technicians	33,000	4	1,200	Because of laborsaving advances, such as computer-controlled programming and remote-controlled transmitters, employment is expected to show little or no change.
Computer programmers	565,000			Employment is expected to grow much faster than average as the number of computer applications continues to increase. Job prospects will be best for college graduates who majored in computer science or a related area and have experience or training in fields such as accounting, management, engineering, or science.
Drafters	326,000	13	44,000	Although large increases in demand for drafting services are expected, they will be partially offset by the widespread use of computer-aided design equipment, which increases the productivity of drafters. Slower than average employment growth is expected.
Engineering technicians	755,000	28	210,000	Well-qualified engineering technicians should experience good opportunities. Anticipated increases in spending on research and development and continued rapid growth in the number of technical products are expected to result in faster than average growth.
Library technicians	65,000	11	7,300	Employment is expected to grow more slowly than average, following the growth pattern of other library workers.

[1]Nearly all estimates are from the BLS industry-occupation matrix.

CLUSTER Subgroup Occupation	Estimated employment 1990[1]	Percent change in employment 1990-2005[1]	Numerical change in employment 1990–2005[1]	Employment prospects
Paralegals	90,000	85	77,000	Much faster than average growth is expected as the use of paralegals to aid lawyers increases. Competition for jobs is expected to increase. Opportunities will be best for graduates of well regarded formal paralegal training programs and paralegals with previous experience.
Science technicians	246,000	24	58,000	Science technicians with good technical and communication skills should experience very good employment opportunities. Expansion in research, development, and the production of technical products will result in average overall growth. The employment of biological technicians is expected to grow faster than most other science technicians; job opportunities for chemical technicians also are expected to be good.
Tool programmers, numerical control	7,800	6	([3])	Despite increased use of numerically controlled machine tools, employment will grow more slowly than average due to expected large increases in productivity.

Marketing and Sales Occupations

CLUSTER Subgroup Occupation	Estimated employment 1990[1]	Percent change in employment 1990-2005[1]	Numerical change in employment 1990–2005[1]	Employment prospects
MARKETING AND SALES OCCUPATIONS				
Cashiers	2,633,000	26	685,000	Faster than average employment growth is expected due to the anticipated increase in retail sales and the popularity of discount and self-service retailing, which has led to the rise of centralized cashier stations. Due to the large size of this occupation and its much higher than average turnover, both part- and full-time job opportunities will be excellent.
Counter and rental clerks	215,000	34	74,000	Faster than average employment growth is expected due to the anticipated growth in rental and leasing services. Prospects for full- and part-time jobs with flexible hours are excellent.
Insurance agents and brokers	439,000	20	88,000	Due to increasing productivity and changing business practices, employment growth will not keep pace with rising insurance sales, but it will still be as fast as average. Many beginners cannot establish a sufficient clientele in this highly competitive business. Opportunities will be best for ambitious people who enjoy selling and develop expertise in a wide range of insurance and financial services.
Manufacturers' and wholesale sales representatives	1,944,000	15	284,000	Average employment growth is expected as the economy expands and as demand for goods increases. Job prospects will be good for qualified persons.

[1] Nearly all estimates are from the BLS industry-occupation matrix.
[3] Less than 500.

CLUSTER Subgroup Occupation	Estimated employment 1990[1]	Percent change in employment 1990-2005[1]	Numerical change in employment 1990–2005[1]	Employment prospects
Real estate agents, brokers, and appraisers	413,000	19	79,000	The large proportion of the population between the ages of 25 and 54 is expected to increase sales of residential and commercial properties, resulting in average employment growth. Because turnover is high, positions should continue to be relatively easy to obtain. Well-trained, ambitious people who enjoy selling have the best chance for success in this highly competitive field.
Retail sales workers	4,754,000	29	1,381,000	Employment is expected to grow faster than average due to anticipated growth in retail sales. Job placement will be excellent for full-time, part-time, and temporary workers.
Securities and financial services sales representatives	191,000	40	76,000	Employment is expected to grow much faster than average as economic growth and rising personal incomes increase the funds available for investment and as banks and other financial institutions offer an increasing array of financial services. However, job competition will remain keen, particularly in large firms, due to the potential for high earnings. Many beginners leave securities sales jobs because they are unable to establish a sufficient clientele.
Services sales representatives	588,000	55	325,000	The continued rapid increase in the demand for services will result in much faster than average employment growth. Applicants with college training or a proven sales record have the best job prospects.
Travel agents	132,000	62	82,000	Much faster than average employment growth is projected due to the large increases expected in both vacation and business-related travel.

Administrative Support Occupations Including Clerical

CLUSTER Subgroup Occupation	Estimated employment 1990[1]	Percent change in employment 1990-2005[1]	Numerical change in employment 1990–2005[1]	Employment prospects
ADMINISTRATIVE SUPPORT OCCUPATIONS INCLUDING CLERICAL				
Adjusters, investigators, and collectors	1,088,000	24	264,000	Employment is expected to grow about as fast as average, in line with a growing population and a rising number of business transactions. Growth should be slightly faster for claim representatives and bill and account collectors than for insurance clerks, adjustment clerks, or welfare eligibility workers.
Bank tellers	517,000	-5	-25,000	Employment is expected to decline due to the increasing use of automatic teller machines by customers and on-line video terminals by tellers, thus increasing their efficiency. Despite declining employment, qualified applicants should have good prospects because the number of job openings is large.

[1] Nearly all estimates are from the BLS industry-occupation matrix.

CLUSTER Subgroup Occupation	Estimated employment 1990[1]	Percent change in employment 1990-2005[1]	Numerical change in employment 1990–2005[1]	Employment prospects
Clerical supervisors and managers	1,218,000	22	263,000	The expanding volume of clerical work is expected to generate average job growth. With slower employment growth in some clerical occupations, clerical supervisors and managers may have smaller staffs and perform more professional tasks. Job openings will be numerous mainly due to replacement needs.
Computer and peripheral equipment operators	320,000	13	42,000	Slower than average employment growth is expected as data centers become increasingly automated.
Credit clerks and authorizers	240,000	24	58,000	Employment will increase as fast as average as the volume of credit in the economy continues to grow. The personal nature of loan clerking and the judgment required of authorizers ensure that computers will not significantly affect employment.
General office clerks	2,737,000	24	670,000	Average employment growth is expected as more employers, especially in small business, opt for the flexibility offered by these workers. In addition, high turnover will provide a large number of job openings.
Information clerks	1,418,000	41	584,000	Overall employment is expected to increase much faster than average due to the rapid growth of industries such as business, professional, and other services. Replacement needs will create an exceptionally large number of job openings because the occupation is large and turnover is high.
Hotel and motel desk clerks	118,000	34	40,000	Employment is expected to grow faster than average as the number of hotels, motels, and other lodging establishments increases. Opportunities for part-time work should be plentiful.
Interviewing and new accounts clerks	250,000	28	71,000	Employment is expected to increase faster than average. Interviewing clerks are expected to grow rapidly due to growth in marketing research, telemarketing, and health care. New accounts clerks, on the other hand, will grow slowly, reflecting slow growth in banking.
Receptionists and information clerks	900,000	47	422,000	As business and professional services continue to expand, employment is expected to grow much faster than average. Job prospects should be better for those with typing and other office skills.
Reservation and transportation ticket agents and travel clerks	150,000	34	52,000	Growing demand for travel services is expected to lead to a faster than average increase in employment. However, applicants can anticipate considerable competition because of the relatively low turnover and large supply of these workers. The airline industry, in particular, attracts many applicants because of its travel benefits and glamour.
Mail clerks and messengers	280,000	9	26,000	Employment is expected to grow more slowly than average due to greater use of electronic forms of communication and more efficient mail handling equipment. Job opportunities should be plentiful due to high turnover in these jobs.
Material recording, scheduling dispatching, and distributing occupations	3,756,000	12	443,000	Overall employment is expected to grow more slowly than average. Demand for workers to carry out these functions will increase as the economy grows, but computers will allow them to be performed more efficiently. Prospects for individual occupations vary.
Dispatchers	209,000	29	60,000	Overall employment of dispatchers is expected to grow faster than average to meet the service, emergency response, and delivery needs of a growing population. Opportunities for jobs should be good.

[1] Nearly all estimates are from the BLS industry-occupation matrix.

CLUSTER Subgroup Occupation	Estimated employment 1990[1]	Percent change in employment 1990-2005[1]	Numerical change in employment 1990–2005[1]	Employment prospects
Stock clerks	2,191,000	12	257,000	Employment is expected to grow more slowly than average as automation increases productivity in warehouses and stockrooms. However, job opportunities should be good in this large occupation because turnover is high.
Traffic, shipping, and receiving clerks	762,000	13	97,000	Employment is expected to grow more slowly than average as the growing use of computerized equipment should allow some functions to be automated. Nevertheless, job opportunities should be good due to the need to replace workers who transfer to other jobs.
Postal clerks and mail carriers	607,000	17	101,000	Overall employment is expected to increase about as fast as average. Automation will increase the productivity of clerks, causing their employment to grow more slowly than average. Employment of mail carriers, however, is closely tied to the amount of new housing and should increase as fast as average. Competition is expected to be keen as the number of applicants continues to exceed the number of openings by far.
Record clerks	3,809,000	([6])	-15,000	Despite the rise in the number of business transactions, little or no employment growth is expected as office automation continues to make these workers more productive. Thousands of openings will arise to replace those who transfer or leave the labor force.
Billing clerks	413,000	4	18,000	Little change in employment is expected as computers are increasingly used to manage account information. More individualized and complex billing applications will require workers with greater technical expertise.
Bookkeeping, accounting, and auditing clerks	2,276,000	-6	-133,000	Employment is expected to decline because of the automation of bookkeeping, accounting, and auditing functions. Large organizations may continue to consolidate and eliminate duplicate functions, further reducing demand for these workers.
Brokerage clerks and statement clerks	93,000	10	9,000	Slower than average employment growth is expected as computers and changes in business practices reduce demand for these workers.
File clerks	271,000	11	29,000	Employment is expected to grow more slowly than average as recordkeeping systems become more automated. Opportunities should be good for part-time and temporary work, and in the health, legal, and computer service industries.
Library assistants and bookmobile drivers	117,000	11	13,000	Slower than average employment growth is expected, reflecting the slow growth in funding that is anticipated for local governments and schools.
Order clerks	291,000	3	8,700	Little change in employment is expected. The growing number of orders being placed for goods and services will be offset by a greater use of sophisticated inventory control, automatic billing, and other advanced systems. Prospects will be best for outside order clerks who deal directly with the public.
Payroll and timekeeping clerks	171,000	3	4,700	Little change in employment is expected as office automation facilitates calculation and recording of information. These tasks are increasingly being assigned to other workers in smaller offices.
Personnel clerks	129,000	21	27,000	Average employment growth is expected. Despite increasing workloads, rising productivity through automation will moderate demand for personnel clerks. Many job openings will arise as workers transfer to other occupations or leave the labor force.

[1] Nearly all estimates are from the BLS industry-occupation matrix.
[6] Less than 1.

CLUSTER Subgroup Occupation	Estimated employment 1990[1]	Percent change in employment 1990-2005[1]	Numerical change in employment 1990–2005[1]	Employment prospects
Secretaries	3,576,000	15	540,000	Average employment growth is expected as the labor force grows and more workers are employed in offices. Productivity increases brought about by office automation will be offset somewhat by the trend to have secretaries assume responsibilities traditionally reserved for managers and professionals. Job prospects should be good.
Stenographers and court reporters	132,000	-5	-7,100	Overall employment is expected to decline because of the widespread use of dictation machines and continuing developments in voice-activated transcription equipment. Demand should be strong for court reporters, however, due to the growing number of court cases and the use of court reporters to record business proceedings.
Teacher aides	808,000	34	278,000	Employment is expected to grow faster than average, reflecting rising enrollments and greater use of aides.
Telephone operators	325,000	-32	-104,000	Employment is expected to decline due to innovations, such as voice recognition technologies and automotive switching, that will reduce labor requirements.
Typists, word processors, and data entry keyers	1,448,000	-3	-46,000	Little or no change in employment is expected because of the widespread use of personal computers, further developments in electronic equipment, and the trend towards professionals and other office workers doing more of their own word processing. Job opportunities will be best for those with good keyboard skills and knowledge of computer software packages.

Service Occupations

CLUSTER Subgroup Occupation	Estimated employment 1990[1]	Percent change in employment 1990-2005[1]	Numerical change in employment 1990–2005[1]	Employment prospects
SERVICE OCCUPATIONS				
Protective service occupations				
Correction officers	230,000	61	142,000	As correctional facilities expand and additional officers are hired to supervise and counsel a growing number of inmates, employment is expected to increase much faster than average. Rapid growth in demand coupled with job openings resulting from turnover should mean favorable opportunities.
Firefighting occupations	280,000	24	68,000	Due to population growth and the increasing need for protection from fires, employment will grow about as fast as average. Keen competition is expected in most areas; the best opportunities are likely to be found in smaller communities with expanding populations.

[1]Nearly all estimates are from the BLS industry-occupation matrix.

OCCUPATIONAL OUTLOOK QUARTERLY

CLUSTER Subgroup Occupation	Estimated employment 1990[1]	Percent change in employment 1990-2005[1]	Numerical change in employment 1990–2005[1]	Employment prospects
Guards	883,000	34	298,000	Increasing concern about crime, vandalism, and terrorism will stimulate the need for guards, resulting in faster than average growth. Overall, job opportunities are expected to be plentiful. Opportunities will be best for those who work for contract security agencies. Some competition is expected for in-house guard jobs, which generally have higher salaries, more benefits, better job security, and greater potential for advancement.
Police, detectives, and special agents	655,000	24	160,000	Employment is expected to rise about as fast as average due to an increase in the population, the need for police protection, and the growing concern about drugs and drug-related crimes. Keen competition is expected for higher paying jobs in large police departments and Federal law enforcement agencies, such as the FBI, Drug Enforcement Administration, and the Secret Service.

Food and beverage preparation and service occupations

Chefs, cooks, and other kitchen workers	3,069,000	34	1,035,000	Faster than average growth is expected due to the increasing size of the population and economy, while higher incomes and increased leisure time allow people to dine out more often. High turnover in these jobs will result in plentiful job openings.
Food and beverage service workers	4,400,000	28	1,223,000	Employment is expected to grow faster than average due to the anticipated increase in the population, personal income, and leisure time. Replacement needs because of high turnover will result in plentiful job openings.

Health service occupations

Dental assistants	176,000	34	60,000	Faster than average growth is expected as demand for dental care increases in response to population growth, greater retention of natural teeth by the middle-aged and older population, and greater ability to pay for services. Also, dentists are expected to rely on assistants to provide more services.
Medical assistants	165,000	74	122,000	Much faster than average growth is anticipated due to expansion of the health services industry. Job opportunities should be very good. Most job openings will result from replacement needs.
Nursing aides and psychiatric aides	1,374,000	43	587,000	Job prospects are expected to be very good. Overall employment is projected to grow much faster than average. Employment of nursing aides will grow much faster than average as a result of the anticipated expansion of nursing and personal care facilities. Employment of psychiatric aides is expected to grow faster than average in response to the needs of the very old and those suffering from acute psychiatric and substance abuse problems. Replacement needs will be high.

Personal service and cleaning occupations

Animal caretakers except farm	106,000	38	40,000	Employment is expected to grow much faster than average, reflecting a growing population and economy. The number of dogs and cats has increased significantly over the last 10 years and is expected to continue to increase. Graduates of training programs in veterinary technology have the best prospects.

[1] Nearly all estimates are from the BLS industry-occupation matrix.

CLUSTER Subgroup Occupation	Estimated employment 1990[1]	Percent change in employment 1990-2005[1]	Numerical change in employment 1990–2005[1]	Employment prospects
Barbers and cosmetologists	713,000	22	156,000	Although average overall employment growth is expected, changing consumer preferences will result in distinctly different employment trends. Little growth is expected for barbers, while cosmetologist employment will rise faster than average. Job opportunities are expected to be plentiful, especially for hairstylists and those who specialize in nail and skin care. Part-time work should also be plentiful.
Flight attendants	101,000	59	59,000	Increases in the number and size of planes will result in much faster than average employment growth. Applicants with some college training and experience dealing with the public have the best job prospects because competition for jobs is likely to remain very keen.
Gardeners and groundskeepers	874,000	40	348,000	Employment is expected to grow much faster than average due to greater use of landscaping in and around buildings, shopping malls, homes, and other structures.
Homemaker–home health aides	391,000	88	343,000	A substantial increase in the elderly population, greater efforts to care for the chronically ill at home, and development of in-home medical technologies should spur much faster than average growth. Job opportunities are excellent.
Janitors and cleaners	3,007,000	18	555,000	Employment is projected to grow as fast as average as the number of office buildings, medical facilities, schools, and other structures increases. Entry to the job is easy because little formal education or training is required, turnover is high, and many part-time positions are available.
Preschool workers	990,000	49	490,000	Employment is expected to grow much faster than average, reflecting the growth anticipated in the number of young children who will need care and a shift in the type of child-care arrangements parents choose.
Private household workers	782,000	-29	-227,000	Employment is expected to decline due to a limited supply of workers. Also, child-care service firms are expanding rapidly at the expense of private household child-care workers. Job prospects should be excellent.

Agriculture-Forestry-Fishing and Related Occupations

CLUSTER Subgroup Occupation	Estimated employment 1990[1]	Percent change in employment 1990-2005[1]	Numerical change in employment 1990–2005[1]	Employment prospects
AGRICULTURE, FORESTRY, FISHING, AND RELATED OCCUPATIONS				
Farm operators and managers	1,223,000	-16	-200,000	The trend toward fewer and larger farms will result in declining employment of farm operators. However, the increasing complexity of farming should increase demand for highly trained and experienced farm managers.

[1] Nearly all estimates are from the BLS industry-occupation matrix.

CLUSTER Subgroup Occupation	Estimated employment 1990[1]	Percent change in employment 1990-2005[1]	Numerical change in employment 1990–2005[1]	Employment prospects
Fishers, hunters, and trappers	61,000	13	7,800	Overall, slower than average employment growth is expected. However, demand for captains and mates should be spurred by increases in commercial and recreational fishing. Slower growth is expected for deckhands, hunters, and trappers.
Timber cutting and logging workers	108,000	-2	-1,800	The increased mechanization of logging operations and improvements in equipment will result in little or no employment growth, despite an increase in demand for lumber and wood products.

Mechanics-Installers-Repairers

CLUSTER Subgroup Occupation	Estimated employment 1990[1]	Percent change in employment 1990-2005[1]	Numerical change in employment 1990–2005[1]	Employment prospects
MECHANICS, INSTALLERS, AND REPAIRERS				
Aircraft mechanics and engine specialists	122,000	24	29,000	Average employment growth is expected due to an increase in air traffic. Because airlines offer relatively high wages and attractive travel benefits, competition can be anticipated for jobs with them; general aviation, however, will offer excellent job opportunities, particularly for experienced mechanics.
Automotive body repairers	219,000	22	48,000	Employment is expected to increase about as fast as the average due to increases in the number of vehicles, the popularity of lighter weight cars more easily damaged in collisions, and the greater difficulty of repairing such cars. Opportunities should be best for persons with formal training in automotive body repair or mechanics.
Automotive mechanics	757,000	22	166,000	Employment is expected to increase about as fast as average as the decreasing need for routine service offsets the increase in the number of motor vehicles on the road. Most of the new jobs will be with automotive repair shops and automobile dealerships as fewer gasoline service stations provide repair services. Opportunities should be plentiful for people who complete formal automotive mechanic training programs.
Diesel mechanics	268,000	22	58,000	Employment is expected to rise about as fast as average, reflecting the growing use of trucks to transport freight. However, the majority of job openings will arise from the need to replace retirees. Those who complete formal diesel mechanic training programs should have the best job prospects.
Electronic equipment repairers	444,000	1	4,100	Overall employment is expected to show little change. Despite the rapidly increasing amount of electronic equipment, improvements in product reliability and lower equipment prices—resulting in more purchases of new equipment and fewer repairs of old equipment—will limit employment growth among repairers.

[1]Nearly all estimates are from the BLS industry-occupation matrix.

CLUSTER Subgroup Occupation	Estimated employment 1990[1]	Percent change in employment 1990-2005[1]	Numerical change in employment 1990–2005[1]	Employment prospects
Commercial and industrial electronic equipment repairers	75,000	17	13,000	Overall, average growth is expected. Employment in government is expected to grow slowly, because of limits on defense spending. In other sectors, employment is expected to grow faster than average as more electronic equipment is used.
Communication equipment mechanics	125,000	-38	-48,000	Employment is expected to decline due to the tremendous productivity increases associated with the computerization of telecommunications equipment.
Computer and office machine repairers	156,000	38	60,000	Much faster than average growth is expected as more computers and office machines are used in homes and offices. All growth will be among computer repairers. Employment of office machine repairers is not expected to grow at all.
Electronic home entertainment equipment repairers	41,000	13	5,100	Despite the growing number of television sets, recorders, video games, disk players, and other home entertainment products in use, employment is expected to increase more slowly than average as improvements in technology reduce service requirements. However, job opportunities should be good as many people transfer to higher paying jobs also requiring knowledge of electronics.
Telephone installers and repairers	47,000	-55	-26,000	Employment is expected to decline due to laborsaving advances, such as plug-in telephones, more efficient equipment testing procedures, and modular assembly of telephone equipment.
Elevator installers and repairers	19,000	17	3,100	The increased number of structures with elevators and escalators—along with the increased stock of equipment needing maintenance, repair, and modernization—is expected to result in average growth.
Farm equipment mechanics	48,000	9	4,500	Employment is expected to increase more slowly than the average. Demand should be limited by the consolidation of farm land, which enables farmers to produce more with less equipment. However, the growing stock of newer, more complex equipment should force farmers to rely more on skilled mechanics. Opportunities should be best for persons who complete formal training in farm equipment repair or diesel mechanics.
General maintenance mechanics	1,128,000	22	251,000	Average growth is expected in response to the increasing number of office buildings, apartment houses, stores, schools, hospitals, hotels, and factories.
Heating, air-conditioning, and refrigeration technicians	219,000	21	46,000	Employment is expected to increase as fast as average due to demand for new industrial, commercial, and residential climate control systems. Maintenance of existing systems also should create job opportunities.
Home appliance and power tool repairers	71,000	-1	-700	Little or no change is expected due to the increasing use of electronic parts—such as solid-state circuits, micro-processors, and sensing devices—that make appliances more reliable. Job prospects are expected to be best for those who have a strong background in electronics.
Industrial machinery repairers	474,000	10	46,000	Due to the increased use of automated machinery that needs much preventive maintenance, employment is expected to increase more slowly than average in contrast to many other manufacturing occupations, which are expected to decline. Because maintenance and repair of machinery is crucial despite the level of production, repairers generally are less subject to layoffs than other workers in poor economic conditions.

[1] Nearly all estimates are from the BLS industry-occupation matrix.

CLUSTER Subgroup Occupation	Estimated employment 1990[1]	Percent change in employment 1990-2005[1]	Numerical change in employment 1990–2005[1]	Employment prospects
Line installers and cable splicers	232,000	-14	-32,000	Overall employment is expected to decline due to technological changes, such as fiber optic cable, and the saturation of the cable TV market. However, the employment of power line installers is expected to grow slowly.
Millwrights	73,000	12	8,900	Employment is expected to increase more slowly than the average. Opportunities will be best with service firms that employ millwrights who work on contract for other companies.
Mobile heavy equipment mechanics	104,000	13	13,000	Employment growth is expected to increase more slowly than the average due to slow growth in the amount of mobile heavy equipment in operation. Job prospects are expected to be best for persons with formal training as diesel or heavy equipment mechanics.
Motorcycle, boat, and small engine mechanics	50,000	10	4,900	Overall employment is expected to increase more slowly than average. Rising incomes enable more families to buy boats and outdoor power equipment. The employment of motorcycle mechanics is expected to increase more slowly than average, reflecting the slow growth in the number of persons between the ages of 18 and 24.
Musical instrument repairers and tuners	8,700	2	([3])	Employment is expected to show little or no change, reflecting slow growth in the number of students playing musical instruments and the number of professional musicians.
Vending machine servicers and repairers	26,000	-1	([3])	Despite the expected rise in the number of vending machines in use, the greater reliability of new equipment should result in little or no change in employment.

Construction Trades and Extractive Occupations

CLUSTER Subgroup Occupation	Estimated employment 1990[1]	Percent change in employment 1990-2005[1]	Numerical change in employment 1990–2005[1]	Employment prospects
CONSTRUCTION TRADES AND EXTRACTIVE OCCUPATIONS				
Bricklayers and stonemasons	152,000	20	31,000	Increased construction of industrial, institutional, and residential structures will result in average employment growth. Also stimulating demand will be the increasing use of brick on building fronts and in lobbies and foyers.
Carpenters	1,077,000	14	154,000	Demand for new housing and industrial plants and the need to renovate existing structures will result in average employment growth. Employment growth may not be as fast as in the past because of expected productivity gains due to an increasing use of prefabricated components and better tools.

[1] Nearly all estimates are from the BLS industry-occupation matrix.
[3] Less than 500.

CLUSTER Subgroup Occupation	Estimated employment 1990[1]	Percent change in employment 1990-2005[1]	Numerical change in employment 1990–2005[1]	Employment prospects
Carpet installers	73,000	21	15,000	Demand for wall-to-wall carpet in new construction and the need to replace existing carpet will result in average employment growth.
Concrete masons and terrazzo workers	113,000	13	15,000	Employment is expected to grow more slowly than average because of productivity gains due to better equipment, tools, and materials.
Drywall workers and lathers	143,000	23	33,000	Employment is expected to grow as fast as average due to increased construction. Many job opportunities will be available because of replacement needs.
Electricians	548,000	29	158,000	Faster than average employment growth should result from the need to install and maintain electrical wiring in new facilities and replace existing wiring. Increased use of telecommunications and computer equipment also should create job opportunities.
Glaziers	42,000	22	9,300	Increasing use of glass for new commercial and industrial buildings and the need to replace glass in all types of buildings should result in average employment growth.
Insulation workers	70,000	24	17,000	Demand for insulation associated with new construction and renovation as well as the demand for asbestos removal and consequent insulation needs in existing structures should result in average employment growth.
Painters and paperhangers	453,000	24	111,000	Employment is expected to grow about as fast as average as construction activity increases and the number of buildings needing repainting grows. Thousands of jobs will become available each year as painters transfer to other jobs or leave the labor force.
Plasterers	28,000	13	3,700	The continued preference for drywall over plaster should result in slower than average employment growth. However, plaster is regaining some share of the market because of its durability, the innovative coatings available, and the architectural effects it makes possible.
Plumbers and pipefitters	379,000	21	80,000	Construction of new industrial, commercial, and residential structures and maintenance of existing ones are expected to result in average employment growth.
Roofers	138,000	23	31,000	New construction and the need to repair and replace roofs will cause employment to increase as fast as average.
Roustabouts	38,000	-4	-1,400	Reduced exploration and production in the oil industry and increased automation in oil fields will result in little or no change in employment. Job opportunities are best for roustabouts with previous experience or formal training in petroleum technology.
Sheet-metal workers	98,000	3	22,000	Employment is expected to grow as fast as average as more factories, shopping malls, homes, and other structures using sheet metal are built. Additional job opportunities will be created as more efficient air-conditioning and heating systems are installed in existing buildings.
Structural and reinforcing ironworkers	92,000	21	20,000	Growing demand for nonresidential buildings—as well as rehabilitation and maintenance of manufacturing and power plants, highways, and bridges—should result in average employment growth.
Tilesetters	28,000	24	6,700	Employment is expected to increase about as fast as average, reflecting the increasing popularity of tile entranceways, foyers, and common areas of shopping malls and buildings.

[1]Nearly all estimates are from the BLS industry-occupation matrix.

CLUSTER Subgroup Occupation	Estimated employment 1990[1]	Percent change in employment 1990-2005[1]	Numerical change in employment 1990–2005[1]	Employment prospects
Numerical-control machine-tool operations	70,000	23	16,000	The increased use of numerically controlled machines will result in average employment growth.

Production Occupations

CLUSTER Subgroup Occupation	Estimated employment 1990[1]	Percent change in employment 1990-2005[1]	Numerical change in employment 1990–2005[1]	Employment prospects
PRODUCTION OCCUPATIONS				
Assemblers				
Precision assemblers	352,000	-33	-116,000	Despite increasing manufacturing activity, a decline in employment is projected because factories will be more automated and more products will be assembled overseas.
Blue-collar worker supervisors	1,792,000	7	120,000	Overall employment is expected to increase more slowly than average. While little change is expected in manufacturing, faster growth is expected in construction, wholesale and retail trade, and services as a result of industry growth.
Food processing occupations				
Butchers and meat, poultry, and fish cutters	355,000	([6])	1,200	Due to technological advances and the growing popularity of "ready-to-heat" foods, employment will shift from the store to the factory. The consequent increase in semiskilled production workers in the factory will be balanced by a decrease in skilled retail butchers, resulting in little or no overall employment change.
Inspectors, testers, and graders	668,000	-1	-9,200	Little change in employment is expected because of automation and the increasing assignment of inspection, testing, and grading duties to all workers involved in the production process.
Metalworking and plastics-working occupations				
Boilermakers	22,000	3	700	Little change in employment is expected due to the trend to repair defective boilers, rather than replace them.
Jewelers	40,000	20	8,000	Average employment growth is expected as the demand for jewelry and jewelry repair increases. Because of rising imports, those interested in jewelry manufacturing will encounter keen competition. Graduates of jeweler training programs have the best opportunities.
Machinists	386,000	10	41,000	Growth of imports, improved technology, increased use of nonmetal parts, and difficulty attracting entrants into this occupation should result in slower than average employment growth. However, opportunities will be very good for those with the necessary skills and training.
Metalworking and plastics-working machine operators	1,473,000	-8	-122,000	The increased use of automated manufacturing systems and growth of foreign competition are expected to cause overall employment to decline. However, the substitution of plastic for metal should create average growth and ample opportunities for plastics-working machine operators.

[1] Nearly all estimates are from the BLS industry-occupation matrix.
[6] Less than 1.

CLUSTER Subgroup Occupation	Estimated employment 1990[1]	Percent change in employment 1990-2005[1]	Numerical change in employment 1990–2005[1]	Employment prospects
Tool and die makers	141,000	3	3,900	Employment is expected to remain about the same because of increased automation and imports of machined products. However, due to the lengthy training required and difficulty attracting entrants, shortages will exist in some areas, and those with appropriate skills and background should find excellent opportunities.
Welders, cutters, and welding machine operators	427,000	4	18,000	Little or no change in overall employment is expected. In construction, wholesale trade, and services, however, employment of skilled welders will grow, because automation will have little or no impact. In manufacturing, greater use of welding robots should cause the employment of welding machine operators to increase.
Plant and systems operators				
Electric power generating plant operators and power distributors and dispatchers	44,000	9	3,900	Employment is expected to grow more slowly than average. The use of automatic controls and more efficient equipment will keep employment from growing as fast as the demand for electric power. Although few, if any, nuclear powerplants are likely to be ordered before the year 2,005, some additional operators will be needed to staff plants under construction and to meet regulatory requirements for increased staffing at existing plants.
Stationary engineers	35,000	1	([3])	Despite commercial and industrial development, which will increase the amount of equipment to be operated and maintained, employment is expected to change little because automated and computerized controls will make newly installed equipment more efficient. Job opportunities will be best for those with technical school or apprenticeship training.
Water and wastewater treatment plant operators	78,000	29	23,000	Employment is expected to grow faster than average as new treatment plants are built and existing ones are expanded to meet the needs of a growing population and economy.
Printing Occupations				
Prepress workers	186,000	22	40,000	Employment is expected to grow as fast as average, spurred by rising demand for printed materials. Experienced individuals and graduates of postsecondary programs in printing and computer graphics technology will have the best prospects.
Printing press operators	251,000	19	49,000	Expansion in the printing and publishing industry should contribute to average employment growth. While employment of offset, gravure, and flexographic nnoperators will increase, employment of letterpress operators will decline. Job prospects will be best for experienced workers. Apprenticeship or other training is likely to be required of new entrants.
Bindery workers	78,000	11	8,900	Slower than average job growth is expected due to technological advances in bindery operations. Opportunities are very limited for hand bookbinders.
Textile, apparel, and furnishings occupations				
Apparel workers	1,037,000	-8	-81,000	Employment is expected to decline due to increases in imports, offshore assembly, and automation. Job prospects will be best for custom tailors and pressing machine operators for whom employment opportunities exist in nonmanufacturing industries, such as retail clothing stores, laundries, and drycleaners.

[1] Nearly all estimates are from the BLS industry-occupation matrix.
[3] Less than 500.

CLUSTER Subgroup Occupation	Estimated employment 1990[1]	Percent change in employment 1990-2005[1]	Numerical change in employment 1990–2005[1]	Employment prospects
Shoe and leather workers and repairers	27,000	-19	-5,200	Inexpensive imports have made the cost of replacing shoes and leather goods cheaper or more convenient than repairing them, so employment is expected to decline. Prospects are better for workers employed in the manufacture and modification of custom-made molded or orthopedic shoes.
Textile machinery operators	289,000	-28	-81,000	Growth of imports and greater use of automated equipment are expected to result in employment declines.
Upholsterers	64,000	10	6,100	Employment is expected to increase more slowly than average due to slow growth in furniture manufacturing. Nevertheless, job opportunities should be good for highly skilled upholsterers due to the lengthy training required to master the craft.
Woodworking occupations	349,000	12	43,000	The substitution of other materials for wood, growth of imports, and improvement of machinery will result in slower than average employment growth.
Miscellaneous production occupations				
Dental laboratory technicians	57,000	4	2,500	Little change is expected in employment, because of better preventive dental care, including fluoridation. This means people keep their teeth longer or need only a bridge or a crown instead of full or partial dentures.
Ophthalmic laboratory technicians	19,000	29	5,600	Faster than average growth is expected in response to the demand for corrective lenses and fashionable glasses.
Painting and coating machine operators	160,000	-1	-1,600	Little change in employment is expected as industrial robots and new painting processes become more widely used. Employment is expected to decline in manufacturing but automotive painters who do more customized work in automotive body repair and paint shops will experience much faster than average growth.
Photographic process workers	76,000	19	14,000	Average growth is projected due to the rising demand for photographs from individuals and businesses. Replacement needs are particularly high for machine operators.

Transportation and Material Moving Occupations

CLUSTER Subgroup Occupation	Estimated employment 1990[1]	Percent change in employment 1990-2005[1]	Numerical change in employment 1990–2005[1]	Employment prospects
TRANSPORTATION AND MATERIAL MOVING OCCUPATIONS				
Busdrivers	561,000	32	177,000	Employment of busdrivers is projected to increase faster than average as school enrollments and bus ridership increase. Job opportunities will be best for school busdrivers.

[1] Nearly all estimates are from the BLS industry-occupation matrix.

CLUSTER Subgroup Occupation	Estimated employment 1990[1]	Percent change in employment 1990-2005[1]	Numerical change in employment 1990–2005[1]	Employment prospects
Material moving equipment operators	1,019,000	12	123,000	Employment is expected to increase more slowly than average because of equipment improvements and automation.
Rail transportation workers	107,000	-4	-4,600	Little change is expected in the overall employment of rail transportation workers. Railroad industry employment will continue to decline as a result of competition from other modes of transportation and the implementation of labor-saving innovations. However, employment of subway operators should grow much faster than the average due to the rapid expansion of intercity rail systems.
Truckdrivers	2,701,000	24	659,000	Employment is expected to grow about as fast as average. Job opportunities in this large occupation should be plentiful because of the growing demand for truck transportation services and the need to replace drivers who leave the occupation. However, competition is expected for jobs that offer the earnings or best working conditions.
Water transportation occupations	49,000	-13	-6,600	Employment is projected to decline due to intense foreign competition and new technology that allows vessels to be operated by fewer workers. Keen competition for jobs is expected to continue.

[1] Nearly all estimates are from the BLS industry-occupation matrix.

Matching Yourself with the World of Work

Source: *Occupational Outlook Quarterly*, Fall, 1992

Occupational Outlook Quarterly

U.S. Department of Labor
Bureau of Labor Statistics
Fall 1992

Matching Yourself With the World of Work in 1992

OCCUPATIONAL OUTLOOK QUARTERLY

Solving the Job Puzzle

by Anne W. Clymer and Elizabeth McGregor

"I am myself reminded that we are not alike; there are diversities of natures among us which are adapted to different occupations." These words, which Plato attributed to Socrates, are still true today.

Choosing a career is one of the hardest jobs you will ever have. You should devote extensive time, energy, and thought to make a decision with which you will be happy. Even though undertaking this task means hard work, view a career as an opportunity to do something you enjoy, not simply as a necessity or as a means of earning a living. Taking the time to thoroughly explore career options can mean the difference between finding a stimulating and fulfilling career or hopping from one job to the next in search of the right job. Finding the best occupation for you also is important because work influences many aspects of your life—from your choice of friends and recreational activities to where you live.

Choosing a career is work that should be done carefully. As you gain experience and mature, however, you may develop new interests and skills which open doors to new opportunities. Work is an educational experience and can further focus your interests or perhaps change your career preferences. The choice you make today may not be your last. In fact, most people change occupations several times during their careers. With careful consideration of the wide range of occupations available, you should be able to find the right career.

There are many factors to consider when exploring career options and many ways to begin solving your job puzzle. Everyone has certain expectations of his or her job—these may include career advancement, self expression or creativity, a sense of accomplishment, or a high salary. Deciding what you want most from your job will make choosing a career easier.

This article can assist you in your search for a suitable career. It discusses things to consider—personal interests, educational and skill requirements, and job outlook—and lists sources of additional information. The accompanying chart (which begins on page 469) is an exploratory tool to help you pair personal interests, skills, and educational qualifications with those usually associated with a particular occupation. This will help you identify some potential occupational choices.

Interests

Identifying your interests will help in your search for a stimulating career. You might start by assessing your likes and dislikes, strengths and weaknesses. If you have trouble identifying them, consider the school subjects, activities, and surroundings that appeal to you. Would you prefer a job that involves travel? Do you want to work with children? Do you like science and mathematics? Do you need flexible working hours? Does a particular industry, such as health services, appeal to you? These are just a few questions to ask yourself. There are no right or wrong answers, and only you know what's important. Decide what job characteristics you require, which ones you prefer, and which ones you would not accept. Then rank these characteristics in order of importance to you.

Perhaps job setting ranks high on your list of important job characteristics. You may not want to work behind a desk all day. The chart indicates many diverse occupations—from building inspectors, to surveyors,

---

Anne W. Clymer and Elizabeth McGregor are economists in the Office of Employment Projections, BLS

to real estate agents—that require work away from an office. Or maybe you always dreamed of a job that involves instructing and helping others; in this case, child care workers, teachers, and physicians are among the occupations that might interest you.

Geographic location may also concern you. If so, it could influence your career decision because employment in some occupations and industries is concentrated in certain regions or localities. For example, aerospace jobs are concentrated in three States—California, Texas, and Washington—while advertising jobs are concentrated in large cities. If you choose to work in one of these fields, you probably will have to live in one of these States or in a large city. Or, if you live in Denver or the Southeast, for instance, you should learn which industries and occupations are found in those locations. On the other hand, many industries such as hotels and motels, legal services, and retail trade, as well as occupations such as teachers, secretaries, and computer analysts, are found in all areas of the country.

Earnings potential varies from occupation to occupation, and each person must determine his or her needs and goals. If high earnings are important to you, look beyond the starting wages. Some occupations offer relatively low starting salaries, but earnings substantially increase with experience, additional training, and promotions. In the end, your earnings may be higher in one of these occupations. For example, insurance sales workers may have relatively low earnings at first; after years of building a clientele, however, their earnings may increase substantially.

Job setting, working with a specific group of people, geographic location, and earnings are just a few occupational characteristics that you may consider. Be open minded. Consider occupations related to your initial interests. For example, you may be interested in health care, and certain qualities of nursing may appeal to you, such as patient care and frequent public contact. Exploring other health occupations that share these characteristics—including doctors, respiratory therapists, and emergency medical technicians—may stimulate your interest in a health field other than nursing.

Don't eliminate any occupation or industry before you learn more about it. Some occupations and industries invoke certain positive or negative images. For some people, fashion designers produce a glamorous image, while production occupations in manufacturing industries bring to mind a less attractive image. However, jobs often are not what they first appear to be, and misconceptions are common. Exciting jobs may have dull aspects, while less glamorous occupations may interest you once you learn about them. For example, the opportunity to travel makes a flight attendant's job seem exciting, but the work is strenuous and tiring; flight attendants stand for long periods and must remain friendly when they are tired and passengers are unpleasant. On the other hand, many people consider automotive assembly work dirty and dull; however, production workers in the motor vehicle manufacturing industry are among the highest paid in the Nation.

Skills

One way to choose an occupation is to examine the skills required to perform the job well. Consider the skills you already have, or your ability and interest in obtaining the skills or training required for specific occupations. Some occupations that require mechanical ability, for instance, include elevator installers and repairers and automotive mechanics. If you do not plan to attend college, consider occupations that require less formal education. If you are interested in engineering, for example, but do not want to pursue a college degree. drafters and engineering technicians are two occupations you can enter with 1 or 2 years of postsecondary training.

Some skills—analysis, persuading, and mechanical ability, for example—are specific to certain occupations and are included in the accompanying chart. However, certain skills are needed, in varying degrees, in virtually all occupations, from factory workers to top executives. Because these skills apply to so many occupations, they are not found in the chart, but are discussed here.

Skills Common to All Jobs

As the marketplace becomes increasingly competitive, a company's ability to succeed depends upon its workers' skills—in particular, basic skills in reading, writing, and mathematics. These skills allow workers to learn and adapt to rapid technological advances and changing business practices in their jobs. This adaptability is crucial to one's survival in the job market.

Reading skills are essential to perform most jobs. Workers must often read and understand text, graphs, charts, manuals, and instructional materials. Writing skills are necessary to communicate thoughts, ideas, and information in written forms such as memorandums, invoices, schedules, letters, or information requests. Many jobs require basic mathematical skills to take measurements and perform simple calculations. Lack of these skills can lead to many problems, including poor quality products and missed deadlines. These problems can then result in a decline in sales and increased customer complaints.

Reading, writing, and mathematical skills are as important for a research scientist as they are for occupations that require little formal education, such as a stockroom clerk at a manufacturing plant. Although a computer system may be designed to track inventory by electronically recording all transactions, the clerk is responsible for verifying the information. The clerk must be able to read and do simple calculations to confirm that stockroom inventory matches what the computer registers. Any inaccuracies in counting, computing, or recording of this inventory could result in a slowdown in production.

Workers also need good listening and speaking skills to interact with others. Greater interaction among workers is evident in factories, offices, and laboratories. Problems often are solved through communication, cooperation, and discussion, and workers must be able to listen, speak, and think on their feet. When dealing with customers, workers must listen and understand customers' needs and communicate solutions and ideas. It is not good enough to merely take a customer's order; workers must provide customers with useful information.

The banking industry illustrates the importance of listening and speaking skills. Banks face competition from other industries—including insurance companies, credit unions, and investment houses—that offer a growing array of financial products. Tellers, customer service representatives, and bank managers need strong communication skills to explain, promote, and sell the bank's services to potential customers. Customer satisfaction can only be achieved by understanding what the customer wants and by providing that service as quickly as possible.

Good interpersonal skills are critical as the workplace becomes more team-oriented. Apparel plants, for instance, are replacing the traditional assembly line with modular manufacturing. On the traditional assembly line, workers performed a specific task independent of other workers and were compensated accordingly. Today, groups of workers, called modules, work as a team to produce garments, solve problems as they occur, and make suggestions to improve production or working conditions. Group interaction is important because an individual's earnings are based upon the group's performance.

Workers at all levels must be willing to learn new techniques. Computers, for instance, were once found primarily in office settings; today, computers are found in every work setting from factories to classrooms. The introduction of computers into the manufacturing process is transforming many craft and factory occupations; many of these jobs now require the use of computer-controlled equipment. For example, most elevators are computerized and electronically controlled. In order to install, repair, and maintain modern elevators, elevator repairers need a thorough knowledge of electronics, electricity, and computer applications. Even though a high school education generally is the minimum requirement for entering this field, workers with postsecondary training in electronics usually have better advancement opportunities than those with less training. As technological changes continue, retraining will be essential for workers in many fields.

Outlook

When matching your interests and skills to an occupation, you should also consider the employment outlook for that occupation or related industry. For instance, stiff competition is expected for jobs as advertising managers because the number of applicants greatly exceeds the number of job openings. On the other hand, job openings for preschool workers should be plentiful due to rapidly growing demand for this occupation and relatively high turnover among preschool workers. Outlook is not addressed in the table but is discussed in detail in the *Occupational Outlook Handbook* and *Career Guide to Industries*, which are revised every two years.

Information about job openings, supply/demand conditions, and susceptibility to layoffs indicate, in part, the ease or difficulty of landing a job. Many factors affect the demand for an occupation, including changes in consumer spending, demographics, and technology. Researching an occupation or industry will help you identify key factors and their impact on employment. For example, increased use of computers has contributed to the rapid growth of computer service technician jobs. On the other hand, the growing use of computers in offices has greatly reduced the demand for typists. This illustrates the diverse effects that technological advances can have on different occupations and emphasizes the importance of learning about specific occupations.

Job growth is a good indicator of favorable opportunities, but the fastest growing occupations do not always equate with the largest numbers of job opportunities. Most job openings result from the need to replace workers who leave their jobs. Consequently, larger occupations—which usually have the highest replacement needs—generally provide the most job openings. As a result of replacement needs, even occupations that are declining can provide employment opportunities.

Knowledge of the industries in which occupations are found also is important in looking for a job. Job opportunities generally are favorable in an occupation found in a wide range of industries, such as receptionists. On the other hand, employment prospects are likely to be unfavorable, and workers more subject to layoffs, in an occupation that is concentrated in a declining industry, such as machine operators in the textile industry. Some workers also may be subject to layoffs because of the nature of the industry. For example, the demand for construction workers is cyclical—employment rises and falls with changes in construction activity—and motor vehicle manufacturing workers may be laid off during periods of slack sales.

Additional Information

"Matching Yourself With the World of Work in 1992" can educate you about factors that affect occupational choices and help you match your interests and skills to specific occupations. However, it is only a first step—its purpose is to facilitate career exploration, not to provide all the answers.

Once you identify an interest in one or more occupations or industries, many sources of additional information are available. The specific sources may vary, depending on the fields which interest you. Use common sense and resourcefulness to learn about potential jobs. For example, local television or radio stations may be a good source of information and, perhaps, work experience if broadcasting interests you. The following sources may serve as starting points in your career search.

Libraries. A library is a great place to find information about jobs. Libraries have career guidance publications that present occupational information covering job duties, training requirements, working conditions, employment outlook, and earnings. Librarians can direct you to the information you need.

Career centers. Many career centers have computerized job information systems that match jobs to your skills and interests. These systems usually are easy to use and generate a list of suggested occupations. Career centers often have career literature that may interest you. Also, career counselors at these centers can help you develop jobseeking skills, such as resume writing or interviewing.

State employment service offices. State employment service offices can provide you with information concerning the industrial and occupational composition of specific areas. This is a good place to start if you need to find out what job opportunities a particular area offers.

Guidance counselors. Counselors interview, test, and counsel students to help them discover their skills and interests and how these relate to career opportunities. If you have a particular aptitude for certain subjects, a counselor can direct you toward occupations that require these talents. If you are interested in art, your counselor might provide information on becoming a designer or graphic artist; if you are good at mathematics, a counselor may suggest that engineer or statistician might be a good occupational choice for you. Counselors may also direct students to career information centers or career education programs.

Informational interviews. Interviewing individuals to gather information about their occupation or industry is a very effective way to find out about jobs that may interest you. An informational interview is not a job interview. Rather, it's your opportunity to learn from a person who knows the pros and cons of an occupation or industry.

If you don't know someone in the occupation that interests you, network! Ask your parents, neighbors, teachers, or friends if they know someone in the occupation. Most people enjoy talking about their jobs and are pleased to have an audience. Your network could lead to internships, volunteer work, or other opportunities in your field of interest.

Before you talk to someone about a particular occupation, think about what you want to know. You may ask questions about job duties, educational or training requirements, advancement opportunities, and average wages. You may also ask for his or her opinion of your qualifications for a particular job.

Internships/volunteer work. There is no substitute for practical experience. Internship programs and volunteer work help students explore a field and develop career skills at the same time. For example, someone interested in politics may volunteer to help a local, State, or national campaign elect a candidate to office.

Many local government planning offices offer internships to college and graduate students specializing in urban and regional planning. Through these programs, students gain planning experience that not only improves their chances of finding a full-time job after graduation but also helps them decide whether or not the field interests them.

Cooperative education. This program is similar to internships; students gain practical experience by working in their chosen fields. Students enrolled in cooperative education programs divide their time between school and work, applying the knowledge and theory gained in class to practical situations on the job. Credit and grades are given for both the worksite learning and the related school instruction. Not all cooperative education programs are alike. In some programs, students switch from school to job each quarter or semester; in others, students may work for a couple of months a year. Through these programs, students earn money, gain experience, test their interest in particular careers, and learn how they fit into the world of work. Your counselor, financial aid office, or career center may have information on these opportunities.

Trade unions and associations. These organizations specialize in a particular field and are well informed on the issues affecting the employment of workers in occupations or industries that they represent. They can provide information about training and skill requirements. Local unions sponsor apprenticeships and formal training programs for many occupations.

Matching Personal and Job Characteristics

Having looked at the job puzzle, you can now focus your career search. The accompanying table matches 18 job characteristics to over 200 occupations studied in the occupational outlook program. You can use it to match yourself with the characteristics associated with various occupations. Be realistic when matching your interests, skills, and goals to a career. For example, you can't become a neurosurgeon without completing college and many years of advanced study, and elementary school teachers do not make $100,000 per year. Being realistic will help you eliminate some possible career choices and identify others that may interest you.

The table can be used in various ways. If you are interested in a specific occupation, you can find out some general characteristics of that occupation. If you are considering psychology, for example, the table indicates that psychologists need a college degree, treat and advise others, and do analysis and evaluation. If the field of education appeals to you, the table provides information about various jobs in that field. If you have no idea about an occupation or field but do know what skills you possess, the table can help you identify careers that might interest you.

Although this table presents information on occupations and skills, it is intended only as a general guide. Don't rule out an occupation because one or two characteristics don't appeal to you. The table addresses primary characteristics of a typical job in that occupation. Not all jobs in an occupation are alike. There may be some differences by specialty, employment setting, or level of experience. For example, jewelers in retail stores deal with the public daily, while those in manufacturing rarely have contact with the public. Counseling psychologists work with people in offices, while experimental psychologists may work with animals in laboratories. Furthermore, you could find two dissimilar occupations that share some characteristics. For example, public relations specialists and dietitians are unrelated occupations, but both require analyzing and troubleshooting ability.

Most occupations cannot be easily categorized by job characteristics. The process of selecting and defining occupational characteristics relies upon the best judgment of analysts who study trends of the selected occupations. Because final decisions rely upon judgment, there may be some questions as to which characteristics apply to a particular occupation. For instance, teachers spend much of their day on their feet, which is physically tiring. However, the table does not indicate physical stamina as a key characteristic of teachers because they can teach while sitting at a desk. Construction laborers, in comparison, must lift heavy objects and endure physical stress and strain to perform their work. Take the time to learn more about occupations that interest you; this may include following the suggestions mentioned in the section on additional information.

The characteristics matched in the table with occupations studied in the occupational outlook program are defined below. The characteristics are grouped under five headings: Education, data/information, people, things, and working conditions. Specific occupations are mentioned with the definitions to illustrate how the characteristics apply to the job.

Education

- High school diploma (HS)—requires a high school diploma or the equivalent.
- Postsecondary training (PS)—requires training beyond high school but less than a bachelor's degree, including formal on-the-job training, technical or vocational school, or junior or community college.
- College and above (C)—requires at least a bachelor's degree.
- No educational level indicated—occupation may be entered with less than a high school education.

In some cases, more than one level of educational attainment is indicated for an occupation, reflecting a range of formal educational requirements. For example, some high school graduates become administrative services managers by advancing through the ranks of an organization. Even though a higher degree is not always required for administrative services managers, postsecondary or college education usually enhances their chance of advancing to top-level management positions. Educational requirements may also vary within an occupation. For instance, registered nursing can be entered by earning a diploma, associate degree, or bachelor's degree.

Data/Information

Researching and compiling: Gathering and organizing information or data by reading, conducting tests or experiments, or interviewing experts. Through research, scientists gather information to develop new theories, products, and processes, such as a new medicine to cure a disease. Paralegals conduct research and compile information to identify appropriate laws, legal articles, and judicial decisions that might be used in a client's case. Credit clerks and authorizers compile and update information for credit reports.

Analyzing and evaluating: Examining data or information to develop conclusions or interpretations. After conducting research and compiling data, paralegals may analyze the information and write reports that are used by attorneys to decide how a case should be handled. Retail buyers study sales data to determine purchasing trends, and budget analysts examine financial data to determine the most efficient distribution of funds and resources for their company.

Troubleshooting: Identifying, diagnosing, and solving problems. A degree of analysis may be required to form opinions and make decisions. Involves a reaction to a situation or problem that arises. Elevator repairers diagnose and repair electrical defects quickly to ensure that elevators continue running smoothly. Automotive mechanics diagnose problems with cars and make adjustments or repairs. Managers must deal with various problems, such as a decline in an employee's performance or budget reductions requiring layoffs.

Artistic expression: Designing, composing, drawing, writing, or creating original works or concepts. Interior designers need creativity to develop designs to use

in preparing working drawings and specifications for interior construction of buildings. They need an artistic sense to coordinate colors, select furniture and floor coverings, and design lighting and architectural details. Newspaper columnists convey their views on political, social, and economic issues.

People

Instructing: Teaching people by explaining or showing. Often requires ability to develop new methods and approaches. Adult education teachers demonstrate various techniques to students, including the use of tools or equipment. Manufacturers' and wholesale sales representatives show their customers how to operate and maintain new equipment.

Treating and advising: Counseling or caring for others. Dietitians advise people on proper nutrition. Psychologists and counselors help people deal with vocational and marital problems. Securities and financial services sales representatives advise people on financial investments and planning.

Supervising: Directing, organizing, and motivating people and groups. Blue-collar worker supervisors coordinate and supervise the activities of subordinates. Education administrators provide direction, leadership, and day-to-day management of educational activities in schools and instructional organizations in private businesses.

Persuading: Influencing the feelings of others. Preaching, selling, promoting, speechmaking, negotiating, and mediating are among the skills included in this occupational characteristic. Lawyers attempt to persuade a jury to believe a client's case. Advertising executives try to influence consumers to buy the products they are promoting.

Public contact: Meeting, assisting, and dealing directly with the public frequently on a daily basis. Reference librarians work directly with people, helping them locate information. Bank tellers cash checks and process deposits and withdrawals for customers. Real estate agents help customers find homes that meet their needs.

Things

Mechanical ability: Extensively using and understanding machines or tools. Setting up, operating, adjusting, and repairing machines may also be required. Textile machinery operators make minor repairs and restart looms when malfunctions occur. Musical instrument repairers tune and adjust pianos and other instruments. Marine engineers maintain and repair engines, boilers, generators, and other machinery on boats and ships.

Operating a vehicle: Driving and controlling vehicles or equipment. Busdrivers, industrial truck operators, and aircraft pilots are several examples.

Working Conditions

Repetitious: Work in which the same duties are performed continuously in a short period of time. Sometimes a machine sets the pace of work. Examples include workers on automotive assembly lines, as well as cashiers and bank tellers.

Geographically concentrated: Occupations concentrated in a particular region or locality. Most textile workers are concentrated in a few states. Advertising workers are found mainly in large cities.

Mobile: Requires frequent movement between various work locations, such as office buildings and construction sites. Can involve a combination of different work settings. Workers do not stay in a single office, factory, or laboratory. For example, in addition to working in an office, property and real estate managers frequently visit properties they oversee, while manufacturing sales representatives travel to different cities to visit customers. Messengers deliver packages to various locations.

Physical stamina: Physically demanding. Workers must endure significant physical stress and strain, including lifting heavy objects. Construction work is often strenuous, and workers spend most of the day on their feet—bending, kneeling, lifting, and maneuvering heavy objects.

Part time: Opportunities for part-time work are favorable. Most waiters and waitresses work part time, as do retail salesworkers.

Irregular hours: Working a schedule other than the standard 8-hour day, including night or weekend shifts, rotating schedules, or working for several days and then having several days off. Many nurses and security guards work nights or weekends. Other occupations that work on shifts include firefighters, pilots, and roustabouts.

OCCUPATIONAL OUTLOOK QUARTERLY

	Education	Researching and compiling	Analyzing and evaluating	Troubleshooting	Artistic expression	Instructing	Treating and advising	Supervising	Persuading	Public contact	Mechanical ability	Operating a vehicle	Repetitious	Geographically concentrated	Mobile	Physical stamina	Part-time	Irregular hours
Management and Financial Occupations																		
General management occupations																		
Administrative services managers	HS, PS, C		•	•				•										
Employment interviewers	PS		•						•	•								
Hotel managers and assistants	C		•	•				•		•								•
Inspectors and compliance officers, except construction	C	•	•	•						•					•			
General managers and top executives	C		•	•				•	•									
Government chief executives and legislators	C		•	•				•	•	•					•		•	•
Management analysts and consultants	C	•	•	•														
Personnel, training, and labor relations specialists and managers	C		•	•				•	•									
Purchasing agents and managers	PS, C	•	•	•				•	•									
Financial occupations																		
Accountants and auditors	C	•	•	•														
Budget analysts	C	•	•	•														
Cost estimators	PS, C	•	•															
Financial managers	C	•	•	•				•										
Mathematical, Scientific, and Related Occupations																		
Mathematical occupations																		
Actuaries	C	•	•															
Computer systems analysts	C	•	•	•														
Computer programmers	C		•	•														
Mathematicians	C	•	•															
Operations research analysts	C	•	•	•														
Statisticians	C	•	•															
Engineering occupations																		
Drafters	PS		•	•														
Engineers (aerospace, chemical, civil, electrical and electronic, industrial, mechanical, metallurgical, mining, nuclear, petroleum)	C	•	•	•														
Engineering, science, and data processing managers	C	•	•	•				•										
Engineering technicians	PS	•	•	•							•							
Scientists and related occupations																		
Life scientists																		
Agricultural scientists	C	•	•															
Biological scientists	C	•	•															
Foresters	C	•	•												•	•	•	

OCCUPATIONAL OUTLOOK QUARTERLY

	Education	Researching and compiling	Analyzing and evaluating	Troubleshooting	Artistic expression	Instructing	Treating and advising	Supervising	Persuading	Public contact	Mechanical ability	Operating a vehicle	Repetitious	Geographically concentrated	Mobile	Physical stamina	Part-time	Irregular hours
		Data/Information				People					Things		Working conditions					
Physical scientists (chemists, geologists and geophysicists, meteorologists, physicists, astronomers)	C	•	•															
Cartographers and geographers	C	•	•															
Science technicians	PS	•																
Architects and surveyors																		
Architects	C	•	•		•													
Landscape architects	C	•	•		•										•			
Surveyors and surveying technicians	PS, C	•	•	•											•			
Legal, Social Science, and Human Service Occupations																		
Legal occupations (also see stenographers and court reporters under administrative support occupations)																		
Lawyers and judges	C	•	•	•			•		•	•								
Paralegals	PS	•	•							•								
Social scientists and urban planners																		
Anthropologists and archaeologists	C	•	•												•	•		
Archivists, curators, and historians	C	•	•															
Economists	C	•	•															
Marketing research analysts	C	•	•							•								
Psychologists	C	•	•	•			•		•	•								
Urban and regional planners	C	•	•	•					•	•								
Sociologists	C	•	•							•								
Social and recreation workers																		
Human services workers	PS, C	•	•				•			•					•			•
Recreation workers	HS, PS, C					•				•					•	•	•	•
Social workers	C	•	•	•			•		•	•					•			
Religious workers (ministers, rabbis, priests)	PS, C					•	•	•	•	•					•			•
Education and Related Occupations																		
Education occupations																		
Adult education teachers and college faculty	C	•	•	•		•	•										•	•
Counselors	C		•	•		•	•		•	•								
Education administrators	C		•	•		•		•	•	•								
Kindergarten, elementary, and secondary school teachers	C		•	•		•	•											
Preschool workers	HS, PS, C			•		•	•			•						•		
Teacher aides	HS, PS					•										•		
Library occupations																		
Librarians	C	•		•						•							•	•
Library assistants and bookmobile drivers	HS									•		•				•	•	•

OCCUPATIONAL OUTLOOK QUARTERLY

	Education	Researching and compiling	Analyzing and evaluating	Troubleshooting	Artistic expression	Instructing	Treating and advising	Supervising	Persuading	Public contact	Mechanical ability	Operating a vehicle	Repetitious	Geographically concentrated	Mobile	Physical stamina	Part-time	Irregular hours
Library technicians	HS	•								•							•	•
Health Care Occupations (chiropractors, dentists, optometrists, physicians, podiatrists, veterinarians)																		
Health diagnosing practitioners	C	•	•	•		•	•			•								•
Health services managers	C	•	•	•				•	•									
Health assessment and treating occupations																		
Dietitians and nutritionists	C		•	•		•	•			•							•	
Occupational therapists	C		•	•		•	•			•								
Pharmacists	C		•	•		•	•			•								•
Physical therapists	C		•	•		•	•			•					•	•		
Physician assistants	C		•	•		•	•			•								•
Recreational therapists	C		•	•		•	•			•					•	•	•	
Registered nurses	PS, C		•	•		•	•			•					•	•	•	
Respiratory therapists	PS, C		•	•		•	•			•								
Speech-language pathologists and audiologists	C		•	•		•	•			•								
Health technologists and technicians																		
Clinical laboratory technologists and technicians	PS, C		•										•					
Dental hygienists	PS					•	•			•							•	
Dispensing opticians	HS, PS									•								
EEG technologists	PS	•								•			•					
EKG technicians	HS	•								•			•					
Emergency medical technicians	PS		•	•			•			•					•		•	•
Licensed practical nurses	PS						•			•						•	•	•
Medical record technicians	PS	•	•							•								•
Nuclear medicine technologists	PS	•								•								
Radiologic technologists	PS	•								•				•				
Surgical technicians	PS						•			•								
Health service occupations																		
Dental and medical assistants	HS						•			•							•	
Nursing and psychiatric aides	HS, PS						•			•							•	•
Homemaker–health aides							•			•					•		•	
Communication, Visual Arts, and Performing Arts Occupations																		
Communications occupations																		
Broadcast technicians	PS			•							•							•
Marketing, advertising, and public relations managers	C		•	•	•			•	•	•				•				
Public relations specialists	C	•	•	•	•				•	•				•				
Radio and television announcers and newscasters	HS, PS, C	•	•		•				•	•								•
Reporters and correspondents	C	•	•		•				•	•					•			•

OCCUPATIONAL OUTLOOK QUARTERLY

	Education	Researching and compiling	Analyzing and evaluating	Troubleshooting	Artistic expression	Instructing	Treating and advising	Supervising	Persuading	Public contact	Mechanical ability	Operating a vehicle	Repetitious	Geographically concentrated	Mobile	Physical stamina	Part-time	Irregular hours
		Data/Information				People					Things		Working conditions					
Writers and editors	PS, C	•	•		•				•	•								
Visual arts occupations																		
Designers	HS, PS, C				•					•								
Photographers and camera operators	PS				•				•	•	•				•			
Visual artists	HS, PS, C				•													
Performing artists																		
Actors, dancers, musicians					•					•					•	•	•	•
Directors, choreographers, and conductors		•	•	•	•	•		•	•	•						•		•
Sales and Related Occupations																		
Marketing, retail, and sales occupations																		
Cashiers										•			•				•	•
Counter and rental clerks										•			•				•	•
Manufacturers' and wholesale sales representatives	C	•	•	•		•			•	•					•			
Retail salesworkers									•	•							•	•
Securities and financial services sales representatives	C	•	•				•		•	•								
Services sales representatives	HS						•		•	•								
Travel agents	HS	•		•					•	•							•	•
Wholesale and retail buyers and merchandise managers	PS, C	•	•	•				•		•								
Insurance occupations																		
(also see adjusters, investigators, and collectors under administrative support occupations, and actuaries under mathematical occupations)																		
Insurance agents and brokers	PS, C	•	•				•		•	•								
Underwriters	PS, C	•	•															
Real estate occupations																		
Property and real estate managers	C	•	•	•				•	•	•					•			
Real estate agents, brokers, and appraisers	HS, PS	•	•	•			•		•	•					•		•	•
Administrative Support Occupations																		
Adjusters, investigators, and collectors	HS, PS, C	•	•							•								
Bank tellers	HS, PS									•				•			•	
Clerical supervisors and managers	HS, PS, C		•	•				•										
Computer and peripheral equipment operators	PS			•														•
Credit clerks and authorizers	HS	•												•				
Dispatchers	HS			•						•				•				•
General office clerks	HS																•	
Mail carriers	HS									•		•		•		•	•	•

OCCUPATIONAL OUTLOOK QUARTERLY

	Education	Researching and compiling	Analyzing and evaluating	Troubleshooting	Artistic expression	Instructing	Treating and advising	Supervising	Persuading	Public contact	Mechanical ability	Operating a vehicle	Repetitious	Geographically concentrated	Mobile	Physical stamina	Part-time	Irregular hours
		Data/Information				People					Things		Working conditions					
Mail clerks	HS												•					
Material recording, scheduling, and distributing occupations (stock clerks, shipping and receiving clerks)	HS												•					
Messengers	HS									•		•	•	•	•	•	•	
Postal clerks	HS									•			•				•	
Receptionists and other information clerks (hotel and motel clerks, interviewing and new account clerks, receptionists, reservation and ticket clerks)	HS									•			•					
Record clerks (billing, bookkeeping, accounting, brokerage, file, order, payroll, and personnel clerks)	HS	•											•					
Secretaries	HS			•						•								
Stenographers and court reporters	PS												•				•	
Telephone, telegraph, and teletype operators	HS									•			•					•
Typists, word processors, and data entry keyers	HS												•					

Service Occupations

Protective service occupations

	Education	Researching and compiling	Analyzing and evaluating	Troubleshooting	Artistic expression	Instructing	Treating and advising	Supervising	Persuading	Public contact	Mechanical ability	Operating a vehicle	Repetitious	Geographically concentrated	Mobile	Physical stamina	Part-time	Irregular hours
Correction officers	HS							•										•
Firefighting occupations	HS			•				•		•		•			•	•		•
Guards	HS							•		•			•				•	•
Police, detectives, and special agents	HS	•	•	•				•		•		•			•	•		

Food and beverage preparation and service occupations

	Education	Researching and compiling	Analyzing and evaluating	Troubleshooting	Artistic expression	Instructing	Treating and advising	Supervising	Persuading	Public contact	Mechanical ability	Operating a vehicle	Repetitious	Geographically concentrated	Mobile	Physical stamina	Part-time	Irregular hours
Chefs	PS					•		•										•
Cooks and other kitchen workers	HS												•				•	•
Food and beverage service occupations	HS									•			•				•	•
Restaurant and food service managers	C		•	•				•		•								•

Personal service and facility maintenance occupations

	Education	Researching and compiling	Analyzing and evaluating	Troubleshooting	Artistic expression	Instructing	Treating and advising	Supervising	Persuading	Public contact	Mechanical ability	Operating a vehicle	Repetitious	Geographically concentrated	Mobile	Physical stamina	Part-time	Irregular hours
Animal caretakers, except farm	HS														•	•		
Barbers and cosmetologists	PS									•			•				•	•
Gardeners and groundskeepers												•	•		•	•	•	•
Janitors and cleaners													•			•	•	•
Private household workers															•	•	•	•

Agricultural, Forestry, Fishing, and Related Occupations

	Education	Researching and compiling	Analyzing and evaluating	Troubleshooting	Artistic expression	Instructing	Treating and advising	Supervising	Persuading	Public contact	Mechanical ability	Operating a vehicle	Repetitious	Geographically concentrated	Mobile	Physical stamina	Part-time	Irregular hours
Farm operators and managers			•	•				•				•			•	•	•	•
Fishers, hunters, and trappers															•	•	•	•
Timber cutting and logging workers															•	•	•	•

OCCUPATIONAL OUTLOOK QUARTERLY

	Education	Researching and compiling	Analyzing and evaluating	Troubleshooting	Artistic expression	Instructing	Treating and advising	Supervising	Persuading	Public contact	Mechanical ability	Operating a vehicle	Repetitious	Geographically concentrated	Mobile	Physical stamina	Part-time	Irregular hours
		Data/Information				People					Things		Working conditions					
Mechanics, Installers, and Repairers (also see aircraft mechanics under air transportation occupations)																		
Automotive body repairers	PS			•							•					•		
Electronic equipment repairers (commercial and industrial electronic equipment, communications equipment, computer and office machines, home entertainment, and telephone repairers)	PS			•						•	•				•	•		
Home appliance and power tool repairers				•						•	•				•	•		
Mechanics (automotive, diesel, farm equipment, mobile heavy equipment, motorcycle, boat, small engine, and general maintenance mechanics)	PS			•						•	•					•		
Musical instrument repairers and tuners				•						•	•				•	•		
Vending machine servicers and repairers	HS			•						•	•				•	•		
Construction and Related Occupations																		
Bricklayers and stonemasons	HS, PS													•		•	•	
Carpenters	HS, PS														•	•		
Carpet installers	HS, PS													•	•	•		
Concrete masons and terrazzo workers	HS, PS														•	•		
Construction and building inspectors	HS, PS		•	•						•					•	•		
Construction contractors and managers	PS, C	•	•	•				•	•	•					•			
Drywall workers and lathers	HS, PS														•	•		
Electricians	HS, PS			•							•				•	•		
Elevator installers and repairers	HS			•							•				•	•		
Glaziers	HS, PS														•	•		
Heating, air-conditioning, and refrigeration technicians	HS, PS			•							•				•	•		
Insulation workers	HS, PS													•	•	•		
Line installers and cable splicers				•							•				•	•		
Painters and paperhangers	HS, PS													•	•	•	•	
Plasterers	HS, PS													•	•	•		
Plumbers and pipefitters	PS			•							•				•	•		
Roofers	HS, PS													•	•	•		
Roustabouts											•			•	•	•		•
Sheet-metal workers	PS														•	•		
Structural and reinforcing ironworkers	HS, PS										•			•	•	•		
Tilesetters	HS, PS													•	•	•		
Production Occupations																		
Plant and systems operators																		
Electric power generating plant operators and power dispatchers	HS		•	•							•							•
Stationary engineers	HS			•							•							•

OCCUPATIONAL OUTLOOK QUARTERLY

	Education	Researching and compiling	Analyzing and evaluating	Troubleshooting	Artistic expression	Instructing	Treating and advising	Supervising	Persuading	Public contact	Mechanical ability	Operating a vehicle	Repetitious	Geographically concentrated	Mobile	Physical stamina	Part-time	Irregular hours
		Data/Information				People					Things		Working conditions					
Water and wastewater treatment plant operators	HS	•	•	•							•							•
Printing occupations																		
Prepress workers	HS			•							•							•
Printing press operators	HS			•							•		•					•
Bindery workers	HS			•							•		•					
Textile, apparel, and furnishings occupations																		
Apparel workers													•					
Shoe and leather workers and repairers								•					•					•
Textile machinery operators	HS			•							•		•	•				•
Upholsterers	HS																	
Miscellaneous production occupations																		
Blue-collar supervisors	HS			•				•										•
Boilermakers	HS		•	•							•				•	•		
Butcher and meat and poultry cutters	HS							•			•							
Handlers, equipment cleaners, helpers, and laborers													•			•		
Industrial machinery repairers and millwrights	PS	•	•								•				•	•		•
Industrial production managers	C	•	•					•										
Inspectors, testers, and graders	HS	•	•								•							•
Jewelers	PS			•					•	•	•							
Machinists and tool and tie makers	PS			•							•							•
Metal and plastics-working machine operators	HS			•							•		•					•
Numerical-control machine tool operators	HS			•							•		•					•
Painting and coating machine operators													•					
Photographic process workers	HS												•				•	•
Precision assemblers	HS			•							•		•					
Tool programmers, numerical control	PS, C	•	•								•							
Welders, cutters, and welding machine operators	PS										•		•			•		•
Woodworking occupations	HS										•		•					
Transportation Occupations																		
Air transportation occupations																		
Aircraft pilots	C			•								•			•			•
Air traffic controllers	HS, PS, C			•														•
Aircraft mechanics and engine specialists	PS			•							•					•		•
Flight attendants	HS, PS			•						•					•			•
Ground transportation occupations																		
Busdrivers	HS			•						•		•	•		•		•	•
Material moving equipment operators	HS, PS										•	•			•			

OCCUPATIONAL OUTLOOK QUARTERLY

	Education	Data/Information				People					Things		Working conditions					
		Researching and compiling	Analyzing and evaluating	Troubleshooting	Artistic expression	Instructing	Treating and advising	Supervising	Persuading	Public contact	Mechanical ability	Operating a vehicle	Repetitious	Geographically concentrated	Mobile	Physical stamina	Part-time	Irregular hours
Rail transportation occupations	HS			•								•			•			•
Truckdrivers	HS			•								•	•		•	•		•
Water transportation occupations																		
Marine engineers and captains	C			•				•			•	•			•			•
Mates and seamen	HS			•							•				•	•		•

Optional Software Supplement

Program Overview

*T*he *Career Guide* does not require any software for its use as a career exploration tool. However, for those instructors who wish to use it, the Software Supplement is designed to complement the text.

Program Descriptions

*T*he software supplement is composed of several programs that are directly keyed to the *Career Guide*. Because these programs are under continual revision and refinement, a detailed description is not provided.

The **Career Profile** uses the input from the Assessment Summary Sheet in Chapter Two to generate a narrative career exploration report. The user is given the option of supplementing the self-assessment results with additional, more objective data, if available.

The **OOH Info** program is a tool that provides assistance with access to information from the *Occupational Outlook Handbook*, in terms of occupational categories used within the *Career Guide*.

A **Program Update** option is provided if any updates have been issued since this printing.

Program Requirements

*T*he Software Supplement requires one of the following hardware configurations:

1. Preferably, an IBM-compatible personal computer running under DOS 3.3 (or later version) or Windows 3.3 (or higher version), or

2. An Apple MacIntosh running under a version of Insignia's *Soft PC* program, or containing an Orange Card, or otherwise able to run MS-DOS software (see your Apple dealer if you need additional information).

You will need at least one disk drive and a (non-Postscript) printer.

NOTE: Instructions are provided in accordance with IBM-compatible parameters. The user may have to vary somewhat from these instructions if he or she is operating an Apple computer in DOS emulation mode.

The Career Profile requires that you input the information from the Assessment Summary Sheet in Chapter Two of the *Career Guide*. The program will then generate a narrative printout based upon these results, compatible with the clusters used in the *Career Guide*.

If you choose to supplement your results with objective skills data, you may request that your instructor or counselor see if funds are available to order the Career Ability Placement Survey—an objective battery of eight skills tests that can be completed within about an hour. Ordering and price information may be obtained from EdITs Publishers, P.O. Box 7234, San Diego, CA 92167, (800) 416-1666. Your instructor or counselor should order the *self-scoring booklets*.

Operating Procedures

Before You Begin

Make sure that you are using a computer that is compatible with the program (see Program Requirements). You should be familiar with the basic operational features of the computer itself before you attempt to run the Software Supplement. You need to know the drive designation for the disk drive you will be using (typically A or B). If you are not familiar with computer hardware and operation, it is suggested that you enlist the assistance of someone who is more knowledgeable about such things.

You will also need some assessment results (from the self-assessment in Chapter Two of the *Career Guide*) to generate a report.

Check to see that you have an adequate supply of paper for your printer (each profile is 10–15 pages long) and that the printer is in the "On line" mode. If you have a choice, use a high-speed printer.

To Start the Program

To use the Software Supplement, follow these instructions:

1. Power-up all your computer hardware. Obtain a DOS prompt.

2. If you are using an Apple computer, do what must be done to get into the DOS emulation mode.

3. When you are in DOS, you should have a "prompt" on your screen—usually a C:> prompt. Your computer may automatically start in this mode, or it may load another program through an "Autoexec" file. If another program is loaded automatically, exit to DOS.

4. Place the program disk in your disk drive. Make your disk drive (not your hard drive) the default drive. You do this by typing in the designation of the drive, followed by a colon, and then hitting the [Enter] key. Typically this would involve typing **A:** and then pushing the [Enter] key. If done correctly, your prompt should change to the letter of your disk drive (e.g., **A:>**).

5. Type the word **GO** and push the [Enter] key. The program should automatically load and the Main Menu should appear on the screen.

   NOTE: If you are operating under the Windows environment, you can get to this point by selecting **File** from the Program Manager menu bar, then selecting the **Run** option, and then typing in **A:Go** and pushing the [Enter] key.

6. Never remove the program disk from the disk drive until you have fully exited the program (explained in a following segment).

From the Main Menu you can access all the primary functions of the Software Supplement. If the Main Menu does not appear, check that you correctly followed steps 1 through 6 above.

All of the programs are menu-driven. If you follow the instructions within the program, you should have no difficulty using this software. Pay special attention to the "status line" at the bottom of the screen; it will often provide operational instructions.

To Exit the Program

When you have finished using the program, return to the Main Menu. From the Main Menu:

1. Push the [Esc] key. This should return you to the P2T logo screen.

2. Push the [Esc] key again. This should clear the screen and provide you with a prompt for your disk drive (e.g., **A:>**). You may now remove the program disk.

3. If this procedure does not work, *remove the program disk* and perform a "warm boot" of your computer. In the unlikely event that this does not work, you may have to power-down and then power-up again. If this still does not work, you might try tapping the CPU a few times with a 22-ounce hammer (just kidding!).

Troubleshooting

*T*he Software Supplement has been thoroughly reviewed to eliminate program errors. However, as Murphy's Law tells us, error is often inevitable. The following suggestions are provided to help you do some initial troubleshooting.

If the program disk will not load at all (i.e., the screen remains "frozen" and the disk drive continues to spin, check the following:

■ Be sure that you are using a computer and operating system that is compatible with the program (see Program Requirements).

■ Make sure that the program disk is not write-protected.

■ Be sure that you have designated the disk drive containing the program disk as the default drive (see Operating Procedures) and that you are running the program from that drive.

■ Reboot the computer, remove the program disk immediately once the disk drive "in-use" light goes out, and try to start up the program once again.

■ Try the program on a different computer.

If you cannot print the program printouts:

■ Be sure that the hardware and software configuration meets the program requirements.

■ Be sure that the printer is properly connected to your computer.

■ Be sure that the printer is in an "On-line" mode.

■ Exit the Software Supplement and try to print something else to make sure your printer is otherwise operational.

If your screen becomes "frozen" or displays an error message:

■ Be sure that you are following the operating procedures properly.

■ Remove the program disk and reboot your computer. Re-initiate start-up procedures and try it again.

■ If the same thing happens more than once, write down exactly what you did (step by step) and make a note of any error messages that are displayed (exact wording is important). Send this information to Brooks/Cole.

■ Shut down your computer, start it up again and use another software program to verify that your computer is operating as it should.

If none of these suggestions resolves the problem, your program disk may have been damaged in some way. Write or call Brooks/Cole to obtain a replacement disk.

Bibliography

NOTE: The following resources are related to the topics covered in *Career Guide*. The author does not necessarily endorse any listing. You should review the resources that you think may be helpful.

Adult Development

Branden, N. (1983). *Honoring the self.* Los Angeles: Tarcher.

Chickering, A. (1969). *Education and identity.* San Francisco: Jossey-Bass.

Creamer, D. (ed.) (1980). *Student development in higher education.* American College Personnel Association.

De Ropp, R. (1979). *Warrior's way: The challenging life games.* New York: Dell.

Erikson, E. (1968). *Identity, youth, and crisis.* New York: Norton.

Knefelkamp, L., et al. (1978). *Applying new developmental findings.* San Francisco: Jossey-Bass.

Kolb, D. (1984). *Experiential learning: Experience as the source of learning and development.* Englewood Cliffs, NJ: Prentice-Hall.

Marcia, J. (1966). Development and validation of ego-identity status. *Journal of Personality and Social Psychology, 3,* 551–558.

Maslow, A. (1968). *Toward a psychology of being.* (2nd ed.). New York: Van Nostrand.

Maslow, A. (1970). *Motivation and personality.* (2nd ed.) New York: Harper & Row.

Okun, B. (1984). *Working with adults: Individual, family, and career development.* Pacific Grove, CA: Brooks/Cole.

Rotter, J. (1966). Generalized expectencies for internal versus external control of reinforcement. *Psychological Monographs, 80,* 1–28.

Career Planning

Appalachia Educational Laboratory. (1978). *Worker trait group guide.* Charleston, WV.

Bolles, R. (1987). *What color is your parachute?* Berkeley, CA: Ten Speed Press.

Chronicle Guidance. (1993–1994). *Chronicle career index.* (1993). Moravia, NY.

Chronicle Guidance. (1993–1994). *Chronicle financial aid guide.* (1993). Moravia, NY.

Chronicle Guidance. (1993–1994). *Chronicle four-year college databook.* (1993). Moravia, NY.

Chronicle Guidance. (1993–1994). *Chronicle two-year college databook.* (1993). Moravia, NY.

Chronicle Guidance. (1993–1994). *Chronicle vocational school manual.* (1993). Moravia, NY.

Firth-Cozens, J., & West, M. (eds.) (1991). *Women at work: Psychological and organizational perspectives.* Philadelphia: Open University Press.

Handy, C. (1989). *The age of unreason.* Boston, MA: Harvard Business School Press.

Holland, J. (1985). *Making vocational choices: A theory of personalities and work environments* (2nd ed.). Englewood Cliffs, NJ: Prentice-Hall.

Johnston, W., & Packer, A. (1987). *Workforce 2000.* Indianapolis, IN: Hudson Institute.

MacMillan Publishing Co. (1991). *College blue book.* New York.

Morrison, A., White, R., & Van Velsor, E. (1987). *Breaking the glass ceiling.* Reading, MA: Addison-Wesley.

Myers, J., & Scott, E. (1989). *Getting skilled, getting ahead: Your guide for choosing a career and a private career school.* Princeton, NJ: Peterson's Guides.

Naisbitt, J., & Aburdene, P. (1985). *Re-inventing the corporation.* New York: Warner.

Naisbitt, J., & Aburdene, P. (1990). *Megatrends 2000: Ten new directions for the 1990's.* New York: Avon.

Olympus Publishing. (1977). *Career emphasis series.* Salt Lake City, UT.

Peterson's Guides. (1989). *Peterson's two-year colleges.* Princeton, NJ.

Sekaran, U., & Leong, F. (1992). *Womanpower: Managing in times of demographic turbulence.* Newbury Park, CA: Sage.

Sharf, R. (1993). *Occupational information overview.* Pacific Grove, CA: Brooks/Cole.

Sourcebooks Trade. (1991). *Future Vision: The 189 most important trends of the 1990s.* Naperville, IL.

Terkel, S. (1974). *Working: People talk about what they do all day and how they feel about what they do.* New York: Avon.

Toffler, A. (1970). *Future shock.* New York: Random House.

Toffler, A. (1980). *The third wave.* New York: Morrow.

Toffler, A. (1983). *Previews and premises.* New York: Morrow.

Toffler, A. (1985). *The adaptive corporation.* New York: McGraw-Hill.

U.S. Department of Defense. (1988). *Military career guide.* Washington, DC: U.S. Government Printing Office.

U.S. Department of Labor. (1979). *Guide for occupational exploration.* Washington, DC: U.S. Government Printing Office.

U.S. Department of Labor. (1994). *Occupational outlook handbook, 1994–1995.* Washington, DC: U.S. Government Printing Office.

U.S. Department of Labor. *Occupational outlook quarterly.* Washington, DC: U.S. Government Printing Office.

U.S. Department of Labor. (1988). *Opportunity 2000.* Washington, DC: U.S. Government Printing Office.

U.S. Employment Service. (1991). *Dictionary of occupational titles.* Washington, DC: U.S. Government Printing Office.

Winterle, M. (1992). *Workforce diversity: Corporate challenges, corporate responses.* New York: The Conference Board.

Yankelovich, D. (1983). *Putting the work ethic to work: A Public Agenda report on restoring America's competitive vitality.* New York: The Public Agenda Foundation.

Critical and Creative Thinking

Agor, W. (1986). *The logic of intuitive decision making.* New York: Quorum Books.

Albrecht, K. (1980). *Brain power: Learn to improve your thinking skills.* Englewood Cliffs, NJ: Prentice-Hall.

De Bono, E. (1970). *Lateral thinking: Creativity step by step.* New York: Harper & Row.

De Bono, E. (1985). *De Bono's thinking course.* New York: Facts on File.

De Bono, E. (1992). *Serious creativity: Using the power of lateral thinking to create new ideas.* New York: Harper Business.

Gray, W. (1991). *Thinking critically about New Age ideas.* Belmont, CA: Wadsworth.

Halpern, D. (1989). *Thought and knowledge: An introduction to critical thinking.* Hillsdale, NJ: Erlbaum Associates.

Minnich, E. (1990). *Transforming knowledge.* Philadelphia: Temple University Press.

Regal, P. (1990). *The anatomy of judgment.* Minneapolis: University of Minnesota Press.

Ruggiero, V. (1990). *Beyond feelings: A guide to critical thinking.* Mountain View, CA: Mayfield.

Seidel, G. (1966). *The crisis of creativity.* Notre Dame, IN: University of Notre Dame Press.

Shekerjian, D. (1990). *Uncommon genius: How great ideas are born.* New York: Viking.

Smith, F. (1990). *To think.* New York: Teachers College Press.

Von Oech, R. (1983). *A whack on the side of the head: How to unlock your mind for innovation.* New York: Warner.

Von Oech, R. (1986). *A kick in the seat of the pants: Using your explorer, artist, judge, and warrior to be more creative.* New York: Perennial Library.

Employability Skills

Allen, J. (1990). *Jeff Allen's best: Get the interview.* New York: Wiley.

Beatty, R. (1988). *The complete job search book.* New York: Wiley.

Beatty, R. (1991). *Get the right job in 60 days or less.* New York: Wiley.

Beatty, R. (1992). *The new complete job search.* New York: Wiley.

Bloch, D. (1992). *How to have a winning job interview.* Lincolnwood, IL: VGM Career Horizons.

Bolles, R. (1992). *What color is your parachute?* Berkeley, CA: Ten Speed Press.

Farr, J. (1988). *Getting the job you really want.* Indianapolis, IN: JIST Works.

Figler, H. (1988). *The complete job-search handbook: All the skills you need to get any job and have a good time doing it.* New York: Holt.

Fry, W. (1989). *Your first resume.* Hawthorne, NJ: Career Press.

Half, R. (1990). *How to get a better job in this crazy world.* New York: Crown.

Jackson, T. (1991). *Guerrilla tactics in the new job market.* New York: Bantam.

Johnson, W. (1992). *The career match method: Getting the job you want in the 90s.* New York: Wiley.

Krannich, R. (1988). *Interview for success.* Manassas, VA: Impact Publications.

Krannich, R. (1989). *Careering and recareering for the 1990s.* Manassas, VA: Impact Publications.

Leeds, D. (1991). *Marketing yourself: The ultimate job seeker's guide.* New York: Harper Collins.

Parker, Y. (1986). *The damn good resume guide.* Berkeley, CA: Ten Speed Press.

Parker, Y. (1988). *The resume catalog.* Berkeley, CA: Ten Speed Press.

Rafe, S. (1990). *Get hired—It's your job.* New York: Harper Business.

Ries, A. (1991). *Horse sense: The key to success is finding a horse to ride.* New York: McGraw Hill.

Rogers, E. (1982). *Getting hired.* Englewodd Cliffs: Prentice-Hall.

Washington, T. (1990). *Resume power: Selling yourself on paper.* Bellevue, WA: Mount Vernon Press.

Philosophy

Angeles, P. (1992). *The Harper Collins dictionary of philosophy.* New York: Harper Collins.

Charlton, W. (1991). *The analytic ambition: An introduction to philosophy.* Cambridge, MA: B. Blackwell.

Frankl, V. (1959). *Man's search for meaning.* New York: Washington Square.

Hoffer, E. (1951). *The true believer: Thoughts on the nature of mass movements.* New York: Harper & Row.

Hoffer, E. (1982). *Between the devil and the dragon.* New York: Harper & Row.

Hollingdale, R. (1977). *A Nietzsche reader.* New York: Penguin.

Kolb, D. (1976). *Learning style inventory: Technical manual.* Boston: McBer.

Kolb, D. (1984). *Experiential learning.* Englewood Cliffs, NJ: Prentice-Hall.

Mackenzie, P. (1989). *The problems of philosophers: An introduction.* Buffalo, NY: Prometheus Books.

Magill, F. (ed.). (1990). *Masterpieces of world philosophy.* New York: Harper Collins.

May, R. (1953). *Man's search for himself.* New York: Norton.

May, R. (1975). *The courage to create.* New York: Norton.

May, R. (1981). *Freedom and destiny.* New York: Dell.

Nietzsche, F. (1969). *Thus spake Zarathustra.* London: Penguin.

Peikoff, L. (1991). *Objectivism: The philosophy of Ayn Rand.* New York: Dutton.

Rader, M. (1991). *The enduring questions: Main problems of philosophy.* Fort Worth: Holt, Rinehart & Winston.

Rand, A. (1957). *Atlas shrugged.* New York: Dutton.

Rand, A. (1961). *For the new intellectual.* New York: Signet.

Rand, A. (1971). *The New Left: The anti-industrial revolution*. New York: Signet.

Rand, A. (1971). *The Romantic manifesto*. New York: Penguin.

Rand, A. (1982). *Philosophy: Who needs it*. Indianapolis, IN: Bobbs-Merrill.

Rand, A. (1989). *The voice of reason*. New York: Penguin/Meridean.

Ruf, H. (1987). *Investigating philosophy: A holistic introduction to its heritage, traditions, and practices*. Lanham, MD: University Press of America.

Tarnas, R. (1991). *The passion of the Western mind: Understanding the ideas that have shaped our world view*. New York: Harmony Books.

Thoreau, H. (1959). *Walden*. New York: New American Library.

Study Skills

Baddeley, A. (1982). *Your memory, a user's guide*. New York: Macmillan.

Berry, M. (1985). *Help is on the way for tests*. Chicago: Children's Press.

Brooks, W. (1989). *High impact time management*. Englewood Cliffs, NJ: Prentice-Hall.

Buzan, T. (1984). *Use your perfect memory*. New York: Dutton.

Cohen, G. (1989). *Memory in the real world*. London: Erlbaum.

Divine, J. (1982). *How to beat test anxiety and score higher on the SAT and all other exams*. Woodbury, NY: Barron's Educational Series.

Fanning, T. (1979). *Get it all done and still be human: A personal time-management workshop*. Radnor, PA: Chilton.

Haynes, M. (1985). *Practical time management: How to make the most of your most perishable resource*. Tulsa, OK: Pennwell.

Herrmann, D. (1991). *Supermemory: A quick-action program for memory improvement*. Emmaus, PA: Rodale Press.

Higbee, K. (1977). *Your memory: How it works and how to improve it*. Englewood Cliffs, NJ: Prentice-Hall.

Jensen, E. (1982). *Student success secrets*. Woodbury, NY: Barron's Educational Series.

Kanar, C. (1991). *The confident student*. Boston: Houghton Mifflin.

Kesselman-Turkel, J. (1981). *Test taking strategies*. Chicago: Contemporary Books.

Levinson, J. (1990). *The ninety-minute hour*. New York: Dutton.

Logan, A. (1955). *Remembering made easy*. New York: Arco.

Lorayne, H. (1990). *Super memory, super student: How to raise your grades in 30 days*. Boston: Little, Brown.

Mackenzie, R. (1990). *The time trap*. New York: Amacon.

Manwarren, M. (1986). *Test taking techniques: How to take a test*. Dubuque, IA: Kendall/Hunt.

Minninger, J. (1984). *Total recall: How to boost your memory power*. Emmaus, PA: Rodale Press.

Orr, F. (1986). *Test-taking power*. New York: Prentice-Hall.

Van Ness, R. (1988). *Eliminating procrastination without putting it off*. Bloomington, IN: Phi Delta Kappa Educational Foundation.

Testing and Assessment

Aiken, L. (1988). *Psychological testing and assessment*. Boston: Allyn & Bacon.

Walsh, B., & Betz, N. (1990). *Tests and assessment*. Englewood Cliffs, NJ: Prentice-Hall.

Watkins, E., & Campbell, V. (ed.). (1990). *Tests in counseling practice*. Hillsdale, NJ: Erlbaum.

Transitions

Bridges, W. (1980). *Transitions: Making sense of life's changes*. Reading, MA: Addison-Wesley.

Ferguson, M. (1980). *The aquarian conspiracy: Personal and social transformation in the 1980's*. Los Angeles: Tarcher.

Kübler-Ross, E. (1969). *On death and dying*. New York: Macmillan.

Naisbitt, J. and Aburdene, P. (1990). *Megatrends 2000: Ten new directions for the 1990's*. New York: Avon.

Index

Please Let Us Know

We are always interested in the comments of those who have read *Career Guide*. Please be assured that, if you take the time to respond to the questions below, your comments will be carefully reviewed by the author and the publisher.

What do you consider to be the strengths of this book? _____

_____

_____

What do you consider to be the weaknesses of this book? _____

_____

_____

What specific suggestions would you make to improve this book? _____

_____

_____

Do you use this book as part of a class (if so, what was the course title?) or as a guide to self-directed study? _____

_____

What chapters were of particular use to you? _____

Were there any chapters that were not helpful? _____

Would you recommend this book to a friend considering career planning? _____

Was the book about the right length? Was the reading level appropriate? _____

_____

Did the Travelogs help you understand and apply the content? _____

Was the inclusion of occupational reference material helpful? If so, how? _____

_____

Anything else you would like to say to the author or the publisher? _____

_____

_____

_____

_____

Optional:

Your name: _____ Date: _____

Is it okay if Brooks/Cole quotes your comments to promote this book?

Sincerely,

Gary Harr

Brooks/Cole is dedicated to publishing quality publications for the helping professions. If you would like to learn more about our publications, please use this mailer to request our catalogue.

Name: _____

Street Address: _____

City, State, and Zip Code: _____

FOLD HERE

FOLD HERE